WHEN SPECIES MEET

posthumanities
3

CARY WOLFE, SERIES EDITOR

WHEN SPECIES MEET

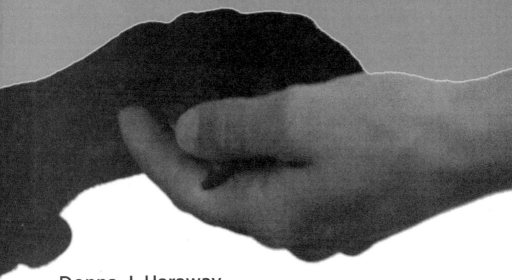

Donna J. Haraway

Posthumanities, Volume 3

 University of Minnesota Press
Minneapolis
London

Published by the University of Minnesota Press
111 Third Avenue South, Suite 290
Minneapolis, MN 55401-2520
http://www.upress.umn.edu

Library of Congress Cataloging-in-Publication Data

Haraway, Donna Jeanne.
　When species meet / Donna J. Haraway.
　　p. cm. — (Posthumanities)
　Includes bibliographical references and index.
　ISBN: 978-0-8166-5045-3 (hc : alk. paper)
　ISBN-10: 0-8166-5045-4 (hc : alk. paper)
　ISBN: 978-0-8166-5046-0 (pb : alk. paper)
　ISBN-10: 0-8166-5046-2 (pb : alk. paper)
1. Human-animal relationships. I. Title.
　QL85.H37 2008
　179′.3—dc22

2007029022

Printed in the United States of America on acid-free paper

The University of Minnesota is an equal-opportunity educator and employer.

15 14 13 12 11 10 09 08   10 9 8 7 6 5 4 3 2 1

CONTENTS

ACKNOWLEDGMENTS

When Species Meet is an acknowledgment of the lively knottings that tie together the world I inhabit, but here I want to name some of the human and nonhuman animals who are especially entwined in the tissues of this book. All those I call my animal people and their companions must come first—the scholars, artists, friends, sports buddies, and scientists whose work is directly shaped by the critters they love and know. These people and critters helped me materially to write this book by becoming ethnographic subjects and, in the case of the humans, also by reading chapter drafts and listening critically to my rants.

Agility friends: those special buddies with whom Cayenne and I study and play agility include Pam Richards and Cappuccino, Suzanne Cogen and Amigo, Barbara McElhiney and Bud, June Bogdan and Chloe, Liza Buckner with Annabelle and Taiko, Annette Thomason and Sydney, Sharon Kennedy and Dena, Susan Cochran and Aiko, Gail and Ralph Frazier with Squeeze and Tally Ho, Derede Arthur and Soja, Susie Buford and Zipper, Connie Tuft with Tag and Keeper, Faith Bugely with Rio and Gracie, Garril Page and Cali, Clare Price and Jazz, David Connet and Megan, Joan Jamison and Boomer, Marion and Mike Bashista with Merlin and Kelli, Laurie Raz-Astrakhan and Blue, Chris Hempel and Keeper, Laura Hartwick with Ruby and Otterpup, Diana Wilson and Callie, Dee Hutton and Izzy, Luanne Vidak and Jiffy, Crissy Hastings Baugh and Gracie, Karen Plemens Lucas and Nikki, Gayle Dalmau and a skein of silky terriers (Kismet, Sprite, and Toot), and Linda Lang with Rosie and Tyler. My agility instructors are Gail Frazier, Rob Michalski (with Hobbes and Fate), and Lauri Plummer. Ziji Scott, with Ashe, knows how much she has given Cayenne and me with her spirit and her magic chiropractor's hands.

Animals in science: the dogs helping with this book who came into the world through the practices of science include Spike and Bruno (and their human Gwen Tatsuno), agility athletes who are Newfoundland–border collie crosses from breeding for the dog genome project. My dog Cayenne contributed DNA for both the merle gene identification project and a drug sensitivity test. But most of the dogs who work in science do so anonymously, live in kennels rather than homes, and all too often are in pain. They and all the other critters whose lives and deaths are built into knowledge making deserve acknowledgment, but that is only the beginning of what we owe them. Working animals, including food- and fiber-producing critters, haunt me throughout this book. Response has hardly begun.

Graduate students and visiting postdocs in my seminars linking science studies, animal studies, and feminist theory at the University of California at Santa Cruz deserve a special thanks. They include Rebecca Herzig, Thomas van Dooren, Cressida Limon, Maria Puig de la Bellacasa, Natasha Myers, Heather Swanson, Jake Metcalf, Shannon Brownlee, Raissa Burns, Scout Calvert, Lindsey Collins, Lindsay Kelley, Sandra Koelle, Natalie Loveless, Matt Moore, Astrid Schrader, Mari Spira, Kalindi Vora, Eric Stanley, Matthew Moore, Marcos Becquer, Eben Kirksey, Martha Kenney, Chloe Medina, Cora Stratton, Natalie Hansen, Danny Solomon, Anna Higgins, Eunice Blavascunas, Nicole Archer, Mary Weaver, Jennifer Watanabe, Kris Weller, Sha LaBare, Adam Reed, and Carrie Friese (UCSF). I owe a huge debt of thanks in this book also to former students, now colleagues, especially Eva Hayward, Chris Rose, Gillian Goslinga, Kami Chisholm, Alexis Shotwell, Joe Dumit, Sarah Jain, Karen Hoffman, Barbara Ley, Anjie Rosga, Adam Geary, David

Delgado Shorter, Thyrza Goodeve, Rebecca Hall, Cori Hayden, Kim TallBear, Kaushik Sunder Rajan, Dawn Coppin, and Delcianna Winders. Colleagues at UCSC have been crucial to my thinking about animal–human encounters, especially Gopal Balakrishnan, Karen Barad, Nancy Chen, Jim Clifford, Angela Davis, Dorothea Ditchfield, Barbara Epstein, Carla Freccero, Wlad Godzich, Jody Greene, Susan Harding (with Bijou and Lulu Moppet, not to mention Marco!), Lisbeth Haas, Emily Honig, David and Jocelyn Hoy, Gary Lease, David Marriott, Tyrus Miller, Jim McCloskey, Karen McNally, Helene Moglen, Sheila Namir, Vicki and John Pearse, Ravi Rajan, Jennifer Reardon, Neferti Tadiar, Dick Terdiman, and Anna Tsing.

Scholars, biologists, and artists from many places helped me in diverse ways with *When Species Meet*, including Carol Adams, Marc Bekoff, Nick Bingham, Lynda Birke, Geoff Bowker, Rosi Braidotti, Jonathan Burt, Rebecca Cassidy, Adele Clarke, Sheila Conant, Istvan Csicsery-Ronay, Beatriz da Costa, Troy Duster, Mike Fischer, Adrian Franklin, Sarah Franklin, Erica Fudge, Joan Fujimura, Scott Gilbert, Faye Ginsburg, Michael Hadfield, Nancy Hartsock, Deborah Heath, Stefan Helmreich, Laura Hobgood-Oster, Don Ihde, Lupicinio Íñiguez, Alison Jolly, Margaretta Jolly, Caroline Jones, Eduardo Kohn, Donna Landry, Tom Laqueur, Bruno Latour, Ann Leffler, Diana Long, Lynn Margulis, Garry Marvin, Donald McCaig, Susan McHugh, Eduardo Mendietta, Alyce Miller, Gregg Mitman, Donald Moore, Darcy Morey, Molly Mullin, Aihwa Ong, Benjamin Orlove, Patricia Piccinini, Annie Potts, Beatriz Preciado, Paul Rabinow, Lynn Randolph, Karen Rader, Rayna Rapp, Jonah Raskin, Manuela Rossini, Joe Rouse, Thelma Rowell, Marshall Sahlins, Juliana Schiesari, Wolfgang Schirmacher, Joseph Schneider, Gabrielle Schwab, Evan Selinger, Barbara Smuts, Susan Squier, Leigh Star, Peter Steeves, Isabelle Stengers, Marilyn Strathern, Lucy Suchman, Anna-Liisa Syrjnen, Karen-Sue Taussig, Jesse Tesser, Charis Thompson, Nick Trujillo, Albian Urdank, Ian Wedde, Steve Woolgar, and Brian Wynne.

I have given invited papers, seminars, and lectures at too many places to name while I was thinking about this book. All of the people who read, listened, and responded made a difference. I also know how much I owe to the institutions that made research and writing possible, especially my department, History of Consciousness and the Center for Cultural Studies, at the University of California at Santa Cruz.

At a critical time, Cary Wolfe asked me if my book were committed, and then he helped me think through my chapters. His writing had already shaped me, and I am deeply grateful. The readers for the University of Minnesota Press, Isabelle Stengers and Erica Fudge, made themselves known to me after their reviews; their comments helped me immensely.

My brothers, Rick Miller-Haraway and Bill Haraway, helped me feel and think through how to write about our father, Frank Haraway, after his death. Dad's willingness to listen to my sports reports from agility underpins this book.

Sheila Peuse, Cheryl VanDeVeer, Laura McShane, and Kathy Durcan hold a special place in my soul for all their help with letters of recommendation, manuscripts, classes, students, and life.

For thinking with me about dogs and much else over many years, I owe sincere thanks to Rusten Hogness, Suze Rutherford, Susan Caudill, C. A. Sharp, Linda Weisser, Catherine de la Cruz, Katie King, Val Hartouni (and Grace), and Sharon Ghamari-Tabrizi. With Susan, I mourn the loss of Willem, the Great Pyrenees, from our lives and land. Rusten not only helped me think and write better; he also used his computer savvy to nurture every stage of the process technically, and he agreed with considerable grace to our inviting a puppy dynamo into our lives in 1999 when we both knew better.

David Schneider and his standard poodle, George, taught me about Anglo-American kinship in life and death. David and I first confronted dog training together through reading Vicki Hearne and studying the awful art of obedience in classes with our long-suffering canine companions, George, Sojourner, and Alexander Berkman.

How can I acknowledge Cayenne and Roland, the dogs of my heart? This book is for them, even if they might prefer a scratch-and-sniff version, one without endnotes.

I. WE HAVE NEVER BEEN HUMAN

1. WHEN SPECIES MEET
Introductions

Two questions guide this book: (1) Whom and what do I touch
when I touch my dog? and (2) How is "becoming with" a practice
of becoming worldly? I tie these questions together in expressions I
learned in Barcelona from a Spanish lover of French bulldogs, *alter-
globalisation* and *autre-mondialisation*.[1] These terms were invented by
European activists to stress that their approaches to militarized neoliberal models of world building are not about antiglobalization but about
nurturing a more just and peaceful other-globalization. There is a promising autre-mondialisation to be learned in retying some of the knots of
ordinary multispecies living on earth.

I think we learn to be worldly from grappling with, rather than gen-
eralizing from, the ordinary. I am a creature of the mud, not the sky. I am
a biologist who has always found edification in the amazing abilities
of slime to hold things in touch and to lubricate passages for living
beings and their parts. I love the fact that human genomes can be
found in only about 10 percent of all the cells that occupy the mundane space I call my body; the other 90 percent of the cells are
filled with the genomes of bacteria, fungi, protists, and such,

some of which play in a symphony necessary to my being alive at all, and some of which are hitching a ride and doing the rest of me, of us, no harm. I am vastly outnumbered by my tiny companions; better put, I become an adult human being in company with these tiny messmates. To be one is always to *become with* many. Some of these personal microscopic biota are dangerous to the me who is writing this sentence; they are held in check for now by the measures of the coordinated symphony of all the others, human cells and not, that make the conscious me possible. I love that when "I" die, all these benign and dangerous symbionts will take over and use whatever is left of "my" body, if only for a while, since "we" are necessary to one another in real time. As a little girl, I loved to inhabit miniature worlds brimming with even more tiny real and imagined entities. I loved the play of scales in time and space that children's toys and stories made patent for me. I did not know then that this love prepared me for meeting my companion species, who are my maker.

Figures help me grapple inside the flesh of mortal world-making entanglements that I call contact zones.[2] The *Oxford English Dictionary* records the meaning of "chimerical vision" for "figuration" in an eighteenth-century source, and that meaning is still implicit in my sense of *figure*.[3] Figures collect the people through their invitation to inhabit the corporeal story told in their lineaments. Figures are not representations or didactic illustrations, but rather material–semiotic nodes or knots in which diverse bodies and meanings coshape one another. For me, figures have always been where the biological and literary or artistic come together with all of the force of lived reality. My body itself is just such a figure, literally.

For many years I have written from the belly of powerful figures such as cyborgs, monkeys and apes, oncomice, and, more recently, dogs. In every case, the figures are at the same time creatures of imagined possibility and creatures of fierce and ordinary reality; the dimensions tangle and require response. *When Species Meet* is about that kind of doubleness, but it is even more about the cat's cradle games in which those who are to be in the world are constituted in intra- and interaction. The partners do not precede the meeting; species of all kinds, living and not, are consequent on a subject- and object-shaping dance of encounters. Neither the partners nor the meetings in this book are merely literary

Jim's Dog. Courtesy of James Clifford.

conceits; rather, they are ordinary beings-in-encounter in the house, lab, field, zoo, park, office, prison, ocean, stadium, barn, or factory. As ordinary knotted beings, they are also always meaning-making figures that gather up those who respond to them into unpredictable kinds of "we." Among the myriad of entangled, coshaping species of the earth, contemporary human beings' meetings with other critters and, especially, but not only, with those called "domestic" are the focus of this book.

And so in the chapters to follow, readers will meet cloned dogs, databased tigers, a baseball writer on crutches, a health and genetics activist in Fresno, wolves and dogs in Syria and the French Alps, Chicken Little and Bush legs in Moldavia, tsetse flies and guinea pigs in a Zimbabwean lab in a young adult novel, feral cats, whales wearing cameras, felons and pooches in training in prison, and a talented dog and middle-aged woman playing a sport together in California. All of these are figures, and all are mundanely here, on this earth, now, asking who "we" will become when species meet.

JIM'S DOG AND LEONARDO'S DOG

Meet Jim's dog. My colleague and friend Jim Clifford took this photograph during a December walk in one of the damp canyons of the Santa Cruz greenbelt near his home. This attentive, sitting dog endured for only one season. The next winter the shapes and light in the canyon did not vouchsafe a canine soul to animate the burned-out redwood stump covered with redwood needles, mosses, ferns, lichens—and even a little California bay laurel seedling for a docked tail—that a friend's eye had found for me the year before. So many species, so many kinds, meet in Jim's dog, who suggests an answer to my question, Whom and what do we touch when we touch this dog? How does this touch make us more worldly, in alliance with all the beings who work and play for an alter-globalization that can endure more than one season?

We touch Jim's dog with fingery eyes made possible by a fine digital camera, computers, servers, and e-mail programs through which the high-density jpg was sent to me.[4] Infolded into the metal, plastic, and electronic flesh of the digital apparatus is the primate visual system that Jim and I have inherited, with its vivid color sense and sharp focal power.

Our kind of capacity for perception and sensual pleasure ties us to the lives of our primate kin. Touching this heritage, our worldliness must answer to and for those other primate beings, both in their ordinary habitats and in labs, television and film studios, and zoos. Also, the biological colonizing opportunism of organisms, from the glowing but invisible viruses and bacteria to the crown of ferns on top of this pooch's head, is palpable in the touch. Biological species diversity and all that asks in our time come with this found dog.

In this camera-begot canid's haptic–optic touch, we are inside the histories of IT engineering, electronic product assembly-line labor, mining and IT waste disposal, plastics research and manufacturing, transnational markets, communications systems, and technocultural consumer habits. The people and the things are in mutually constituting, intra-active touch.[5] Visually and tactically, I am in the presence of the intersectional race-, sex-, age-, class-, and region-differentiated systems of labor that made Jim's dog live. Response seems the least that is required in this kind of worldliness.

This dog could not have come to me without the leisure-time promenading practices of the early twenty-first century in a university town on the central California coast. Those urban walking pleasures touch the labor practices of late nineteenth-century loggers who, without chainsaws, cut the tree whose burned stump took on a postarboreal life. Where did the lumber from that tree go? The historically deliberate firing by the loggers or the lightning-caused fires in dry-season California carved Jim's dog from the tree's blackened remains. Indebted to the histories of both environmentalism and class, the greenbelt policies of California cities resisting the fate of Silicon Valley ensured that Jim's dog was not bulldozed for housing at the western edge of real-estate hungry Santa Cruz. The water-eroded and earthquake-sculpted ruggedness of the canyons helped too. The same civic policies and earth histories also allow cougars to stroll down from the campus woodlands through the brushy canyons defining this part of town. Walking with my furry dogs off leash in these canyons makes me think about these possible feline presences. I reclip the leashes. Visually fingering Jim's dog involves touching all the important ecological and political histories and struggles of ordinary small cities that have asked, Who should eat whom, and who should cohabit? The rich naturalcultural contact zones multiply with each tactile look. Jim's dog is a provocation to curiosity, which I regard as one of the first obligations and deepest pleasures of worldly companion species.[6]

· Jim's seeing the mutt in the first place was an act of friendship from a man who had not sought dogs in his life and for whom they had not been particularly present before his colleague seemed to think about and respond to little else. Furry dogs were not the ones who then came to him, but another sort of canid quite as wonderful dogged his path. As my informants in U.S. dog culture would say, Jim's is a real dog, a one-off, like a fine mixed-ancestry dog who could never be replicated but must be encountered. Surely, there is no question about the mixed and myriad ancestors, as well as contemporaries, in this encrusted charcoal dog. I think this is what Alfred North Whitehead might have meant by a concrescence of prehensions.[7] It is definitely at the heart of what I learn when I ask whom I touch when I touch a dog. I learn something about how to inherit in the flesh. Woof . . .

Leonardo's dog hardly needs an introduction. Painted between 1485 and 1490, da Vinci's *Vitruvian Man*, the Man of Perfect Proportions, has paved his way in the imaginations of technoculture and canine pet culture alike. Sydney Harris's 1996 cartoon of Man's celebrated canine companion mimes a figure that has come to mean Renaissance humanism; to mean modernity; to mean the generative tie of art, science, technology, genius, progress, and money. I cannot count the number of times da Vinci's *Vitruvian Man* appeared in the conference brochures for genomics meetings or advertisements for molecular biological instruments and lab reagents in the 1990s. The only close competitors for illustrations and ads were Vesalius's anatomical drawings of dissected human figures and Michelangelo's *Creation of Adam* from the ceiling of the Sistine Chapel.[8] High Art, High Science: genius, progress, beauty, power, money. The Man of Perfect Proportions brings both the number magic and the real-life organic ubiquity of the Fibonacci sequence to the fore. Transmuted into the form of his master, the Dog of Perfect Proportions helps me think about why this preeminently humanist figure cannot work for the kind of autre-mondialisation I seek with earthly companions in the way that Jim's dog does. Harris's cartoon is funny, but laughter is not enough. Leonardo's dog is the companion species for technohumanism and its dreams of purification and transcendence. I want to walk instead with the motley crowd called Jim's dog, where the clean lines between traditional and modern, organic and technological, human and nonhuman give way to the infoldings of the flesh that powerful figures such as the cyborgs and dogs I know both signify and enact.[9] Maybe that is why Jim's dog is now the screen saver on my computer.

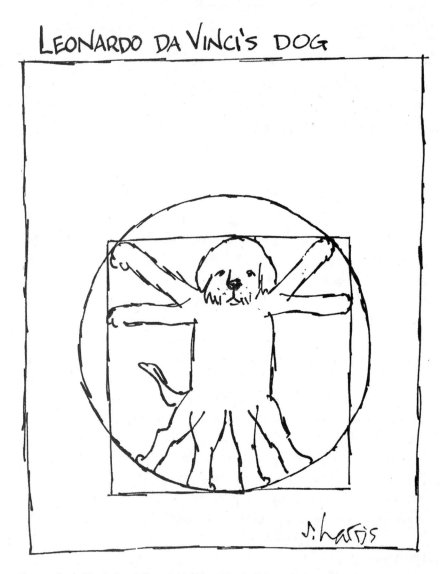

"Leonardo da Vinci's Dog." Copyright Sidney Harris, ScienceCartoonsPlus.com.

PROFESSIONAL MEETINGS

That brings us to the more usual encounters of dogs and cyborgs, in which their supposed enmity is onstage. Dan Piraro's *Bizarro* Sunday cartoon from 1999 caught the rules of engagement perfectly. Welcoming the attendees, the small dog keynote speaker at the American Association of Lapdogs points to the illuminated slide of an open laptop computer, solemnly intoning, "Ladies and Gentlemen. . . behold the enemy!" The pun that simultaneously joins and separates lapdogs and laptops is wonderful, and it opens a world of inquiry. A real dog person might first ask how capacious human laps can actually be for holding even sizable pooches and a computer at the same time. That sort of question tends to arise in the late afternoon in a home office if a human being is still at the computer and neglecting important obligations to go for a walk with the effectively importuning beast-no-longer-on-the-floor. However, more philosophically weighty, if not more practically urgent, questions also lurk in this *Bizarro* cartoon.

Modernist versions of humanism and posthumanism alike have taproots in a series of what Bruno Latour calls the Great Divides between what counts as nature and as society, as nonhuman and as human.[10] Whelped in the Great Divides, the principal Others to Man, including his "posts," are well documented in ontological breed registries in both

Copyright Dan Piraro, King Features Syndicate.

past and present Western cultures: gods, machines, animals, monsters, creepy crawlies, women, servants and slaves, and noncitizens in general. Outside the security checkpoint of bright reason, outside the apparatuses of reproduction of the sacred image of the same, these "others" have a remarkable capacity to induce panic in the centers of power and self-certainty. Terrors are regularly expressed in hyperphilias and hyperphobias, and examples of this are no richer than in the panics roused by the Great Divide between animals (lapdogs) and machines (laptops) in the early twenty-first century C.E.

Technophilias and technophobias vie with organophilias and organophobias, and taking sides is not left to chance. If one loves organic nature, to express a love of technology makes one suspect. If one finds cyborgs to be promising sorts of monsters, then one is an unreliable ally in the fight against the destruction of all things organic.[11] I was quite personally made to understand this point at a professional meeting, a wonderful conference called "Taking Nature Seriously" in 2001, at which I was a keynote speaker. I was subjected to a fantasy of my own public rape by name in a pamphlet distributed by a small group of self-identified deep ecology, anarchist activists, because, it seemed, my commitment to the mixed organic–technological hybrids figured in cyborgs made me worse than a researcher at Monsanto, who at least claims no alliance with ecofeminism. I am made to recall those researchers even at Monsanto who may well take antiracist environmental feminism seriously and to imagine how alliances might be built with them. I was also in the presence of the many deep ecologists and anarchists who have no truck with the action or analysis of my hecklers' self-righteous and incurious stance. In addition to reminding me that I am a woman (see the Great Divides above)—something class and color privilege bonded to professional status can mute for long periods of time—the rape scenario reminded me forcibly why I seek my siblings in the nonarboreal, laterally communicating, fungal shapes of the queer kin group that finds lapdogs and laptops in the same commodious laps.

At one of the conference panels, I heard a sad man in the audience say that rape seems a legitimate instrument against those who rape the earth; he seemed to regard this as an ecofeminist position, to the horror of the men and women of that political persuasion in the room. Everyone

I heard at the session thought the guy was slightly dangerous and definitely politically embarrassing, but mainly crazy in the colloquial sense if not the clinical. Nonetheless, the quasi-psychotic panic quality of the man's threatening remarks is worth some attention because of the way the extreme shows the underside of the normal. In particular, this would-be rapist-in-defense-of-mother-earth seems shaped by the culturally normal fantasy of human exceptionalism. This is the premise that humanity alone is not a spatial and temporal web of interspecies dependencies. Thus, to be human is to be on the opposite side of the Great Divide from all the others and so to be afraid of—and in bloody love with—what goes bump in the night. The threatening man at the conference was well marinated in the institutionalized, long dominant Western fantasy that all that is fully human is fallen from Eden, separated from the mother, in the domain of the artificial, deracinated, alienated, and therefore free. For this man, the way out of his culture's deep commitments to human exceptionalism requires a one-way rapture to the other side of the divide. To return to the mother is to return to nature and stand against Man-the-Destroyer, by advocating the rape of women scientists at Monsanto, if available, or of a traitorous keynote environmentalist feminist, if one is on the spot.

Freud is our great theorist of panics of the Western psyche, and because of Derrida's commitment to track down "the whole anthropomorphic reinstitution of the superiority of the human order over the animal order, of the law over the living," he is my guide to Freud's approach on this question.[12] Freud described three great historical wounds to the primary narcissism of the self-centered human subject, who tries to hold panic at bay by the fantasy of human exceptionalism. First is the Copernican wound that removed Earth itself, man's home world, from the center of the cosmos and indeed paved the way for that cosmos to burst open into a universe of inhumane, nonteleological times and spaces. Science made that decentering cut. The second wound is the Darwinian, which put *Homo sapiens* firmly in the world of other critters, all trying to make an earthly living and so evolving in relation to one another without the sureties of directional signposts that culminate in Man.[13] Science inflicted that cruel cut too. The third wound is the Freudian, which posited an unconscious that undid the primacy of conscious processes, including the reason that comforted Man with his unique excellence, with dire consequences for teleology once again. Science seems to hold that blade too. I want to add a fourth wound, the informatic or cyborgian, which infolds organic and technological flesh and so melds that Great Divide as well.

Is it any wonder that in every other election cycle the Kansas Board of Education wants this stuff out of the science text books, even if almost all of modern science has to go to accomplish this suturing of rending wounds to the coherence of a fantastic, but well-endowed, being? Notoriously, in the last decade voters in Kansas elected opponents of teaching Darwinian evolution to the state board in one election and then replaced them in the next cycle with what the press calls moderates.[14] Kansas is not exceptional; it figured more than half the public in the United States in 2006.[15] Freud knew Darwinism is not moderate, and a good thing too. Doing without both teleology and human exceptionalism is, in my opinion, essential to getting laptops and lapdogs into one lap. More to the point, these wounds to self-certainty are necessary, if not yet sufficient, to no longer easily uttering the sentence in any domain, "Ladies and gentlemen, behold the enemy!" Instead, I want my people, those collected by figures of mortal relatedness, to go back to that old political button from the late 1980s, "Cyborgs for earthly survival," joined to my newer bumper sticker from *Bark* magazine, "Dog is my co-pilot." Both critters ride the earth on the back of the Darwin fish.[16]

That cyborg and dog come together in the next professional meeting in these introductions. A few years ago, Faye Ginsburg, an eminent anthropologist and filmmaker and the daughter of Benson Ginsburg, a pioneering student of canine behavior, sent me a cartoon by Warren Miller from the March 29, 1993, *New Yorker.* Faye's childhood had been spent with the wolves her father studied in his lab at the University of Chicago and the animals at the Jackson Memorial Laboratories in Bar Harbor, Maine, where J. P. Scott and J. L. Fuller also carried out their famous inquiries into dog genetics and social behavior from the late 1940s.[17] In the cartoon a member of a wild wolf pack introduces a conspecific visitor wearing an electronic communications pack, complete with an antenna for sending and receiving data, with the words, "We found her wandering at the edge of the forest. She was raised by scientists." A student of Indigenous media in a digital age, Faye Ginsburg was easily drawn to the join of ethnography and communications technology in Miller's cartoon. Since childhood a veteran of integrating into wolf social life through the rituals of polite introductions, she was triply hailed. She is in my kin group in feminist theory as well, and so it is no surprise that I find myself also in that female telecommunications-packing wolf. This figure collects its people through friendship networks, animal–human histories, science and technology studies, politics, anthropology and animal behavior studies, and the *New Yorker*'s sense of humor.

This wolf found at the edge of the forest and raised by scientists figures who I find myself to be in the world—that is, an *organism* shaped by a post–World War II biology that is saturated with information sciences and technologies, a *biologist* schooled in those discourses, and a *practitioner* of the humanities and ethnographic social sciences. All three

"We found her wandering at the edge of the forest. She was raised by scientists."

of those subject formations are crucial to this book's questions about worldliness and touch across difference. The found wolf is meeting other wolves, but she cannot take her welcome for granted. She must be introduced, and her odd communications pack must be explained. She brings science and technology into the open in this forest. The wolf pack is politely approached, not invaded, and these wolves will decide her fate. This pack is not one of florid wild-wolf nature fantasies, but a savvy,

Faye Ginsburg and the wolf Remus greeting and playing in Benson Ginsburg's laboratory at the University of Chicago. Published in *Look* magazine, "A Wolf Can Be a Girl's Best Friend," by Jack Star, 1963. Photograph by Archie Lieberman. *Look* Magazine Collection, Library of Congress, Prints and Photographs Division, LC-L9-60-8812, frame 8.

cosmopolitan, curious lot of free-ranging canids. The wolf mentor and sponsor of the visitor is generous, willing to forgive some degree of ignorance, but it is up to the visitor to learn about her new acquaintances. If all goes well, they will become messmates, companion species, and significant others to one another, as well as conspecifics. The scientist–wolf will send back data as well as bring data to the wolves in the forest. These encounters will shape naturecultures for them all.

A great deal is at stake in such meetings, and outcomes are not guaranteed. There is no teleological warrant here, no assured happy or unhappy ending, socially, ecologically, or scientifically. There is only the chance for getting on together with some grace. The Great Divides of animal/human, nature/culture, organic/technical, and wild/domestic flatten into mundane differences—the kinds that have consequences and demand respect and response—rather than rising to sublime and final ends.

COMPANION SPECIES

Ms Cayenne Pepper continues to colonize all my cells—a sure case of what the biologist Lynn Margulis calls symbiogenesis. I bet if you were to check our DNA, you'd find some potent transfections between us. Her saliva must have the viral vectors. Surely, her darter-tongue kisses have been irresistible. Even though we share placement in the phylum of vertebrates, we inhabit not just different genera and divergent families but altogether different orders.

How would we sort things out? Canid, hominid; pet, professor; bitch, woman; animal, human; athlete, handler. One of us has a microchip injected under her neck skin for identification; the other has a photo ID California driver's license. One of us has a written record of her ancestors for twenty generations; one of us does not know her great grandparents' names. One of us, product of a vast genetic mixture, is called "purebred." One of us, equally a product of a vast mixture, is called "white." Each of these names designates a different racial discourse, and we both inherit their consequences in our flesh.

One of us is at the cusp of flaming, youthful, physical achievement; the other is lusty but over the hill. And we play a team sport called agility on the same expropriated Native land where Cayenne's ancestors herded sheep. These sheep were imported from the already colonial pastoral economy of Australia to feed the California gold rush forty-niners. In layers of history, layers of biology, layers of naturecultures, complexity is the name of our game. We are both the freedom-hungry offspring of conquest, products of white settler colonies, leaping over hurdles and crawling through tunnels on the playing field.

I'm sure our genomes are more alike than they should be. Some molecular record of our touch in the codes of living will surely leave traces in the world, no matter that we are each reproductively silenced females, one by age and choice, one by surgery without consultation. Her red merle Australian shepherd's quick and lithe tongue has swabbed the tissues of my tonsils, with all their eager immune system receptors. Who knows where my chemical receptors carried her messages or what she took from my cellular system for distinguishing self from other and binding outside to inside?

We have had forbidden conversation; we have had oral intercourse; we are bound in telling story on story with nothing but the facts. We are training each other in acts of communication we barely understand. We are, constitutively, companion species. We make each other up, in the flesh. Significantly other to each other, in specific difference, we signify in the flesh a nasty developmental infection called love. This love is a historical aberration and a naturalcultural legacy.[18]

In my experience, when people hear the term *companion species*, they tend to start talking about "companion animals," such as dogs, cats, horses, miniature donkeys, tropical fish, fancy bunnies, dying baby turtles, ant farms, parrots, tarantulas in harness, and Vietnamese potbellied pigs. Many of those critters, but far from all and none without very noninnocent histories, do fit readily into the early twenty-first-century globalized and flexible category of companion animals. Historically situated animals in companionate relations with equally situated humans are, of course, major players in *When Species Meet*. But the category "companion species" is less shapely and more rambunctious than that. Indeed, I find that notion, which is less a category than a pointer to an ongoing "becoming with," to be a much richer web to inhabit than any of the posthumanisms

on display after (or in reference to) the ever-deferred demise of man.[19] I
never wanted to be posthuman, or posthumanist, any more than I wanted
to be postfeminist. For one thing, urgent work still remains to be done in
reference to those who must inhabit the troubled categories of woman
and human, properly pluralized, reformulated, and brought into constitutive intersection with other asymmetrical differences.[20] Fundamentally,
however, it is the patterns of relationality and, in Karen Barad's terms,
intra-actions at many scales of space–time that need rethinking, not getting beyond one troubled category for a worse one even more likely to go
postal.[21] The partners do not precede their relating; all that is, is the fruit
of becoming with: those are the mantras of companion species. Even the
Oxford English Dictionary says as much. Gorging on etymologies, I will
taste my key words for their flavors.

    Companion comes from the Latin *cum panis*, "with bread." Mess-
mates at table are companions. Comrades are political companions. A
companion in literary contexts is a vade mecum or handbook, like the
Oxford Companion to wine or English verse; such companions help
readers to consume well. Business and commercial associates form a *company*, a term that is also used for the lowest rank in an order of knights,
a guest, a medieval trade guild, a fleet of merchant ships, a local unit of the
Girl Guides, a military unit, and colloquially for the Central Intelligence
Agency. As a verb, *to companion* is "to consort, to keep company," with sexual and generative connotations always ready to erupt.

    Species, like all the old and important words, is equally promiscuous,
but in the visual register rather than the gustatory. The Latin *specere* is
at the root of things here, with its tones of "to look" and "to behold." In
logic, *species* refers to a mental impression or idea, strengthening the
notion that thinking and seeing are clones. Referring both to the relentlessly "specific" or particular and to a class of individuals with the same
characteristics, *species* contains its own opposite in the most promising—
or special—way. Debates about whether species are earthly organic entities or taxonomic conveniences are coextensive with the discourse we call
"biology." Species is about the dance linking kin and kind. The ability to
interbreed reproductively is the rough and ready requirement for members of the same biological species; all those lateral gene exchangers such
as bacteria have never made very good species. Also, biotechnologically

mediated gene transfers redo kin and kind at rates and in patterns unprecedented on earth, generating messmates at table who do not know
how to eat well and, in my judgment, often should not be guests together
at all. Which companion species will, and should, live and die, and how,
is at stake.

The word *species* also structures conservation and environmental
discourses, with their "endangered species" that function simultaneously
to locate value and to evoke death and extinction in ways familiar in colonial representations of the always vanishing indigene. The discursive tie
between the colonized, the enslaved, the noncitizen, and the animal—all
reduced to type, all Others to rational man, and all essential to his bright
constitution—is at the heart of racism and flourishes, lethally, in the en-
trails of humanism. Woven into that tie in all the categories is "woman's"
putative self-defining responsibility to "the species," as this singular and
typological female is reduced to her reproductive function. Fecund, she
lies outside the bright territory of man even as she is his conduit. The
labeling of African American men in the United States as an "endangered
species" makes palpable the ongoing animalization that fuels liberal and
conservative racialization alike. *Species* reeks of race and sex; and where
and when species meet, that heritage must be untied and better knots of
companion species attempted within and across differences. Loosening the
grip of analogies that issue in the collapse of all of man's others into one
another, companion species must instead learn to live intersectionally.[22]

Raised a Roman Catholic, I grew up knowing that the Real Presence was present under both "species," the visible form of the bread and
the wine. Sign and flesh, sight and food, never came apart for me again
after seeing and eating that hearty meal. Secular semiotics never nourished as well or caused as much indigestion. That fact made me ready to
learn that species is related to spice. A kind of atom or molecule, species is also a composition used in embalming. "The species" often means
the human race, unless one is attuned to science fiction, where species
abound.[23] It would be a mistake to assume much about species in advance of encounter. Finally, we come to metal coinage, "specie," stamped
in the proper shape and kind. Like *company*, *species* also signifies and
embodies wealth. I remember Marx on the topic of gold, alert to all its
filth and glitter.

Looking back in this way takes us to seeing again, to *respecere*, to the act of respect. To hold in regard, to respond, to look back reciprocally, to notice, to pay attention, to have courteous regard for, to esteem: all of that is tied to polite greeting, to constituting the polis, where and when species meet. To knot companion and species together in encounter, in regard and respect, is to enter the world of becoming with, where *who and what are* is precisely what is at stake. In "Unruly Edges: Mushrooms as Companion Species," Anna Tsing writes, "Human nature is an interspecies relationship."[24] That realization, in Beatriz Preciado's idiom, promises an autre-mondialisation. Species interdependence is the name of the worlding game on earth, and that game must be one of response and respect. That is the play of companion species learning to pay attention. Not much is excluded from the needed play, not technologies, commerce, organisms, landscapes, peoples, practices. I am not a posthumanist; I am who I become with companion species, who and which make a mess out of categories in the making of kin and kind. Queer messmates in mortal play, indeed.

AND SAY THE PHILOSOPHER RESPONDED?
WHEN ANIMALS LOOK BACK

"And Say the Animal Responded?" is the title Derrida gave his 1997 lecture in which he tracked the old philosophical scandal of judging "the animal" to be capable only of reaction as an animal–machine. That's a wonderful title and a crucial question. I think Derrida accomplished important work in that lecture and the published essay that followed, but something that was oddly missing became clearer in another lecture in the same series, translated into English as "The Animal That Therefore I Am (More to Follow)."[25] He understood that actual animals look back at actual human beings; he wrote at length about a cat, his small female cat, in a particular bathroom on a real morning actually looking at him. "The cat I am talking about is a real cat, truly, believe me, *a little cat*. It isn't the *figure* of a cat. It doesn't silently enter the room as an allegory for all the cats on the earth, the felines that traverse myths and religions, literatures and fables" (374). Further, Derrida knew he was in the presence of someone, not of a machine reacting. "I see it as *this* irreplaceable living being that one day enters my space, enters this place where it can encounter me, see me, see me naked" (378–79). He identified the key question as being not whether the cat could "speak" but whether it is possible to know what *respond* means and how to distinguish a response from a reaction, for human beings as well as for anyone else. He did not fall into the trap of making the subaltern speak: "It would not be a matter of 'giving speech back' to animals but perhaps acceding to a thinking . . . that thinks the absence of the name as something other than a privation" (416). Yet he did not seriously consider an alternative form of engagement either, one that risked knowing something more about cats and *how to look back*, perhaps even scientifically, biologically, and *therefore* also philosophically and intimately.

He came right to the edge of respect, of the move to *respecere*, but he was sidetracked by his textual canon of Western philosophy and literature and by his own linked worries about being naked in front of his cat. He knew there is no nudity among animals, that the worry was his, even as he understood the fantastic lure of imagining he could write naked words. Somehow in all this worrying and longing, the cat was never heard from again in the long essay dedicated to the crime against animals perpetrated by the great Singularities separating the Animal and the Human in the canon Derrida so passionately read and reread so that it could never be read the same way again.[26] For those readings I and my people are permanently in his debt.

But with his cat, Derrida failed a simple obligation of companion species; he did not become curious about what the cat might actually be doing, feeling, thinking, or perhaps making available to him in looking back at him that morning. Derrida is among the most curious of men, among the most committed and able of philosophers to spot what arrests curiosity, instead nurturing an entanglement and a generative interruption called response. Derrida is relentlessly attentive to and humble before what he does not know. Besides all that, his own deep interest in animals is coextensive with his practice as a philosopher. The textual evidence is ubiquitous. What happened that morning was, to me, shocking *because* of what I know this philosopher can do. Incurious, he missed a possible invitation, a possible introduction to other-worlding. Or, if he was curious when he first really noticed his cat looking at him that morning, he

arrested that lure to deconstructive communication with the sort of critical gesture that he would never have allowed to stop him in his canonical philosophical reading and writing practices.

Rejecting the facile and basically imperialist, if generally well-
intentioned, move of claiming to see from the point of view of the other,
Derrida correctly criticized two kinds of representations, one set from
those who observe real animals and write about them but never meet
their gaze, and the other set from those who engage animals only as literary and mythological figures (382–83). He did not explicitly consider
ethologists and other animal behavioral scientists, but inasmuch as they
engage animals as objects of their vision, not as beings who look back and
whose look their own intersects, with consequences for all that follows,
the same criticism would apply. Why, though, should that criticism be the
end of the matter for Derrida?

What if not all such Western human workers with animals have
refused the risk of an intersecting gaze, even if it usually has to be teased
out from the repressive literary conventions of scientific publishing and
descriptions of method? This is not an impossible question; the literature
is large, complemented by a much larger oral culture among biologists as
well as others who earn their livings in interaction with animals. Some
astute thinkers who work and play with animals scientifically and professionally have discussed at some length this sort of issue. I am leaving aside
entirely the *philosophical* thinking that goes on in popular idioms and
publishing, not to mention the entire world of people thinking and engaging with animals who are not shaped by the institutionalized so-called
Western philosophical and literary canon.

Positive knowledge of and with animals might just be possible,
knowledge that is positive in quite a radical sense if it is not built on the
Great Divides. Why did Derrida not ask, even in principle, if a Gregory
Bateson or Jane Goodall or Marc Bekoff or Barbara Smuts or many others
have met the gaze of living, diverse animals and in response undone and
redone themselves and their sciences? Their kind of positive knowledge
might even be what Derrida would recognize as a mortal and finite knowing that understands "the absence of the name as something other than a
privation." Why did Derrida leave unexamined the practices of communication outside the writing technologies he did know how to talk about?

Leaving this query unasked, he had nowhere else to go with his keen recognition of the gaze of his cat than to Jeremy Bentham's question: "The *first* and *decisive* question will rather be to know whether animals *can suffer*. . . . Once its protocol is established, the form of this question changes everything" (396). I would not for a minute deny the importance of the question of animals' suffering and the criminal disregard of it throughout human orders, but I do not think that is the decisive question, the one that turns the order of things around, the one that promises an autre-mondialisation. The question of suffering led Derrida to the virtue of pity, and that is not a small thing. But how much more promise is in the questions, Can animals play? Or work? And even, can I learn to play with *this* cat? Can I, the philosopher, respond to an invitation or recognize one when it is offered? What if work and play, and not just pity, open up when the possibility of mutual response, without names, is taken seriously as an everyday practice available to philosophy and to science? What if a usable word for this is *joy*? And what if the question of how animals engage *one another's* gaze *responsively* takes center stage for people? What if that is the query, *once its protocol is properly established*, whose form changes everything?[27] My guess is that Derrida the man in the bathroom grasped all this, but Derrida the philosopher had no idea how to practice this sort of curiosity that morning with his highly visual cat.

Therefore, as a philosopher he knew nothing more *from, about, and with* the cat at the end of the morning than he knew at the beginning, no matter how much better he understood the root scandal as well as the enduring achievements of his textual legacy. Actually to respond to the cat's response to his presence would have required his joining that flawed but rich philosophical canon to the risky project of asking what this cat on this morning cared about, what these bodily postures and visual entanglements might mean and might invite, as well as reading what people who study cats have to say and delving into the developing knowledges of both cat–cat and cat–human behavioral semiotics when species meet. Instead, he concentrated on his shame in being naked before this cat. Shame trumped curiosity, and that does not bode well for an autre-mondialisation. Knowing that in the gaze of the cat was "an existence that refuses to be conceptualized," Derrida did not "go on as if he had never been looked at," never addressed, which was the fundamental gaffe he teased out of his canonical tradition (379, 383). Unlike Emmanuel Lévinas, Derrida, to his credit, recognized in his small cat "the absolute alterity of the neighbor" (380).[28] Further, instead of a primal scene of Man confronting Animal, Derrida gave us the provocation of a historically located look. Still, shame is not an adequate response to our inheritance of multispecies histories, even at their most brutal. Even if the cat did not become a symbol of all cats, the naked man's shame quickly became a figure for the shame of philosophy before all of the animals. That figure generated an important essay. "The animal looks at us, and we are naked before it. Thinking perhaps begins there" (397).

But whatever else the cat might have been doing, Derrida's full human male frontal nudity before an Other, which was of such interest in his philosophical tradition, was of no consequence to her, except as the distraction that kept her human from giving or receiving an ordinary polite greeting. I am prepared to believe that he did know how to greet this cat and began each morning in that mutually responsive and polite dance, but if so, that embodied mindful encounter did not motivate his philosophy in public. That is a pity.

For help, I turn to someone who did learn to look back, as well as to recognize that she was looked at, as a core work-practice for doing her science. To respond was to respect; the practice of "becoming with" rewove the fibers of the scientist's being. Barbara Smuts is now a bioanthropologist at the University of Michigan, but as a Stanford University graduate student in 1975, she went to Tanzania's Gombe Stream preserve to study chimpanzees. After being kidnapped and ransomed in the turbulent nationalist and anticolonial human politics of that area of the world in the mid-1970s, she ended up studying baboons in Kenya for her PhD.[29] About 135 baboons called the Eburru Cliffs troop lived around a rocky outcropping of the Great Rift Valley near Lake Naivasha. In a wonderful understatement, Smuts writes, "At the beginning of my study, the baboons and I definitely did not see eye to eye."[30]

She wanted to get as close as possible to the baboons to collect data to address her research questions; the monkeys wanted to get as far away from her threatening self as possible. Trained in the conventions of objective science, Smuts had been advised to be as neutral as possible, to be like a rock, to be unavailable, so that eventually the baboons would go on about their business in nature as if data-collecting humankind were not present. Good scientists were those who, learning to be invisible themselves, could see the scene of nature close up, as if through a peephole. The scientists could query but not be queried. People could ask if baboons are or are not social subjects, or ask anything else for that matter, without any ontological risk either to themselves, except maybe being bitten by an angry baboon or contracting a dire parasitic infection, or to their culture's dominant epistemologies about what are named nature and culture.

Along with more than a few other primatologists who talk, if not write in professional journals, about how the animals come to accept the presence of working scientists, Smuts recognized that the baboons were unimpressed by her rock act. They frequently looked at her, and the more she ignored their looks, the less satisfied they seemed. Progress in what scientists call "habituation" of the animals to the human being's would-be nonpresence was painfully slow. It seemed like the only critter to whom the supposedly neutral scientist was invisible was herself. Ignoring social cues is far from neutral social behavior. I imagine the baboons as seeing somebody off-category, not something, and asking if that being were or were not educable to the standard of a polite guest. The monkeys, in short, inquired if the woman was as good a social subject as an ordinary baboon, with whom one could figure out how to carry on relationships, whether hostile, neutral, or friendly. The question was not, Are the baboons social subjects? but, Is the human being? Not, Do the baboons have "face"? but, Do people?

Smuts began adjusting what she did—and who she was—according to the baboons' social semiotics directed both to her and to one another. "I . . . in the process of gaining their trust, changed almost everything about me, including the way I walked and sat, the way I held my body, and the way I used my eyes and voice. I was learning a whole new way of being in the world—the way of the baboon. . . . I was responding to the cues the baboons used to indicate their emotions, motivations and intentions to one another, and I was gradually learning to send such signals back to them. As a result, instead of avoiding me when I got too close, they started giving me very deliberate dirty looks, which made me move away. This may sound like a small shift, but in fact it signaled a profound change from being treated like an *object* that elicited a unilateral response (avoidable), to being recognized as a *subject* with whom they could communicate" (295). In the philosopher's idiom, the human being acquired a face. The result was that the baboons treated her more and more as a reliable social being who would move away when told to do so and around whom it might be safe to carry on monkey life without a lot of fuss over her presence.

Having earned status as a baboon-literate casual acquaintance and sometimes even a familiar friend, Smuts was able to collect data and earn a PhD. She did not shift her questions to study baboon–human interactions, but only through mutual acknowledgment could the human being and baboons go on about their business. If she really wanted to study something other than how human beings are in the way, if she was really interested in these baboons, Smuts had to enter into, not shun, a responsive relationship. "By acknowledging a baboon's presence, I expressed respect, and by responding in ways I picked up from them, I let the baboons know that my intentions were benign and that I assumed they likewise meant me no harm. Once this was clearly established in both directions, we could relax in each other's company" (297).

Writing about these introductions to baboon social niceties, Smuts said, "The baboons remained themselves, doing what they always did in the world they always lived in" (295). In other words, her idiom leaves the baboons in nature, where change involves only the time of evolution, and perhaps ecological crisis, and the human being in history, where all other sorts of time come into play. Here is where I think Derrida and Smuts need each other. Or maybe it is just my monomania to place baboons and humans together in situated histories, situated naturecultures, in which all the actors become who they are *in the dance of relating*, not from scratch, not ex nihilo, but full of the patterns of their sometimes-joined, sometimes-separate heritages both before and lateral to *this* encounter. All the dancers are redone through the patterns they enact. The temporalities of companion species comprehend all the possibilities activated in becoming with, including the heterogeneous scales of evolutionary time for everybody but also the many other rhythms of conjoined process. If we know how to look, I think we would see that the baboons of Eburru Cliffs were redone too, in baboon ways, by having entangled their gaze with that of this young clipboard-toting human female. The relationships are the smallest possible patterns for analysis;[31] the partners and actors are their still-ongoing products. It is all extremely prosaic, relentlessly mundane, and exactly how worlds come into being.[32]

Smuts herself holds a theory very like this one in "Embodied Communication in Nonhuman Animals," a 2006 reprise of her study of the Eburru Cliffs baboons and elaboration of daily, ongoing negotiated responses between herself and her dog Bahati.[33] In this study, Smuts is struck by the frequent enactments of brief greeting rituals between beings who know each other well, such as between baboons in the same troop and between herself and Bahati. Among baboons, both friends and nonfriends greet one another all the time, and who they are is in constant becoming in these rituals. Greeting rituals are flexible and dynamic, rearranging pace and elements within the repertoire that the partners already share or can cobble together. Smuts defines a greeting ritual as a kind of embodied communication, which takes place in entwined, semiotic, overlapping, somatic patterning over time, not as discrete, denotative signals emitted by individuals. An embodied communication is more like a dance than a word. The flow of entangled meaningful bodies in time—whether jerky and nervous or flaming and flowing, whether both partners move in harmony or painfully out of synch or something else altogether—is communication about relationship, the relationship itself, and the means of reshaping relationship and so its enacters.[34] Gregory Bateson would say that this is what human and nonhuman mammalian nonlinguistic communication fundamentally is, that is, communication about relationship and the material–semiotic means of relating.[35] As Smuts puts it, "Changes in greetings *are* a change in the relationship" (6). She goes further: "With language, it is possible to lie and say we like someone when we don't. However, if the above speculations are correct, closely interacting bodies tend to tell the truth" (7).

This is a very interesting definition of truth, one rooted in material–semiotic dancing in which all the partners have face, but no one relies on names. That kind of truth does not fit easily into any of the inherited categories of human or nonhuman, nature or culture. I like to think that this is one treasure for Derrida's hunt to "think the absence of the name as something other than a privation." I suspect this is one of the things my fellow competitors and I in the dog–human sport called agility mean when we say our dogs are "honest." I am certain we are not referring to the tired philosophical and linguistic arguments about whether dogs can lie, and if so, lie about lying. The truth or honesty of nonlinguistic embodied communication depends on looking back and greeting significant others, again and again. This sort of truth or honesty is not some trope-free, fantastic kind of natural authenticity that only animals can have while humans are defined by the happy fault of lying denotatively and knowing it. Rather, this truth telling is about co-constitutive naturalcultural dancing, holding in esteem, and regard open to those who look back reciprocally. Always tripping, this kind of truth has a multispecies future. *Respecere*.

BECOMING-ANIMAL OR SETTING OUT THE TWENTY-THIRD BOWL?

The making each other available to events that is the dance of "becoming with" has no truck with the fantasy wolf-pack version of "becoming-animal" figured in Gilles Deleuze and Félix Guattari's famous section of *A Thousand Plateaus*, "1730: Becoming-Intense, Becoming-Animal, Becoming-Imperceptible."[36] Mundane, prosaic, living wolves have no truck with that kind of wolf pack, as we will see at the end of these introductions, when dogs, wolves, and people become available to one another in risky worldings. But first, I want to explain why writing in which I had hoped to find an ally for the tasks of companion species instead made me come as close as I get to announcing, "Ladies and Gentlemen, behold the enemy!"

I want to stay a while with "Becoming-Intense, Becoming-Animal, Becoming-Imperceptible," because it works so hard to get beyond the Great Divide between humans and other critters to find the rich multiplicities and topologies of a heterogeneously and nonteleologically connected world. I want to understand why Deleuze and Guattari here leave me so angry when what we want seems so similar. Despite much that I love in other work of Deleuze, here I find little but the two writers' scorn for all that is mundane and ordinary and the profound absence of curiosity about or respect for and with actual animals, even as innumerable references to diverse animals are invoked to figure the authors' anti-Oedipal and anticapitalist project. Derrida's actual little cat is decidedly not invited into this encounter. No earthly animal would look twice at these authors, at least not in their textual garb in this chapter.

A Thousand Plateaus is a part of the writers' sustained work against the monomaniacal, cyclopean, individuated Oedipal subject, who is riveted on daddy and lethal in culture, politics, and philosophy. Patrilineal thinking, which sees all the world as a tree of filiations ruled by genealogy and identity, wars with rhizomatic thinking, which is open to nonhierarchical becomings and contagions. So far, so good. Deleuze and Guattari sketch a quick history of European ideas from eighteenth-century natural history (relations recognized through proportionality and resemblance, series and structure), through evolutionism (relations ordered through descent and filiation), to becomings (relations patterned through "sorcery" or alliance). "Becoming is always of a different order than filiation. It concerns alliance" (238). The normal and abnormal rule in evolutionism; the anomaly, which is outside rules, is freed in the lines of flight of becomings. "Molar unities" must give way to "molecular multiplicities." "The anomalous is neither individual nor species; it has only affects, infections, horror . . . a phenomenon of bordering" (244–45). And then, "We oppose epidemic to filiation, contagion to heredity, peopling by contagion to sexual reproduction, sexual production. Bands, human or animal, proliferate by contagion, epidemics, battlefields, and catastrophes. . . . All we are saying is that animals are packs, and packs form, develop, and are transformed by contagion. . . . Wherever there is multiplicity, you will find also an exceptional individual, and it is with that individual that an alliance must be made in order to become-animal" (241–42). This is a philosophy of the sublime, not the earthly, not the mud; becoming-animal is not an autre-mondialisation.

Earlier in *A Thousand Plateaus*, Deleuze and Guattari conducted a smart, mean critique of Freud's analysis of the famous case of the Wolf-Man, in which their opposition of dog and wolf gave me the key to how D&G's associational web of anomalous becoming-animal feeds off a series of primary dichotomies figured by the opposition between the wild and the domestic. "That day the Wolf-Man rose from the couch particularly tired. He knew that Freud had a genius for brushing up against the truth and passing it by, and then filling the void with associations. He knew that Freud knew nothing about wolves, or anuses for that matter.

The only thing Freud understood was what a dog is, and a dog's tail" (26). This gibe is the first of a crowd of oppositions of dog and wolf in *A Thousand Plateaus*, which taken together are a symptomatic morass for how not to take earthly animals—wild or domestic—seriously. In honor of Freud's famously irascible chows, no doubt sleeping on the floor during the Wolf-Man's sessions, I brace myself to go on by studying the artist David Gojnes's Chinese Year of the Dog poster for 2006: one of the most gorgeous chow chows I have ever seen. Indifferent to the charms of a blue-purple tongue, D&G knew how to kick the psychoanalyst where it would hurt, but they had no eye for the elegant curve of a good chow's tail, much less the courage to look such a dog in the eye.

But the wolf/dog opposition is not funny. D&G express horror at the "individuated animals, family pets, sentimental Oedipal animals each with its own petty history" who invite only regression (240).[37] All worthy animals are a pack; all the rest are either pets of the bourgeoisie or state animals symbolizing some kind of divine myth.[38] The pack, or pure-affect animals, are intensive, not extensive, molecular and exceptional, not petty and molar—sublime wolf packs, in short. I don't think it needs comment that we will learn nothing about actual wolves in all this. I know that D&G set out to write not a biological treatise but rather a philosophical, psychoanalytic, and literary one requiring different reading habits for the always nonmimetic play of life and narrative. But no reading strategies can mute the scorn for the homely and the ordinary in this book. Leaving behind the traps of singularity and identity is possible without the lubrication of sublime ecstasy bordering on the intensive affect of the 1909 Futurist Manifesto. D&G continue, "*Anyone who likes cats or dogs is a fool*" (240, italics in original). I don't think Deleuze here is thinking of Dostoevsky's idiot, who slows things down and whom Deleuze loves. D&G go on: Freud knows only the "dog in the kennel, the analyst's bow wow." Never have I felt more loyal to Freud. D&G go even further in their disdain for the daily, the ordinary, the affectional rather than the sublime. The Unique, the one in a pact with a demon, the sorcerer's anomaly, is both pack and Ahab's leviathan in *Moby Dick*, the exceptional, not in the sense of a competent and skillful animal webbed in the open with others, but in the sense of what is without characteristics and without tenderness (244). From the point of view of the animal worlds I inhabit, this is not about a good run but about a bad trip. Along with the Beatles, I need a little more help than that from my friends.

Little house dogs and the people who love them are the ultimate figure of abjection for D&G, especially if those people are elderly women, the very type of the sentimental. "Ahab's Moby Dick is not like the little cat or dog owned by an elderly woman who honors and cherishes it. Lawrence's becoming-tortoise has nothing to do with a sentimental or domestic relation. . . . But the objection is raised against Lawrence: 'Your tortoises are not real!' And he answers: 'Possibly, but my becoming is, . . . even and especially if you have no way of judging it, because you're just little house dogs'" (244). "My becoming" seems awfully important in a theory opposed to the strictures of individuation and subject. The old, female, small, dog- and cat-loving: these are who and what must be vomited out by those who will become-animal. Despite the keen competition, I am not sure I can find in philosophy a clearer display of misogyny, fear of aging, incuriosity about animals, and horror at the ordinariness of flesh, here covered by the alibi of an anti-Oedipal and anticapitalist project. It took some nerve for D&G to write about becoming-woman just a few pages later! (291–309).[39] It is almost enough to make me go out and get a toy poodle for my next agility dog; I know a remarkable one playing with her human for the World Cup these days. That *is* exceptional.

It is a relief to return from my own flights of fancy of becoming-intense in the agility World Cup competitions to the mud and the slime of my proper home world, where my biological soul travels with that wolf found near the edge of the forest who was raised by scientists. At least as many nonarboreal shapes of relatedness can be found in these not-always-salubrious viscous fluids as among Deleuze and Guattari's rhizomatic anomalies. Playing in the mud, I can even appreciate a great deal of *A Thousand Plateaus*. Companion species are familiar with oddly shaped figures of kin and kind, in which arboreal descent is both a latecomer to the play of bodies and never uniquely in charge of the material–semiotic action. In their controversial theory of *Acquiring Genomes*, Lynn Margulis and her son and collaborator, Dorion Sagan, give me the flesh and figures that companion species need to understand their messmates.[40]

Reading Margulis over the years, I get the idea that she believes everything interesting on earth happened among the bacteria, and all the rest is just elaboration, most certainly including wolf packs. Bacteria pass genes back and forth all the time and do not resolve into well-bounded species, giving the taxonomist either an ecstatic moment or a headache. "The creative force of symbiosis produced eukaryotic cells from bacteria. Hence all larger organisms—protests, fungi, animals, and plants—originated symbiogenetically. But creation of novelty by symbiosis did not end with the evolution of the earliest nucleated cells. Symbiosis still is everywhere" (55–56). Margulis and Sagan give examples from Pacific coral reefs, squid and their luminescent symbionts, New England lichens, milk cows, and New Guinea ant plants, among others. The basic story is simple: ever more complex life forms are the continual result of ever more intricate and multidirectional acts of association of and with other life forms. Trying to make a living, critters eat critters but can only partly digest one another. Quite a lot of indigestion, not to mention excretion, is the natural result, some of which is the vehicle for new sorts of complex patternings of ones and manys in entangled association. And some of that indigestion and voiding are just acidic reminders of mortality made vivid in the experience of pain and systemic breakdown, from the lowliest among us to the most eminent. Organisms are ecosystems of genomes, consortia, communities, partly digested dinners, mortal boundary formations. Even toy dogs and fat old ladies on city streets are such boundary formations; studying them "ecologically" would show it.

Eating one another and developing indigestion are only one kind of transformative merger practice; living critters form consortia in a baroque medley of inter- and intra-actions. Margulis and Sagan put it more eloquently when they write that to be an organism is to be the fruit of "the co-opting of strangers, the involvement and infolding of others into ever more complex and miscegenous genomes. . . . The acquisition of the reproducing other, of the microbe and the genome, is no mere sideshow. Attraction, merger, fusion, incorporation, co-habitation, recombination— both permanent and cyclical—and other forms of forbidden couplings, are the main sources of Darwin's missing variation" (205). Yoking together all the way down is what sym-bio-genesis means. The shape and temporality of life on earth are more like a liquid–crystal consortium folding on itself again and again than a well-branched tree. Ordinary identities emerge and are rightly cherished, but they remain always a relational web opening to non-Euclidean pasts, presents, and futures. The ordinary is a multipartner mud dance issuing from and in entangled species. It is turtles all the way down; the partners do not preexist their constitutive intra-action at every folded layer of time and space.[41] These are the contagions and infections that wound the primary narcissism of those who still dream of human exceptionalism. These are also the cobblings together that give meaning to the "becoming with" of companion species in naturecultures. *Cum panis,* messmates, to look and to look back, to have truck with: those are the names of my game.

One aspect of Margulis and Sagan's exposition seems unnecessarily hard for companion species to digest, however, and a more easily assimilated theory is cooking. In opposition to various mechanistic theories of the organism, Margulis has long been committed to the notion of autopoiesis. Autopoiesis is self-making, in which self-maintaining entities (the smallest biological unit of which is a living cell) develop and sustain their own form, drawing on the enveloping flows of matter and energy.[42] In this case, I think Margulis would do better with Deleuze and Guattari, whose world did not build on complex self-referential units of differentiation or on Gaian systems, cybernetic or otherwise, but built on a different kind of "turtles all the way down," figuring relentless otherness knotted into never fully bounded or fully self-referential entities. I am instructed by developmental biologist Scott Gilbert's critique of autopoiesis for its emphasis on self-building and self-maintaining systems, closed except for nourishing flows of matter and energy. Gilbert stresses that nothing makes itself in the biological world, but rather reciprocal induction within and between always-in-process critters ramifies through space and time on both large and small scales in cascades of inter- and intra-action. In embryology, Gilbert calls this "interspecies epigenesis."[43] Gilbert writes: "I think that the ideas that Lynn [Margulis] and I have are very similar; it's just that she was focusing on adults and I want to extend the concept (as I think the science allows it to be fully extended) to embryos. I believe that the *embryonic* co-construction of the physical bodies has many more implications because it means that we were 'never' individuals." Like Margulis and Sagan, Gilbert stresses that the cell (not the genome) is the smallest unit of structure and function in the biological world, and he argues that "the morphogenetic field can be seen as a major unit of onto-genetic and evolutionary change."[44]

As I read him, Gilbert's approach is not a holistic systems theory in the sense that Margulis and Sagan lean toward, and his fractal "turtles all the way down" arguments do not posit a self-referential unit of differentiation. Such a unit cheats on the turtles pile, whether up or down. Software engineer Rusten Hogness suggests the term *turtling all the way down* might better express Gilbert's kind of recursivity.[45] I think that for Gilbert the noun *differentiation* is permanently a verb, within which mortal knots of partly structured difference are in play. In my view, Margulis and Sagan's symbiogenesis is not really compatible with their theory of autopoiesis, and the alternative is not an additive mechanistic theory but a going even more deeply into differentiation.[46] A nice touch is that Gilbert and his students literally work on turtle embryogeny, studying the inductions and cell migrations that result in the turtle's plastron on its belly surface. Layers of turtling, indeed.

All of that takes us to the ethologist Thelma Rowell's practice of setting out a twenty-third bowl in her farmyard in Lancashire when she has only twenty-two sheep to feed. Her Soay sheep crunch grass on the hillsides most of the day, forming their own social groups without a lot of interference. Such restraint is a revolutionary act among most sheep farmers, who rob sheep of virtually every decision until whole breeds may well have lost the capacity to find their way in life without overweening human supervision. Rowell's empowered sheep, belonging to a so-called primitive breed recalcitrant to meat–industrial standardization and be-havioral ruination, have addressed many of her questions, not least telling her that even domesticated sheep have social lives and abilities as complex as those of the baboons and other monkeys she studied for decades. Probably descended from a population of feral sheep thought to have been deposited on the island of Soay in the St. Kilda archipelago some-time in the Bronze Age, Soay sheep are today the subject of attention by rare breed societies in the United Kingdom and the United States.[47]

Focused on weighty matters such as feed conversion rates, scandal-ized sheep scientists with an agribusiness emphasis rejected Rowell's first papers on feral ram groups when she submitted them (the manuscripts, not the sheep) for publication. But good scientists have a way of nibbling away at prejudice with mutated questions and lovely data, which works at least sometimes.[48] Scottish blackface hill sheep, Rowell's numerically dominant ovine neighbors in Lancashire, and the lowland Dorset white-faced breed, mostly on the English Downs, seem to have forgotten how to testify to a great deal of sheep competence. They and their equivalents around the world are the sorts of ovids most familiar to the sheep experts reviewing papers for the journals—at least for the journals in which sheep usually show up, that is, *not* the behavioral ecology, integrative biology, and evolution journals in which nondomestic species seem the "natural" subjects of attention. But in the context of the ranching and farming practices that led to today's global agribusiness, maybe those "domestic" ovine eating machines are rarely asked an interesting question. Not brought into the open with their people, and so with no experience of jointly becoming available, these sheep do not "become with" a curious scientist.

There is a disarmingly literal quality to having truck with Rowell and her critters. Rowell brings her competent sheep into the yard most days so that she can ask them some more questions while they snack. There, the twenty-two sheep find twenty-three bowls spaced around the yard. That homely twenty-third bowl is the open,[49] the space of what is not yet and may or may not ever be; it is a making available to events; it is asking the sheep and the scientists to be smart in their exchanges by making it possible for something unexpected to happen. Rowell practices the virtue of worldly politeness—not a particularly gentle art—with her colleagues and her sheep, just as she used to do with her primate subjects. "Interesting research is research on the conditions that make something interesting."[50] Always having a bowl that is not occupied provides an extra place to go for any sheep displaced by his or her socially assertive fellow ovid. Rowell's approach is deceptively simple. Competition is so easy to see; eating is so readily observed and of such consuming interest to farmers. What else might be happening? Might what is not so easy to learn to see be what is of the utmost importance to the sheep in their daily doings and their evolutionary history? Might it be that thinking again about the history of predation and the smart predilections of prey will tell us something surprising and important about ovine worlds even on Lancashire hillsides, or on islands off the coast of Scotland, where a wolf has not been seen for centuries?

Always a maverick alert to complexity in its details rather than in grand pronouncements, Rowell regularly discomfited her human colleagues when she studied monkeys, beginning with her 1960s accounts of forest baboons in Uganda who did not act according to their supposed species script.[51] Rowell is among the most satisfyingly opinionated, empirically grounded, theoretically savvy, unself-impressed, and unsparingly anti-ideological people I have ever met. Forgetting her head-over-heels interest in her sheep, seeing her patent love for her obstreperous male adolescent turkeys on her Lancashire farm in 2003, whom she unconvincingly threatened with untimely slaughter for their misdeeds,[52] told me a great deal about how she treats both unwary human colleagues and the opinionated animals whom she has studied over a lifetime. As Vinciane Despret emphasizes in her study, Rowell poses the question of the collective in relation to both sheep and people: "Do we prefer living with predictable sheep or with sheep that surprise us and that add to our definitions of what 'being social' means?"[53] This is a fundamental worldly question, or what Despret's colleague Isabelle Stengers might call a cosmopolitical query, in which "the cosmos refers to the unknown constituted by these multiple divergent worlds, and to the articulations of which they could eventually be capable, as opposed to the temptation of a peace intended to be final."[54] Eating lunch with the circa sixty-five-year-old Rowell and her elderly, cherished, nonherding, pet dog in her farmhouse kitchen strewn with scientific papers and heterogeneous books, my would-be ethnographic self had the distinct sense that Oedipal regression was not on the menu among these companion species. Woolf!

LIVING HISTORIES IN THE CONTACT ZONE: WOLF TRACKS

Whom and what do I touch when I touch my dog? How is becoming with a practice of becoming worldly? When species meet, the question of how to inherit histories is pressing, and how to get on together is at stake. Because I become with dogs, I am drawn into the multispecies knots that they are tied into and that they retie by their reciprocal action.

My premise is that touch ramifies and shapes accountability. Accountability, caring for, being affected, and entering into responsibility are not ethical abstractions; these mundane, prosaic things are the result of having truck with each other.[55] Touch does not make one small; it peppers its partners with attachment sites for world making. Touch, regard, looking back, becoming with—all these make us responsible in unpredictable ways for which worlds take shape. In touch and regard, partners willy nilly are in the miscegenous mud that infuses our bodies with all that brought that contact into being. Touch and regard have consequences. Thus, my introductions in this chapter end in three knots of entangled companion species—wolves, dogs, human beings, and more—in three places where an autre-mondialisation is at stake: South Africa, the Golan Heights in Syria, and the countryside of the French Alps.

At the off-leash dog park in Santa Cruz, California, which I frequent, people sometimes boast that their largish, prick-eared, shepherd-like mutts are "half wolf." Sometimes the humans claim that they know this for sure but more often rest content with an account that makes their dogs seem special, close to their storied wild selves. I find the genealogical speculations highly unlikely in most cases, partly because it is not easy to have at hand a breeding wolf with whom a willing dog might mate, and partly because of the same agnosticism with which I and most of my dogland informants greet identification of any largish black dog of uncertain provenance as a "half Labrador retriever." Still, I know wolf–dog hybrids do exist rather widely, and my dogs' playing with a few motley claimants tied me into a web of caring. Caring means becoming subject to the unsettling obligation of curiosity, which requires knowing more at the end of the day than at the beginning. Learning something of the behavioral biology of wolf–dog hybrids seemed the least that was required. One of the places that led me, via an article by Robyn Dixon in the *Los Angeles Times* on October 17, 2004, "Orphaned Wolves Face Grim Future," was to the Tsitsikamma Wolf Sanctuary on the southern coast of South Africa near the town of Storm River.[56]

During the apartheid era, in quasi-secret experiments, scientists in the service of the white state imported northern gray wolves from North America with the intent of breeding an attack dog with a wolf's smarts, stamina, and sense of smell to track down "insurgents" in the harsh border areas. But the security-apparatus scientists at Roodeplaat Breeding Enterprises found to their dismay that wolf–dog hybrids make particularly bad trained attack dogs, not because of aggressivity or unpredictability (both issues with many of the hybrids discussed in the general literature), but because, besides being hard to train, the wolf–dogs generally defer to their human pack leaders and fail to take the lead when ordered to do so on counterinsurgency or police patrols. Members of an endangered species in much of its former range in North America became failed mixed-blood immigrants in the apartheid state intent on enforcing racial purity.

After the end of apartheid, both the wolves and the hybrids became signifiers of security once again, as people terrified for their personal safety in the ripe, still racialized discourses of criminality rampant in South Africa engaged in a brisk newspaper- and Internet-mediated trade in the animals. The predictable result has been thousands of animals unable to be "repatriated" to their continent of origin. Both epidemiologically and genetically categorically "impure," these canids enter the cultural category of the disposable "homeless," or in ecological terms "nicheless." The new state could not care less what happens to these animate tools of a former racist regime. Running on private money from rich donors and middle-class, mostly white people, a rescue and sanctuary apparatus of a sort that is familiar globally to dog people does what it can. This is not an honored truth and reconciliation process trying to meet a socially recognized obligation to those nonhumans forced into "becoming with" a scientific racial state apparatus. The sanctuary practices are private charity directed to nonhumans whom many people would see as better killed (euthanized? Is there any "good death" here?) in a nation where unaddressed human economic misery remains immense. Further, the financially strapped sanctuaries accept only "pure wolves," though only about two hundred canids could probably have passed that test in 2004 in South Africa, and have no resources for the possibly tens of thousands of hybrids who face, as the newspaper article headlined, a "grim future."

So, what have I and others who touch and are touched by this story inherited? Which histories must we live? A short list includes the racial discourses endemic to the history of both biology and the nation; the collision of endangered species worlds, with their conservation apparatuses,

and security discourse worlds, with their criminality and terrorist apparatuses; the actual lives and deaths of differentially situated human beings
and animals shaped by these knots; contending popular and professional
narratives about wolves and dogs and their consequences for who lives
and dies and how; the coshaped histories of human social welfare and
animal welfare organizations; the class-saturated funding apparatuses of
private and public animal–human worlds; the development of the categories to contain those, human and nonhuman, who are disposable and
killable; the inextricable tie between North America and South Africa in
all these matters; and the stories and actual practices that continue to produce wolf–dog hybrids in unlivable knots, even on a romping-dog beach
in Santa Cruz, California. Curiosity gets one into thick mud, but I believe
that is the kind of "looking back" and "becoming-with-companions" that
might matter in making autres-mondialisations more possible.

Heading to the Golan Heights after running with the wolves in
South Africa is hardly restful. Among the last companion-species knots
in which I imagined living was one that in 2004 featured Israeli cowboys
in occupied Syrian territory riding kibbutz horses to manage their Euro-
pean-style cattle among the ruins of Syrian villages and military bases.
All I have is a snapshot, one newspaper article in the midst of an ongoing
complex, bloody, and tragic history.[57] That snapshot was enough to reshape
my sense of touch while playing with my dogs. The first cattle-ranching
kibbutz was founded shortly after 1967; by 2004 about seventeen thousand Israelis in thirty-three various sorts of settlements held the territory,
pending removal by an ever-receding peace treaty with Syria. Learning
their new skills on the job, the neophyte ranchers share the land with the
Israeli military and their tanks. Mine fields still pose dangers for cattle,
horses, and people, and firing-range practice vies with grazing for space.
The cattle are guarded from the resourceful Syrian wolves, not to mention Syrian people periodically repatriating stock, by large white livestock
guardian dogs (LGDs), namely, Turkish Akbash dogs. Turkey does play
an odd role in the Middle East! With the dogs on duty, the ranchers
do not shoot the wolves. Nothing was said in this *Times* article about
whether they shoot the Syrian "rustlers." The cattle that the Israelis took
over after the expulsion of the Syrian villagers were small, wiry, capable
in the same kinds of ways as Rowell's nonsheepish sheep, and resistant to

the local tick-borne diseases. The European cattle who were imported to replace the supposedly unmodern Syrian beasts are none of those things. The Israeli ranchers brought the guardian dogs into their operation in the 1990s in response to the large number of gray wolves, whose number on the Golan Heights grew significantly after the defeat of Syria in 1967 reduced the Arab villagers' hunting pressure on them.

The Akbash dogs were the prosaic touch that made the story in the newspaper of more than passing interest in the huge canvas of fraught naturecultures and war in the Middle East. I was a kind of "godhuman" to Willem, a Great Pyrenees livestock guardian dog who worked on land in California that my family owns with a friend. Willem, his human, Susan, and his breeder and her health and genetics activist peers in dogland have been major informants for this book. Willem's livestock guardian dog people are astute participants in the hotly contested dog–wolf–rancher–herbivore–environmentalist–hunter naturecultures of the contemporary U.S. northern Rocky Mountain region. Willem and my dog Cayenne played as puppies and added to the stock of the world's joy.[58] This is all quite small and unexceptional—not much of a "line of flight" to delight Deleuze and Guattari here. But it was enough to hail me and maybe us into curiosity about the naturalcultural politics of wolves, dogs, cattle, ticks, pathogens, tanks, mine fields, soldiers, displaced villagers, cattle thieves, and settlers become cowboy-style ranchers on still another bit of earth made into a frontier by war, expulsion, occupation, the history of genocides, and ramifying insecurity all around. There is no happy ending to offer, no conclusion to this ongoing entanglement, only a sharp reminder that anywhere one really looks actual living wolves and dogs are waiting to guide humans into contested worldings. "We found her at the edge of the city; she was raised by wolves." Like her forest-immigrant cousin, this wolf wore a communications pack that was no stranger to the development of military technology for command, control, communication, and intelligence.

Of course, by the first decade of the new millennium, that kind of telecommunications pack could be ordinary equipment for day walkers in the mountains, and that is where these introductions will end, but with the printed word rather than a personal GPS system situating the hiker. In 2005 primatologist Allison Jolly, knowing my livestock-guardian-dog passions, sent me a brochure she had picked up on her walking tour through the French Alps that summer with her family. The brochure was in Italian, French, and English, already setting it off from unaccommodating monolingual U.S. aids to mountain outings. The transnational paths through the Alps and the urbane, leisured, international hikers expected on the paths were vividly present. On the cover was an alert, calm Great Pyrenees guardian dog, surrounded by text: "Important notice to walkers and hikers [or on the flip side, 'Promeneurs, Randonneurs,' etc.]: In the course of your walk, you may encounter the local guarding-dogs. These are large white dogs whose task is to guard the flocks."

We are in the midst of reinvented pastoral–tourist economies linking foot-traveling humans, meat and fiber niche markets that are complexly both local and global, restoration ecology and heritage culture projects of the European Union, shepherds, flocks, dogs, wolves, bears, and lynxes. The return of previously extirpated predators to parts of their old ranges is a major story of transnational environmental politics and biology. Some of the animals have been deliberately reintroduced after intense captive breeding programs or with transplants from less-developed countries in the previous Soviet sphere, where progress-indicating extinctions sometimes have not gone as far as in western Europe. Some predators reestablished populations on their own when people began trapping and shooting returnees less often. The wolves newly welcome in the French Alps seem to be offspring of opportunistic canids sidling over from unreliably progressive Italy, which never completely wiped out its wolves. The wolves gave the LGDs a job deterring lupine (and tourist) depredations on the shepherds' flocks. After the near destruction of the Great Pyrenees during the two world wars and the pastoral economic collapse in the Basque regions, the breed came to the Alps from the mountains for which they are named, by way of their rescue by the purebred dog fancy, especially through the collecting practices of wealthy women in England and the eastern United States. French dog fanciers learned some of what they needed to know about reintroducing their dogs to guarding work from U.S. LGD people, who had placed dogs on ranches in western states in recent decades and communicated with their European peers.

The knots of technocultural, reinvented pastoral–tourist economies and ecologies are all over North America too, raising the most basic questions of who belongs where and what flourishing means for whom. Following the dogs and their herbivores and people in order to respond to those questions attaches me again and again to ranching, farming, and eating. In principle if not always in personal and collective action, it is easy to know that factory farming and its sciences and politics must be undone. But what then? How can food security for everybody (not just for the rich, who can forget how important cheap and abundant food is) and multispecies' coflourishing be linked in practice? How can remembering the conquest of the western states by Anglo settlers and their plants and animals become part of the solution and not another occasion for the pleasurable and individualizing frisson of guilt? Much collaborative and inventive work is under way on these matters, if only we take touch seriously. Both vegan and nonvegan community food projects with a local and translocal analysis have made clear the links among safe and fair working conditions for people, physically and behaviorally healthy agricultural animals, genetic and other research directed to health and diversity, urban and rural food security, and enhanced wildlife habitat.[59] No easy unity is to be found on these matters, and no answers will make one feel good for long. But those are not the goals of companion species. Rather, there are vastly more attachment sites for participating in the search for more livable "other worlds" (autres-mondialisations) inside earthly complexity than one could ever have imagined when first reaching out to pet one's dog.

The kinds of relatings that these introductions perform entangle a motley crowd of differentially situated species, including landscapes, animals, plants, microorganisms, people, and technologies. Sometimes a polite introduction brings together two quasi-individuated beings, maybe even with personal names printed in major newspapers, whose histories can recall comfortable narratives of subjects in encounter, two by two. More often, the configurations of critters have other patterns more reminiscent of a cat's cradle game of the sort taken for granted by good ecologists, military strategists, political economists, and ethnographers. Whether grasped two-by-two or tangle-by-tangle, attachment sites needed for meeting species redo everything they touch. The point is not to celebrate complexity but to become worldly and to respond. Considering still live metaphors for this work, John Law and Annemarie Mol help me think: "Multiplicity, oscillation, mediation, material heterogeneity, performativity, interference . . . there is no resting place in a multiple and partially connected world."[60]

My point is simple: Once again we are in a knot of species coshaping one another in layers of reciprocating complexity all the way down. Response and respect are possible only in those knots, with actual animals and people looking back at each other, sticky with all their muddled histories. Appreciation of the complexity is, of course, invited. But more is required too. Figuring what that more might be is the work of situated companion species. It is a question of cosmopolitics, of learning to be "polite" in responsible relation to always asymmetrical living and dying, and nurturing and killing. And so I end with the alpine tourist brochure's severe injunction to the hiker to "be on your best countryside behavior," or "sorveguate il vostro comportamento," followed by specific instructions about what polite behavior toward the working dogs and flocks entails. A prosaic detail: The exercise of good manners makes *the competent working animals* those whom *the people* need to learn to recognize.[61] The ones with face were not all human.

And say the philosopher responded?

Mike Peters, *Mother Goose and Grimm,* copyright 2004 Grimmy, Inc. All rights reserved. Reprinted with permission of Grimmy, Inc., in conjunction with the Cartoonist Group.

2. VALUE-ADDED DOGS
AND LIVELY CAPITAL

Marx dissected the commodity form into the doublet of exchange value and use value. But what happens when the undead but always generative commodity becomes the living, breathing, rights-endowed, doggish bit of property sleeping on my bed, or giving cheek swabs for your genome project, or getting a computer-readable ID chip injected under the neck skin before the local dog shelter lets my neighbor adopt her new family member? *Canis lupus familiaris*, indeed; the familiar is always where the uncanny lurks. Further, the uncanny is where value becomes flesh again, in spite of all the dematerializations and objectifications inherent in market valuation.

Marx always understood that use and exchange value were names for relationships; that was precisely the insight that led beneath the layer of appearances of market equivalences into the messy domain of extraction, accumulation, and human exploitation. Turning all the world into commodities for exchange is central to the process. Indeed, remaking the world so that new opportunities for commodity production and circulation are ever generated is the name of this game. This is the game that absorbs living human labor power without mercy. In Marx's own colorful, precise language that still gives capitalism's apologists apoplexy, capital comes into the world "dripping from head to toe, from every pore, with blood and dirt."[1]

What, however, if *human* labor power turns out to be only part of the story of lively capital? Of all philosophers, Marx understood relational sensuousness, and he thought deeply about the metabolism between human beings and the rest of the world enacted in living labor. As I read him, however, he was finally unable to escape from the humanist teleology of that labor—the making of man himself. In the end, no companion species, reciprocal inductions, or multispecies epigenetics are in his story.[2] But what if the commodities of interest to those who live within the regime of Lively Capital cannot be understood within the categories of the natural and the social that Marx came so close to reworking but was finally unable to do under the goad of human exceptionalism? These are hardly new questions, but I propose to approach them through relationships inherent in contemporary U.S. dog–human doings that raise issues not usually associated with the term *biocapital*, if, nonetheless, crucial to it.

We have no shortage of proof that classic rabid commodification is alive and well in consumer-crazy, technoscientifically exuberant dog worlds in the United States. I will give my readers plenty of reassuring fact-packages on this point, sufficient to create all the moral outrage that we lefties seem to need for breakfast and all the judgment-resistant desires that we cultural analysts seem to enjoy even more. However, if a Marx-equivalent were writing *Biocapital*, volume 1, today, insofar as dogs in the United States are commodities as well as consumers of commodities, the analyst would have to examine a tripartite structure: use value, exchange value, and encounter value, without the problematic solace of human exceptionalism.[3] Trans-species encounter value is about relationships among a motley array of lively beings, in which commerce and consciousness, evolution and bioengineering, and ethics and utilities are all in play. I am especially interested here in "encounters" that involve, in a nontrivial but hard-to-characterize way, *subjects* of different biological species. My goal is to make a little headway in characterizing these relationships in the historically specific context of lively capital. I would like to tie my Marx-equivalent into the knots of value for companion species, especially for

dogs and people in capitalist technoculture in the early twenty-first century, in which the insight that to be a situated human being is to be
shaped by and with animal familiars might deepen our abilities to understand value-added encounters.

VALUING DOGS: MARKETS AND COMMODITIES

Like a 1950s TV show, companion-animal worlds are all about family.
If European and American bourgeois families were among the products
of nineteenth-century capital accumulation, the human–animal companionate family is a key indicator for today's lively capital practices. That
nineteenth-century family invented middle-class pet keeping, but what a
pale shadow of today's doings that was! Kin and brand are tied in productive embrace as never before. In 2006, about 69 million U.S. households (63 percent of all households) had pets, giving homes to about 73.9
million dogs, 90.5 million cats, 16.6 million birds, and many other critters.[4] As an online report on the pet food and supplies market from
MindBranch, Inc., for 2004 stated, "In the past, people may have said their
pet 'is like a member of the family,' but during 1998–2003 this attitude
has strengthened, at least in terms of money spent on food with quality
ingredients, toys, supplies, services, and healthcare."[5] The consumer habits
of families have long been the locus for critical theory's efforts to understand the category formations that shape social beings (such as gender,
race, and class). Companion-species kin patterns of consumerism should
be a rich place to get at the relations that shape emergent subjects, not all
of whom are people, in lively capital's naturecultures. Properly mutated,
the classics, such as gender, race, and class, hardly disappear in this world—
far from it; but the most interesting emergent categories of relationality are going to have to acquire some new names, and not just for the dogs
and cats.

The global companion-animal industry is big, and the United States
is a major player. I know this because I have dogs and cats who live in the
style in which my whole post-Lassie generation and I have become in-
doctrinated. Like any scholar, however, I tried to get some hard figures
to go with the coming examples. The Business Communications Company publishes an annual analysis of market opportunities and segments,

company fortunes, rates of expansion or contraction, and other such data dear to the hearts of investors. So for the first draft of this chapter I tried to consult *The Pet Industry: Accessories, Products, and Services* for 2004 online. Indeed, I could have downloaded any of the alluring chapters, but all of them are proprietary, and so to peek is to pay. To obtain access to the whole package would have cost me over five thousand dollars, a nice piece of evidence all by itself for my assertion in the first sentence of this paragraph. An alternative data source, Global Information, Inc. (the self-described online "vertical markets research portal"), offers twenty-four-hour, five-day-per-week updates for pet marketers on forecasts, shares, R&D, sales and marketing, and competitive analysis. Ignore these services at your peril.

In the end, I settled for training-sized statistical tidbits from Business Communications and from the 2006 free summaries on the Web site of the American Pet Products Manufacturers Association, Inc.[6] In the United States alone in 2006, pet owners spent about $38.4 billion overall on companion animals, compared with $21 billion in 1996 (constant dollars). The global figure for pet food and pet care products for 2002 was U.S.$46 billion, which is an inflation-adjusted increase of 8 percent over the period 1998–2002. The inflation-adjusted growth rate for 2003 alone was 3.4 percent, driven, we are told, by pet owners' demand for premium foods and supplies.

Consider just pet food. ICON Group International published a world market report in February 2004. The report was written for "strategic planners, international executives and import/export managers who are concerned with the market for dog and cat food for retail sale." The point was that "with the globalization of the market, managers can no longer be contented with a local view." Thus, the report paid special attention to which countries supply dog and cat food for retail sale, what the dollar value of the imports is, how market shares are apportioned country by country, which countries are the biggest buyers, how regional markets are evolving, and so how managers might prioritize their marketing strategies. Over 150 countries are analyzed, and the report makes clear that its figures are estimates of potential that can be drastically altered by such things as "'mad cow' disease, foot-and-mouth disease, trade embargoes, labor disputes, military conflicts, acts of terrorism, and other events that will certainly affect the actual trade flows."[7] Indeed. Nonetheless, the report neglected to state the underlying obvious fact: industrial pet food is a strong link in the multispecies chain of global factory farming.

The *News York Times* for Sunday, November 30, 2003, is my source for the $12.5 billion figure for the size of the 2003 pet food market in the United States ($15 billion in 2006). I did not know how to think about the size of that sum until I read another *New York Times* story (December 2, 2003) telling me that in 2003 the human cholesterol-lowering statin market was worth $12.5 billion to the pharmaceutical industry. How much human blood-lipid control is worth how many dog dinners? I'd throw away my Lipitor before I shorted my dogs and cats. Marx told us how the purely objective nature of exchange value obviates the trouble springing from such use-value comparisons. He also told us how such things as statins and premium dog food become historically situated bodily needs. For my taste, he didn't pay nearly enough attention to *which* needy bodies in the multispecies web link slaughter labor, chicken cages, pet dinners, human medicine, and much more.

I cannot now forget these things as I decide how to evaluate both the latest niche-marketed dog food purported to maximize the sports performance of my agility dog and the difference between her nutritional needs and those of my older but still active pooch. A large and growing portion of pet food products addresses specific conditions, such as joint and urinary tract health, tartar control, obesity, physiological demands, age-related needs, and so on. I cannot go to an agility meet to run with my dog without tripping over brochures and booths for natural foods, scientifically formulated foods, immune-function enhancing foods, foods containing homemade ingredients, foods for doggy vegans, raw organic foods that would not please vegans at all, freeze-dried carrot-fortified foods, food-delivery devices to help out dogs who are alone too much, and on and on. Indeed, diets are like drugs in this nutritional ecology, and creating demand for "treatment" is crucial to market success. Besides diets, I feel obligated to investigate and buy all the appropriate supplements that ride the wavering line between foods and drugs (chondroitin sulfate and glucosamine sulfate or omega-3 fatty acid–rich flaxseed oil, for example). Dogs in capitalist technoculture have acquired the "right to health," and the economic (as well as legal) implications are legion.

Food is not the whole story. The Business Communications Company stressed the growth occurring in all segments of the companion-animal industry, with rich opportunities for existing players and new entrants. Health is a giant component of this diversifying doggy version of lively capital. Small-animal veterinarians are well aware of this fact as they struggle to incorporate the latest (very expensive) diagnostic and treatment equipment into a small practice in order to remain competitive. A special study done in 1998 revealed that vets' income was not growing at the rate of comparable professionals, because they did not know how to adjust their fees to the rapidly expanding services they routinely offer.[8] My family's credit card records tell me that at least one of the vet practices we frequent got the point in spades. In 2006, people in the United States spent about $9.4 billion for vet care for pets. As a reality check, I turned to the "World Animal Health Markets to 2010," a report that profiles animal health markets in fifteen countries, accounting for 80 percent of the world share.[9] The conclusion: in the affluent parts of the globe, the pet health market is robust and growing.

Consider a few figures and stories. Mary Battiata wrote a feature article for the *Washington Post* in August 2004; it followed her search for a diagnosis for her aging family member, her beloved mutt, Bear, who showed troubling neurological symptoms. After the first sick visit to the vet cost nine hundred dollars, she began to understand her situation. She was referred to Washington, D.C.'s Iams Pet Imaging Center for an MRI. Or rather, Bear was referred, and his guardian–owner, Mary, wrestled with the ethical, political, affectional, and economic dilemmas. How does a companion animal's human make judgments about the right time to let her dog die or, indeed, to kill her dog? How much care is too much? Is the issue quality of life? Money? Pain? Whose? Does paying fourteen hundred dollars for an MRI for Bear add to the world's injustice, or is the comparison between what it costs to run decent public schools or to repair wetlands and what it costs for Bear's diagnosis and treatment the wrong comparison? What about the comparison between people who love their pet kin and can afford an MRI and people who love their pet kin and can't afford annual vet exams, good training education, and the latest tick and flea products, much less hospice care (now available in a few places for dogs and cats)? What comparisons are the right ones in the regime of lively capital?

Other high-end treatments now available for pets include kidney transplants, cancer chemotherapy, and titanium joint-replacement surgeries. The University of California at Davis recently opened an up-to-the-minute treatment and research hospital for companion animals with the kind of cancer care expected in the best human medical centers. New veterinary drugs—and human drugs redirected to companion animals—emphasize pain relief and behavior modification, matters that hardly appeared on the radar screens of Lassie's people but involve serious money and serious ethical dilemmas today. In addition, vets in training today take courses in the human–animal bond, and this diversifying region of the affectional family economy is as richly commodified and socially stratified as is any other family-making practice, say, for example, assisted reproduction for making human babies and parents.[10]

Pet health insurance has become common, as is malpractice insurance for vets, partly fueled by the success of court arguments that companion animals cannot be valued as ordinary property. "Replacement value" for a companion dog is not the market price of the animal. Neither is the dog the same as a child nor an aged parent. In case we missed the point in all the other aspects of daily life, efforts both to establish money damages and to pay the bills for our companions tell us that *parent–child*, *guardian–ward*, and *owner–property* are all lousy terms for the sorts of multispecies relationships emerging among us. The categories need a makeover.

Besides vets, other sorts of health professionals have also emerged to meet companion-animal needs. I get regular professional adjustments for my Australian shepherd sports partner, Cayenne, from Ziji Scott, an animal chiropractic-certified practitioner with magic hands. No one could convince me that this practice reflects bourgeois decadence at the expense of my other obligations. Some relationships are zero sum games, and some are not. But a central fact shapes the whole question: rights to health and family-making practices are heavily capitalized and stratified, for dogs as well as for their humans.

Beyond the domains of dog medical services, nutrition, or pedagogical offerings, canine consumer culture of another sort seems truly boundless. Consider vacation packages, adventure trips, camp experiences, cruises, holiday clothing, toys of all kinds, day care services, designer beds and other animal-adapted furniture, doggy sleeping bags and special tents and backpacks, and published guides to all of the above. On September 24, 2004, the *New York Times* ran ads for dog shopping that featured a $225 raincoat and $114 designer collar. Toy dogs as fashion accessories to the wealthy and famous are a common newspaper topic and a serious worry for those who think those dogs have doggish needs.[11] The American Kennel and Boarding Association in 2006 reported that the significant industry growth is in the high-end pet lodgings, such as the new San Francisco hotel, Wag, which charges eighty-five dollars per night and offers massage, facials, and swimming pools. Webcam TV for traveling humans to watch their pets in real time in communal play areas is standard at San Francisco's middle-of-the-market forty-dollar-a-night Fog City Dogs Lodge.[12] For those whose commodity preferences are more bookish, look at the companion-animal print culture. Besides a huge companion-species book market in categories from anthropology to zoology and the whole alphabet in between, two new general-audience magazines make my point. *Bark* is a Berkeley, California, dog literary, arts, and culture rag that I read avidly, and not just because it favorably reviewed my *Companion Species Manifesto.* The East Coast finally faced its responsibilities in this market segment, and so, with articles on such matters as how to win a dog custody battle and where to find the best ten places to walk with your dog in Manhattan, the *New York Dog* appeared in November–December 2004, aiming to rival *Vogue* and *Cosmopolitan* for glossy values.[13] And all of this hardly touches the media markets crucial to hunting with dogs, playing dog–human sports, working with dogs in volunteer search and rescue, and much more. It seems to me that it is all too easy in dogland to forget that resistance to human exceptionalism *requires* resistance to humanization of our partners. Furry, market-weary, rights bearers deserve a break.

Enough, or rather, almost enough; after all, in lively capital markets "value-added" dogs aren't just familial co-consumers (or coworkers, for which you must go to the next section of this chapter). In the flesh and in the sign, dogs *are* commodities, and commodities of a type central to the history of capitalism, especially of technoscientifically saturated agribusiness. Here I will consider only kennel-club registered "purebred" dogs, even though those surely aren't the canines that come first to mind in connection with the term *agribusiness*, no matter how much pedigree-packing dogs return us to crucial nineteenth-century economic and cultural innovations rooted in the biosocial body. In *Bred for Perfection*, Margaret Derry explains that the public data keeping of lineage (the written, standardized, and guaranteed pedigree) is the innovation that fostered international trade in both livestock such as sheep and cattle and fancy stock such as show dogs and chickens.[14] And, I might add, race- and family-making stock. Institutionally recorded purity of descent, emphasizing both inbreeding and male lines that made female reproductive labor all but invisible, was the issue. The state, private corporations, research institutions, and clubs all played their roles in moving practices for controlling animal reproduction from pockets of memory and local endeavors of both elites and working people to rationalized national and international markets tied to registries. The breeding system that evolved with the data-keeping system was called scientific breeding, and in myriad ways this paper-plus-flesh system is behind the histories of eugenics and genetics, as well as other sciences (and politics) of animal and human reproduction.

Dog breeds, not variously differentiated and stabilized kinds, but breeds with written pedigrees, were one result. Across continents, dogs with those credentials could command very nice prices as well as fuel amazing practices of heritage invention, standards writing and maintenance, sales contract development, germ plasm trading, health surveillance and activism, reproductive-technology innovation, and the passionate commitment of individuals, groups, and even whole nations.[15]

The proliferation of dog breeds and their movement into every social class and geographical region of the world are part of the story. Many breeds have been specifically produced for the pet market, some quite new, such as the cross of Borzois and long-haired whippets to make the little sight hound called the silken windhound. Witness today's explosion in toy breeds and teacup breeds as fashion accessories (and too often, medical disasters). Or the popularity of the puppy mill–produced dogs because they carry an AKC purebred dog pedigree. Or, as I move away from outrage to love affair, I am reminded both of the knowledgeable, talented, self-critical dog people whom I have met in performance dog worlds, as well as in conformation show dog scenes, and of their accomplished, beautiful dogs. And of my dogs, including Roland, the one

with the fraudulent (that chow chow dad) AKC Australian shepherd registration, acquired so that he can play agility in their sandbox, as long as
he is reproductively sterilized.

But is he necessarily reproductively silenced? What happens when
pedigree, or lack of it, meets petri dish? Consider the Dolly technique so
insightfully written about by Sarah Franklin in *Dolly Mixtures*. Dolly the
pedigreed sheep might have been the first mammal who was the fruit of
somatic cell nuclear transfer cloning, but she was at the head of a growing
parade of critters. By tracing the many biosocial threads in Dolly's genealogy across continents, markets, species, sciences, and narratives, Franklin
argues that emergent ways of fleshly becoming are at the heart of biocapital, both as commodities and as modes of production.[16] Franklin
maintains that breedwealth was the crucial new kind of reproductive
wealth in the late eighteenth and nineteenth centuries, and control over
the reproduction (or generation by other means) of plants and animals
(and, to varying degrees, people) is fundamental to contemporary biocapital's promises and threats. The traffic between industrialized agriculture
and scientific medicine for people and animals is especially thick in Dolly
mixtures and spillovers. Current innovations and controversies in stem
cell research and therapeutic as well as reproductive cloning are at the
heart of the transnational, transspecific action.

Stem cells and dogs take us inevitably to Hwang Woo-Suk and Seoul
National University. The international scandal surrounding Hwang's an-
nouncement in *Science* magazine in 2004 and 2005 of achieving the
globalized biomedical grail of human embryonic stem cell clones and the
subsequent revelation in December 2005 of fabricated data, bioethics vio-
lations in egg donation, and possible embezzlement have a more authentic canine backstory that only makes sense in light of *Dolly Mixtures*. In
the United States, the well-hyped dog-cloning Missyplicity Project was
directed to the affectional commodity pet market.[17] Not so the biomedical dog-cloning efforts of Hwang and his nine South Korean associates,
plus Gerald Schatten, a stem cell researcher at the University of Pitts-
burgh, who announced Snuppy, an Afghan hound puppy cloned with the
Dolly technique, in August 2005.[18] Snuppy is a biotechnical splice to his
core, his name fabricated of S(eoul) N(ational) U(niversity) and (pu)ppy.
Hwang's research career must be understood in the context of agribusiness

animal research moved to human biomedicine. His professorship is in the Department of Theriogenology and Biotechnology in the College of Veterinary Medicine at Seoul National University. Before Snuppy, Hwang reported a cloned dairy cow in 1999, and he was widely regarded as a world leader in the field. A great deal about Hwang's dramatic rise and fall is not clear, but what is clear is the thick cross-species travel between agribusiness research and human biomedicine often obscured in the U.S. "ethical" debates over human stem cell technologies and imagined therapies or reproductive marvels.

Pricey U.S. dog cryopreservation services, university–private company collaborations for canine-cloning research geared to the pet market, and Korean national efforts to become first in a major area of biomedical research are not the only arias in this lively capital opera. However, even if freezing the cells of my AKC-mutt Roland in anticipation of making a nuclear clone of him could happen only over the dead bodies of my whole polyspecific and polysexual family, these Dolly spillovers, especially Snuppy, do suggest just the right segue to the next section of "Value-Added Dogs."

VALUING DOGS: TECHNOLOGIES, WORKERS, KNOWLEDGES

Referring to advertisements for the sale of working sheepdogs, Donald McCaig, the Virginia sheep farmer and astute writer on the history and current state of herding border collies in Britain and the United States, noted that categorically the dogs fall somewhere between livestock and coworkers for the human shepherds.[19] These dogs are not pets or family members, although they are still commodities. Working dogs are tools that are part of the farm's capital stock, and they are laborers who produce surplus value by giving more than they get in a market-driven economic system. I think that is more than an analogy, but it is not an identity. Working dogs produce and they reproduce, and in neither process are they their own "self-directed" creatures in relation to lively capital, even though enlisting their active cooperation (self-direction) is essential to their productive and reproductive jobs. But they are not human slaves or wage laborers, and it would be a serious mistake to theorize their labor within those frameworks. They are paws, not hands. Let's see if we can sort through the implications of the difference, even in spite of the evolutionary homology of the forelimbs.

To do so, I turn to Edmund Russell's arguments about the evolutionary history of technology in his introduction to the collection *Industrializing Organisms*.[20] Far from keeping organic beings and artifactual technologies separate, putting one in nature and the other in society, Russell adopts recent science and technology studies' insistence on the coproduction of natures and cultures and the interpenetration of bodies and technologies. He defines organisms shaped for functional performance in human worlds as biotechnologies—"biological artifacts shaped by humans to serve human ends."[21] He goes on to distinguish macrobiotechnologies, such as whole organisms, from microbiotechnologies, such as the cells and molecules that draw all the attention as biotechnology itself in the current science and business press.

In that sense, dogs deliberately selected and enhanced for their working capacities, for example, as herders, are biotechnologies in a system of market farming that became contemporary capital-intensive agribusiness through a welter of nonlinear processes and assemblages. Russell is interested in how the ways in which human beings have shaped evolution have changed both themselves and other species. The tight boxes of nature and society do not allow much serious investigation of this question. Russell's major efforts are directed at analyzing organisms as technologies, and he looks at biotechnologies as factories, as workers, and as products. Even though Russell gives almost all the agency to humans—who, I admit readily, make the deliberate plans to change things—I find his framework rich for thinking about valuing dogs as biotechnologies, workers, and agents of technoscientific knowledge production in the regime of lively capital.

Aside from such critters of the past as spit-turning dogs or cart-hauling dogs, whole dogs are simultaneously biotechnologies and workers in several kinds of contemporary material–semiotic reality. Herding dogs are still at work on profit-making (or, more likely, money-losing) farms and ranches, although job loss has been acute. Their work in sheep trials is robust but located in the zone between work and sport, as is the labor of most sled dogs. Livestock guardian dogs have expanding job opportunities in sheep-raising areas of the French Alps and Pyrenees because of the reintroduction of ecotourism-linked heritage predators (wolves, bears, and lynxes), as well as on U.S. ranches no longer allowed to use poisons for predator control. Dogs have state jobs and jobs franchised to private providers as airport security laborers, drug and bomb sniffers, and pigeon-clearing officers on runways.

The popular television show *Dogs with Jobs*, using the classified help-wanted ads in newspapers as the visual icon for the show, is a good place to get a grip on dogs as workers.[22] Most of the dogs seem to be unpaid voluntary labor, but not all. Jobs include warning of epileptic seizures, detecting cancer, guiding the blind, serving as aides for the hearing impaired and the wheelchair-bound and as psychotherapeutic aides for traumatized children and adults, visiting the aged, aiding in rescues in extreme environments, and more. Dogs can be and are studied and specifically bred to enhance their readiness to learn and perform these kinds of jobs. For all of these jobs, dogs and people have to train together in subject-changing ways. But more of that later.

Part dogs (or delegated dog wholes or parts in material bases other than carbon, nitrogen, and water) might have more work in lively capital than whole dogs. Consider, in addition to Snuppy's stem cell scene, dog genome projects. Archived canine genomes are repositories useful for research in product development by veterinary pharmaceutical enterprises and human biomedical interests, as well as for research in—a gleam in researchers' eyes—behavioral genetics.[23] This is "normal" biotechnology. Sequencing and databasing the complete dog genome were made a priority of the U.S. National Human Genome Research Institute in June 2003. Based on a poodle, the first rough dog genome sequence, about 75 percent complete, was published that year. The first full draft of the dog genome was published and deposited in a free public database for biomedical and vet researchers in July 2004. In May 2005, a 99 percent complete sequence of the genome of a boxer named Tasha, with comparisons to ten other kinds of dogs, was released. Dogs belonging to researchers, members of breed clubs, and colonies at vet schools provided DNA samples. The team that produced this draft, in the process developing procedures that might speed the deposition of many more mammalian genomes, was headed by Kerstin Lindblad-Toh, of the Broad Institute of MIT and

Harvard as well as the Agencourt Bioscience Corporation. Part of the National Human Genome Research Institute's Large-Scale Sequencing Research Network, the Broad Institute received a thirty-million-dollar grant for the work. These are the kinds of public–private arrangements typical of microbiotechnology in the United States and, with variations, internationally.[24]

Further, once the genome was published, the Center for Veterinary Genetics, at the University of California School of Veterinary Medicine, called for individual dog people and clubs to contribute to a full repository of many of the different breeds of dogs in order to address the needs of different domains of dogdom. The goal was to enlarge the DNA data bank from its then current sampling of the genetic legacy of one hundred breeds to more than four hundred international canine populations. Many research projects involving dog genes, organs, diseases, and molecules could be addressed to canine questions as well as to comparative queries for humans. The part dogs are reagents (workers), tools, and products, just as whole dogs are in macrobiotechnological kinds of knowledge and production projects.

Dogs are valuable workers in technoculture in another sense as well. In laboratories, they labor as research models both for their own and for human conditions, especially for diseases that could be "enclosed" for medical commodity production, including for previously unknown sorts of services to address newly articulated needs. That, of course, is what their archived genomes are doing, but I want to look more closely at another mode of this scientific medical canine labor in the context of lively capital. Stephen Pemberton explores how dogs suffering from hemophilia became model patients, as well as surrogates and technologies for studying a human disease, over the course of years beginning in the late 1940s in the laboratory of Kenneth Brinkhous at the University of North Carolina at Chapel Hill. This research is what made human hemophilia a manageable disease by the early 1970s with the availability of standardized clotting factors.[25]

Bleeder dogs did not just appear at the lab doorstep as ready-made models and machine tools for making things for humans. The canine hemophiliac was made through representational strategies, dog care practices, breeding and selection, biochemical characterization, development of novel measurement devices, and the semiotic and material joining of hemophilia to other metabolic deficiency disorders (especially diabetes and pernicious anemia, both treatable by administering something functionally absent in the patient and both diseases in which dogs played a large role in the research, with crucial payoff in techniques and devices for working with dog organs and tissues). The principal problem Brinkhous faced in his lab when he brought in male Irish setter puppies who showed the stigmata of bleeding into joints and body cavities was keeping them alive. The puppies had to become patients if they were to become technologies and models. The entire labor organization of the laboratory addressed the priority of treating the dogs before anything else. A bleeding dog was given transfusions and supportive care. Lab staff could not function as researchers if they did not function as caregivers. Dogs could not work as models if they did not work as patients. Thus, the lab became a clinical microcosm for its research subjects as an essential part of the last century's revolution in experimental biomedicine. As Pemberton put it, "We cannot understand how scientists discipline their experimental organisms without understanding how these organisms also discipline scientists, forcing them to care."[26]

In the late twentieth century, drugs developed for people (and surely tested on rodents) came to be agents of relief for dogs too, in a kind of patient-to-patient cross-species transfusion. This kind of dogs-as-patients scene is part of my own adult origin tale in dogland. My middle-class childhood tale had more to do with the confining of the multispecies civic commons through leash laws in the 1950s than with biomedicine. Toward the end of her sixteenth, and last, year of life in 1995, my half-Lab mutt, Sojourner (that grace-giving whelp of an irresponsible backyard breeder, a dog whom we named for a great human liberator), and I began to frequent her vet's office in Santa Cruz. I had read Michel Foucault, and I knew all about biopower and the proliferative powers of biological discourses. I knew modern power was productive above all else. I knew how important it was to have a body pumped up, petted, and managed by the apparatuses of medicine, psychology, and pedagogy. I knew that modern subjects had such bodies and that the rich got them before the laboring classes. I was prepared for a modest extension of my clinical privileges to any sentient being and some insentient ones. I had read *Birth of the Clinic* and *The History of Sexuality*, and I had written about the technobiopolitics of cyborgs. I felt I could not be surprised by anything. But I was wrong. Foucault's own species chauvinism had fooled me into forgetting that dogs too might live in the domains of technobiopower. *The Birth of the Kennel* might be the book I needed to write, I imagined. *When Species Meet* is the mutated spawn of that moment.

While Sojourner and I waited to be seen by her vet, a lovely Afghan hound pranced around at the checkout desk while his human discussed recommended treatments. The dog had a difficult problem—obsessive self-wounding when his human was off making a living, or engaging in less justifiable nondog activities, for several hours a day. The afflicted dog had a nasty open sore on his hind leg. The vet recommended that the dog take Prozac. I had read *Listening to Prozac*;[27] so I knew this was the drug that promised, or threatened, to give its recipient a new self in place of the drab, depressive, obsessive one who had proved so lucrative for the non-pharmaceutical branches of the psychological professions. For years, I had insisted that dogs and people were much alike and that other animals had complex minds and social lives, as well as physiologies and genomes largely shared with humans. Why did hearing that a pooch should take Prozac warp my sense of reality in the way that makes one see what was hidden before? Surely Saul, on the way to Damascus, had more to his turnaround than a Prozac prescription for his neighbor's ass!

The Afghan's human was as nonplussed as I was. She chose instead to put a large cone, called an Elizabethan collar, around her dog's head so that he couldn't reach his favorite licking spot to suck out his unhappiness. I was even more shocked by that choice; I fumed internally, Can't you get more time to exercise and play with your dog and solve this problem without chemicals or restraints? I remained deaf to the human's defensive explanation to the vet that her health policy covered her own Prozac, but the pills were too expensive for her dog. In truth, I was hooked into the mechanisms of proliferating discourse that Foucault should have prepared me for. Drugs, restraints, exercise, retraining, altered schedules, searching for improper puppy socialization, scrutinizing the genetic background of the dog for evidence of canine familial obsessions, wondering about psychological or physical abuse, finding an unethical breeder who turns out inbred dogs without regard to temperament, getting a good toy that would occupy the dog's attention when the human was gone, accusations about the workaholic and stress-filled human lives that are out of tune with the more natural dog rhythms of ceaseless demands for human attention: all these moves and more filled my neo-enlightened mind.

I was on the road to the fully embodied, modern, value-added dog–human relationship. There could be no end to the search for ways to relieve the psychophysiological suffering of dogs and, more, to help them achieve their full canine potential. Furthermore, I am convinced that is actually the ethical obligation of the human who lives with a companion animal in affluent, so-called first-world circumstances. I can no longer make myself feel surprise that a dog might need Prozac and should get it—or its improved, still-on-patent offshoots.

Caring for experimental dogs as patients has taken on intensified meaning and ambiguities in twenty-first-century biopolitics. A leading cause of death for older dogs and people is cancer. Enabled by comparative postgenomics tying humans and dogs together as never before, the National Cancer Institute set up a consortium of over a dozen veterinary teaching hospitals in 2006 to conduct drug trials on pet dogs living at home, to test for possible benefit in fighting the same malignancies they share with humans. A parallel nonprofit group will collect tissue samples and DNA from these pet dogs to pinpoint genes associated with cancer in dogs and people. The companion dogs will be clinic patients and not kenneled lab pooches, possibly relieving some of the latter of their burden, and grants and companies will pay for the experimental drugs. Dogs may benefit from the drugs, but they will get them with lower standards of safety than required in human testing. That's the point, after all, for enlisting dogs in National Cancer Institute state-of-the-art testing in the first place. Pet owners may have to pay for things like biopsies and imaging, which can be very expensive. Researchers will not have either the animal rights scrutiny or the financial burden of caring for lab dogs, including paying for those MRIs.[28] Pet owners and guardians will have the power to call a halt to further experimental treatment on the basis of their sense of their dogs' experiences. This system of drug testing seems to me superior to the current one, because it places the burden of suffering (and opportunity of participating in scientific research) on those specific individuals, humans and dogs, who might reap the benefit of relief. In addition, experimentation will take place much more in the open than can ever be possible or desirable with lab animals, perhaps encouraging deeper thinking and feeling by a diverse human population of pet owners, as well as clinicians and scientists.

What I find troubling here is a growing ethos that subjects pet dogs to the same search for "cures" that human cancer patients endure, rather than continuing to work within and improve current standards of care in vet practice to reduce cancer burdens and provide supportive care guided by quality-of-life criteria, not by the goal of maximally prolonging life. Chemotherapy that dogs currently get rarely aims to eliminate the cancer, and dogs consequently generally do not experience the terrible sickness from drug toxicity that most people, in the United States at least, seem to feel obligated to accept. How long can that moderate veterinary approach to dog illness, and acceptance of death as profoundly sad and hard but also normal, endure in the face of the power of comparative postgenomic medicine and its associated affectional and commercial biopolitics?

So, dogs have become patients, workers, technologies, and family members by their action, if not choice, in very large industries and exchange systems in lively capital: (1) pet foods, products, and services; (2) agribusiness; and (3) scientific biomedicine. Dogs' roles have been multifaceted, and they have not been passive raw material to the action of others. Further, dogs have not been unchangeable animals confined to the supposedly ahistorical order of nature. Nor have people emerged unaltered from the interactions. Relations are constitutive; dogs and people are emergent as historical beings, as subjects and objects to each other, precisely through the verbs of their relating. People and dogs emerge as mutually adapted partners in the naturecultures of lively capital. It is time to think harder about encounter value.

VALUING DOGS: ENCOUNTERS

In considering the value of encounters, why not start with prisons, since we have been touring other large industries in lively capital, and this one is immense? There are many places we might go—dogs terrorizing detainees in Iraq, for example, where the encounters that shaped enemies, torturers, and attack dogs made use of the social meanings of all the "partners" to produce definite value in lively capital. International human rights apparatuses (and where were the animal rights outcries on this one?); franchised interrogation functions; and the moral, psychological, and financial economies of contemporary imperialist wars: who could deny that all these are at the heart of enterprise and investment? Or we could travel to the high-security, high-technology, soul-destroying prison in California's Pelican Bay to track the attack-dog production, dog-fighting culture, and Aryan gang operations run from the prison, resulting in the dog-mauling death of a young woman in her apartment hallway in San Francisco and an outcry for exclusion of dogs from public space in general (but not from apartment hallways).[29]

All of these prison dog–human encounters depend on the face-to-face meeting of living, meaning-generating beings across species; that is the encounters' power to terrorize and to reach into the core of all the partners to produce both dogs condemned to euthanasia when their usefulness is ended and people fit to carry on the profitable enterprise of the prison–industrial complex, as inmates, lawyers, and guards. However, I want to think about coshaping dog–human encounters in another prison context, one that makes me pay a different kind of attention to coming face-to-face across species and so to encounter value. Therefore, let's go to Animal Planet television again, this time to watch *Cell Dogs*.[30] If dogs became technologies and patients in the world of hemophilia, then they have become therapists, companions, students, and inmates in the world of prison cells. It's all in the job description.[31]

Animal Planet focuses each week on a different prison work project that has reforming prisoners teaching reforming pooches their manners in order to place them in various occupations outside the prison. The narrative and visual semiotics are fascinating. First, the entering dogs have to be made into inmates in need of pedagogy if they are to have productive lives outside. Fast frame cuts have cell doors clanging behind the dogs, each of whom is then assigned to one prisoner–apprentice teacher, to live in the same cell with this individual human inmate for the duration of his or her joint subject-transforming relationship. Dog trainers teach the prisoners to teach the dogs basic obedience for placement as family member house pets and sometimes higher-order skills for placement as assistance dogs or therapy dogs. The screen shows the incarcerated dogs preparing for life outside by becoming willing, active, achieving obedience subjects. The pooches are obviously surrogates and models for the prisoners in the very act of becoming the prisoners' students and cell mates.

The technologies of animal training are crucial to the cell dog programs. These technologies include the postbehaviorist discourses and the equipment of so-called positive training methods (not unlike many of the pedagogies in practice in contemporary schools and child-counseling centers); some older technologies from the military-style, Koehler training methods based on frank coercion and punishment; and the apparatuses and bodily and mental habits crucial to making family members and happy roommates in close quarters. Another sense of technology is operating here too: in their personal bodies themselves, the dogs and people are freedom-making technologies for each other. They are each other's machine tools for making other selves. Face-to-face encounter is how those machines grind souls with new tolerance limits.

The canines must be modern subjects in many senses for the cell dog program to work. The dogs both require and model nonviolent, nonoptional, and finally self-rewarding discipline from legitimate authority. Both dogs and people model nonviolent, nonoptional, and self-rewarding obedience to an authority that each must earn in relation to the other. That is the route to freedom and work outside—and to survival. That death awaits the failed dog is a leitmotif in many of the programs, and the lesson for their teachers is not subtle. The traffic between performing and modeling is thick for both the humans and the dogs, who are teachers and students, docile bodies and open souls to each other. Life and death are the stakes in the prison–industrial complex. Prison reform discourse has never been more transparent. Arbeit macht frei.

Leaving the prison through the mutual self-transformation of dogs and people is the nonstop theme. The humans must stay behind to finish their sentences (some are lifers); nonetheless, when their dogs are successful canine citizen–workers outside, the human inmates leave jail in two senses. First, through their dog students, the convicts give themselves to another human person, to someone free, someone outside, and so they taste freedom and self-respect both by proxy and in their *substantial* presence in the flesh of both dog and human being. Second, they demonstrate their own reformed status as obedient, working subjects who can be trusted with freedom in a society divided into the outside and the inside. Part of the proof of worthiness is the human prisoners' act of surrendering, for the benefit of another, the companion and cell mate with whom they have lived for weeks or months in the only physically intimate, touching, face-to-face relationship they are allowed. The graduation scenes, which involve the human inmates sacrificing themselves by giving their intimate companions to another to achieve a better life for both, are always intensely emotional. I dare you to be cynical, even if all the knives of critical discourse are in your hands. Maybe it's not all "arbeit macht frei" here, but something more like "touch makes possible." Since I can't be outside ideology, I'll take that one, face-to-face and eyes open. The rhetoric that connects categories of the oppressed in these programs is not subtle (prisoners, animals, the disabled, women in jail, black men, strays, etc.); all belong to categories that discursively need much more than remedial training. However, these projects hold potential for much more promising entanglements that question the terms of these tropes and the conditions of those who must live them.

Perhaps it would be possible to rethink and retool cell dogs to work their magic to build subjects for a world not so fiercely divided into outside and inside. Marx understood the analysis of the commodity form into exchange value and use value to be a practice crucial to freedom projects. Maybe if we take seriously encounter value as the underanalyzed axis of lively capital and its "biotechnologies in circulation"—in the form of commodities, consumers, models, technologies, workers, kin, and knowledges—we can see how something more than the reproduction of the same and its deadly logics-in-the-flesh of exploitation might be going on in what I call "making companions."

In *Making Parents: The Ontological Choreography of Reproductive Technologies*, Charis Thompson compares and contrasts capitalist production with what she calls a "biomedical mode of reproduction," which I think of as core to the regime of lively capital. Thompson is studying the making of parents and children through the subject- and object-making technologies of biomedically assisted reproduction, a very lively area of contemporary investments of bodily, narratival, desiring, moral, epistemological, institutional, and financial kinds. She is acutely alert to the classical processes of production, investment, commodification, and so on, in contemporary human-assisted reproduction practices in the United States. But she is adamant that the *end* of the practices makes a difference; that is, the whole point is to make parents by making living babies. *Capital*, volumes 1–3, did not cover that topic. *Biocapital*, volume 1, must do so.

In two columns, Thompson sets out the following lists, which I borrow, abbreviate, and abuse:[32]

Production	Reproduction
Alienated from one's labor	Alienated from one's body parts
Capital accumulated	Capital promissory
Efficiency/productivity	Success/reproductivity
Life course finite and descent linear	Loss of finitude/linearity in life course and descent
Essentialism of natural kinds/social construction of social kinds	Strategic naturalization/ socialization of all kinds

In practice, parents-in-the-making selectively seek out, endure, elaborate, and narrate various objectifications and commodifications of their body parts. Women do this much more than men do because of the fleshly realities of assisted conception and gestation. Many sorts of social stratification and injustice are in play, but they are often not of the kinds found by those seeking their fix of outrage whenever they smell the commodification of humans or part humans. Properly assigned, living babies make living parents content with their objectifications. Other actors in this mode of reproduction may be made invisible in order to ensure their status as nonkin and as reproductively impotent. The lure of kin making is the name of this promissory game of reproduction.

I am interested in these matters when the kin-making beings are not all human and literal children or parents are not the issue. Companion species are the issue. They are the promise, the process, and the product. These matters are mundane, and this chapter has been replete with examples. Add to those many more proliferations of naturalsocial relationalities in companion-species worlds linking humans and animals in myriad ways in the regime of lively capital. None of this is innocent, bloodless, or unfit for serious critical investigation. But none of it can be approached if the fleshly historical reality of face-to-face, body-to-body subject making across species is denied or forgotten in the humanist doctrine that holds only humans to be true subjects with real histories. But what does *subject* or *history* mean when the rules are changed like this? We do not get very far with the categories generally used by animal rights discourses, in which animals end up permanent dependents ("lesser humans"), utterly natural ("nonhuman"), or exactly the same ("humans in fur suits").

The categories for subjects are part of the problem. I have stressed kin making and family membership but rejected all the names of human kin for these dogs, especially the name "children." I have stressed dogs as workers and commodities but rejected the analogies of wage labor, slavery, dependent ward, and nonliving property. I have insisted that dogs are made to be models and technologies, patients and reformers, consumers and breedwealth, but I am needy for ways to specify these matters in nonhumanist terms in which specific difference is at least as crucial as continuities and similarities across kinds.

Biocapital, volume 1, cannot be written just with dogs and people. I face up to my disappointment in this sad fact by rejoicing in the work of my fellow animal (and other critter) studies and lively capital analysts across lifeworlds and disciplines.[33] Most of all, I am convinced that actual encounters are what make beings; this is the ontological choreography that tells me about value-added dogs in the lifeworlds of biocapital.

"McTrap." Copyright Dan Piraro, 2004. Reprinted with permission. All rights reserved.

3. SHARING SUFFERING
Instrumental Relations between Laboratory Animals and Their People

Reading Nancy Farmer's young adult novel *A Girl Named Disaster*, I was arrested by the story of the relationship between an old African Vapostori man and the guinea pigs he cared for in a little scientific outpost in Zimbabwe around 1980. Used for sleeping sickness research, the lab rodents were at the center of a knot tying together tsetse flies, trypanosomes, cattle, and people. During their working hours, the guinea pigs were held in tight little baskets while wire cages filled with biting flies were placed over them, their skin shaved and painted with poisons that might sicken the offending insects with their protozoan parasites. The flies gorged themselves on the guinea pigs' blood. A young Shona adolescent girl, Nhamo, new to the practices of science, watched.

> "It's cruel," agreed Baba Joseph, "but one day the things we learn will
> keep our cattle from dying." He stuck his own arm into a tsetse cage.
> Nhamo covered her mouth to keep from crying out. The flies
> settled all over the old man's skin and began swelling up. "I do this
> to learn what the guinea pigs are suffering," he explained. "It's
> wicked to cause pain, but if I share it, God may forgive me."[1]

Baba Joseph seems to me to offer a deep insight into how to think about the labor of animals and their people in scientific practices, especially in experimental labs. The experimental animal science inhabited in this chapter is largely medical and veterinary research in which animals bear diseases of interest to people. A great deal of animal experimental science is not of this type, and for me the most interesting biological research, in and out of labs, does not have the human species much in mind. The notion that "the proper study of man is mankind" is risible among most of the biologists I know, whose curiosity is actually for and about other critters. Curiosity, not just functional benefit, may warrant the risk of "wicked action." Baba Joseph, however, is worried about sick cattle, coerced guinea pigs, and their people.

The animal caretaker is engaged not in the heroics of self-experimentation (a common trope in tropical medicine histories)[2] but in the practical and moral obligation to mitigate suffering among mortals—and not just human mortals—where possible and to share the conditions of work, including the suffering, of the most vulnerable lab actors. Baba Joseph's bitten arm is not the fruit of a heroic fantasy of ending all suffering or not causing suffering, but the result of remaining at risk and in solidarity in instrumental relationships that one does not disavow. Using a model organism in an experiment is a common necessity in research. The necessity and the justifications, no matter how strong, do not obviate the obligations of care and sharing pain. How else could necessity and justice (justification) be evaluated in a mortal world in which acquiring knowledge is never innocent? There are, of course, more standards for evaluation than this one, but forgetting the criterion of sharing pain to learn what animals' suffering is and what to do about it is not tolerable anymore, if it ever was.

SHARING AND RESPONSE

It is important that the "shared conditions of work" in an experimental lab make us understand that entities with fully secured boundaries called possessive individuals (imagined as human or animal) are the wrong units for considering what is going on.[3] That means not that a particular animal does not matter but that mattering is always inside connections that demand and enable response, not bare calculation or ranking. Response, of course, grows with the capacity to respond, that is, responsibility. Such a capacity can be shaped only in and for multidirectional relationships, in which always more than one responsive entity is in the process of becoming. That means that human beings are not uniquely obligated to and gifted with responsibility; animals as workers in labs, animals in all their worlds, are response-able in the same sense as people are; that is, responsibility is a relationship crafted in intra-action through which entities, subjects and objects, come into being.[4] People and animals in labs are both subjects and objects to each other in ongoing intra-action. If this structure of material–semiotic relating breaks down or is not permitted to be born, then nothing but objectification and oppression remains. The parties in intra-action do not admit of preset taxonomic calculation; responders are themselves co-constituted in the responding and do not have in advance a proper checklist of properties. Further, the capacity to respond, and so to be responsible, should not be expected to take on symmetrical shapes and textures for all the parties. Response cannot emerge within relationships of self-similarity.

Calculation, such as a risk–benefit comparison weighted by taxonomic rank, suffices within relations of bounded self-similarity, such as humanism and its offspring. Answering to no checklist, response is always riskier than that. If an experimental lab becomes a scene only of calculation in relation to animals or people, that lab should be shut down. Minimizing cruelty, while necessary, is not enough; responsibility demands more than that. I am arguing that instrumental relations of people and animals are not themselves the root of turning animals (or people) into dead things, into machines whose *reactions* are of interest but who have no *presence*, no *face*, that demands recognition, caring, and shared pain. Instrumental intra-action itself is not the enemy; indeed, I will argue below that work, use, and instrumentality are intrinsic to bodily webbed mortal earthly being and becoming. Unidirectional relations of use, ruled by practices of calculation and self-sure of hierarchy, are quite another matter. Such self-satisfied calculation takes heart from the primary dualism that parses body one way and mind another. That dualism should have withered long ago in the light of feminist and many other criticisms, but the fantastic mind/body binary has proved remarkably resilient.

Failing, indeed refusing, to come face-to-face with animals, I believe, is one of the reasons.

We are in the midst of webbed existences, multiple beings in relationship, this animal, this sick child, this village, these herds, these labs, these neighborhoods in a city, these industries and economies, these ecologies linking natures and cultures without end. This is a ramifying tapestry of shared being/becoming among critters (including humans) in which living well, flourishing, and being "polite" (political/ethical/in right relation) mean staying inside shared semiotic materiality, including the suffering inherent in unequal and ontologically multiple instrumental relationships. In that sense, experimental animal research is, or can be, necessary, indeed good, but it can never "legitimate" a relation to the suffering in purely regulatory or disengaged and unaffected ways. The interesting question, then, becomes, What might a responsible "sharing of suffering" look like in historically situated practices?

The sense of sharing I am trying to think about is both epistemological and practical.[5] It's not about being a surrogate for the surrogate or taking the place of the suffering "other" that we need to consider. We do not need some New Age version of the facile and untrue claim "I feel your pain." Sometimes, perhaps, "taking the place of the victim" is a kind of action ethically required, but I do not think that is sharing, and, further, those who suffer, including animals, are not necessarily victims. What happens if we do not regard or treat lab animals as victims, or as other to the human, or relate to their suffering and deaths as sacrifice? What happens if experimental animals are not mechanical substitutes but significantly unfree partners, whose differences and similarities to human beings, to one another, and to other organisms are crucial to the work of the lab and, indeed, are partly constructed by the work of the lab? What happens if the working animals are significant others with whom we are in consequential relationship in an irreducible world of embodied and lived partial differences, rather than the Other across the gulf from the One?

In addition, what does "unfree" mean here in relation to animals who are in an instrumental relation with people? Where is our zoological Marx when we need him? Lab animals are not "unfree" in some abstract and transcendental sense. Indeed, they have many degrees of freedom in a more mundane sense, including the inability of experiments to work if animals and other organisms do not cooperate. I like the metaphor "degrees of freedom"; there really are unfilled spaces; something outside calculation can still happen. Even factory meat industries have to face the disaster of chickens' or pigs' refusal to live when their cooperation is utterly disregarded in an excess of human engineering arrogance. But that is a very low standard for thinking about animal freedom in instrumental relations.

LABOR AND INEQUALITY

The Marx in my soul keeps making me return to the category of labor, including examining the actual practices of extraction of value from workers. My suspicion is that we might nurture responsibility with and for other animals better by plumbing the category of labor more than the category of rights, with its inevitable preoccupation with similarity, analogy, calculation, and honorary membership in the expanded abstraction of the Human. Regarding animals as systems of production and as technologies is hardly new.[6] Taking animals seriously as workers without the comforts of humanist frameworks for people or animals is perhaps new and might help stem the killing machines.[7] The posthumanist whispering in my ear reminds me that animals work in labs, but not under conditions of their own design, and that Marxist humanism is no more help for thinking about this for either people or other animals than other kinds of humanist formulae. Best of all, the Marxist feminist in my history and community reminds me that freedom cannot be defined as the opposite of necessity if the mindful body in all its thickness is not to be disavowed, with all the vile consequences of such disavowal for those assigned to bodily entrammelment, such as women, the colonized, and the whole list of "others" who cannot live inside the illusion that freedom comes only when work and necessity are shuffled off onto someone else. Instrumental relations have to be revalued, rethought, lived another way.

Marxist feminists, however, were not leaders in coming face to face with animals; they tended to be all too happy with categories of society, culture, and humanity and all too suspicious of nature, biology, and co-constitutive human relationships with other critters. Marxist feminists and their brothers both tended to reserve the category of labor (and desire and sexuality, if not sex) for people. Other feminists, however, did take the lead many years ago in seriously cohabiting and understanding the earth with animals—or, as Val Plumwood called the vast heterogeneity of presences besides human beings, "earth others."[8] These feminist theorists paid attention to slimy, furry, scaly, fleshy animals of great variety (and other organisms too), not just literary, mythological, philosophic, and linguistic ones, although they had a lot to say about those as well.[9] I am inside these feminists' work, nourished and instructed by it, even as I resist the tendency to condemn all relations of instrumentality between animals and people as necessarily involving objectification and oppression of a kind similar to the objectifications and oppressions of sexism, colonialism, and racism. I think in view of the terrible similarities, too much sway has been given to critique and not enough to seeing what else is going on in instrumental human–animal world makings and what else is needed.[10]

To be in a relation of use to each other is not the definition of unfreedom and violation. Such relations are almost never symmetrical ("equal" or calculable). Rather, relations of use are exactly what companion species are about: the ecologies of significant others involve messmates at table, with indigestion and without the comfort of teleological purpose from above, below, in front, or behind. This is not some kind of naturalistic reductionism; this is about living responsively as mortal beings where dying and killing are not optional or able to be laundered like stolen money by creating unbridgeable gaps in the pathways through which the flows of value can be tracked. Flows of value can be tracked, thanks to Marx and his heirs; but response has to go into trackless territory, without even the orienting signposts of reliable chasms.

None of this lets me forget that I called the lab animals unfree in some sense not undone by remembering that relations of utility are not the source of that ascription. Baba Joseph did not say that understanding the animals' suffering made the wickedness of causing them pain go away. He said only that his God "may forgive" him. May. When I say "unfree," I mean that real pain, physical and mental, including a great deal of killing, is often directly caused by the instrumental apparatus, and the pain is not borne symmetrically. Neither *can* the suffering and dying be borne symmetrically, in most cases, no matter how hard the people work to respond. To me that does not mean people cannot ever engage in experimental animal lab practices, including causing pain and killing. It does mean that these practices should never leave their practitioners in moral comfort, sure of their righteousness. Neither does the category of "guilty" apply, even though with Baba Joseph I am convinced the word *wicked* remains apt.[11] The moral sensibility needed here is ruthlessly mundane and will not be stilled by calculations about ends and means. The needed morality, in my view, is culturing a radical ability to remember and feel what is going on and performing the epistemological, emotional, and technical work to respond practically in the face of the permanent complexity not resolved by taxonomic hierarchies and with no humanist philosophical or religious guarantees. Degrees of freedom, indeed; the open is not comfortable.

NONMIMETIC SHARING

Baba Joseph did not stand in for the guinea pigs; rather, he tried to understand their pain in the most literal way. There is an element of mimesis in his actions that I affirm: feeling in his flesh what the guinea pigs in his charge feel.[12] I am most interested, however, in another aspect of Baba Joseph's practice, an element I will call nonmimetic sharing. He sustained bites not to stand in as experimental object but to understand the rodents' pain so as to do what he could about it, even if that was only to serve as witness to the need for something properly called forgiveness even in the most thoroughly justified instances of causing suffering. He did not resign his job (and so starve? or "just" lose his status in his community?) or try to convince Nhamo not to help out in the lab with Dr. van Heerden. He did not "free" the guinea pigs or worry about the flies. Joseph encouraged and instructed Nhamo's curiosity about and with animals of all sorts, in and out of the lab. Still, Joseph had his God from whom he hoped for forgiveness. What might standing in need of forgiveness mean when God is not addressed and sacrifice is not practiced? My suspicion is that the kind of forgiveness that we fellow mortals living with other animals hope for is the mundane grace to eschew separation, self-certainty, and innocence even in our most creditable practices that enforce unequal vulnerability.

In an essay called "FemaleMan©_Meets_OncoMouse™," I confronted a genetically engineered lab critter, patented under the name OncoMouse, whose work was to serve as a breast cancer model for women. Commanded by her suffering and moved by Lynn Randolph's painting *The Passion of OncoMouse*, which showed a chimeric mouse with the breasts of a white woman and a crown of thorns in a multinational observation chamber that was a laboratory, I argued: "OncoMouse™ is my sibling, and more properly, male or female, s/he is my sister. . . . Although her promise is decidedly secular, s/he is a figure in the sense developed within Christian realism: s/he is our scapegoat; s/he bears our suffering; s/he signifies and enacts our mortality in a powerful, historically specific way that promises a culturally privileged kind of secular salvation—a 'cure for cancer.' Whether I agree to her existence and use or not, s/he suffers, physically, repeatedly, and profoundly, that I and my sisters might live. In the experimental way of life, s/he is the experiment. . . . If not in my own body, surely in those of my friends, I will someday owe to OncoMouse™ or her subsequently designed rodent kin a large debt. So, who is s/he?"[13] It is tempting to see my sister OncoMouse as a sacrifice, and certainly the barely secular Christian theater of the suffering servant in science and the everyday lab idiom of sacrificing experimental animals invite that thinking. OncoMouse is definitely a model substituted for human experimental bodies. But something the biologist Barbara Smuts calls copresence with animals is what keeps me from resting easily with the idiom of sacrifice.[14] The animals in the labs, including the oncomice, have face; they are somebody as well as something, just as we humans are both subject and object all the time. To be in response to that is to recognize copresence in relations of use and therefore to remember that no balance sheet of benefit and cost will suffice. I may (or may not) have good reasons to kill, or to make, oncomice, but I do not have the majesty of Reason and the solace of Sacrifice. I do not have *sufficient reason*, only the risk of doing something wicked because it may also be good in the context of *mundane reasons*. Further, those mundane reasons are inextricably affective and cognitive if they are worth their salt. Felt reason is not sufficient reason, but it is what we mortals have. The grace of felt reason is that it is always open to reconsideration with care.

I am trying to think about what is required of people who use other animals unequally (in experiments, directly or indirectly, in daily living, knowing, and eating because of animals' sensuous labor). Some instrumental relations should be ended, some should be nurtured, but none of this without response, that is, nonmechanical and morally alert consequences for all the parties, human and not, in the relation of unequal use. I don't think we will ever have a general principle for what sharing suffering means, but it has to be material, practical, and consequential, the sort of engagement that keeps the inequality from becoming commonsensical or taken as obviously okay. The inequality is in the precise and *changeable* labor practices of the lab, not in some transcendent excellence of the Human over the Animal, which can then be killed without the charge of murder being brought. Neither the pure light of sacrifice nor the night vision of the power of domination illuminates the relationships involved.

Inequality in the lab is, in short, not of a humanist kind, whether religious or secular, but of a relentlessly historical and contingent kind that never stills the murmur of nonteleological and nonhierarchical multiplicity that the world is. The questions that then interest me are, How can the multispecies labor practices of the lab be less deadly, less painful, and freer for all the workers? How can responsibility be practiced among earthlings? Labor as such, which is always proper to instrumental relations, is not the problem; it is the always pressing question of nonsymmetrical suffering and death. And nonmimetic well-being.

KILLING

Jacques Derrida has been lurking in this reflection for quite some time, and it is time to invite him in directly. Not least, Derrida eloquently and relentlessly reminds his readers that responsibility is never calculable. There is no formula for response; precisely, to respond is not merely to react with a fixed calculus proper to machines, logic, and—most Western philosophy has insisted—animals. In the lineage of Western philosophers with and against whom Derrida struggled all his life, only the Human can respond; animals react. The Animal is forever positioned on the other side of an unbridgeable gap, a gap that reassures the Human of his excellence by the very ontological impoverishment of a lifeworld that cannot be its own end or know its own condition. Following Lévinas on the subjectivity of the hostage, Derrida remembers that in this gap lies the logic of sacrifice, within which there is no responsibility toward the living world other than the human.[15]

Within the logic of sacrifice, only human beings can be murdered. Humans can and must respond to one another and maybe avoid deliberate cruelty to other living beings, when it is convenient, in order to avoid damaging their own humanity, which is Kant's scandalous best effort on the topic, or at best recognize that other animals feel pain even if they cannot respond or in their own right obligate response. Every living being except Man can be killed but not murdered. To make Man merely killable is the height of moral outrage; indeed, it is the definition of genocide. Reaction is for and toward the unfree; response is for and toward the open.[16] Everything but Man lives in the realm of reaction and so calculation; so much animal pain, so much human good, add it up, kill so many animals, call it sacrifice. Do the same for people, and they lose their humanity. A great deal of history demonstrates how all this works; just check out the latest list of genocides-in-progress. Or read the rolls of death rows in U.S. prisons.

Derrida understood that this structure, this logic of sacrifice and this exclusive possession of the capacity for response, is what produces the Animal, and he called that production criminal, a crime against beings we call animals. "The confusion of all nonhuman living creatures within the general and common category of the animal is not simply a sin against rigorous thinking, vigilance, lucidity, or empirical authority; it is also a crime. Not against animality precisely, but a crime of the first order against the animals, against animals."[17] Such criminality takes on special historical force in view of the immense, systematized violence against animals that deserves the name "exterminism." As Derrida put it, "No one can deny this event any more, no one can deny the *unprecedented* proportions of the subjection of the animal. . . . Everybody knows what terrifying and intolerable pictures a realist painting could give to the industrial, mechanical, chemical, hormonal, and genetic violence to which man has been submitting animal life for the past two centuries."[18] Everyone may know, but there is not nearly enough indigestion.[19]

Within the logic of sacrifice that undergrids all versions of religious or secular humanism, animals are sacrificed precisely because they can be killed and then ingested symbolically and materially in acts saved from cannibalism or murder of the brother by the logic of surrogacy and substitution. (Derrida understood that patricide and fratricide are the only real murders in the logic of humanism; everybody else to whom the law is applied is covered by courtesy.) The substitute, the scapegoat, is not Man but Animal.[20] Sacrifice works; there is a whole world of those who can be killed, because finally they are only something, not somebody, close enough to "being" in order to be a model, substitute, sufficiently self-similar and so nourishing food, but not close enough to compel response. Not the Same, but Different; not One, but Other. Derrida repudiates this trap with all the considerable technical power of deconstruction and all the moral sensitivity of a man who is affected by shared mortality. Judging that the crime that posits the Animal is more than idiotic (a *bêtise*), Derrida goes much further: "The gesture seems to me to constitute philosophy as such, the philosopheme itself."[21]

Derrida argues that the problem is not human beings' denying something to other critters—whether that be language, or knowledge of death, or whatever is the theoretico-empirical sign of the Big Gap popular at the moment—but rather the death-defying arrogance of ascribing such wondrous positivities to the Human. "The question of the said animal in its entirety comes down to knowing not whether the animal speaks but whether one can know what *respond* means. And how to distinguish a response from a reaction."[22] Taking as given the irreducible multiplicity of living beings, *Homo sapiens* and other species, who are entangled together, I suggest that this question of discernment pivots on the unresolved dilemmas of killing and relationships of use.

I am afraid to start writing what I have been thinking about all this, because I will get it wrong—emotionally, intellectually, and morally—and the issue is consequential. Haltingly, I will try. I suggest that it is a misstep to separate the world's beings into those who may be killed and those who may not and a misstep to pretend to live outside killing. The same kind of mistake saw freedom only in the absence of labor and necessity, that is, the mistake of forgetting the ecologies of all mortal beings, who live in and through the use of one another's bodies. This is not saying that nature is red in tooth and claw and so anything goes. The naturalistic fallacy is the mirror-image misstep to transcendental humanism.

I think what my people and I need to let go of if we are to learn to stop exterminism and genocide, through either direct participation or indirect benefit and acquiescence, is the command "Thou shalt not kill." The problem is not figuring out to whom such a command applies so that "other" killing can go on as usual and reach unprecedented historical proportions. The problem is to learn to live responsibly within the multiplicitous necessity and labor of killing, so as to be in the open, in quest of the capacity to respond in relentless historical, nonteleological, multispecies contingency. Perhaps the commandment should read, "Thou shalt not make killable."

The problem is actually to understand that human beings do not get a pass on the necessity of killing significant others, who are themselves responding, not just reacting. In the idiom of labor, animals are working subjects, not just worked objects. Try as we might to distance ourselves, there is no way of living that is not also a way of someone, not just something, else dying differentially. Vegans come as close as anyone, and their work to avoid eating or wearing any animal products would consign most domestic animals to the status of curated heritage collections or to just plain extermination as kinds and as individuals. I do not disagree that vegetarianism, veganism, and opposition to sentient animal experimentation can be powerful feminist positions; I do disagree that they are Feminist Doxa. Further, I think feminism outside the logic of sacrifice has to figure out how to honor the entangled labor of humans and animals together in science and in many other domains, including animal husbandry right up to the table. It is not killing that gets us into exterminism, but making beings killable. Baba Joseph understood that the guinea pigs were not killable; he had the obligation to respond.

I think that is exactly what David Lurie, the sexually harassing, middle-aged scholar of poetry, understood in J. M. Coetzee's *Disgrace*. Working with a vet who fulfilled her duty to untold numbers of stray and sick animals by killing them in her clinic, Lurie brought the dog he had bonded with to her for euthanasia at the end of the novel. He could have delayed the death of that one dog. That one dog mattered. He did not sacrifice that dog; he took responsibility for killing without, maybe for the first time in his life, leaving. He did not take comfort in a language of humane killing; he was, at the end, more honest and capable of love than that. That incalculable moral response is what, for me, distinguishes David Lurie in *Disgrace* from Elizabeth Costello in *The Lives of Animals*, for whom actually existing animals do not seem present. Elizabeth Costello, the fictional Tanner Lecturer in Coetzee's *Lives of Animals*, inhabits a radical language of animal rights. Armed with a fierce commitment to sovereign reason, she flinches at none of this discourse's universal claims, and she embraces all of its power to name extreme atrocity. She practices the enlightenment method of comparative history in order to fix the awful equality of slaughter. Meat eating is like the Holocaust; meat eating is the Holocaust. What would Elizabeth Costello do if she were in the place of Bev Shaw, the volunteer animal caretaker in *Disgrace*, whose daily service of love is to escort large numbers of abandoned dogs and cats to the solace of death? Maybe there is no solace for those animals, but only dying. What would Costello do in the place of *Disgrace*'s Lucy Lurie, whose face-to-face life with dogs and human neighbors in postapartheid South Africa arrests the categorical power of words in midutterance? Or even of David Lurie, Lucy's disgraced father, who finally inhabits a discourse of desire at least as fierce and authentic as Elizabeth Costello's distinction-obliterating discourse of universal suffering? How do the relentlessly face-to-face, historically situated, language-defeating suffering and moral dilemmas of *Disgrace* meet the searingly generic, category-sated moral demands of *The Lives of Animals*? And who lives and who dies—animals and humans—in the very different ways of inheriting the histories of atrocity that Coetzee proposes in these novels' practices of moral inquiry?[23]

I suggest that what follows from the feminist insight that embraced historically situated, mindful bodies as the site not just of first (maternal) birth but also of full life and all its projects, failed and achieved, is that human beings must learn to kill responsibly. And to be killed responsibly, yearning for the capacity to respond and to recognize response, always with reasons but knowing there will never be sufficient reason. We can never do without technique, without calculation, without reasons, but these practices will never take us into that kind of open where multispecies responsibility is at stake. For that open, we will not cease to require a forgiveness we cannot exact. I do not think we can nurture living until we get better at facing killing. But also get better at dying instead of killing.

Sometimes a "cure" for whatever kills us is just not enough reason to keep the killing machines going at the scale to which we (who?) have become accustomed.

CARING

It is always bracing to go back to the lab after a visit with great philosophers and the awful places one gets into because of them. Let me revisit the hemophilic canines in "Value-Added Dogs and Lively Capital" (chapter 2). There we saw how dogs suffering from hemophilia became model patients, as well as surrogates and technologies for studying a human disease, over the course of years beginning in the late 1940s in the laboratory of Kenneth Brinkhous at the University of North Carolina at Chapel Hill.[24] To share the dogs' suffering, or that of participants in today's experiments, would be not to mimic what the canines go through in a kind of heroic masochistic fantasy but to do the *work* of paying attention and making sure that the suffering is minimal, necessary, and consequential. If any of those assurances are found impossible, which is always a risky judgment made on the basis of reasons but without the guarantee of Reason, then the responsible work is to bring the enterprise to a halt. Breaking the sacrificial logic that parses who is killable and who isn't might just lead to a lot more change than the practices of analogy, rights extension, denunciation, and prohibition. Examples could include making sure experiments are well planned and executed; taking the time to practice care among and for all the people and organisms in the lab and in the worlds reached by that lab, even if results come more slowly or cost more or careers aren't as smooth; and practicing the civic skills of political engagement and cultural presence in these sorts of issues, including the skills of responding, not reacting, to the discourse of those who do not grant the goodness or necessity of one's scientific practices. None of this makes the word *wicked* go away; I am not advocating cleaning the soul by hygienic reformism. I am advocating the understanding that earthly heterogeneous beings are in this web together for all time, and no one gets to be Man.

If the plant molecular biologist Martha Crouch was right that some of the pleasures of lab science that tend to make practitioners less able to engage in full cosmopolitics come from a Peter Pan–like preadolescence, in which one never really has to engage the full semiotic materiality of one's scientific practices,[25] then maybe sharing suffering is about growing up to do the kind of time-consuming, expensive, hard work, as well as play, of staying with all the complexities for all of the actors, even knowing that will never be fully possible, fully calculable. Staying with the complexities does not mean not acting, not doing research, not engaging in some, indeed many, unequal instrumental relationships; it does mean learning to live and think in practical opening to shared pain and mortality and learning what that living and thinking teach.

The sense of cosmopolitics I draw from is Isabelle Stengers's. She invoked Deleuze's idiot, the one who knew how to slow things down, to stop the rush to consensus or to a new dogmatism or to denunciation, in order to open up the chance of a common world. Stengers insists we cannot denounce the world in the name of an ideal world. Idiots know that. For Stengers, the cosmos is the possible unknown constructed by multiple, diverse entities. Full of the promise of articulations that diverse beings might eventually make, the cosmos is the opposite of a place of transcendent peace. Stengers's cosmopolitical proposal, in the spirit of feminist communitarian anarchism and the idiom of Whitehead's philosophy, is that decisions must take place somehow in the presence of those who will bear their consequences. Making that "somehow" concrete is the work of practicing artful combinations. Stengers is a chemist by training, and artful combinations are her métier. To get "in the presence of" demands work, speculative invention, and ontological risks. No one knows how to do that in advance of coming together in composition.[26]

For those hemophilic dogs in the mid-twentieth century, their physiological labor demanded from human lab people the answering labor of caring for the dogs as patients in minute detail before addressing questions to them as experimental subjects. Of course, the research would have failed otherwise, but that was not the whole story—or should not be allowed to be the whole story when the consequences of sharing suffering nonmimetically become clearer. For example, what sorts of lab arrangements would minimize the number of dogs needed? Make the dogs' lives as full as possible? Engage them as mindful bodies, in relationships of response? How to get the funding for a biobehavioral specialist as part of the lab staff for training both lab animals and people on all levels, from

principal investigators to animal room workers?[27] How to involve humans
with hemophilia or humans who care for people with hemophilia in the
care of the dogs? How to ask in actual practice, without knowing the
answer through a calculus of how much and whose pain matters, whether
these sorts of experiments deserve to flourish anymore at all? If not, whose
suffering then will require the practical labor of nonmimetic sharing? All
of this is my own imagined scenario, of course, but I am trying to picture
what sharing could look like if it were built into any decision to use
another sentient being where unequal power and benefit are (or should
be) undeniable and not innocent or transparent.

The Belgian philosopher and psychologist Vinciane Despret argued
that "articulating bodies to other bodies" is always a political matter. The
same must be said about disarticulating bodies to rearticulate other bodies. Despret reformulated ways for thinking about domestication between
people and animals.[28] My study inhabits one of the major sites where
domestic animals and their people meet: the experimental laboratory. I
have made side trips into the agricultural animal pen and abattoir, propelled by the cattle in Baba Joseph's story, beasts loved and cultivated intensely by Nhamo and her people, beasts used cruelly by the tsetse flies
and their trypanosomes, and beasts turned into efficient, healthy enough,
parasite-free, meat-making machines in the death camps of industrial
agribusiness. The language of nonmimetic sharing and work is not going
to be adequate, I am sure, even if it is part of a needed toolkit. When our
humanist or religious soporifics no longer satisfy us, we require a rich
array of ways to make vivid and practical the material–ethical–political–
epistemological necessities that must be lived and developed inside unequal, instrumental relations linking human and nonhuman animals in
research as well as in other sorts of activities. Human beings' learning
to share other animals' pain nonmimetically is, in my view, an ethical obligation, a practical problem, and an ontological opening. Sharing pain
promises disclosure, promises becoming. The capacity to respond may yet
be recognized and nourished on this earth.

I end in the company of another arresting writer, Hélène Cixous,
who remembers how she failed her childhood dog with abject betrayal.
Many years later, she knew only that she loved him, knew only how to love
him, recognized only how he loved. Bitten hard on the foot by her crazed

dog, Fips, who had been brought to the insanity of the bite by the daily pelting of rocks into the family's compound in Algiers after World War II, the twelve-year-old Cixous, subject like all her family to the insupportable pain of the death of her father and the repudiation visited on the scapegoat outsiders by the colonized Arabs all around them, could not face the awful fate of her dog. No complexity of lived history saved her family from the label of doubly hated French Jews. The Cixous family, like the colonized Arabs, were made categorically killable. No grace of a happy ending saved Fips from the consequences. The leashed dog, apparently expecting the girl Hélène to step on him, savaged her foot, holding on despite her desperate beating to make him let go; after this, Cixous could no longer face Fips. The dog, ill and neglected, died in the company of her brother; Hélène was not there. As an adult, Cixous learned to tell the story of Job the Dog.

> The story ends in tragedy. . . . I wanted him to love me like this and not that. . . . But if they told me I wanted a slave I would have responded indignantly that I only wanted the pure ideal dog I had heard of. He loved me as an animal and far from my ideal. . . . I have his rage painted on my left foot and on my hands. . . . I did not make light in his obscurity. I did not murmur to him the words that all animals understand. . . . But he had ticks, big as chickpeas. . . . They ate him alive, those blood drinking inventions created to kill a victim entirely lacking in possibilities to escape them, those proofs of the existence of the devil soft vampires that laugh at the dog's lack of hands, they suckle it to death, Fips feels his life flow into their tribe of stomachs and without the chance of combat. . . . I did not accompany him. A foul fear of seeing the one I did not love strong enough die, and as I would not give my life for him, I could no longer share his death.[29]

My story ends where it began, with the dilemmas posed by bloodsucking insects, when the logic of sacrifice makes no sense and the hope for forgiveness depends on learning a love that escapes calculation but requires the invention of speculative thought and the practice of remembering, of rearticulating bodies to bodies. Not an ideal love, not an obedient love, but one that might even recognize the noncompliant multiplicity of insects. And the taste of blood.

CODA: REARTICULATING

I wrote "Sharing Suffering" acutely conscious that a few weeks later I was to give a keynote address at the conference Kindred Spirits, at which most of the speakers and attendees would be vegans, animal activists, and other thoughtful people, including some biologists, suspicious of most animal lab research.[30] I did not plan to give this paper there, but if I was going to be able to say anything in good faith at that conference, I needed to write publicly on the hard issues in response to and with that community. Talking about conducting responsive field research or training with dogs and horses, while serious and important, would not fulfill my obligation to people or animals. I am a part of the Kindred Spirits human and non-human animal community in many of the same ways in which I have been part of the ecofeminist world, in response to whom I wrote the "Cyborg Manifesto" in 1985. I also was and am part of the experimental biological science community to whom that cyborg paper was equally addressed.

My friend and colleague Sharon Ghamari-Tabrizi read "Sharing Suffering" in manuscript and forced me to come face-to-face with, as she put it, "the hardest case for the theory of co-presence and response":

> It's much easier to make use of a notion of trans-species relationality in field studies where the scientist/knower can hang out in the animal's habitat. But the harder question is when the site is wholly humanly-constructed, where the lab is a total environment. In the lab, not only is the relationship unequal and asymmetrical; it is wholly framed and justified, legitimated, and meaningful within the rationalist materials of early modern humanism. Why? Because it is conditioned on the human ability to capture, breed, manipulate, and compel animals to live, behave, die within its apparatus. How has it been justified? By human power over the animal. Justified in the past by divine right and hierarchy of domination, or by human reason's gloss on necessary human predation over other beings.
>
> So if you were going to abandon humanism, in favor of the post-humanism, ahumanism, non-humanism of the process philosophers, of the phenomenologists, of Derrida and Whitehead, I still want to know how specifically laboratory experimental practices get done and get justified. These details, these mundane practices, are the place where the politics of successor science get worked out.

What I'm trying to say is, Donna, the hardest case of all will be struggled over in the actual details of prohibition and license and the details of practice in the procedures in the lab during experiments.

I want to know what you would say when someone buttonholes you and says: I challenge you to defend the slaughter of lab animals in biomedical experiments. No matter how carefully you guard them from extraordinary pain, in the end, they are subject to pain inflicted by you for the social goods of: knowledge-seeking in itself, or applications for human purposes. You did it. You killed the animals. Defend yourself.

What do you say then?[31]

I wrote her back:

Yes, all the calculations still apply; yes, I will defend animal killing for reasons and in detailed material–semiotic conditions that I judge tolerable because of a greater good calculation. And no, that is never enough. I refuse the choice of "inviolable animal rights" versus "human good is more important." Both of those proceed as if calculation solved the dilemma, and all I or we have to do is choose. I have never regarded that as enough in abortion politics either. Because we did not learn how to shape the public discourse well enough, in legal and popular battles feminists have had little choice but to use the language of rationalist choice as if that settled *our* prolife politics, but it does not and we know it. In Susan Harding's terms, we feminists who protect access to abortion, we who kill that way, need to learn to revoice life and death in our terms and not accept the rationalist dichotomy that rules most ethical dispute.[32]

Calculation also demands another series of questions, ones feminists struggling with abortion decisions know intimately too: *for whom, for what,* and *by whom* should a cost–benefit calculation be made, since more than one always entangled being is at stake and in play in all of these hard cases? When I questioned the biologist Marc Bekoff in a panel session at the Kindred Spirits conference, he stated uncategorically that his make-or-break question is, "Does the research benefit the animals?" In light of the history of the reduction of lab animals to machine tools and products for big pharma (the technoscientific pharmaceutical research–industrial complex), agribusiness, cosmetics, art performances, and much else, that question has particular force. *Not* asking that question seriously is, or ought to be, outside the pale of scientific practice.

The practice of holding nonhuman animals at the center of attention is necessary but not sufficient, not just because other moral and ontological goods compete in that kind of cost–benefit frame, but more important because companion-species worldliness works otherwise. A question like Bekoff's is not a moral absolute but a needed, mortal, focusing practice in a soul-numbing, situated history. That practice does not reduce the force of the question but locates it on earth, in real places, where judgment and action are at stake. Further, individual animals, human and nonhuman, are themselves entangled assemblages of relatings knotted at many scales and times with other assemblages, organic and not. Individuated critters matter; they are mortal and fleshly knottings, not ultimate units of being. Kinds matter; they are also mortal and fleshly knottings, not typological units of being. Individuals and kinds at whatever scale of time and space are not autopoietic wholes; they are sticky dynamic openings and closures in finite, mortal, world-making, ontological play.

Ways of living and dying matter: Which historically situated practices of multispecies living and dying should flourish? There is no outside from which to answer that mandatory question; we must give the best answers we come to know how to articulate, and take action, without the god trick of self-certainty. Companion-species worlds are turtles all the way down. Far from reducing everything to a soup of post- (or pre-) modern complexity in which anything ends up permitted, companion-species approaches *must* actually engage in cosmopolitics, articulating bodies to some bodies and not others, nourishing some worlds and not others, and bearing the mortal consequences. Respect is *respecere*—looking back, holding in regard, understanding that meeting the look of the other is a condition of having face oneself. All of this is what I am calling "sharing suffering." It is not a game but more like what Charis Thompson calls ontological choreography.[33]

I act; I do not hide my calculations that motivate the action. I am not thereby quit of my debts, and it's more than just debts. I am not quit of response-ability, which demands calculations but is not finished when the best cost–benefit analysis of the day is done and not finished when the best animal welfare regulations are followed to the letter. Calculations—reasons—are obligatory and radically insufficient for companion-species worldliness. The space opened up by words like *forgive* and *wicked* remains, although I grant that overripe religious tones cling to those words like a bad smell, and so we need other words too. We have reasons but not sufficient reasons. To refuse to engage the practices for getting good reasons (in this case, for doing particular experimental lab science) is not just stupid but also criminal. Neither "the greater human good trumps animal pain" camp nor the "sentient animals are always ends in themselves and so cannot be used that way" camp sees that the claim to have Sufficient Reasons is a dangerous fantasy rooted in the dualisms and misplaced concretenesses of religious and secular humanism.

Obviously, trying to figure out who falls below the radar of sentience and so is killable while we build retirement homes for apes is also an embarrassing caricature of what must be done. We damn well do have the obligation to make those lab apes' lives as full as we can (raise taxes to cover the cost!) and to take them out of the situations into which we have inexcusably placed them. Improved comparative biobehavioral sciences, in and out of labs, as well as affective political and ethical reflection and action, tell us that no conditions are good enough to continue permitting many kinds of experiments and practices of captivity for many animals, not only apes. Note, I think we now know this, at least in serious part, *because* of research. But again, those calculations—necessary, obligatory, and grounding action out loud and in public—are not sufficient.

Now, how to address that response-ability (which is always experienced in the company of significant others, in this case, the animals)? As you say, Sharon, the issue lies not in Principles and Ethical Universals but in practices and imaginative politics of the sort that rearticulates the relations of minds and bodies, in this case critters and their lab people and scientific apparatuses. For example, what about instituting changes in daily lab schedules so that even rats or mice get to learn how to do new things that make their lives more interesting. (A trainer to enhance the lives of subjects is a little thing but a consequential one.) After all, in the world of biotechnology, rodents bear the brunt of increased invasive use worldwide.[34] Besides the provision of good human child care attached to labs, I'd love to see many jobs open up for good animal trainers and environmental enrichment practitioners. I imagine the lab people having to pass a positive-methods training proficiency test and lab-oriented biobehavioral ecology test for the species they work with in order to keep their jobs or obtain approval for their research. Experimenters would have to pass such tests for the same reasons that bosses and workers these days have to learn that sexual harassment is real (even if the regulatory apparatus often seems to be a caricature of what feminists intended); that is, unless retrained, people, like other animals, keep seeing and doing what they already know how to see and do, and that's not good enough.

Of course, imagining that reforms will settle the matter is a failure of affective and effective thinking and a denial of responsibility. New openings will appear because of changes in practices, and the open is about response. I think this actually happens all the time with good experimenters and their critters. For most of this chapter, I have concentrated on instrumental, unequal, scientific relations among human and nonhuman vertebrates with sizable brains that people identify as being like their own in critical ways. However, the vast majority of animals are not like that; nonmimetic caring and significant otherness are my lures for trying to think and feel more adequately; and multispecies flourishing requires a robust nonanthropomorphic sensibility that is accountable to irreducible differences.

In a doctoral exam committee with my colleague, marine invertebrate zoologist Vicki Pearse, I learned how she looks for ways to make her cup corals in the lab more comfortable by figuring out which wave lengths and periods of light they enjoy. Getting good data matters to her, and so do happy animals, that is, actual *animal* well-being in the lab.[35] Inspired by Pearse, I asked some of my biologist friends who work with invertebrates to tell me stories about their practices of care that are central to their labor as scientists. I wrote:

> Do you have an example from your own practice or those close to you of how the well being of the animals, always important for good data, of course, but not only for that, matters in the daily life of the lab? I want to argue that such care is not instead of experiments that might also involve killing and/or pain, but is intrinsic to the complex felt responsibility (and mundane non-anthropomorphic kinship) many researchers have for their animals. How do you make your animals happy in the lab (and vice versa)? How do good zoologists learn to see when animals are not flourishing? The interesting stories are in the details more than the grand principles!

Michael Hadfield, professor of zoology at the University of Hawaii and director of the Kewalo Marine Laboratory (the Pacific Biosciences Research Center), responded:

What your questions draw to mind for me lies more in my work with the Hawaiian tree snails than our small beasts at the marine lab. I have worked very hard to provide laboratory environments for these endangered snails that approach a field setting as closely as possible. To that end, we buy expensive "environmental chambers," wherein we can set up day lengths and temperature–humidity regimes that approach those of the snails' field habitats as much as possible. We also try to provide a leafy world and the mold they scrape from leaves in abundance. Most importantly, we provide all of this in a predator-free world, to "save" them from the aliens [highly destructive introduced species such as predatory snails and rats] that are eating them up in the mountains. I also find the snails to be beautiful and their babies to be "cute," but that's not very scientific, is it? For many reasons—not least being their legally protected status—we work very hard to keep from injuring or killing any of the snails in the lab. I truly want to see these species persist in the world, and what we do in the lab is the only way I know to make that happen, at present. We are now caring for more than 1,500 tree snails in the lab, at great expense and personal effort, with the goal of staving off even more extinctions than have already occurred. A major part of this is keeping the snails as healthy and "natural" as possible ("natural," because they must someday go back to—and survive in—the field). If that's "keeping them happy," then it's our driving force.

How do we see (assuming we are "good zoologists") that our animals are not flourishing? Ah, well, usually it's when they die. Snails and worms don't emit cries of anguish, nor typically show signs of illness for very long before they die. For the tree snails, I watch the demographic trends in each terrarium very carefully (we census them at least bi-weekly) to note whether there are births, if death rates are greater than birth rates, etc. At the first hint of something wrong, I force the lab crew to immediately stop and review every step in the maintenance-culture regime. We often have to check an entire environmental chamber (10+ different terraria, with several species) to see if something is wrong with the entire environment. And we take immediate steps to remedy situations, even when we don't fully understand them. E.g., I recently concluded that my lab group was over-filling the terraria with leafy branches from ohi'a trees at each cleaning/changing session. They had concluded that, since the snails' food is the mold growing on the leaves, the more leaves the better. I explained that the snails needed more air flow through the terraria, and that their activities were strongly regulated by light, little of which reached the centers of the leaf-crammed terraria. So, we've fixed that and are now looking for the next problem and "remedy."[36]

Scott Gilbert, whose work I have drawn from constantly over many years, also gave me a story rooted in his experimental investigation, with his Swarthmore undergrad students, of the embryonic origin of the turtle plastron from neural crest cells:

I usually don't allow my students to kill any animals. That's always been one of my jobs. I don't particularly mind dissecting turtle embryos off their yolks and consigning them to 4 percent paraformaldehyde. I'd probably tolerate a day of that more than I'd tolerate dispatching one adult or hatchling turtle. I don't know of any story as provocative as the one you mentioned concerning the man who had his arm bitten by tsetse flies. The founder of this department, Joseph Leidy, was a remarkable person, and one legend is that he walked from Philadelphia to Swarthmore because he had forgotten to ask a student to feed the frogs and lizards.[37]

I like the language of "politics" as used by Despret, Latour, and Stengers, which I see related to *polis* and *polite*: good manners (politesse), response to and with. Hadfield, Gilbert, and Pearse are "polite"; theirs is the biological cosmopolitical practice of articulating bodies to other bodies with care so that significant others might flourish. Their work is immersed in the daily minutiae of life and death for the animals (and the students and postdocs) they care for and learn with and from. I am suspicious of assimilating this labor to the category of "bioethics," but I am not ready to give over the word *ethics* to the enemy either. It's my old refusal to give up what folks say I can't have, such as *cyborg*. I don't duck the decision to kill animals for the best reasons that persuade me or duck what it takes to formulate those best reasons. I am just saying that does not end the question; it opens it up. Maybe that's all *nonhumanism* means. But in that little "all" lies permanent refusal of innocence and self-satisfaction with one's reasons and the invitation to speculate, imagine, feel, build something better. This is the sf worlding that has always lured me. It is a real worlding.

Indeed, Whitehead in Stengers's hands talks of abstractions as lures when our previous abstractions break down.[38] Loving our abstractions seems to me really important; understanding that they break down even as we lovingly craft them is part of response-ability. Abstractions, which require our best calculations, mathematics, reasons, are built in order to be able to break down so that richer and more responsive invention, speculation, and proposing—worlding—can go on. A Whiteheadian proposition, says Stengers, is a risk, an opening to what is not yet. A proposition is also an opening to become with those with whom we are not yet. Put that into the dilemma ensuing from killing experimental organisms or meat animals, and the mandatory "ethical" or "political" call is to reimagine, to speculate again, to remain open, because we are (reasonably, if we built good abstractions; badly, if we were lazy, unskillful, or dishonest) killing someone, not just something.

We are face-to-face, in the company of significant others, companion species to one another. That is not romantic or idealist but mundane and consequential in the little things that make lives. Instead of being finished when we say this experimental science is good, including the kind that kills animals when necessary and according to the highest standards we collectively know how to bring into play, our debt is just opening up to speculative and so possible material, affective, practical reworlding in the concrete and detailed situation of *here*, in this tradition of research, not everywhere all the time. This "here" might be quite big, even global, if abstractions are really well built and full of grappling hooks for connections. Maybe sf worlding—speculative fiction and speculative fact—is the language I need instead of *forgiveness* and *wickedness*. Maybe even Baba Joseph and Cixous would think so, if probably not the ticks and tsetse flies. Perhaps best of all, in the lab and in the field, Hawaiian tree snails might actually have a chance to live naturally because an experimental invertebrate zoologist cared in nonanthropomorphic, nonmimetic, painstaking detail.

4. EXAMINED LIVES
Practices of Love and Knowledge
in Purebred Dogland

CURIOSITY AND THE LOVE OF KINDS

I need to ask again: Whom and what do I touch when I touch my dogs? How is "becoming with" a practice of "becoming worldly"? What do these questions mean when the entangled knots of companion species join *kinds* of dogs with their *collectively organized* people as fiercely as individual dogs interlace with particular humans? Kinds of companion species come in many flavors, but in this chapter, I need to break bread with a particularly contaminated and controversial kind of kind—an institutionalized "purebred" dog breed, in particular, Australian shepherds in the United States. Right from the start, my typological convention has taken a position in the fray, because I cannot bring myself to write about kinds of dogs as *the* dog, *the* Australian Shepherd, the only sort to get capital letters in the idiom of purebred dogland and elsewhere, while all nominative plurals are lowercased as collectives (Australian shepherds) or given scare quotes around call names for mere individual dogs, as in "Cayenne" rather than Cayenne, while I am unmarked Donna, empowered by honorary membership in the category Man to live textually outside scare quotes. Little privileges tell big stories. Typological errors suggest revisions. *Respecere.*

In the beginning of everything that led to this book, I was pure of heart, at least in relation to dog breeds. I knew they were an affectation, an abuse, an abomination, the embodiment of animalizing racist eugenics, everything that represents modern people's misuse of other sentient beings for their own instrumental ends. Besides, so-called purebreds got sick all the time, as well they should from all that genetic manipulation. Really bad, in short. Mutts were good as long as they were sterilized; trained to a low standard—lest human control play too big a role—by positive methods; and off leash in every possible situation. Fertile street and village dogs were good because they lived in the third world or its moral and symbolic equivalent in doggish humanism, but they needed to be rescued nonetheless. At home, in my progressive, American middle-class, white bubble, I was a true believer in the Church of the Shelter Dog, that ideal victim and scapegoat and therefore the uniquely proper recipient of love, care, and population control. Without giving anyone quarter about our collective and personal obligations to mutts and shelter dogs, I have become an apostate. I am promiscuously tied with both my old and new objects of affection, two kinds of kinds, mutts and purebreds. Two terrible things caused this unregenerate state: I got curious, and I fell in love. Even worse, I fell in love with kinds as well as with individuals. Parasitized by paraphilias and epistemophilias, I labor on.[1]

Research can be calming in such circumstances. Tantalized by questions about kinds of dogs, and especially by questions about the people and the dogs involved in health and genetics activism inside biotechnological natureculture, I was told to talk to a woman in Fresno, California, named C. A. Sharp, who, I was assured, was the diva of dog genetic health in Australian shepherd land. All of that fit nicely into my alibi as a science studies scholar and look-alike anthropologist. It helped that, tempted to excess by the modest success of my Aussie–chow cross mutt, Roland, in the sport of agility—an activity that my husband, Rusten, and I innocently began with our politically correct, rehomed, adult pooch to help him socialize and gain confidence with other dogs—I was also told that Sharp, a lady into a herding breed, albeit the conformation end of things, might be able to help me find a great agility prospect, a.k.a., a high-drive, purpose-bred, puppy athlete. My informants were right; C.A. was all this and more. Not only did she direct me to the stock dog breeders who helped bring Cayenne into the world; in 1998 Sharp and I began a research exchange and friendship in dogland that tied new companion-species knots in my heart and mind. In "Examined Lives" I will track Sharp's practices of curiosity and care over several decades to tease out how becoming worldly can work when kinds are at stake.

First, however, I need to tell how that material–semiotic kind called Australian shepherds came to be in the world at all. Knowing and living with these dogs means inheriting all of the conditions of their possibility, all of what makes relating with these beings actual, all of the prehensions that constitute us as companion species. To be in love means to be worldly, to be in connection with significant otherness and signifying others, on many scales, in layers of locals and globals, in ramifying webs. I want to know how to live with the histories I am coming to know. Once one has been in touch, obligations and possibilities for response change.

BREED STORIES: AUSTRALIAN SHEPHERDS

If anything is certain about Australian shepherd origins, it is that no one knows how the name came about, and no one knows all of the kinds of dogs tied into the ancestry of these talented herders. Perhaps the surest thing is that the dogs should be called the United States western ranch dog. Not "American," but "United States." Let me explain why that matters, especially since most (but far from all) of the ancestors are probably varieties of collie types that emigrated with their people from the British Isles to the East Coast of North America from early colonial times on. The California gold rush and the aftermath of the Civil War are the keys to my regional national story. These epic events made vast swathes of the North American West into part of the United States. I don't want to inherit these violent histories, as Cayenne, Roland, and I run our agility courses and conduct our cross-species family affairs. But, like it or not, flesh-to-flesh and face-to-face, I have inherited these histories through touch with my dogs, and my obligations in the world are different because of that fact. That's why I have to tell these stories—to tease out the personal and collective response required now, not centuries ago. Companion species cannot afford evolutionary, personal, or historical amnesia. Amnesia will corrupt sign and flesh and make love petty. If I tell the story of the gold rush and the Civil War, then maybe I can also remember the other stories about the dogs and their people—stories about immigration, indigenous worlds, work, hope, love, play, and the possibility of cohabitation through reconsidering sovereignty and ecological developmental naturecultures.

Romantic-origin stories about Aussies tell of late nineteenth- and early twentieth-century Basque herders bringing their little blue merle dogs with them in steerage as they headed for the ranches of California and Nevada to tend the sheep of a timeless pastoral West after a sojourn of herding sheep in Australia. "In steerage" gives the game away; working-class men in steerage were in no position to bring their dogs to Australia or to California. Besides, the Basques who immigrated to Australia did not become herders; they became sugarcane workers; and they did not go to that frontier called Down Under until the twentieth century. Not necessarily shepherds before, the Basques came to California, sometimes via South America and Mexico, in the nineteenth century with the millions lusting for gold, and ended up herding sheep to feed other disappointed miners. The Basques also established popular restaurants, heavy on lamb dishes, in Nevada on what became the interstate highway system after World War II. The Basques acquired their sheep dogs from among local working herding dogs, who were a mixed lot, to say the least.[2]

Spanish missions favored the coercion of sheep ranching to "civilize" the Indians, but in her online history of Australian shepherds, Linda Rorem notes that by the 1840s the number of sheep in the far West had greatly declined (not to mention human reductions from the killing and dislocation of Native peoples), and the pastoral economy was depressed.[3] The mission sheep were descendants of the Iberian Churra, which the Spanish valued for hardiness, fecundity, and adaptability. Originally accompanying the conquistadors for food and fiber, the Churra (called Churro by Anglos and later by Native Americans too) were the mainstay of New Spain's ranches and villages by the seventeenth century. Acquiring these sheep for themselves through both raids and trade, other Native American peoples bred them for over three hundred years for adaptation to rugged native pastoral conditions. The Churro became the famous Pueblo and Navajo sheep, whose wool was spun and woven into the Southwest

Indians' exquisite textiles. In Navajo communities, sheep are primarily owned by women, and weaving has always been women's labor. Further, hopeful projects to reintegrate twenty-first-century Navajo young people into the community by splicing the so-called modern and traditional rely on a reinvigorated, cosmopolitan Navajo–Churro sheep culture. Gender and generation grow with the fibers of a lamb's coat and muscle.

In the 1850s, thousands of Churro were herded into the West to supply the people of the gold rush. The U.S. Army slaughtered most of the Navajo flocks in the 1860s in retribution for Indian resistance to conquest and relocation to Bosque Redondo, and "improved" European sheep breeds and stock reductions were forced on the Navajo throughout the early decades of the twentieth century. In the 1930s, in response to drought, U.S. federal government agents went hogan-to-hogan to shoot mandated percentages of sheep. In front of their human households, the agents killed every Navajo–Churro sheep they found under the mistaken belief that these tough-looking animals were especially worthless. In both experiential and scientific fact, Navajo–Churro ovines need less grass and water, thrive on less human labor, produce a higher-quality wool fiber and a meat of higher protein and less fat content than "progressive" European breeds in comparable naturalcultural conditions. Even in the early twenty-first-century, Navajo elders can narrate the details of each sheep shot. Few survived, and in the 1970s, there were only around 450 of this hardy kind of sheep in Diné Bikéyah, also known as the Navaho Nation. In the first decade of the 2000s, the kind of sheep, the people committed to them, and the traditional–modern ways of life that these companion species knit together seem to have a chance for a multispecies future in technocultural agropastoralism and its many-threaded coalitions and freedom projects.

My California historian colleagues tell me they find very little mention of herding dogs associated with Spanish missionization and Indian labor. However, at some point the Navajo did enlist the work of dogs for their sheep, mostly for protection from predators who surely came from the same motley of dogs in the West, both English and Iberian in lineage and imaginably even some preconquest dogs,[4] who contributed to Australian shepherds. Never standardized into a closed breed and always open to the contributions of whatever dogs proved useful to the Navajo, these hardy, diverse dogs still labor today for the Diné, protecting their miraculously still-surviving but endangered Navajo–Churro sheep, as well as their "improved" sheep flocks. Restoration and preservation projects involving the Navajo–Churro sheep breed are now part of the biopolitics of the West and Southwest, including online and local niche-marketing of their meat and fiber, festivals crucial both to indigenous community building and to transregional tourism, rare-sheep breeding labs, written ovine breed standards and genetic databases (for example, the Navajo–Churro genetic material collections of the National Center for Genetic Resources Preservation [NCGRP] in Fort Collins, Colorado), Hispano and Navajo cultural–political action and educational projects, guard lamas favored over working livestock guardian dogs, spay–neuter projects for surplus Navajo Nation dogs, and range restoration work. Started in 1977 by Lyle McNeal, an Anglo animal scientist working with the Navajo Nation, the Navajo Sheep Project aimed "to establish a breeding Navajo–Churro flock, from which livestock is returned to Navajo and Hispanic weavers and sheep raisers. Recognizing the intimate relationship between sheep, wool, weaving, land, and traditional cultures, the project seeks to support agro-pastoralism and create culturally-relevant economic support for the continuation of these cultures."[5] In 1991, the Diné bí' íína' (Navajo Lifeways) registered as a nonprofit organization in Arizona. "Diné bí' íína' represents the Navajo Nation Sheep and Goat Producers, providing leadership, technical information, and economic development assistance to individuals and families and supporting traditional lifeways associated with sheep, wool, and goat producing. The organization seeks to restore status to sheep herding and to promote the education that is necessary for its pursuit in the modern world."[6]

This story tells me again that following the dogs (and their herbivores) cannot help but make their human traveling companions more worldly, more enmeshed in webs of history that demand response today. In my view, response should include, but not be limited to, supporting agroecological ranching; opposing factory-system meat and fiber production; working for genetic diversity and ecological restoration for many domestic and wild species; joining with indigenous economic and political struggles over land and biowealth; becoming smarter about the complex biopolitics of human class, nation, and ethnicity that are entangled with kinds as well as with institutionalized breeds of nonhuman animals; and, hardly least, taking personal and collective action for the animals' well-being in their relations with diverse contemporary people. Alerted by that minimal checklist for response, I return to the branch of the story that led to Australian shepherds and some of the responses enmeshed in telling the tale.

Discovery of gold radically and permanently changed the food economy, species assemblages, politics, human and more-than-human demographies, and naturalsocial ecology of California and other parts of the North American West.[7] Large sheep flocks were transported by sailing them from the east coast around Cape Horn, driving them overland from the Midwest and New Mexico, and shipping them from that other white settler colony with a strong market-oriented pastoral economy, Australia.[8] What the gold rush began, the aftermath of the Civil War finished, with the military reduction and containment of western Native Americans; consolidations of land expropriated from Mexicans, Californios, and Indians; and the vast influx of Anglo (and significant numbers of always parenthetical African American) settlers.

All of these movements of sheep also meant movements of their herding dogs. These were not the guardian dogs of the old transhumant Eurasian pastoral ecologies and economies, with their established market routes, seasonal pasturages, and local bears and wolves (who were, nonetheless, heavily depleted, especially where progress held sway). The white settler colonies in Australia and the United States adopted an even more aggressive attitude than their European forebears to nonhuman predators, building fences around most of Queensland to keep out dingoes and trapping, poisoning, and shooting anything with serious canine teeth that moved on the land in the U.S. West.[9] Guardian breeds, such as Great Pyrenees and Akbash dogs, did not appear in the U.S. western sheep economy until after these eradication tactics became illegal in the queer times of effective environmental movements from the 1970s onward, when collaboration with the slightly mad white women of purebred livestock guardian dog land began to seem rational to at least some manly ranchers of both genders. But that is another story, more wolfish in nature and consequences.

The herding dogs accompanying the immigrant sheep from both the U.S. East Coast and Australia were mainly of the old working collie or shepherd types. These were strong, multipurpose dogs with a "loose eye" and upstanding working posture—rather than with a sheep trial–selected, border collie hard eye and crouch—from which several kennel-club breeds derive. Among the dogs coming to the U.S. West from Australia were the frequently merle-colored "German coulies," who look a lot like modern Australian shepherds. These were British-derived, all-purpose herding "collies," called German because German settlers lived in an area of Australia where these dogs were common. Dogs that look like contemporary Aussies might have acquired their name early from association with flocks arriving on boats from Down Under, whether or not they, too, came on those ships. Or, associated with later immigrant dogs, these types might have acquired the name "Australian shepherd" as late as World War I. Written records are scarce. And there wasn't a "purebred" in sight for a long time.

Identifiable lines, however, were developing in California, Washington, Oregon, Colorado, and Arizona by the 1940s. The Australian Shepherd Club of America met for the first time in 1957 in Himmel Park, Arizona, and comprising about twenty people, the new parent club asked the National Stock Dog Registry to handle the breed. Registration was not common until the mid- to late 1970s.[10] The range of types was still wide, and styles of dogs were associated with particular families and ranches. Curiously, a rodeo performer from Idaho named Jay Sisler is part of the story of molding a kind of dog into a contemporary breed, complete with its clubs and politics. He began training two smart pups, Shorty and Stub, in 1949 on an Idaho ranch, and he subsequently worked with several other Aussies and with a high-jumping greyhound. For over twenty years, Sisler's "blue dogs" performed for his popular rodeo trick show.[11] Although many of his dogs are behind Australian shepherd pedigrees, he was proud of never owning a registered dog. He knew the parents of most of these dogs, but that is as deep as genealogy went in the beginning. Sisler obtained his dogs from various ranchers, several of whose Aussies became foundation stock of the breed. Among the identified 1,371 dogs out of 2,046 ancestors in my Cayenne's ten-generation pedigree, I count seven Sisler dogs in her family. (Many with names such as "Redding Ranch Dog" and "Blue Dog," 6,170 out of over 1 million ancestors are known in her twenty-generation tree; that leaves a few gaps. Most of the really early Aussies were never registered.)

An accomplished trainer of the type Vicki Hearne would have loved,[12] Sisler considered Keno, whom he acquired around 1945, to be his first really good dog. Keno contributed offspring to what became the breed, but the Sisler dog who made the biggest impact (percentage ancestry) to the current population of Aussies was John, a dog with unknown antecedents who wandered one day onto the Sisler ranch and into written pedigrees. There are many such stories of foundation dogs. They could all be microcosms for thinking about companion species and the invention of tradition in the flesh as well as in the text.

The Aussie parent club, ASCA, wrote a preliminary standard in 1961 and a firm one in 1977 and got its own breed club registry going in 1971. Organized in 1969, the ASCA Stock Dog Committee organized herding trials and titles, and working ranch dogs began their considerable reeducation for the trial ring.[13] Conformation competitions and other events became popular, and sizable numbers of Aussie people saw AKC

Jay Sisler and some of his rodeo performing canine partners.

affiliation as the next step. Other Aussie people saw AKC recognition as the road to perdition for any working breed. The pro-AKC people broke away to found their own club, the United States Australian Shepherd Association (USASA), which was given full AKC recognition in 1993.

All of the biosocial apparatus of modern breeds emerged, including savvy lay health and genetics activists; scientists researching gene-linked illnesses common in the breed and establishing companies to market resultant vet biomedical products; scientists and entrepreneurs engaged in comparative genomics, postgenomics, and stem cell research hinged on the published complete DNA sequences of a growing array of taxonomic species as well as of entities such as distinct breeds of dogs; Aussie-themed small businesses; performers passionate about the dogs in agility, flyball, obedience, and dancing; both suburban weekend and rural ranching stock dog trialers; search and rescue workers, both dogs and humans; therapy dogs and their people; termite-detection businesses employing Aussies as sniffer dogs; breeders committed to maintaining the versatile and diverse herding dogs they inherited; other breeders enamored of big-coated, gorgeous show dogs with untested herding talent; puppy millers

Beret's Dogon Grit winning High in Sheep at the 2002 Australian Shepherd Club of America National Stock Dog Finals in Bakersfield, California. Courtesy of Glo Photo and Gayle Oxford.

cashing in on a popular breed no matter the suffering of their reproducing dog "stock" or their offspring; abundant backyard breeders despised by all of the above but self-justified by the fantasy (and sometimes reality) of their children witnessing the "miracle of birth" just once; and much more.

Cayenne's breeders, Gayle and Shannon Oxford in California's Central Valley, are active in both the USASA and ASCA. Committed to breeding and training working stock dogs and also showing in conformation and agility, the Oxfords taught me about "the versatile Aussie," a discourse that I see as analogous to the Great Pyrenees people's "dual purpose" or "whole dog." These idioms work to prevent the splitting up of breeds into ever more isolated gene pools, each dedicated to a specialist's limited goal, whether that be sports, beauty, or something else. The bedrock test of an Australian shepherd, however, remains the ability to herd with consummate skill. If "versatility" does not start there, the working breed will not survive.

That fact concentrates my question about how to inherit the history of touch with these dogs and so how to shape becoming with them in a potentially less violent future. The working dogs are the means and offspring of colonial conquest, the international meat and fiber animal trade, U.S. western ranch economies and ecologies, Native American resistance to the U.S. Army, and sports and entertainment cultures. The nonworking dogs are the offspring of class, race, and gender formations that are rooted in the conformation show world and affectional pet culture.[14] Further, no one can live with a herding (or hunting) dog seriously and remain above the debates about their working partners, the domestic and wild meat- and fiber-producing herbivores. Living in response to these histories is not about guilt and its resultant exterminationist nonsolutions, such as shutting down all stock ranching, encouraging only vegan diets, and working against the deliberate breeding of herding, pet, and show dogs.

I believe that ethical veganism, for example, enacts a necessary truth, as well as bears crucial witness to the extremity of the brutality in our "normal" relations with other animals.[15] However, I also am also convinced that multispecies coflourishing requires simultaneous, contradictory truths if we take seriously *not* the command that grounds human exceptionalism, "Thou shalt not kill," but rather the command that makes us face nurturing and killing as an inescapable part of mortal companion species entanglements, namely, "Thou shalt not make killable." There is no category that makes killing innocent; there is no category or strategy that removes one from killing. Killing sentient animals is killing someone, not something; knowing this is not the end but the beginning of serious accountability inside worldly complexities. Facing up to the outrage of human exceptionalism will, in my view, require severely reducing human demands on the more-than-human world and also radically reducing the number of human beings (*not* by murder, genocide, racism, war, neglect, disease, and starvation—all means that the daily news shows to be common as sand grains on the beach).

Facing up to the outrage of human exceptionalism also requires working for the mortal entanglements of human beings and other organisms in ways that one judges, without guarantees, to be good, that is, to deserve a future. From the point of view of situated histories in the United States, I have proposed modern agropastoralism connected to indigenous as well as other struggles, and also embedded in technoculture, as something I find good, that is, requiring response, feeling, and work. Except as museum, rescue, or novelty heritage critters, most kinds (and individuals) of domestic animals and their ways of living and dying with people would disappear unless this hard matter is approached without moral absolutes. I find that disappearance to be as unacceptable as human murder, genocide, racism, and war. Moral absolutes contribute to what I mean by exterminism. Faced with hard origin stories and irreducible entanglement, we should not go postal, wiping out the source of our well-earned disease, but instead deepen responsibility to get on together without the dream of past, present, or future peace.

That is part of what the philosopher Isabelle Stengers means by cosmopolitics. Forbidding both the dream (and nightmare) of a final solution and also the fantasy of transparent and innocent communication, cosmopolitics is a practice for going on, for remaining exposed to consequences, for entangling materially with as many of the messy players as possible.[16] Unwilling to denounce the present world in favor of an ideal world, the dog people I admire are those who act in companion-species webs with complexity, care, and curiosity. To explore further this kind of examined life, I will tell a story about one remarkable dog woman who began in the conformation culture of the show Aussies but who serves the whole dogland community through her health and genetics knowledge and activism.

ACCOUNTING FOR GENES:
C. A. SHARP IN AUSTRALIAN SHEPHERD LAND

C. A. Sharp embodies for me the practice of love of a breed in its historical complexity.[17] Evident in her kitchen table–produced *Double Helix Network News* and the Australian Shepherd Health and Genetics Institute, which she helped found—not to mention in her critical reflection on her own practices as a breeder and her adoption of a too-small Aussie rescue pooch, Sydney, after the death of the last dog of her breeding—Sharp practices a love that seeks knowledge, nurtures nondogmatic curiosity, and takes action for the well-being of dogs and people. Sharp's world is a good place to look for people who know more at the end of the day than they did in the morning, because they owe it to their beloved, both as kinds and as individuals.

C. A. Sharp and her rescue Australian shepherd, Sydney, in 2006. Photograph by Larry Green.

The dog-activist scene, or canine cosmopolitics, is also a good place to look for examples of some of the major themes in contemporary science and technology studies, such as the fashioning, care, and feeding of "epistemic objects" like the dog genome or genetic diversity; the consolidation and strengthening of facts important for dog health for communities stratified by scientific status hierarchies; the power of boundary objects such as disease genes to stitch together diverse social worlds, including those of pet owners, kennel club breeders, veterinarians, lay health activists, entrepreneurs, and bench researchers; online community formation in digital culture; and the development of open health registries and databases that complexly operationalize the meaning of democratic, companion-species data apparatuses. Multitasking social activism in technoculture characterizes the work of dog people like Sharp, who are in the distinct minority in their breed clubs but who develop robust networks with the potential to change business as usual. Their multitasking includes such action as building grief support systems, peer enforcement of new standards of ethical behavior, above- and below-the-radar networking in highly gendered worlds, nurturing sophisticated lay scientific and medical knowledge, juggling the threat of lawsuits with risky open information sharing, running advertising campaigns, raising money, and acting as dog health advocates in science in a way that has become familiar in patient advocacy groups in human biomedical naturecultures.

Sharp begins her own origin story as a breeder with a traumatic memory that she mobilizes rhetorically to establish grounds for a better Aussie community. She recounts finding herself in the vet's office confronted with bad news about the very first bitch she hoped to breed for a litter of her own. "Within a year and a half of obtaining my first Aussie for show and breeding, I slammed up against the reality of canine genetic disease."[18] Her dog Patte failed to get a hip rating of "good" or better from the Orthopedic Foundation for Animals, a necessary imprimatur for responsible use of a dog in a breeding program.[19] A naive Sharp called Patte's breeder, who was also her mentor in Australian shepherds. The mentor agreed immediately that Patte could not be allowed to have the planned litter. But when Sharp said she'd call the owner of the proposed stud dog and explain why she was canceling the breeding, the mentor capitalized on her power as friend and teacher and pushed Sharp's guilt buttons. The mentor told C.A. that if she told anyone the real reason, she would damage her mentor's reputation as a breeder as well as that of the owners of the prospective sire. That last bit especially, Sharp reminded me, flew in the face of all logic, since the candidate father was unrelated to her Patte, but stress has a way of quelling logic. Properly intimidated, Sharp writes of her phone conversation with the owner of the stud dog, "I don't remember what I said, but I know it was a lie. . . . I felt dirty."[20] From that shaming experience, fortified with a growing knowledge of genetics (and, I would add, no small amount of sheer guts in the face of retaliation), Sharp became a breed health advocate and lay genetic counselor.

This story is a classic conversion narrative. It is also a moving factual account of how denial, culpable ignorance, intimidation to enforce silence, and outright lies work to damage the dogs people claim to love. Sharp named this redolent complex the "Ostrich Syndrome." It and the people she calls "the Incorrigibles" run like a red thread through the rest of my story, providing the friction against which a more progressive future of dog and human coflourishing can be imagined and brought into being in some of the earth's technocultural neighborhoods. It should not need saying, but in case any reader thinks that noticing or mobilizing a narrative form somehow saps the juice of reality from the world, I insist that co-whelped meaning making and world making are material–semiotic littermates, that is, the stuff of robust, frolicking, bumptious, fleshly reality.

I will track Sharp's ways of living and promoting examined lives through three transformative, storied events: (1) establishing the fact of the collie eye anomaly (CEA) gene in Aussies in the early 1990s;[21] (2) redoing the Mendelian self through engagement with genetic diversity discourse in the late 1990s; and (3) building a durable collective institution, the Australian Shepherd Health and Genetics Institute (ASHGI) in the early 2000s, thus supporting the struggle to defeat the Incorrigibles and the Ostrich Syndrome once again, this time in the face of epilepsy. Sharp's involvement in determining the mode of inheritance of CEA in her breed shows how "lay" agency can work in "clerical" canine genetics research and publishing. This is a story of how a fact is brought into robust being and changes its people, a favorite topic for science studies scholars. Sharp's participation in the Canine Genetics Discussion Group Listserv, CANGEN-L, in the late 1990s and early 2000s maps a change in her intellectual and moral field, with a mutated emphasis from disease-linked genes to genetic diversity in the context of widespread turn-of-the millennium attention to evolution, ecology, biodiversity, and conservation. Finally, her work to make the ASHGI a reality illustrates the power of digital media coupled with old-fashioned, mostly women's networking to build effective, and affective, technocultural communities.

Sharp began breeding Australian shepherds in the late 1970s, and she served on ASCA's genetics committee from the early 1980s until 1986, when the board eliminated the committee in a controversial and poorly explained move. In the winter of 1993, she began writing and distributing the *Double Helix Network News*. The first issue of the *DHNN* described itself as a "kitchen-table" enterprise. By 1999, about 150 people—mostly breeders, a few dog research professionals, and one or two ringers like me—subscribed.[22] Learning desktop publishing, Sharp emphasized networking, sharing information, educating one another, dealing with the Ostrich Syndrome among breeders about genetic disease, and practicing love of the breed through responsible genetics.

With a BA in radio, TV, and cinema from California State University at Fresno and a job as an accountant, Sharp has never claimed scientific *insider* status. However, she properly claims *expert* status of a rich kind, and she is regarded as an expert in both the breeder and professional scientific communities. She coauthored a paper in the early 1990s with the veterinary ophthalmologist L. F. Rubin on the mode of inheritance of an eye defect (CEA) in Aussies, engaged in collaborative research on the relation of longevity to coefficients of inbreeding in Aussies with Dr. John Armstrong of the University of Ottawa in the 1990s, and coauthored a paper in 2003 with Sheila Schmutz, of the University of Saskatchewan, that mapped a coat-pattern candidate gene (KTLG) to dog chromosome 15 and excluded it as the merle gene. She has functioned as a clearinghouse for genetic data in her breed; performed pedigree analyses for specific conditions; taught breeders the rudiments of Mendelian, molecular, and population genetics and the practical steps that both conformation and working-dog breeders can and should take to detect and reduce genetic disease in their lines; and linked researchers with the lay dog community to advance the ends of both. Sharp occupies a mediating position among communities of practice from her location as a self-educated, practically experienced, savvy activist who is willing and able to express controversial opinions within cross-linked social worlds.

THE BIRTH OF A FACT

Sharp's interest in the genetic basis of eye disorders dates to 1975, when her first bitch was still a puppy. She went to an All Breed Fun Match near Paso Robles, which turned out to have an eye clinic. Sharp asked what it was about and had her dog checked. "I just got interested and started educating myself."[23] She made it a point afterward to get her dogs' eyes checked, which meant going annually to clinics at the local cocker spaniel club or else hauling dogs a few hours away to Stanford to a veterinary ophthalmologist. She started reading in genetics, guided by an Aussie person named Phil Wildhagen, "who is quite literally a rocket scientist, by the way," Sharp laughed gleefully. About 1983, the Genetics Committee of ASCA put out a call for people to assist it in gathering data. "One thing led to another, and I was on the committee."

This was the period when the Genetics Committee was shifting its attention from coat color, which had been of particular interest during the 1970s when what counted as an Aussie was codified in the written standard, to the more controversial topic of genetic disease. A breeder gave the Genetics Committee two puppies affected with collie eye anomaly, a condition Aussies were not supposed to have. This breeder also went public with the fact of CEA in her dogs and was vilified for her disclosure by Aussie people terrified of this kind of bad news in the breed. Sharp began writing a regular column in the *Aussie Times* for the Genetics Committee.[24]

Starting with the original donated pair, the committee conducted a series of test matings to determine the mode of inheritance. Involving a couple dozen dogs and their pups, these crosses were conducted in the kennels of two committee members, including Sharp, at their own expense, which amounted to several thousand dollars. Most of the affected test puppies were placed in pet homes, with advice to spay or neuter. Some were placed in a university for further research work. The committee collected pedigree data and CERF (Canine Eye Registry Foundation) exam sheets on their test matings and on dogs brought to their attention by a growing number of interested Aussie breeders touched by the *Times* column and word of mouth. The pattern of inheritance indicated an autosomal recessive gene. It was now *technically* possible to take action to reduce the incidence of the condition.[25] But *real* possibility remained another matter.

First, it was more than Aussie breeders who denied the existence of CEA in these dogs. Simply put, Sharp explained, "collie eye anomaly in Aussies wasn't 'real' when we started working with it." For example, Sharp brought a couple of puppies from test matings to an eye clinic at a show in Fresno only to be told by the ophthalmologist that Aussies did not have the condition. Sharp obtained the exam by mobilizing her technical vocabulary—a familiar move for lay activists in health and genetics advocacy. "Their mother has an optic discoloboma; [another relative] has choroidal hyperplasia; please check these dogs. . . . Grumble, grumble, then he checked the puppies." Sharp recalled breeders around the country telling her about attempting to get genetic advice from vets who told them to relax—Aussies don't have CEA; it's not in the literature. Finally, armed with "nearly forty pedigrees with varying degrees of relationships, plus the test-mating data, I went in search of an American College of Veterinary Ophthalmology vet who might be interested in what I had."

A natural to what took science studies scholars a palace coup to establish, Sharp emphasized that she could not make CEA "real" on her own—"certainly not with a BA in radio, television, and cinema." The data had to be published in the right place by the right person. "It's not recessive until someone out there says it is; then it's recessive." "Out there" meant inside institutionalized science. No science studies scholar is surprised now by this social history of truth or by the recognition of it by a savvy "lay" knowledge producer working within a "clerical" culture.

The popular but controversial ASCA Genetics Committee had ceased to be, so Sharp began looking for a collaborator to legitimate the data and analysis she already had. She talked to several likely scientists, but they had other priorities. Frustrated, Sharp recalled insisting, "Look, until one of you people writes it up, it isn't real." Effective corrective action depended on the reality of the fact. The chain finally led to Dr. Lionel Rubin, at the University of Pennsylvania, who was in the process of publishing his book on inherited eye disease in dogs.[26] The book was already in galleys, so the Aussie story did not make that publication. Sharp assembled the data and did the genealogy charts from the committee's crosses and turned that over to Rubin, who hired a professional pedigree analyst for the final charts. From the time Rubin began working with Sharp, publication took two years.[27] With a proper pedigree at last, CEA in Aussies as an autosomal recessive condition was on its way to becoming a fact.

But the reality of the fact remained tenuous. In our 1999 interview, Sharp noted that the demand for independently replicated experiments seems to have kept the "fact" out of the Aussie section of the handbook of the American College of Veterinary Ophthalmology that came out after 1991. She emphasized that such expensive, ethically fraught research on a large companion animal is unlikely to be replicated. "It wouldn't have happened the first time if those of us out here in the trenches had not been interested enough to gather the data." But she argued, "Why couldn't the ACVO say it's *probably* recessive?" She added, "At least when someone out there asks me now, I can send them a copy of the paper." Finally, George Padgett's bible of inherited dog problems included the fact Sharp's network made real.[28] Sharp had consulted George Padgett, of Michigan State University, an important institution in the apparatus of dog genetics natureculture, when she designed her pedigree analysis service and data system for Aussie breeders once the first phase of the research indicated the mode of inheritance. Padgett confirmed that her approach was scientifically sound, and Sharp put the service in place a year or so before she started the *Double Helix Network News* in 1993.

Sharp related with pride that the veterinary ophthalmologist Greg Acland, at Cornell, told her that the Aussie CEA study provided one of the most impressive data sets on the mode of inheritance of a single-gene trait anywhere in the dog literature. The CEA recessive gene fact became stronger in a robust network that included Rubin, Padgett, Acland, and Sharp's expert lay practices. This is the stuff of objectivity as a precious, situated achievement.[29] This is also the stuff of "science for the people"— and for the dogs. Mendelian genetics is hardly a new science in the late twentieth century, but sustaining and extending its knowledge-production apparatus still take work.

But making the fact hold "inside" official science was not enough. Inside the Aussie breed communities is just as crucial a location for this fact to get real and, thus, potentially effective. Denial here takes a different form from that in the scientific communities, and so the material–semiotic rhetorics for persuading the fact into hard reality have to be different. While Sharp set up her pedigree analysis service, a group of committed breeders in Northern California took an extraordinary step. They developed a test-breeding program and forms to document the breedings. Most important, they went public with their results. "As a group, they purchased a full-page ad in the breed magazine admitting they had produced CEA and listing the names of their carrier dogs. In a subsequent ad they told about the test-breeding they had done to clear their related stock."[30] Their group action forestalled the kind of attack that had been made on the donor of the first pair of affected puppies given to the genetics committee. This time, the Incorrigibles were relegated to the underground, and the test breeders reshaped the explicit community standard of practice. The standard might not always be followed, but the reversal of what is secret and what is public in principle was achieved.

One final bit has helped stabilize CEA as a fact in the Aussie world: emotional support for people who find the disease in their lines. Dog people tend to see any "defect" in their dogs as a defect in themselves. Sharp could not be the emotional support person in the Aussie genetic disease world. "When people call me about genetic problems in their Aussies, I'm the 'expert,' not a kindred spirit." Thus, Sharp asked the Northern Californians who went public with their dogs' and their own names to function as a support group to which she referred quite literally grieving breeders.[31] Biosociality is everywhere.[32]

By the time of our first formal interview in 1999, Sharp received far fewer reports of CEA in Aussies than she had seven to eight years before. Getting puppies checked through CERF had become standard ethical practice, and serious breeders did not breed affected dogs. Puppy buyers from such breeders receive a copy of the CERF report right along with their new dog, as well as strict instructions about checking eyes of breeding stock annually if the new pup does not come with a spay/neuter contract. Facts matter.[33]

By late 2005, the date of our second formal conversation, using data mostly gathered from border collies and with the bulk of the money for research raised by the working border collie club, Cornell's Gregory Acland had found the gene for CEA and marketed a gene test through his com-pany, OptiGen.[34] Despite Sharp's urging in the *DHNN* and in her fre-quent presentations at Aussie shows around the country,[35] Australian shepherd people failed to participate in significant numbers in the Cor-nell study. However, one progressive Aussie breeder, Cully Ray, gave Acland a substantial donation, and a few determined souls maneuvered CEA-affected Aussies into the research that allowed Acland to determine that Aussies and border collies (as well as collies) share the same gene for CEA and so can use the same DNA test. Sharp told me that one gutsy Aussie owner offered Acland a CEA-affected puppy in the face of her breeder's negative reaction that approached stalking. Incorrigibles are not, well, corrigible.

Nonetheless, by 2006, CEA was no longer the significant genetic problem in Aussies that it once was, because effective detection of affected dogs and carriers, followed by action, became common as a result of the work of committed health activists. The DNA test is nice to have, but more traditional methods of detection (an eye exam) and using pedigree analysis to reduce the chance of mating carriers to each other had man-aged the crisis fairly well. The condition had become common because of the overuse in the 1980s of a few popular sires, who happened to be car-riers for the recessive gene. The problem could become common again if a single undetected popular sire cavorts in the gene pool. The knowledge and technology exist now, but genetic health, as well as other kinds of dog–human coflourishing, requires the ongoing work of examined lives.[36]

BORN AGAIN

The world of disease-linked genes is, however, only one component of the story of dog genetics, especially in the era of biodiversity discourse. En-hancing and preserving genetic diversity are not the same thing as avoid-ing and reducing genetically linked illness. The discourses touch in many places, but their divergences are reshaping the intellectual and moral worlds of many dog people. Sharp's story is again instructive.

In the mid-1990s Sharp was a subscriber to an Internet discussion group called K9GENES. On that Listserv, Dr. Robert Jay Russell, a pop-ulation geneticist, rare dog breed activist, and president of the Coton de

Tulear Club of America, criticized breeding practices that reduce genetic diversity in dog breeds and the AKC structure that keeps such practices in place, even though the kennel club funds genetic disease research and mandates DNA-based parentage testing. Russell's controversial postings were blocked from the list several times, prompting him to log on under a different e-mail account and reveal the censorship.

These events led to the founding in 1997 of the Canine Genetics Discussion Group, CANGEN-L, moderated by Dr. John Armstrong, at the University of Ottawa, to allow free genetics discussion among breeders and scientists. Until his death in 2001, Armstrong also maintained the Canine Diversity Project Web site,[37] where one could obtain an elementary education in population genetics, read about conservation projects for endangered wild canids, consider activist positions on dog breeding operating outside the kennel clubs, and follow links to related matters. Concepts such as effective population size, genetic drift, and loss of genetic diversity structured the moral, emotional, and intellectual terrain.

CANGEN-L was an impressive site, where it was possible both to observe and to interact with other dog people learning how to alter their thinking, and possibly their actions, in response to one another. The list started with thirty members, and Armstrong expected it to reach one hundred. Taxing its computer resources at the University of Ottawa, CANGEN had three hundred subscribers in the spring of 2000. Acrimonious and fascinating controversies surfaced on CANGEN. Some participants complained that threads were ignored, and breeders periodically expressed a sense that they were treated with disrespect by some scientists (and vice versa), though breeders and scientists were not mutually exclusive categories on CANGEN. Subscribers, scientists or not, occasionally left the list in a huff or in frustration. A few dogmatists dedicated to the Truth as revealed to themselves cut a wide swath from time to time.

All that said, in my opinion, CANGEN was an extraordinary site of informed, democratic discussion among diverse actors. CANGEN's uncovering of my own yawning ignorance about such things as coefficients of inbreeding prompted me to run back to my graduate school notes on theoretical population genetics and sign up for the Cornell University vet school online canine genetics course, an experience that abruptly ended my elitist disdain for offerings of online distance learning.[38] I was not alone on CANGEN in suddenly understanding that I had to know more than I did if I claimed to love kinds of dogs.

Sharp welcomed the higher level of scientific discourse and the emphasis on evolutionary population genetics on CANGEN. She felt challenged by the statistical arguments and wanted to explore the practical consequences for the kind of breeding advice she gives in the *DHNN*. Beginning with the summer 1998 issue, the newsletter shifted direction. She began with an article explaining the doleful effects of the "popular sire syndrome" on genetic diversity and made clear that line breeding is a form of inbreeding. In the fall 1998 issue, she explored how severe selection against disease-linked genes can worsen the problem of the loss of genetic diversity in a closed population. She cited with approval the success of the basenji club in getting AKC approval for importing African-born dogs outside the stud book, a daunting endeavor given AKC resistance.

Sharp's feature article in the winter 1999 issue of *DHNN* was introduced by a quotation from a fellow CANGEN member who had been especially outspoken, Dr. Hellmuth Wachtel, free collaborator of the Austrian Kennel Club and member of the Scientific Council of the Vienna Schönbrunn Zoo. Sharp explained genetic load, lethal equivalents, population bottlenecks, genetic drift, coefficients of inbreeding, and fragmented gene pools. In the spring 1999 *DHNN*, Sharp published "Speaking Heresy: A Dispassionate Consideration of Cross-Breeding," an article she expected, in her words, to make "the excretory material hit the circulatory apparatus." Love of the breed is messy.

The new genetics is not an abstraction in dog worlds, whether one considers the politics of owning microsatellite markers, the details of a commercial gene test, the problem of funding research, competing narratives of origin and behavior, the pain of watching a dog suffer genetic illness, the personally felt controversies in dog clubs over breeding practices, or the cross-cutting social worlds that tie different kinds of expertise together. When I asked Sharp what she thought breeders, geneticists, dog magazine writers, and others might have learned from one another on CANGEN or other places, she zeroed in on the rapid and deep transformations in genetics over the last decades. Her growth in genetic knowledge, she suggested, including her ability to handle the whole apparatus of molecular genetics, was natural and continuous—until she logged on to CANGEN. "The only epiphany sort of thing I've been through was when I got on CANGEN and started reading all the posts from the professionals. . . . I knew there were problems with inbreeding, but I didn't have a grasp about what the whole problem was until I started learning about population genetics." At that point, the analogies with politically fraught wildlife conservation and biodiversity loss hit home—and she made the connection between her dog work and her volunteering as a docent at her local zoo, a connection that surfaced again in her struggles with animal-rights opponents of a ballot initiative to reorganize and reform the Fresno zoo in 2005. Citizenship across species ties many knots, none of them innocent. Born again, indeed, but into ongoing complexity, curiosity, and care, not grace.

IN THE FACE OF EPILEPSY

By the early 2000s, Sharp had amassed a vast archive of breed health, genetic, and pedigree information, and she had initiated a variety of services for researchers, breeders, and ordinary Aussie people. What would happen to her data if something happened to her? Also, she had been threatened with lawsuits more than once by breeders more worried about their kennels' winning reputations in show culture than about their dogs and their dogs' offspring across future generations. That the threatened suits were very unlikely to have succeeded would not shield her from the personal financial disaster that having to defend against them would bring. In my experience, her discretion and practice of confidentiality were (and are) exemplary,[39] but that might not protect her from well-funded and ill-intentioned Incorrigibles. This matter strikes at the heart of pedigree analysis and database accessibility. Also, her networks had grown way beyond the kitchen-table publishing, personal test breeding, and breed club–committee dimensions of the early years, although the face-to-face (and computer screen-to-screen) quality of dog health activism remains striking.

It was time for another transformation, this time into an incorporated, nonprofit, dog health organization that would operate in cooperation with, but independent from, all the Aussie breed clubs. Sharp's old colleague and friend on the ASCA DNA committee, Pete Adolphson, approached her with a similar idea, and they decided to work together to bring the plan to fruition. With an MS in zoology, Adolphson had published on the effects of aquatic toxicology on population genetics. Sharp and Adolphson recruited another former member of the ASCA DNA committee, George Johnson, a long-term Aussie owner and occasional breeder with a PhD in botany from North Carolina State University, who had published on Australian shepherd genetics in the breed magazine *Aussie Times*. In 2001 the Australian Shepherd Health and Genetics Institute incorporated in the United States as a federal 501(c)(3) organization, and in July 2002 Sharp and her colleagues publicly announced their infant institute. With the donated labor of a talented professional Web designer and Aussie breeder in Arizona, Claire Gustafson, ASHGI went online as www.ashgi.org in January 2003. Sharp serves as president. Joining her and Johnson after Adolphson left the board of directors, Kylie Munyard—then a postdoctoral agricultural genetic analyst at Murdoch University and now an associate lecturer in molecular genetics at Curtin University of Technology, Australia, as well as a competitor with her Aussie in agility, obedience, and, more recently, herding—came on the board. With two other activists, Munyard established the Australian Shepherd Health Registry of Australasia, which, alas, had a short life even as it inspired a project for an international Aussie health database.

From the beginning, ASHGI entered into partnerships with canine genetic researchers on projects that have included epilepsy research, behavioral genetics, multiple drug resistance genes, cataracts, and others.[40] Encouraging people to give samples, ASHGI explains the research, spreads the word, and helps researchers to connect meaningfully in their work with the dog world. With files augmented by those of Sharp's deceased friend Betty Nelson, with whom she had done the original CEA test crosses, ASHGI maintains an extraordinary archive of documents relevant to breed health and genetics. They have a breedwide cancer survey underway as well as plans to develop an international online searchable health database (the International Directory for Australian Shepherd Health, IDASH), drawn from existing open health registries and voluntary submissions from Aussie owners. IDASH will computerize Sharp's pedigree-analysis and make it available as a paid ASHGI service.[41] Gestating the idea for IDASH for about a year already and then further prompted by

BEACON, the bearded collie health organization's Web site, in 2005 Sharp networked at the Canine Health Foundation conference with activists in other breeds, especially bearded collies, Bernese mountain dogs, and malamutes.[42] Each ASHGI project has a hard-working committee coordinating with Sharp. About a dozen very active people make ASHGI work; 90 percent of them are women; 100 percent of them live deeply entwined with cherished individual dogs as well as with the breed. Their labor of love would fall apart without constant Internet-mediated communication and considerable technoscientific professional and self-taught expertise. In my terms, cyborgs are among ASHGI's companion species.

Networking, connecting care with knowledge, and collective commitment are what get my attention in ASHGI. No one could miss the volunteer expertise and labor at the heart of the practice of love of the breed. Three activities make this matter vivid: the "Ask an Expert" feature of the Web site, the Ten Steps to a Healthier Australian Shepherd program for breeders, and support of a broad range of action to address epilepsy in the breed.

Sharp had for years answered an avalanche of e-mail questions about Aussie health and genetics, but with ASHGI she organized a corps of committed volunteer experts with diverse experience in the breed. E-mail links appear on each subject-matter page as well as several other places on the Web site to connect people to the relevant volunteer. One of those volunteers who give their expertise for free is Kim Monti, formerly a research chemist with a career in animal health product research and now a business consultant. Long active in search-and-rescue work with her dogs, as well as conformation and obedience, Monti is an Aussie breeder whose Foxwood Kennel is in New Mexico.[43] The driving force behind and chair of the Ten Steps program, Monti has also been active in the effort to reduce the incidence of epilepsy in the breed. Ten Steps grew from an intense discussion about breeder ethics in the EpiGENES confidential online chat group, whose international membership represents the sweep of health cultures throughout the breed.[44] Participants drew up numerous drafts before settling on a list of ten ethical actions every breeder should take to cultivate a culture of openness about problems, mutual support, health screening, and targeted research. The tone and content are caught by these four pledges: "I support the open disclosure of all health issues that affect Australian Shepherds, utilizing publicly accessible canine health registries in the country of my residence whenever possible"; "I do not speak ill of any breeder or breeding program that has produced affected Australian Shepherds"; "I compassionately support and assist owners of affected dogs in gathering information on the genetic diseases that have stricken their dogs"; and "Before being bred, all of my dogs are DNA profiled with an accredited laboratory and the results made public, if such services are available within my country, or before my stock is exported to a country that has DNA profiling available."

Breeders take the Ten Step pledge on the honor system, of course. No mandatory regulatory structure supports these practices in the breed clubs or elsewhere, for better and for worse. The existence of such a clear set of principles can be a powerful educational tool and a potent instrument of peer pressure. The pledge is taken in the first-person singular—"I"— but the statement is the fruit of rich collective processes among people deeply affected by the issues who see themselves to be directly responsible for making positive change happen. In many senses, Ten Steps is an exemplary instance of bioethics in transnational canine technoculture. For example, the program is simultaneously a response to the geneticization of health and illness across species, with its market-based research, testing, and therapeutic regimes; a model for responsible individual and collective action; an example of social activism in women's communities; a window to the casting of political and scientific action in ethical idioms and instruments; a product of screen-to-screen as well as face-to-face networking in digital culture; an active shaping of the terms of operation of key emergent objects of digital culture, such as open databases; and a fascinating configuration of affective and epistemological engagement with kinds of dogs, individual dogs, and dog people.

Ten Steps emerged from an epilepsy-focused confidential chat group, EpiGENES. Why is epilepsy so important in current dog culture, including Australian shepherd worlds? Why did a chat group have to be confidential? Are purebred dogs really sick all the time, seizing at every opportunity? The answer to the last question for Australian shepherds remains "no"; Aussies are a generally healthy breed, with a mean life expectancy of over twelve years. *But* genetic disease incidence has increased in recent decades, and that is unnecessary and inexcusable.[45] Nonetheless, are we really certain that so-called idiopathic epilepsy definitely is a genetic disease or complex of diseases? What is the incidence of epilepsy in Australian shepherds, and how has that changed over the last twenty years or so? What would it take to know the answer to these questions? Why can epilepsy so concentrate what is at stake in the kind of examined lives C. A. Sharp has worked so hard to promote and practice?

In the 1980s, epilepsy was hardly heard of among Aussies, but twenty-five years later it is one of the two most frequent diseases in the breed, and denying its heritability has become very difficult. Show lines are riddled with it, and at least two nonshow lines are affected.[46] Epilepsy first cropped up in obvious family clusters in the offspring of Aussies exported to the United Kingdom in the early 1990s, and the British breeders reacted with silence, coercion, and threats to those who spoke up. U.S. breeders tended to regard the U.K. scene as of no interest to themselves, but when reports of the disorder in U.S. dogs became more and more frequent, many U.S. breeders proceeded to react the same way that U.K. breeders had. Easy to misrecognize, primary or idiopathic (heritable) epilepsy was still diagnosed in 2006 by excluding other causes. Seizures can be caused by many things; the cause of inherited epilepsy is not yet nailed down to a mapped gene or genes (much less to gene regulation or epigenetic patterning); epilepsy usually does not manifest until well into adulthood, making it hard to breed away from; and living with epilepsy is extremely difficult for the dogs, their companion people, and their breeders. All of this opens the doors wide to the full panoply of Incorrigible antics and the associated Ostrich Syndrome. As Sharp put it, "An example of the Ostrich Syndrome gone malignant can be found in my breed. . . . There are many Ostriches who have or have produced epileptic Aussies, but the testing doesn't get done, they won't cooperate with an on-going research project, and what 'really' happened is the dog hit its head/got into an ant poison/had sun stroke, and so on. Apparently these dogs hit their heads, eat poison, or overheat every three to four weeks."[47] The stakes are high for developing a direct DNA-based screening test, the strongest forceps available in technoculture for pulling ostrich heads into the bracing air on such matters.

Readers of this chapter will have noticed that EpiGENES was a confidential chat group, a powerful clue to the stigmatizing nature of diseases suspected of being hereditary.[48] The evidence for the stigma and the attack response of Incorrigibles is not hard to find. Sharp began a powerful article on epilepsy in the *Australian Shepherd Journal* in 2003 with a horrific seizure log for one young bitch who had to be euthanized in 1993, six months after her first grand mal seizure. The gutsy owner of this dog, Pat Culver, placed a memorial ad in the September/October 1994 issue of the *Aussie Times*, giving the registered name, the cause of death, and two generations of pedigree. Some breeders with closely related dogs exploded and attacked Culver; other people discussed the need for positive response. Along with Culver, another Aussie lover named Ann DeChant, who had produced two litters with epileptic pups (and has since cleared epilepsy from her breeding program), and Sharp tried to rally breed action, but Sharp told me in our interview in November 2005 that people were afraid, and attention died down.

The Incorrigibles attacked those who spoke up and continued to breed first-degree relatives of affected dogs without telling anyone anything. In addition, these people slowed down positive response to the dogs' and their people's suffering by refusing to give samples from affected dogs and their close relatives to the two then-existing research programs, even though those projects held all data confidential. By the time of Sharp's and my interview in 2005, however, things had turned around because of a resolute grassroots movement of Aussie activists, who also came under the umbrella of ASHGI. That grassroots movement is one of the reasons that by the spring of 2006, a DNA test specific to at least one Aussie version of epilepsy seemed likely. (The genetics of the disease is not the same for all breeds, and a single-gene inheritance for any form of epilepsy is a weak fact at this point.)

At the Aussie National Specialty Show in Bakersfield, California, in 2002, three Arizona women and Ann DeChant from Michigan, all of whom had produced dogs who developed epilepsy and were committed to doing something about it, began to hatch a multifaceted, long-range plan. The Arizona gang included Kristin Rush, who became the chairperson of the Australian Shepherd Genetic Epilepsy Network and Education Service (AussieGENES), which came into ASHGI's structure; Claire Gustafson, who was the Web site designer for ASHGI; and Kristina Churchill. Along with Gustafson, Rush, and Churchill, DeChant set up

EpiGENES in 2003, while Gustafson and Heidi Mobley designed an attention-getting ad campaign in the major Aussie breed journals, with the ads bearing the signatures of people who had produced epileptic dogs and who refused to stay quiet any longer. The idea for the fleshed-out organization of AussieGENES came from the chat group EpiGENES. Sharp looked on, cheered, and helped where she could, including writing "The Road to Hell" for the 2003 issue of the *Australian Shepherd Journal* that published the first ads. That article attracted notice, winning a 2003 Dog Writers Association of America Maxwell Award. Also, both of the major breed registries, the ASCA and the United States Australian Shepherd Association, underwrote part of the expenses for the ad campaigns. There was even a Parade of Veterans and Titleholders at the 2005 Aussie National Specialty Show, in which several of the people who submitted bios for their dogs included the information that near kin had epilepsy. Even one of the titleholding dogs proudly walking with its human was listed as suffering from epilepsy. Sharp reported that the crowd was amazed, shocked, and deeply moved, with many people approaching the owner of the affected dog to thank her for her honesty. The attack culture was definitely losing its ability to silence and intimidate.

The Incorrigibles met another formidable force in the pet owner Pam Douglas, her afflicted dog Toby, and the charitable foundation Douglas established to increase public awareness about canine epilepsy and to develop means to fight the disease.[49] A lawyer who had practiced on the East Coast and then moved to California, Douglas had raised three children with her husband, and they found themselves wanting another family member after their human offspring had fledged. And so, after examining all the standard health tests for eyes and hips, they bought an Australian shepherd puppy. The puppy's sire was from a well-regarded "Hall of Fame" kennel with many winners in conformation and versatility competitions. Douglas and her husband did not want a show dog or an athlete; they wanted a pet. Their puppy, Toby, had a series of misdiagnosed difficulties beginning at the age of ten months, culminating in a terrifying grand mal seizure at thirteen months. The process of diagnosis and subsequent efforts to control the disease have been emotionally and physically painful, for humans and dog alike, not to mention expensive for the Douglases. Toby has major difficulties and a troubled prognosis, but the good news is that at over four years of age, Toby has a good life in spite of very serious and only partly controlled epilepsy and debilitating effects from both seizures and medications. The best news is that he has hard-drive, focused human herders for family members, who are not about to be intimidated.

Assuming the best, a still naive Douglas contacted Toby's breeder and the breeder of Toby's sire after the youngster's epilepsy became clear and had what she described as a long series of conversations that went no-where. The *Australian Shepherd Journal* article on Douglas's story reported that these well-known breeders with a beautiful Web site about quality dogs who had all the standard health clearances (a site that, as far as I can tell, has not been updated since April 2003 and received more than twenty thousand unique visitors between December 2002 and December 2006) did not respond to her pleas to contribute blood samples of their dogs who were closely related to Toby to the major dog genetic epilepsy research program at the University of Missouri.[50] Douglas refused to let things go at that. She talked at length with Sharp, who lent an ear and sympathy while Douglas educated herself about the science of canine epilepsy and the realities of supporting dogs and dog people through the illness. Douglas then published a heart-catching full-color ad in both major Aussie breed journals in 2004, asking for owners of Toby's relatives to contribute DNA samples to the Canine Epilepsy Network. The ad was called "The Face of Epilepsy." The advertisements published by Toby's Foundation are radical in dogland. The classic first-person biographical semiotics, portraiture, material signifiers of family, narrative pathos, appeals to take action, enticements to modern selfhood through participation in scientific research, and registered genealogy (even if indicating genetic disease) ought to be effective in U.S. middle-class culture. I for one am caught and proud of it. I contribute to Toby's Foundation and wish my readers would, too. To notice how material–semiotic labor is done does not vitiate it ethically or politically but locates it culturally and histori-cally, within which nonreductive judgment is possible.

No one came forward with information about any of Toby's sib-lings, but one call linked Toby to Shadow, an Aussie puppy who had been

The Face of Epilepsy

Kutabay's Blue Chip Toby

ASCA #N128035 • AKC #DL90828201

Sire: Moonlight's Short Circuit   Dam: Hartke of Kutabay

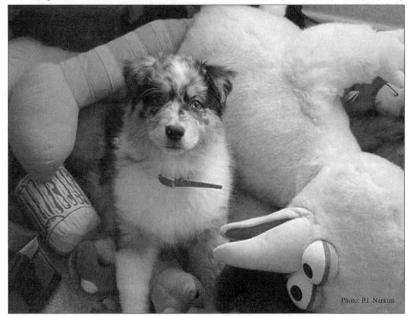

Photo: P.I. Narkun

"At 12 weeks old I caught my first ball.
At 7 months old I went swimming for the first time.
On February 17, 2003, I celebrated my first birthday.
One month later I had my first grand mal seizure."

Epilepsy threatens the future of our breed. Please give blood.

Toby has been diagnosed with Idiopathic (Primary) Epilepsy. If you are related to Toby or any other affected dog, please help by donating a DNA sample to the University of Missouri for research that can lead to a genetic screening test for Aussies to help put an end to this killer disease.

For more information contact Liz Hansen, Research Coordinator, by email at hansenl@missouri.edu or by phone at 573-884-3712 or visit www.canine-epilepsy.net.

For more information about Toby call 949-455-7842 or email DougPCN@yahoo.com.

"The Face of Epilepsy," *Australian Shepherd Journal* (May/June 2004). Courtesy of Toby's Foundation and Pam Douglas.

whelped in November 2000 from the kennel of Toby's sire and who had such bad seizures that he had to be euthanized at eleven months of age. Shadow's humans helped craft a memorial ad for their dog too, asking for cooperation with research by giving blood samples from affected dogs and their close relatives. Including as many of these kin in the samples as possible is crucial for mapping genes of interest. The ad campaign has been very public and very effective. Pet owners, or at least Pam Douglas and her growing networks, have made their power felt in the breeders' purebred scene, where the mere pet buyer can feel decidedly secondary.

One of the labs looking for the gene or genes responsible for heritable epilepsy in Aussies, VetGen, dropped out in 2003,[51] while Gary Johnson's lab in the Canine Epilepsy Network at the University of Missouri continued its research. AussieGENES, the *DHNN*, Toby's Foundation, and ASHGI have made sample submissions to the researchers a high priority. In 2003, the year of Toby's birth, the Canine Epilepsy Network had only ninety-nine samples from Aussies, with sixteen affected dogs. By 2006, they had over a thousand samples, more than for any other breed, including two extended multigenerational families. The patterns began to indicate that an autosomal recessive allele at only one locus might be the main culprit for this form of epilepsy. In early 2006, gene identification seemed near, and fund-raising was under way in Aussie land to obtain seventy thousand dollars to help support that final push. Many knots still remain to be tied in the technocultural assemblages needed to build and stabilize consequential facts, such as an Aussie epilepsy gene, but the activists in ASHGI and Toby's Foundation have invented some very promising cat's cradle patterns.

A DNA screening test is no panacea and certainly no cure for affected dogs, but in dog breeding, where identified mutations do prove strongly causal for a disorder, a reliable screening test can identify carriers and indicate carrier-to-carrier crosses to be avoided. The key is the community's relation to the test and to its technocultural apparatus. The Ashkenazi Jewish community in New York City has virtually eliminated the birth of babies with Tay-Sachs disease by first supporting research and then using a gene test, even while affected children continue to be born to other communities around the world with very different relationships to the cultural apparatuses of research, medicine, and genetic citizenship.[52]

Not all stories about gene tests are so benign, in either human or dog worlds, but maybe this Aussie tale can have a happy ending.

My shaggy dog story about webs of action in the postgenomic age is about an old symbiosis—that among knowledge, love, and responsibility. Dog genetics is a social network as much as a biotechnical one. Neither microsatellite markers, nor ten-generation pedigrees, nor DNA-based gene tests fall from the sky; they are the fruit of historically located natural-cultural work. Breed standards, dog genomes, and canine populations are material–semiotic objects that shape lives across species in historically specific ways. This chapter has asked how heterogeneous sorts of expertise and caring are required to craft and sustain scientific knowledge for the benefit of kinds of dogs, as well as individual pooches, within a particular, noninnocent, naturalcultural context. The story of C. A. Sharp navigates the linkages of lay and professional work as well as the linkages between knowledge and affect in technoculture. Genetic flows in dogs and humans have implications for meanings of species and race; origin stories remain potent in scientific culture; and molecular biotechnology can be mobilized to sustain ideas of diversity and conservation. Internet sociality shapes alliances and controversies in dog worlds, and popular and commercial practices infuse technical and professional worlds and vice versa.

   None of this is breaking news in science studies, and none of it resolves the contradictions of biowealth, biocapital, and biopolitics, but all of it holds my attention as a scholar, a citizen, and a dog person. Sharp and her networks grapple with matters that shape human and nonhuman lives profoundly; they make a difference. Interested in the symbioses of companion species of both organic and inorganic kinds, I end with fusions. The passage of the leash law in Denver, Colorado, in the 1950s enclosed the commons of my childhood dog–human world. The proprietary regimes and DNA-testing surveillance mechanisms at the turn of the millennium map and enclose the commons of the genome and mandate new kinds of relations among breeders, researchers, dog owners and guardians, and dogs. Local and global crises of the depletion of cultural and biological diversity lead to novel kinds of enclosure of lands and bodies in zoos, museums, parks, and nations. Telling about a kind of dog also meant coming to terms with the complexities and consequences of histories of ranching and mining, the dispossession of Californios and Native Americans, and the modern efforts to constitute an economically, biologically, politically, and ethically viable human–animal agropastoralism out of the shards of that inheritance. No wonder that I am looking in the joined story of dogs and people for a vivid sense of a still possible common life and future from which we can continue to build.

DIVERSITY MURDERS

With homage to Charis Thompson for her true fiction story in science studies, "Confessions of a Bioterrorist,"[53] I conclude "Examined Lives" with a foray into detective fiction, starting with my (reedited) post to CANGEN-L on January 26, 2000:

> Okay, List Members, I'll start a shaggy dog murder story for genetic diversity and see if anyone wants to help write this pulp contribution by committee! I'd like three friends to be the sleuths, all human alpha bitches of a certain age and each with different appendages in dog worlds.
>
> One sleuth is a long-term breeder of herding dogs; and since we're speculating, I take the liberty of choosing Australian shepherds, the best example of herders anyway <vbg>. This breeder is an Anglo woman from a ranching family of modest means who lives in California's Central Valley not far from Fresno. She has tried hard over four decades, ever since Aussies became institutionalized as a breed, to produce dogs who could herd with matchless skill, win in conformation, excel in obedience and agility sports, and serve as pets with dignity. This woman graduated from high school, is self-educated, very smart, and richly connected in dog worlds, especially in the herding and working dog breeds. Next to herders, livestock guardian dogs have a special place in her heart, and she's informed herself about the population and ecological history of the various LGDs in Europe and Eurasia and their construction as institutionalized breeds in the United States and Europe. She took the side of the anti-AKC faction in the great Aussie wars of the 1980s, but she's been active in both of the registries for the last few years. Lately, she's made friends with a health and genetics activist in Fresno who publishes a newsletter that's making a lot of people mad. This sleuth has her

doubts about the ways scientists treat breeders and about the hardness
of the data that scientists use to make claims about breeding practices.
She's a hard-headed realist about dogs, and there's not much she
wouldn't do to stay true to her commitment to their well-being.
She's also one of the few people who can talk to both ranchers and
environmentalists about wolf reintroductions in the West. She is
active in the Navajo Sheep Project and in solidarity with Diné bí'
íína'. No friend of People for the Ethical Treatment of Animals,
nonetheless she works with them to expose the conditions of the
factory-farming meat industry.

My second sleuth is a molecular geneticist at UC Davis who is
forming a venture capital start-up company in order to research and
market diagnostic kits for genetic diseases affecting toy breeds mainly.
Her company is called Genes 'R' Us, and Toys 'R' Us is suing her for
trademark infringement after her marketing campaign got toys and
genes a little too confused. She has papillons and competes at a high
level in agility meets, where she met sleuth 1. She has been connected
recently with Southern California assisted reproduction clinics that
are taking steps toward cloning humans. She has a strong interest in
the frozen zoo collection at the San Diego Zoo and in the transnational
world of conservation biology and politics. She's a second-generation
Chinese American, and partly because she has an uncle in China who
works as a panda biologist, she became involved with the politics of
international panda population restoration in both zoos and wildlife
preserves. She's no stranger to the problems of small populations.
Besides her four papillons, she has a Newfoundland puppy and two
aging golden retriever—whippet crosses she got from a shelter fifteen
years ago.

My third sleuth is a nutritional biochemist at Ralston Purina,
and she went to graduate school at Cornell with sleuth 2. Like many
African American women of her generation who earned chemistry
degrees, she took a job in industry rather than academia. Her research
has put her right in the middle of controversies about diets tailored to
metabolic disorders in companion animals, and all the ideological and
commercial battles about dogs made her interested in the genetic
issues in allergies, digestive malfunctions, reproductive ill health, and
metabolic diseases. With sleuth 1, she's trying to get studies funded to
test hypotheses about loss of genetic diversity and ill health. She
started by asking if purebred dogs really are "sicker" now than in the
past, and if so why. She's ended up the target of suspicion by both her
division chief at the company and advocates of unprocessed "natural

foods" for dogs. Her passion has led her to form research consortia with veterinarians, modeled after AIDS community research efforts, to try to get good data on the cheap from vet practices. All of this led her to an analysis of nutrition, hunger, health, and illness for both human and nonhuman animals around the world that has more to do with justice and sustainable agroecology than with genes. When she can get free of all this, she brings her two chow chows to assisted living communities as therapy dogs. She is proving that chows can have great temperaments. This lady takes on hard projects as a way of life.

The three women and their Aussie, chow, and papillon pooches got together for a vacation at a summer dog camp only to discover that they each have more than a few ideas about the recent murder of a famous dog writer who had authored a series of controversial stories in the *New Yorker* about how the Dog Genome Project would finally throw light on behavioral genetics in humans as well as in dogs. The writer had infuriated everyone, from those worried about a new eugenics, to advocates of cloning on demand, to animal rights activists, to bench scientists, to breeders, to those committed to dogs' difference from humans as an ethical principle crucial to canine well-being. But before the murder is solved, the trail takes our sleuths into commercial, laboratory, conservation, and dog breeding and show world science and politics that put genetic diversity on the talk shows all over the country and brought the AKC to its knees.

In response to my e-mailed prompt, "But I am looking for a suspect," C. A. Sharp, my obvious model for the Diversity Murders' "health and genetics activist in Fresno who publishes a newsletter that's making a lot of people mad," posted back:

> Hmmm. Maybe pups.com is also a major shareholder in the corporate lab that does AKC's DNA-PV [parentage verification testing] and has been pushing AKC toward mandatory. Puppy millers don't like this. Many non-commercial breeders are not exactly delighted for a variety of reasons. Maybe a zealot who espouses the need for mandatory DNA and open disease registries has been publicly critical of pups.com's mixed motivations.
>
> You aren't helping, Donna. I've put fiction-writing on hold so I could deal with a backlog of canine genetics projects. Now you're sucking me back in with canine fiction!

I responded to the list:

> C.A., now we're purring! Fabulous ideas. Lists of suspects are
> beginning to suggest themselves. Consider canine genetic fiction
> double tasking and definitely part of getting those genetics
> projects done. . . .
>
> Have you seen the new company name that is associated with
> the [dog-cloning] Missyplicity Project? Genetic Savings and Clone.
> See *Wired*, March 2000. That—plus my new ethical obligation, made
> clear in Lazaron BioTechnologies' ad right next to Thorpe-Vargas
> and Cargill's article on cloning in the March *DogWorld*, of "saving a
> genetic life"—has me thinking CANGEN might also ask how the
> extraordinary genetic popular and commercial culture we are gestating
> in affects our efforts to think clearly about scientific issues. "Right to
> life" discourse always makes me break out in hives, and "saving a
> genetic life" is just such a powerful allergen.

On March 8, C.A. wrote back:

> I'm already multi-tasking (what woman doesn't?). And my processor
> (not to mention my husband) is flashing error messages warning me
> that I am about to exceed my RAM!

To be continued . . . Watch for the series on Amazon.com, where purchases will earn the Australian Shepherd Health and Genetics Institute a percentage. Move over, Susan Conant![54]

5. CLONING MUTTS, SAVING TIGERS
Bioethical Angst and Questions of Flourishing

The breed, any breed, is a river. It began flowing before it got to us and it will continue to flow past where we see it. . . . If we truly love this river we will recognize that it belongs to all of us now and to its future visitors, and that we cannot simply be individuals using it as we please for our personal and immediate benefit only.
—Linda Weisser, January 8, 2000, Pyr-L@apple.ease.lsoft.com

Cloning companion animals is where evolution meets the free market; those who can afford it will save what they like and leave the rest to burn.
—Lou Hawthorne, CEO, Genetic Savings and Clone, Inc., May 12, 2000

EMERGENTS IN TECHNOCULTURE

Pleasures and anxieties over beginnings and endings abound in contemporary dog worlds. When technocultures are awash in millennial discourses, why shouldn't dogs get in an apocalyptic bark at first and last things? Canine tales demand a hearing; they concern the dramatis personae in the ecological theater and the evolutionary play of rescripted naturecultures in technonatural, biosocial modernity.[1] I want to know how the emergence of an ethics of cross-species flourishing, compassion, and responsible action is at stake in technosavvy dog cultures engaged with genetic diversity, on the one hand, and cloning, on the other.

In the past, I wrote about cyborgs, a kind of companion-species congeries of organisms and information machines emergent from the Cold War. Also on my mind have been genetically engineered laboratory organisms such as OncoMouse™, those companion species linking commercial, academic, medical, political, and legal domains. Emergent over the time of "species being" (in the philosopher's idiom) for both participants, dogs and humans as companion species suggest distinct histories and lives compared with cyborgs and engineered mice.

The term *companion species* refers to the old co-constitutive link between dogs and people, where dogs have been actors and not just recipients of action. *Companion species* also points to the sorts of being made possible at interfaces among different human communities of practice for whom "love of the breed" or "love of dogs" is a practical and ethical imperative in an *always* specific, historical context, one that involves science, technology, and medicine at every turn. Further, *companion species* designates webbed bio-social-technical apparatuses of humans, animals, artifacts, and institutions in which particular ways of being emerge and are sustained. Or not.

Trafficking in category making and unmaking, the play between kin and kind is essential to the figure of companion species. What is the cost of kinship, of category making and unmaking, and for whom? The content of any obligation is dependent on the thick and dynamic particularities of relationships-in-progress, that is, of kin and kind. The common matrix for these diverse claims on us is an ethics of flourishing. Chris Cuomo suggests that the core ecological feminist ethical starting point is a "commitment to the *flourishing* or well-being, of individuals, species, and communities."[2] Flourishing, not merely the relief of suffering, is the core value, one I would like to extend to the emergent entities, human and animal, in technocultural dog worlds. Compassionate action is, of course, crucial to an ethics of flourishing.

Living in a companion-species world, where kin and kind are emergent and unsettled and also have unequally distributed life-and-death consequences, is living in a force field subject to "torque." Bowker and Star develop the idea of torque to describe the lives of those who are subject to twisted skeins of conflicting categories and systems of measure or standardization. Where biographies and categories twine in conflicting trajectories, there is torque.[3] The fabric of technocultural dog worlds is torqued along several axes.

In the United States, dogs became "companion animals," both in contrast and in addition to "pets" and "working and sporting dogs," around the late 1970s in the context of social scientific investigations into the relations of animals such as dogs to human health and well-being.[4] Vet schools, such as the one at the University of Pennsylvania, and assistance-dog programs, such as the Delta Society, were key arenas of action. There are many more threads to the story of the transformation from pets to companion animals, but I want only to make three points. First, dogs live in several twisted, braided categories at once; their biographies and their classifications are in a relation of torque. Second, changes in terminology can signal important mutations in the character of relationships—commercially, epistemologically, emotionally, and politically. Third, the term *companion animals* has more than an accidental relationship with other technocultural categories that achieved potency around 1980, such as biodiversity, genome, quality-of-life management, outcomes research, and all-the-world a database. "New" names mark changes in power, symbolically and materially remaking kin and kind.

A peculiar attitude to history characterizes those who live in the timescape of the technopresent. They (we?) tend to describe everything as new, as revolutionary, as future oriented, as a solution to problems of the past. The arrogance and ignorance of this attitude hardly need comment. So much is made to appear "new" in technoculture, linked to "revolutions" such as those in genetics and informatics. Getting through the day in technoculture is impossible without witnessing some old stability wobble and some new category make its claim on us. Dog worlds are hardly immune to this curious form of experience. To give a homely example, where having one's own human teeth cleaned used to qualify one as an upstanding biosocial citizen, hard-hearted are the dog people who have not felt the disapproval of their vets for failing to have their pooches' ivories tended. Similarly, where once being tested for human genetic disease seemed all one could handle, today failure to have testing done and to raise money for research into the most prevalent canine genetic diseases weighs on the conscience. Sharing the risk of gum disease and of genetic biosociality is part of the companion-species bond.

However, if revolutions here are mostly hype, discontinuities and mutated ways of being are not. Categories abound in technocultural worlds that did not exist before; these categories are the sedimentations of processual relationships that matter. Emergents require attention to process, relationship, context, history, possibility, and conditions for flourishing.[5] Emergents are about the apparatuses of emergence, themselves braided of heterogeneous actors and action in torqued relationship. Companion animals, themselves emergent entities, require an inquiry into "what is to be done," that is, into what some call ethics or, in the domains I live in, bioethics. I want to explore this matter in relation to practices and discourses of canine genomic diversity and pet dog cloning.

First, I venture a word on bioethics, perhaps one of the most boring discourses to cross one's path in technoculture. Why is bioethics boring? Because too often it acts as a regulatory discourse after all the really interesting, generative action is over. Bioethics seems usually to be about *not* doing something, about some need to prohibit, limit, police, hold the line against looming technoviolations, to clean up after the action or prevent the action in the first place. Meanwhile, reshaping worlds is accomplished elsewhere. In this unfair cartoon, bioethics is firmly on the side of society, while all the lively, promising monsters are on the side of science and technology. If science studies scholars have learned anything in the last decades, it is that the categorical dualism between society and science, culture and nature, is a setup to block a grasp of what is going on in technoculture, including what is to be done in order that companion species flourish. If bioethics is to be part of science studies, it will have to get real. Bioethics is going to have to become a besmirched ontological laborer in the political economies of *Biocapital*, volume 1.

Bioethics has inserted its speculum into the worlds of reproduction of just about all kin and kinds, sexual and asexual, in vivo and in vitro. Consider the difficulties that independent radio producer Rusten Hogness experienced as he developed a five-minute National Public Radio piece on human cloning for *The DNA Files II*, aired in the fall of 2001. Hogness's interview subjects—developmental biologists, nuclear transfer specialists, and other biologists involved in mammalian-cloning efforts—all argued that the crucial ethical questions in the human case lie in the materialities of the biology of cloning. There, the poorly understood processes of nuclear reprogramming and organismic pattern formation in epigenesis are crucial to the possibility of offspring who could be healthy throughout the life span, assuming they could get through the rigors of fetal development. Human cloning in current conditions of knowledge and practice would cause deep suffering to large numbers of sure-to-be-damaged offspring and to potential parents, medical staff, researchers, teachers, and others. Spontaneous and induced abortions for defective fetuses would be only the beginning of the suffering, in present and, at least near, future conditions of knowledge and practice.

Partly because of the widespread cultural belief, too often fostered by scientists themselves, that genes-as-code determine everything in biology, just as a program is determined by its code, the complexities of development are given short shrift in public discussions of cloning. Hogness and his biologist subjects turned to a metaphor of a musical score and performance, instead of the encyclopedia or the code, to gain a better grip on the layered materialities of genetics and development. In doing so, they directed attention to the collaborative, complex, processual, and performative relationships that make up biological reality. Getting inside that reality could direct ethical attention to the probable lived experience of cloned and cloning subjects. The ethical and the technical here are hand-in-glove or, perhaps better, nucleus-in-cytoplasm.

All of the scientists Hogness interviewed argued that human cloning should be unacceptable for a long time, because the offspring so likely would be hurt, as would the universe of people among whom those offspring would come. The conditions for flourishing are, put mildly, not met. This sort of consideration ought to unsettle the "misplaced concreteness" of conventional discussions of human cloning. Too frequently, bioethical discussion asks whether it is proper to copy an individual, to scramble the generations, to play God, et cetera, as if these were matters for "society," while matters such as our ability to understand the complexity of genomics and epigenetics are relegated to the category of the "scientific and technical." While the bioethicists wax eloquent about supposedly compromised human individual uniqueness or excessive control of natural processes, the scene of ontological reshaping mutates once again under their feet, leaving ethical inquiry to play catch-up with odd abstractions and bio-think-tank scenarios.

Hogness had trouble convincing editors and producers up the line in *The DNA Files* that the crucial ethical issues now in human cloning *are* the biological matters. In a very short program in which even the rudiments of the biological techniques and developmental and genetic processes could barely be sketched, he was repeatedly asked to interview "a bioethicist." Society was on one side; science, on the other. But the biologists wanted to savor a mutated metaphor that let them stress what is really at stake in processes such as nuclear reprogramming in cloning, because that is where many of the conditions for flourishing lie. The ethics is in the whole ontological apparatus, in the thick complexity, in the nature-cultures of being in technoculture that join cells and people in a dance of becoming.

One of the scientists whom Hogness interviewed was Ian Wilmut, who led the effort to clone Dolly the sheep at the Roslin Institute. Referring obliquely to the misplaced concreteness of much bioethical hand wringing, he said, "It does strike me as the supreme irony which escapes some people that one of the reasons they're suggesting for copying people is to bring back a dead child. And one of the most likely outcomes of their cloning exercise is another dead child."[6] Whether or not developmentally damaged sheep should be given similar consideration is a separate, but not empty, question, partly addressed by turning to those banes of living mutton, namely dogs, themselves subjects of an infamous pet-cloning experiment, the Missyplicity Project, which took off in 1998 with a $2.3 million private grant to researchers at Texas A&M University, the largest grant by far ever to be given in the area of canine physiology. The beloved mutt Missy herself died in 2002, the year the project moved from university–corporate collaboration to an entirely corporate ecology in order to develop the "high-throughput technology that only industrial partnerships can offer."[7] Despite success in cloning two very pricey cats (in the range of fifty thousand dollars) for the pet market, the whole effort crashed in 2006 when Genetic Savings and Clone, Inc., went out of business and sold its frozen cells and gametes to an agricultural animal biotech firm, ViaGen, which had no plans to develop commercially cloned dogs.

The kennel has whelped fewer bioethicists than the nursery, but dog worlds also stand in acute need of a different ethical inquiry, one that is at the heart of the action that births emergent species, emergent kinds. As any feminist knows who has survived the biopolitical wars waged about structures and relationships below the diaphragm in human female bodies, "reproduction" is a potent matter. The symbolic load on reproduction in Western philosophy, medicine, and culture at large has required tomes from the most talented anthropological theorists among us.[8] Even partly relocating this power from (properly impregnated and in situ) wombs (of the same species as the being-to-be) to laboratories, clinics, embryos in freezers, stem cell collections, surrogate wombs of anomalous kinds, and genome databases has undergirded industries of academic pronouncements, commercial boosterism, and bioethical angst. Where reproduction is at stake, kin and kind are torqued; biographies and systems of classification, warped. "Cloning Mutts, Saving Tigers" twists inside these symbolic and material forces. Both cloning and genetic diversity discourses are in the warp field of reproduction enterprised up.

Getting inside the apparatus of the production/reproduction of dogs in technoculture starts with the rich communities of breeders and health activists in purebred dog worlds. I will not here address purebred puppy mill producers, backyard breeders, or many other worlds of dog practice, which a wider analysis would require. Instead, I want to begin with a small community of dog breeders who taught me more about respect than about critique, so that I can anchor my anger with the pet-cloning extravaganza with which I end this chapter. Since the beginning of modern "purebred" dog breeds linked to kennel clubs in the last third of the nineteenth century, controversy about the health of dogs and ethical breeding practices has raged. As Foucault taught us for the birth of the clinic, the birth of the kennel had all the constitutive discourses in place from the first appearance of the formation.[9]

Two points need to be highlighted at the outset: (1) Responsible dog breeding is a cottage industry, made up largely of amateur communities and individuals who are not scientific or medical professionals and who breed modest numbers of dogs at considerable cost to themselves over many years and with impressive dedication and passion. I am excluding from my category of responsible dog breeders many of the larger kennels breeding to win in conformation competitions, partly because I have no firsthand ethnographic research on which to draw. Even more, I withhold attention here because what I think I know from both oral dog culture and published scholarly work makes me predictably critical, and I have nothing new to add to the well-worn arguments. I want to start somewhere that gives me an ethical, emotional, and analytical compass; it is a methodological principle for me. My small breeder worlds are not utopian communities, far from it; but the people I have met in my fieldwork, who are trying to do what they call ethical dog breeding, have earned my respect. (2) "Lay" people who breed dogs are often solidly knowledgeable about science, technology, and veterinary medicine, often self-educated, and often effective actors in technoculture for the flourishing of dogs and their humans.

The efforts of Linda Weisser and Catherine de la Cruz, U.S. West Coast breeders of Great Pyrenees livestock guardian dogs as well as health activists, to reshape the habits of Pyr breeders in dealing with canine hip dysplasia are a good example of this technosavvy and its biological and ethical demands.[10] Weisser insists that the moral center of dog breeding is the breed, that is, the dogs themselves, as both a specialized kind and as irreducible individuals, to whom all the participants in Pyr worlds have an obligation. The obligation is to work so that the dogs and their people flourish over as long a time as possible. Hers is an "other-centered" ethics of a resolutely antiromantic sort that despises both anthropomorphism and anthropocentrism as a framework for practicing "love of the breed."

Both respected elders in the breed, Weisser and de la Cruz have encyclopedic knowledge of Pyr history and pedigrees over many decades; they are immersed in a cross-species kinship network of epic proportions. Listening to them talk about Pyr history requires learning idioms of dog form and function, layered national histories, functional and dysfunctional institutions, and human heroes and villains. They have entered thousands of individual Pyr pedigrees, some going back more than twenty generations, into computerized pedigree programs, which they carefully researched for their robustness for their purposes. A tremendous amount of what they know is personal and community knowledge—face-to-face, human-to-dog, and dog-to-dog—in the showing, ordinary living, and working ranch worlds where Great Pyrenees do their jobs. When they place puppies they have bred or dogs they have rescued from shelters into homes or livestock guardian jobs, they take the people and the dogs into their permanent cross-species kinship web. Membership in that web entails concrete demands, all of which are part of "love of the breed."

One of those demands is to breed only those animals who can improve the breed, that is, those who can contribute to the flourishing of Great Pyrenees. Even remembering that "improvement" is one of the most important modernizing and imperializing discourses, I cannot be dismissive of these commitments. What counts as improving the breed in dogland is controversial, to say the least. But since the founding in 1966 of the Orthopedic Foundation for Animals as a closed registry and voluntary diagnostic service addressing the problem of canine hip dysplasia, standards of good breeding practice require at least X-raying potential mates for the soundness of their hips. However, this practice, even coupled with conscientious breeders' mating only dogs whose hips are rated good or excellent by OFA, could not seriously reduce the incidence of this complex genetic and developmental condition for two reasons. First, the registry was voluntary and closed; that is, breeders could not get the record of problems in someone else's dogs, and breeders with a questionable dog did not (and do not) have to get an X-ray to be able to register that dog's offspring with the American Kennel Club or other registry. Second and just as bad, if only potential mates were X-rayed and archived, the rest of the relatives (littermates, aunts and uncles, etc.) went unrecorded. People like Weisser and de la Cruz argued that open registries with complete pedigrees and fully disclosed health records for as many relatives as possible, all accessible to the community of practice, are needed. That is what biological, technical, and ethical "love of the breed" requires.[11]

How could a community be led to a better practice, especially when something like full disclosure of genetic problems could lead to terrible criticism and even ostracism by those with too much to hide or just those who don't know any better? First, an open registry in the United States for canine genetic diseases came on the scene in 1990.[12] The Institute for Genetic Disease Control in Animals (GDC), founded at the University of California at Davis vet school, was modeled after the Swedish Kennel Club's open registry. The GDC tracked several orthopedic and soft tissue diseases. Listing suspected carriers and affected animals and maintaining breed-specific registries and research databases as well as all-breed registries, the GDC issued the KinReport™ to individuals with a valid reason for inquiring. However, by 2000 the GDC faced a problem that threatened to end the service: too few dog people used its registry, and the institute was in financial trouble. In 2001, in coalition with progressive breeders and breed groups, the GDC launched a major effort to develop a grassroots advocacy program to support the institute's work. It needed five thousand breeders and owners to use the service and to work to promote the open registry.

Weisser and de la Cruz were among the most active Great Pyrenees breeders working to persuade their peers to use the GDC's registry instead of a closed registry such as OFA's. Biology and ethics were lived in concert in this dogland biosociality. However, what an open registry implies made for an uphill battle. In August 2001, de la Cruz received "quarterly reports from both OFA and GDC. Discouraging. There were 45 Pyrs listed as cleared by OFA and only THREE from GDC.... I would think any breeder would be proud to be able to point to a product of her breeding and say, 'That dog is producing sounder dogs than the breed average.' Instead we continue to see ads for the numbers of champions produced, the number of shows won.... I would love to hear from other breeders. Why don't you use the GDC?"[13] One of many extended discussions on Pyr-L followed, along with behind-the-scenes work, in which de la Cruz, Weisser, and a few others educated, exhorted, and otherwise tried to make a difference for their breed. The GDC was not a technical fix; it was a biologically and technologically sophisticated whole-dog approach that required difficult changes in human practice for dog well-being.

In summer 2002, the GDC registry merged with the genetic health databases of OFA, preserving breeder access to the GDC's open data, but at a cost. All of the health data of the GDC were open; in the OFA system it was optional for a breeder or owner to allow others access to data on a dog. Negative information stays in short supply in an optional system under current incentives in dogland. Advantages for dogs probably prevailed in the merger. The OFA databases were much larger and had stable financing and wide use. Breeder education continued on the advantages of an open registry for searching whole families. Further, the merger was coordinated with the pooled databases from many breeds of the Canine Health Information Center, the new program jointly sponsored by OFA and the AKC's Canine Health Foundation.

Weisser and de la Cruz's struggle for the open registry exemplifies the technosavvy of "lay" dog people as they live within genetic biosociality. These women and those like them read widely, are knowledgeable about international dog cultures, take online genetics courses from a major vet school, follow medical and veterinary literatures, support wolf reintroduction projects and keep track of Pyrs who might protect livestock on adjoining ranches, engage broadly in conservation politics, and otherwise live well-examined lives in technoculture. Their expertise and action are planted in the soil of generations of particular dogs, whom they know in intimate detail, as kin and kind. What do such people do when they meet emergent demands, not only to deal with genetic disease, but also to breed for canine genetic diversity in the context of global biodiversity science and politics?

SAVING TIGERS

In spite of the long history of population genetics and its importance for the modern theory of natural section, genetic diversity concerns remain news—and hard-to-digest news—for most dog people. Why? Genetic culture for both professionals and nonprofessionals, especially but not only in the United States, has been shaped by medical genetics. Human genetic disease is the moral, technoscientific, ideological, and financial center of the medical genetic universe. Typological thinking reigns almost unchecked in this universe, and nuanced views of developmental biology, behavioral ecology, and genes as nodes in dynamic and multivectorial fields of vital interactions are only some of the crash victims of high-octane medical genetic fuels and gene-jockey racing careers.

Evolutionary biology, biosocial ecology, population biology, and population genetics (not to mention history of science, political economy, and cultural anthropology) have played a woefully small role in shaping public and professional genetic imaginations and all too small a role in drawing the big money for genetic research. Canine genetic diversity research received very little funding up to about 2000 and the explosion of comparative postgenomics. Pioneer canine genetic diversity scientists were Europeans in the early 1980s. Genetic diversity concerns in dog worlds developed as a wavelet in the set of breakers constituting transnational, globalizing, biological, and cultural diversity discourses, in which genomes are major players. Since the 1980s the emergence of biodiversity discourses, environmentalisms, and sustainability doctrines of every political color on the agendas of non-governmental organizations and institutions such as the World Bank, the International Union for the Conservation of Nature and Natural Resources, and the Organization for Economic

Cooperation and Development has been crucial.[14] The notoriously problematic politics and the naturalcultural complexity of diversity discourses require a shelf of books, some of which have been written. I am compelled by the *irreducible* complexity—morally, politically, culturally, and scientifically—of diversity discourses, including those leashed to the genomes and gene pools of purebred dogs and their canine relatives in and out of what counts as "nature."

The last few paragraphs are preparation for logging on to the Canine Diversity Project Web site, owned by Dr. John Armstrong, a lover of standard and miniature poodles and a faculty member in the Department of Biology at the University of Ottawa, until his death on August 26, 2001.[15] Armstrong widely distributed his analyses of the effects that a popular sire and a particular kennel have had on standard poodles. Also, as the owner of the Listserv CANGEN-L, Armstrong conducted collaborative research with dog health and genetics activists to study whether longevity is correlated to the degree of inbreeding. Their conclusion: It is. Aiming in the introductory sentence to draw the attention of dog breeders to "the dangers of inbreeding and the overuse of popular sires," the Diversity Project Web site started in 1997. Used by at least several hundred dog people of many nationalities, from January 2000 to June 2001 the site registered over thirty thousand logons.

Linda Weisser was a frequent visitor and vociferous advocate of this Web site in 2000–2001, but she was not a true believer in all the positions advocated by the population biologists on CANGEN-L. Open to change, she evaluated the diversity discourses in light of her hands-on experience in her breed over several decades. Along with Weisser and other dog people, I have learned a tremendous amount from the Web site. I still appreciate the quality of information, the controversies engaged, the care for dogs and people, the range of material, and the commitments to issues. I remain acutely alert professionally to the semiotics—the meaning-making machinery—of the Canine Diversity Project Web site. Some of that rhetorical machinery caused allergies in people like Weisser in the period around 2000.

Animated by a mission, the site still draws its users into its reform agenda. Some of the rhetorical devices are classical American tropes rooted in popular self-help practices and evangelical Protestant witness, devices so ingrained in U.S. culture that few users would be conscious of their history. For example, right after the introductory paragraph with the initial link terms, the Diversity Project Web site leads its users into a section called "How You Can Help." The heading works on the reader much like questions in advertising and preaching: Have you been saved? Have you taken the Immune Power pledge? (The latter is a slogan from an ad for a vitamin formulation in the 1980s.) Or, as the Diversity Project put the query, "Ask the Question—Do you need a 'Breed Survival Plan?'" This is the stuff of subject-reconstituting, conversion and conviction discourse.[16]

The first four highlighted linkage terms in the opening paragraphs of the Web site are *popular sires,* for many years a common term in pure-bred dog talk about the overuse of certain stud dogs and the consequent spreading of genetic disease; *Species Survival Plans,* a term that serves as a new link for dog breeders to zoos and the preservation of endangered species; *wild cousins,* which places dogs with their taxonomic kin and reinforces the consideration of purebreds within the family of natural (in the sense of "wild") and frequently endangered species; and *inherited disease,* in last place on the list and of concern primarily because a high incidence of double autosomal recessives for particular diseases is an index of lots of homozygosity in purebred dog genomes. Such high incidences of double recessives are related to excessive in- and linebreeding, and especially to overuse of popular sires, all of which are diversity-depleting practices. The soul of the Web site, however, is diversity *itself* in the semiotic framework of evolutionary biology, biodiversity, and biophilia, *not* diversity as an instrument for solving the problem of genetic disease. In that sense, "breeds" become like endangered species, inviting the apparatus of apocalyptic wildlife biology.

Constructed as a teaching instrument, the Web site approaches its audience as engaged lay breeders and other committed dog people. These are the subjects invited to declare support for a breed survival plan. Secondarily, scientists might learn from using the site, but they are more teachers here than researchers or students. Nonetheless, plenty of boundary objects link lay and professional communities of practice in the Canine Diversity Project. Further, a Web site by its nature resists reduction to single purposes and dominating tropes. Links lead many places;

these paths are explored by users, within the webs that designers spin but rapidly lose control over. The Internet is hardly infinitely open, but its degrees of semiotic freedom are many.

Popular sires is well enough recognized that this linking term will appeal to most dog people open to thinking about genetic diversity. For one thing, the link stays with *dogs* as the principal focus of attention and does not launch the user into a universe of marvelous creatures in exotic habitats whose utility as models for dogs is hard to swallow for many breeders, even those interested in such nondog organisms and ecologies in other contexts. *Species Survival Plans*, on the other hand, opens up controversial metaphoric and practical universes for breeders of purebred dogs, and, if such plans are taken seriously, they would require major changes in ways of thinking and acting. First, *survival plans* connotes that something is endangered. The line between a secular crisis and a sacred apocalypse is thin in U.S. discourse, where millennial matters are written into the fabric of the national imagination, from the first Puritan City on a Hill to *Star Trek* and its sequelae. Second, the prominent role given to species survival plans on the Canine Diversity Project Web site invites a reproductive tie between natural species and purebred dogs. In this mongrelizing tie, the natural and the technical keep close company, semiotically and materially.

To illustrate, I dwell on the material on my screen in spring 2000 after I clicked on "Species Survival Plans" and followed up with a click on "Introduction to a Species Survival Plan."[17] I was teleported to the Web site for the Tiger Information Center, and, appreciating a face-front photo of two imposing tigers crossing a stream, I encountered the article "Regional and Global Management of Tigers," by R. Tilson, K. Taylor-Holzer, and G. Brady. Lots of dog people love cats, contrary to stereotypes about folks being either canine or feline in their affections. But tigers in the world's zoos and in shrunken "forest patches spread from India across China to the Russian Far East and south to Indonesia" *is* a leap out of the kennel and the show ring or herding trials. I learned that three of the eight subspecies of tigers are extinct, a fourth is on the brink, and all the wild populations are stressed. Ideally, the goal of an SSP master blueprint for an endangered species is to create viable, managed, captive populations out of existing animals in zoos and some new "founders" brought in from "nature," to maintain as much of the genetic diversity for all the extant taxa of the species as possible. The purpose is to provide a genetic reservoir for reinforcing and reconstituting wild populations. A practical SSP "because of space limitations generally targets 90% of genetic diversity of the wild populations for 100–200 years as a reasonable goal." I recognize both the hopefulness and the despair that inhere in that kind of reasonableness. The "Zoo Ark" for tigers has to be even more modest, because resources are too few and needs are too great.

An SSP is a trademarked complex, cooperative management program of the American Zoo and Aquarium Association (AZA), itself a controversial organization from the point of view of people committed to the well-being of *individual* tigers in captivity who are enlisted in an SSP. Developing and implementing an SSP involve a long list of companion species of organic, organizational, and technological kinds. A minimal account of these includes the World Conservation Union's specialist groups who make assessments of endangerment; member zoos, with their scientists, keepers, and boards of governors; a small management group under the AZA; a database maintained as a regional studbook, using specialized software like SPARKS (single population and records keeping system) and its companion programs for demographic and genetic analysis, produced by the International Species Information System; funders; national governments; international bodies; stratified local human populations; and, hardly least, the flesh-and-blood animals whose kind is categorically "endangered." Crucial operations within an SSP are measurements of diversity and relatedness. One wants to know founder importance coefficients (FIC) as a tool for equalizing relative founder contributions and minimizing inbreeding. Full, accurate pedigrees are precious objects for an SSP. Mean kinship (MK) and kinship values (KV) rule mate choice in this sociobiological system. "Reinforcing" wild species requires a global apparatus of technoscientific production, in which the natural and the technical have very high coefficients of semiotic and practical inbreeding.[18]

Purebred-dog breeders also value deep pedigrees, and they are accustomed to evaluating matings with regard to breed standards, which is a complex, unformulaic art. Inbreeding is not a new concern. So what is so challenging about an SSP as a universe of reference? The definition of populations and founders is perhaps first. Discussions among engaged breeders on CANGEN (i.e., people sufficiently interested in questions of genetic diversity to sign on and post to a specialized Listserv) showed that dog people's terms *lines* and *breeds* are not equivalent to wildlife biologists' and geneticists' *populations*. The behavior associated with these different words is distinct. A dog breeder educated in the traditional mentoring practices of the fancy will attempt through line breeding, with variable frequencies of outcrosses, to maximize the genetic or blood contribution of the truly "great dogs" who are rare and special. The great dogs are the individuals who best embody the type of the breed. The type is not a fixed thing, but a living, imaginative hope and memory. Kennels are recognized for the distinctiveness of their dogs, and breeders point proudly to their kennel's founders, and breed club documents point to the breed's founders. In the population geneticists' sense, the notion of working to *equalize* the contribution of *all* of the founders is truly odd in traditional dog breeders' discourse. Of course, an SSP, unlike nature and unlike dog breeders, is *not* operating with adaptational criteria of selection; the point of an SSP is to preserve *diversity as such* as a banked reservoir. This preservation could have doleful consequences several generations later in a program of reintroduction into demanding habitats in which genetically stabilized details of adaptation matter.

The SSP is a conservation management plan, not nature, however conceptualized, and not a breed's written standard or a breeder's interpretation of that standard. Like an SSP, a breed standard is also a large-scale action blueprint, but for purposes other than genetic diversity. Some breeders talk of those purposes in capital letters, as the Original Purpose of a breed. Other breeders are not typological in that sense; they are attuned to dynamic histories and evolving goals within a partly shared sense of breed history, structure, and function. These breeders are keenly aware of the need for selection on the basis of criteria that are as numerous and holistic as possible to maintain and improve a breed's overall quality and to achieve the rare, special dogs. They take these responsibilities seriously, and they are not virgins to controversy, contradiction, and failure. They are not against learning about genetic diversity in the context of the problems they know or suspect their dogs face. Some breeders—a very few, I think—embrace genetic diversity discourse and population genetics. They worry that the foundation of their breeds might be too narrow and getting narrower.

But the breeder's art does not easily entertain the adoption of the mathematical and software-driven mating systems of an SSP. Several courageous breeders insist on deeper pedigrees and calculations of coefficients of inbreeding, with efforts to hold them down. But the breeders I meet are loath to cede decisions to anything like a master plan. They do not categorize their own dogs or their breed primarily as biological populations. The dominance of specialists over local and lay communities in the SSP world does not escape dog breeders' attention. Most of the breeders I overhear squirm if the discussion stays on the level of theoretical population genetics and if few, if any, of the data come from dogs rather than from a Malagasy lemur population, a lab-bound mouse strain, or, worse still, fruit flies. In short, breeders' discourse and genetic diversity discourse do not hybridize smoothly, at least in the F1 generation. This mating is what breeders call a cold outcross, which they worry risks importing as many problems as it solves.

There is much more to the Canine Diversity Project Web site than the past and current SSP links. If I had space to examine the whole Web site, many more openings, repulsions, inclusions, attractions, and possibilities would be evident for seeing the ways dog breeders, health activists, veterinarians, and geneticists relate to the question of diversity. The serious visitor to the Web site could obtain a decent elementary education in genetics, including Mendelian, medical, and population genetics. Fascinating collaborations among individual scientists and breed club health and genetics activists would emerge. The differences within dog people's ways of thinking about genetic diversity and inbreeding would be inescapable, such as when the apocalyptic and controversial "evolving breeds" of Jeffrey Bragg and the Seppala Siberian sled dogs meet John Armstrong's more modest standard poodles (and his more moderate action plan, "Genetics for Breeders: How to Produce Healthier Dogs") or the differences between Leos Kral's and C. A. Sharp's ways of working in Australian shepherd worlds. Links would take the visitor to the extraordinary Code of Ethics of the Coton de Tulear Club of America and this breed's alpha-male geneticist–activist, Robert Jay Russell, as well as to the online documents with which the border collie Web site teaches genetics relevant to that talented breed. The visitor could follow links to the molecular evolution of the dog family, updated lists of gene tests in dogs, discussions of wolf conservation and taxonomic debates, accounts of a cross-breeding (to a pointer) and backcross project in Dalmatians to eliminate a common genetic disease and of importing new stock in African basenjis to deal with genetic dilemmas. One could click one's way to discussions of infertility, stress, and herpes infections or follow links to endocrine-disrupter discourse for thinking about how environmental degradation might affect dogs, as well as frogs and people, globally. Until Armstrong's death, right in the middle of the Diversity Project Web site was a bold-type invitation to join the Listserv that he ran for three years, the Canine Genetics Discussion Group (CANGEN-L), on which a sometimes rough and tumble exchange among lay and scientific dog people stirred up the Web site's pedagogical order.

So, in the active years of the Canine Diversity Project Web site's construction around 2000, dogs, not tigers—and breeds, not endangered species—dominated on it. But the metaphoric, political, scientific, and practical possibilities of those first links to the AZA's Species Survival Plan attached themselves like ticks on a nice blade of grass, waiting for a passing visitor from purebred dogland. The emergent ontologies of bio-diversity naturecultures are laced with new ethical demands. In many ways, the expertise and practices of dog breeders remain in a relation of torque with the discourses of genetic diversity. Kin and kind mutate in these emergent apparatuses of dog (re)production. Whether companion species will flourish was and still is at stake.

CLONING MUTTS

A well-funded, media-savvy, commercially venturesome project to clone a pet mutt in a major agribusiness-linked U.S. university would seem at the opposite end of the spectrum from the scientific and ethical practices emergent within canine genetic diversity worlds. Yet, such cloning projects raise similar issues: What kinds of collaborations produce the expertise and make the decisions for the biosocial evolution of companion species in technocultural dogland? What constitutes an ethic of flourishing and for which members of the companion-species community? Unlike the canine open health registry debates or the genome diversity discourses, the initial world of pet dog cloning was a surreal mix of state-of-the-art reproductive technoscience, inventive ethics, New Age epistemological pranksterism, and marketing extravagance.[19]

The Missyplicity Project began in 1998 with a $2.3 million grant for the first two years, from a wealthy donor, initially anonymous, to three senior researchers at Texas A&M University and their collaborators from several institutions. The project had an elaborate Web site in 2000, with comments from the public; stories about the mixed-breed dog, Missy, who was to be cloned; a list of research objectives; an account of home adoption and dog-training programs for the surrogate bitches used in the research ("All of our dogs have been trained using only positive reinforcement through clicker training"); and a state-of-the-art code of bioethics.[20]

Marketing was never far from the pet dog–cloning project, and advertising provided an easy, if cheap, window to the trading floor in cultural futures in dog geneticism. In advance of the ability to clone a dog, Animal Cloning Sciences, Inc. (ANCL), made a claim, presenting it over a picture of an elderly white woman holding her beloved terrier: "You no longer have to look forward to heart-rending grief at the death of your pet. If you preserve your pet's DNA now, you will have the option to clone your pet and continue your pet's life in a new body."[21] Alien-identity-transfer experiments were never so successful, even on *X-Files*. Promising cloning technology for companion animals "soon," ANCL offered cryopreservation of cells in 2000 at $595.

In a *DogWorld* ad, another company offering cell cryopreservation, Lazaron BioTechnologies, started by two embryologists and a business associate at the Louisiana Business and Technology Center, on the campus of Louisiana State University, urged readers to take tissue samples from their dogs before it is too late, so that they might "save a genetic life." This was something of an escalation of prolife rhetoric in the Age of Genes™! At the top of its Web site, Lazaron described itself as "saving the genetic life of valued animals."[22] Never did value have more value, in all its kinds. Bioethics, "enterprised up," flourished here, where profit met science, conservation, art, and undying love-on-ice. Both companies dealt in agricultural and endangered species as well as companion animals, and the link to "saving endangered species" lent a value cachet not to be despised.

We met this enhancement in dog genome diversity contexts, which became a boundary object joining conservation and cloning discourses.

Cloning dogs could have a scientific appeal for dog breeders. Prize-winning writers on canine genetics and health as well as breeders themselves, John Cargill and Susan Thorpe-Vargas argued the merits of dog cloning to preserve genetic diversity.[23] They wrote that the depletion of genetic diversity might be mitigated if it were possible to clone desirable dogs, rather than trying to duplicate qualities through excessive line-breeding and overuse of popular sires. Cryopreservation and cloning could then be one tool in the effort to manage the genomes of small populations in the best interests of the breed or species, they argued. In over-wrought technoculture committed to reproduction of the same, cloning seemed an easier sell in some parts of dogland than simply doing more carefully matched outcrosses and committing to open health registries to mitigate the damage of genetic diversity depletion!

High seriousness characterized the rhetoric of the Web site of Genetic Savings and Clone, Inc., the only cryopreservation tissue and gene bank in 2001 directly associated with cloning research, beginning with the Missyplicity Project. Buying out Lazaron's interest in that year, GSC put pets, livestock, wildlife, and assistance and rescue dogs on its agenda. The company's self-perception of its part in ethical, ontological, and episte-mological emergents was grand. Large investment, best science, and aca-demic–business collaboration featured prominently; GSC did not see itself as a "vanity" cloning and biobanking endeavor. Its bioethics statement endorsed an extraordinary collage of progressive commitments: GSC pledged itself to maximize public knowledge and keep as proprietary only the minimum needed for its business goals. Transgenic alterations would be done only under severe scrutiny by the GSC Advisory Board. Biolog-ical weapons (figured as attack dogs!) would not be produced, nor would GSC's animals enter the food chain as genetically modified organisms (GMOs). No information would be knowingly shared with those attempt-ing human cloning. GSC promised to raise its animals in "traditional," not "factory farm," conditions. "This means that the animals will spend part of every day grazing and interacting with humans and other animals—rather than being constantly isolated in sterile pens."[24] GSC even pledged itself to organic farming methods and to other ecologically conscious practices.

So, GSC's traditionally raised, cloned animals and surrogate mothers were to have plenty of organic produce in their diets. Irony had little chance in the context of such high ethical seriousness. True, we had to take the company's word for everything; no public power intruded into this corporate idyll. Still, as the song goes, "Who could ask for anything more?"

We did, in fact, get even more in the Missyplicity Project. Its goals foregrounded basic knowledge of reproductive canine biology crucial to repopulating endangered species (e.g., wolves), basic knowledge of birth control for feral and pet dog populations, and the replication of "specific, exceptional dogs of high societal value—especially seeing-eye and search-and-rescue dogs."[25] How would they ever make a buck, one wondered? Over ten million research dollars later in the ashes of Genetic Savings and Clone, Inc., in 2006, one knew the answer.

In 1998 Missyplicity's scientific founding team was a microcosm of crosscutting technoscience at institutions such as Texas A&M University, a "land- sea- and space-grant institution," with a faculty of twenty-four hundred and a research budget of $367 million.[26] Dr. Mark Westhusin, the principal investigator, was a nuclear transfer specialist with an appointment in the Department of Veterinary Physiology and Pharmacology. He had a large lab and numerous publications from cloning research on agriculturally important mammals. The embryo transfer specialist was Dr. Duane Kraemer, PhD, DVM. "He and his colleagues have transferred embryos in more different species than any other group in the world."[27] Kraemer was a cofounder of Project Noah's Ark, an international effort to bank the genomes of numerous wildlife species in case they become further endangered or extinct. Kraemer wanted to establish mobile satellite labs around the world to perform needed in vitro fertilizations and cryopreservation.[28] Project Noah's Ark originated in the mid-1990s from Texas A&M students' "concerns for the world's endangered species."[29]

At the turn of the millennium, "saving the endangered [fill in the category]" emerged as the rhetorical gold standard for "value" in technoscience, trumping and shunting other considerations of the apparatus for shaping public and private, kin and kind, animation and cessation. "Endangered species" turned out to be a capacious ethical bypass for ontologically heterogeneous traffic in dogland.

Where better could "Cloning Mutts" conclude than at a solemn public program sponsored by Stanford University's Ethics in Society Program? On May 12, 2000, Lou Hawthorne, CEO of GSC and project coordinator of Missyplicity, spoke on the panel "The Ethics of Cloning Companion Animals."[30] Also on the panel were two Stanford philosophy professors, a professor of theology and ethics at the Pacific School of Religion, and Lazaron chief executive, Richard Denniston, who was director of the Louisiana State University Embryology Biotechnology Laboratory. In the questions after the formal presentations, someone asked how the Missyplicity Project, with its mongrel subject, affected purebred dog breeders. Reaching for the gold standard, Denniston called mutts "an endangered species of one"! Hawthorne more modestly said that GSC was a "celebration of the mutt," since these one-of-a-kind pooches could not be bred to type.

A talented polemicist and media expert, Hawthorne was a confidence man in the American traditions so well understood by Herman Melville, P. T. Barnum, and New Age savants. Hawthorne was also a thoughtful and complex actor in cross-species technoscience. A trickster or confidence man tests the goodness of reasoning and valuing, perhaps

"Actually, we're only taking tissue samples."

J. P. Rini, from CartoonBank.com. Copyright *The New Yorker* collection, 1997. All rights reserved.

showing up the baseness of what passes for gold in official knowledges, or at least tweaking the certainties of the pious, those "for" or "against" a technoscientific marvel. A confidence man in twenty-first-century America would also like to make some money, preferably lots of it, while saving the earth. Science studies scholar Joseph Dumit sees such figures to be engaged seriously with "playful truths."[31] Not innocent truths; play is not innocent. Play can open up degrees of freedom in what was fixed. But loss of fixity is not the same thing as opening new possibilities for flourishing among companion species. I read Hawthorne as a master player in technoscience, whose not inconsiderable earnestness is overmatched by his trickster savvy.

At Stanford, Hawthorne staged his discussion of the Missyplicity Project's Code of Ethics with an origin story and travel narrative. He began as a Silicon Valley media and technology consultant with no knowledge of biotechnology or bioethics. In July 1997 his "rich and anonymous client" asked him to explore the feasibility of cloning his aging mutt. This study led to many and marvelous places in biotechnology land, including the conference Transgenic Animals in Agriculture in August 1997 in Tahoe. There Hawthorne heard about animals as "bioreactors," which could be manipulated without moral limit. He emerged "with two epiphanies": (1) Missyplicity would need a strong Code of Bioethics, "if just to distance ourselves from the giddy, anything-goes attitude of most bioengineers," in the words of the preprint; and (2) his lack of scientific training might be an advantage.

Like many seekers in the West, Hawthorne arrived in the East. Returning to his experience of filming a documentary on Zen in 1984, he retrieved "a core value of Buddhism—borrowed from Hinduism—*ahimsa*, commonly translated as 'non-harming.' *Ahimsa*, like most Buddhist ideas, is a koan, or puzzle without clear-cut solution, which can only be fully resolved through a process of personal inquiry. . . . I decided to put non-harming at the top of the Missyplicity Bioethics Code."[32] His search, he believed, led to a way to live responsibly in emergent technocultural worlds, where kin and kind are unfixed.

Hawthorne's explication of the code revealed a wonderful collage of transactional psychology (all the partners—humans and dogs—should benefit); Buddhist borrowings; family values ("at the completion of their

role in the Missyplicity Project, all dogs should be placed in loving homes");
no-kill animal shelter policies; and birth control discourse ("how many
dogs could we save from death—by preventing their births in the first
place—through the development of an effective canine contraceptive?").
If Margaret Sanger had been a dog activist, she would have been proud of
her progeny. Animal rights, disability rights, and right-to-life discourses
had echoes in the Missyplicity Code—with practical consequences for
how the canine research subjects were treated, that is, as subjects, not
objects. No matter how many trips are made to the East, in its soul Western ethics is riveted to rights discourses. In any case, if I were a research
dog, I'd have wanted to be at Texas A&M and GSC in the Missyplicity
Project, where the Zen of Cloning was more than a slogan. Besides, that
is where "best science" lay. As Hawthorne noted, cloning dogs is harder
than cloning humans. Missyplicity was against cloning those bipeds anyway, and as a reward, Missy's hominid companion species was able to do
more leading-edge research.

The clincher in Hawthorne's savvy presentation at Stanford, where
making money has never been a stranger to producing knowledge, was
his introduction of Genetic Savings and Clone, Inc., "which is based in
College Station, Texas, but [which] also heavily leverages the internet."
Distributed networking was not limited to neural nets and activists. GSC
"represents the first step toward commercializing the enormous amount
of information being generated by Missyplicity." There was a backlog of
demand for private cloning services. Hawthorne speculated that the price
of cloning a pet dog (or cat—a project that succeeded in 2001) would "fall
within three years to under $20,000—though at first it may be ten times
as much."

Not surprisingly, these figures led Hawthorne to great works of art,
those conserved, one-of-a-kind creations. "I'd like to end with this thought:
great companion animals are like works of art. . . . Once we've identified
these masterpieces, then arguably it's not just reasonable but imperative
that we capture their unique genetic endowments before they're gone—
just as we would rescue great works of art from a burning museum."
"Unique genetic endowments" become like "vanishing indigenes"—needing the kind of "saving" that comes so easily in white settler colonies.
In addition to saving a genetic life, this Zen bioethics seems to demand

saving genetic art. Science, business, ethics, and art are the familiar renaissance partners at the origin of technopresence, where "evolution meets the free market; those who can afford it will save what they like and leave the rest to burn." That sounds like the play of scary, Peter Pan–like CEOs. Even as he mobilized the resources for bringing cloned dogs into the world, Hawthorne "playfully" tweaked official truths in his well-funded, trickster boosterism in the "Museum of Mutts."

At the end of "Cloning Mutts, Saving Tigers" I return to the homelier metaphors of Linda Weisser and her less dazzling work to persuade Pyr people to use an open health and genetics registry and to try to whelp only dogs who can improve the breed, helping the kin and kind of companion species to flourish. Immersed in emergences of many kinds, I saw value in aspects of the Missyplicity Project—without that fire at the end of things. I am definitely on the side of endangered tigers, as well as the people who inhabit the nations where the big cats (barely) live. Genetic diversity is a precious pattern for dogs as well as people, and cats *are* like dogs. The crucial issues remain, as always, attending to the details. Who makes decisions? What is the apparatus of production of these new sorts of being? Who flourishes, and who does not, and how? How can we stay on Linda Weisser's science-savvy riverbank without choking on the fog of the technopresent? If "saving the endangered [fill in the blank]" means personally and collectively cleaning the rivers so that the earth's always emergent kin can drink without harm or shame, who could ask for anything more?

II. NOTES OF A SPORTSWRITER'S DAUGHTER

6. ABLE BODIES AND COMPANION SPECIES

November 3, 1981
Dear Dad,

Your retirement from the Denver *Post* has been
present to me for weeks now. I want to write to you
about what your work has meant to me since I was a small
girl. I tell all the people who are important to me, "My
father is a sportswriter. He loves his work. He is good at it,
and he passed on to me the center of my feeling about work
as a way of living at least as much as making a living." Your
pleasure in words has been central to your work. I saw you
enjoy words. You showed your children words as tools to
sculpt fuller lives. I read your stories for years, and I learned
a daily, reliable craft to tell important stories. Your work
taught me that "writing a story" is a very fine way to "make
a living." I saw you consistently insist on writing about
the parts of people you could affirm, not because you
hid sordid things, but because you allowed people
their beauty. I think that is why you loved the

game story best. I saw you chronicle dramas, rituals, feats, skills, mindful bodies in motion. In sportswriting, you penned stories that made living bigger, expansive, generous.

I remember going to the old Denver Bears Stadium in the 1950s when Bill and the other boys were bat and ball boys. I regretted not being able to *be* a bat boy in the same way I regretted not being able to *be* a Jesuit, so I heard my dolls' confessions in my closet with the sliding doors and said Mass for them on my dresser. I have changed since then from a junior Catholic theologian to a much less innocent feminist scribbler, from a parochial school basketball forward, to a writer of her own game stories. You gave me the same skills you gave my brothers, Bill and Rick. You taught us all to score about the same time we learned to read.[1] That night in 1958 when you and the *Rocky Mountain News* scribe Chet Nelson asked me how I had scored a contested baseball play on which you couldn't agree, and then used my scoring, you gave me something precious: you recognized me in your work. You gave me your regard.

My father is a sportswriter.

With love,
Donna

Bodies in the making, indeed. This chapter is a note of a sportswriter's daughter. It is writing that I must do, because it's about a legacy, an inheritance in the flesh. To come to accept the body's unmaking, I need to re-member its becoming. I need to recognize all the members, animate and inanimate, that make up the knot of a particular life, my father, Frank Outten Haraway's life.

My husband, Rusten, and I have been privileged to accompany our aging parents in the last months and years of their lives. On September 29, 2005, my brothers and I held my father while he died, alert and present, in our hands. We held him during the process of his no longer being there. This was not a process uniquely of his no longer being present as a soul, or a mind, or a person, or an interior, or a subject. No, as his body cooled, his *body* was no longer there. The corpse is not the body. Rather, the body is always in-the-making; it is always a vital entanglement of heterogeneous scales, times, and kinds of beings webbed into fleshly presence, always a becoming, always constituted in relating. The corpse's consignment to the earth as ashes is, I think, a recognition that, in death, it is not simply the person or the soul who goes. That knotted thing we call the body has left; it is undone. My father is undone, and that is why I must re-member him. I and all those who lived entangled with him become his flesh; we are kin to the dead because their bodies have touched us. The body of my father is the body that I knew as his daughter. I inherit in the flesh, in material troping, tripping, that joins text and body in what I call material semiosis and semiotic materiality.

Mine is a looping set of stories of the generations; my story is about inheriting the craft of writing looping, braided stories, stories of the game. Born in 1916, my father was a sportswriter for the Denver *Post* for forty-four years. After retiring from the paper in 1981, he continued to work in the Denver sports world, as the baseball official scorer for the National League for the Colorado Rockies and as part of the statistics crews for Denver Nuggets basketball and Broncos football. His last working game was in September 2004, when he was eighty-seven years old. Writing his own epitaph, he lived and died as a sportswriter, or as he put it, as a fan who got paid to do what he loved.

I try to be something of a sportswoman; we will come back to that. In the university, I too am paid to do what I love. In this chapter, I write about the inheritance of being a journalist's daughter, a sportswriter's daughter, about my effort to gain the father's regard, to gain his approval, to somehow have his writing be about my sport, my game. I write out of a child's need in order to honor an ongoing adult love.

I'm a heterosexual daughter, more or less, of a relentlessly heterosexual father, a girl child who never had her father's heterosexual gaze. His was a deliberate withholding of the gaze of potential incest, I now think. I both loathed and envied his gender-conventional sexualization of other women and girls. My husband's sister Suze and I talk together about our fathers, who could not look at their daughters as beautiful physically because they dared not. But I had my father's regard in another, life-giving, bodily way: I had his respect. This is a different specular economy of generational passage, no less corporeal and no less full of desire and lure, no less leery of the law, no less in the game, but in an economy that leads the daughter to remember in joy and grief. This kind of look has made my body what it is in life as a writer and as a woman playing a sport. I want to take us, take me, through part of this legacy.

Consider "regard" and "respect" a bit longer. I am drawn by the tones of this kind of active looking at/regard (both as verb, *respecere*, and as *respectus*) that I sought and experienced with and from my father.[2] The specific relationality in this kind of regard holds my attention: to have regard for, to see differently, to esteem, to look back, to hold in regard, to hold in seeing, to be touched by another's regard, to heed, to take care of. This kind of regard aims to release and be released in oxymoronic, necessary, autonomy-in-relation. Autonomy as the fruit of and inside relation. Autonomy as trans-acting. Quite the opposite of the gaze/look usually studied in cultural theory! And certainly not the fruit of the gaze of incest.

In recent speaking and writing on companion species, I have tried to live inside the many tones of regard/respect/seeing each other/looking back at/meeting/optic–haptic encounter. Species and respect are in optic/haptic/affective/cognitive touch: they are at table together; they are messmates, companions, in company, *cum panis*. I also love the oxymoron inherent in "species"—always both logical type and relentlessly particular, always tied to *specere* and yearning/looking toward *respecere*. "Species" includes animal and human as categories, and much more besides; and we would be ill advised to assume which categories are in play and shaping one another in flesh and logic in constitutive encounterings.

In all those senses, I see the regard I am trying to think and feel as part of something not proper to either humanism or posthumanism. *Companion species*—coshapings all the way down, in all sorts of temporalities and corporealities—is my awkward term for a not-humanism in which species of all sorts are in question. For me, even when we speak only of people, the animal/human/living/nonliving category separations fray inside the kind of encountering worthy of regard. The ethical regard that I am trying to speak and write can be experienced across many sorts of species differences.[3] The lovely part is that we can know only by looking and by looking back. *Respecere.*

For the last few years, I have been writing under the sign of companion species, perhaps partly to tweak my colleagues' sense of proper species behavior. They have been remarkably patient; indeed, they understand that "companion species" does not mean smallish animals treated like indulged children-in-fur-coats (or in fins or feathers) in late imperial societies. Companion species is a permanently undecidable category, a category-in-question that insists on the relation as the smallest unit of being and of analysis. By species I mean, with thanks to Karen Barad's theory of agential realism and intra-action, a kind of intra-ontics/intra-antics that does not predetermine the status of the species as artifact, machine, landscape, organism, or human being.[4] Singular and plural, species resonate with the tones of logical types, of the relentlessly specific, of stamped coin, of the real presence in the Catholic Eucharist, of Darwinian kinds, of sf aliens, and of much else. Species, like the body, are internally oxymoronic, full of their own others, full of messmates, of companions.

Every species is a multispecies crowd. Human exceptionalism is what companion species cannot abide. In the face of companion species, human exceptionalism shows itself to be the specter that damns the body to illusion, to reproduction of the same, to incest, and so makes remembering impossible. Under the material–semiotic sign of companion species, I am interested in the ontics and antics of significant otherness, in the ongoing making of the partners through the making itself, in the making of bodied lives in the game. Partners do not preexist their relating; the partners are precisely what come out of the inter- and intra-relating of fleshly, significant, semiotic–material being. This is the ontological choreography that Charis Thompson writes about.[5] I'm telling a looping story of figuration, of ontics, of bodies in the making, of play in which all the messmates are not human.

Indeed, perhaps this is the daughter's knowledge, which is made possible by the kind of regard/respect her father gave—the knowledge that we have never been human and so are not caught in that cyclopean trap of mind and matter, action and passion, actor and instrument. Because we have never been the philosopher's human, we are bodies in braided, ontic, and antic relatings.

And so, we write the game story. In this account, the messmates with my father—the constitutive companion species knots that get my attention—are not myself or any other organism, but a pair of crutches and two wheelchairs. These were his partners in the game of living well.

When he was sixteen months old, my father fell and injured his hip. Tuberculosis set in. It subsided, only to return with a vengeance in 1921, when he slipped on an oiled floor. Tuberculosis lodged in the upper leg, knee, and hip bones, in a period when there was no treatment. We get this version of the history of the body from a tenth-grade school assignment, "The Autobiography of Frank Haraway," which we found after Dad's death in his orderly, but still packrat-inspired, files.[6] His own father had moved to Colorado Springs from Tennessee and Mississippi (the state line actually ran through the family house) in order to heal from pulmonary tuberculosis in a Rocky Mountain spa town that makes me recall *The Magic Mountain*. My father's childhood tuberculosis meant that from an early age he could not move without excruciating pain. He spent the ages of eight to about eleven in bed in a full-length body cast from his chest to his knees, not able to attend school and so learning with a private tutor. Not expected to live, he nonetheless eventually healed. But, the hip joints were permanently calcified, and he was left rigid with no plane of motion, no ability to bend, from the hips. He could not separate his legs in any direction. (This fact made me curious in my adolescent years about how my parents pulled off feats of conception—ordinary epistemophilia, with a twist. There was more than a little joking in our house about these matters.)

My father's father had money until a few years into the Depression. My grandfather was a sports promoter as well as the owner of Piggly Wiggly grocery stores in Colorado. A businessman and community figure, he brought sports figures to Denver such as Babe Ruth and Lou Gehrig, who came to Dad's house and signed a baseball for him while he was still confined to bed. My grandfather and his industrialist colleagues founded the white men's basketball leagues that preceded professional basketball as we now know it. The players for BF Goodrich, Akron Goodyear, Piggly Wiggly, and other midwestern and western industrial basketball teams were all white men destined to be middle-level managers. The bodily practices of racialization come in many forms, not least the braiding of family, sports, and business. My father was a sportswriter; that is part of how I am white; it is part of the game story. Race and money are part of how my father became a sportswriter.

My grandfather gave Dad a wheelchair as soon as he was able to get out of his bed and body cast, so he could go to the old Merchant's Park and watch the ballgames. But he was not just a spectator. From his wheelchair, in his typical semirecumbent seated posture dictated by his unaccommodating hips, Dad played baseball in the neighborhood. I have a picture of him and his younger brother, Jack, at about twelve and thirteen years old, both wearing characteristic pajama-mimic baseball pants, clutching bottles of Coke. Dad is in his wheelchair, flashing his trademark, gap-toothed smile, which showed up years later in the sports page cartoons drawn by Bob Bowie at the beginning of baseball spring training. Another photo shows my pimply-faced father swinging the bat with rather elegant athletic form. Dad was known in the neighborhood, I am told, as a good player, or at least a popular one. That wheelchair was in a companion-species relation to the boy; the whole body was organic flesh as well as wood and metal; the player was on wheels, grinning. Yet, perhaps not always grinning. At the end of a neighborhood game, so the family story goes, when their ancient baseball fell apart definitively and for the last time, the other kids persuaded Dad to bring out his Babe Ruth–Lou Gehrig autographed treasure. Sure, Dad thought, we only have one out to go. Dad watched the batter hit the ball past the fielder's outreached glove. The ball rolled down the urban gutter into the sewers, where it continues to fertilize narratives of loss and nostalgia—and narratives of the dramatic plays in a game.

When he graduated from Randall, the private high school he attended in his wheelchair, Dad got his crutches and galloped off to Denver University, where he became student sports editor of the DU *Clarion*. His track career at DU was cut short after an unauthorized race with a broken-legged football player, who was temporarily locomoting with crutches, a race that was set up by the other athletes on the track around the football field, starting gun and all. With his trusty cherrywood crutches under his armpits, swinging in long arcs, my father won the race handily, but his opponent fell and broke his other leg, prompting the coach to warn Dad off any further competitive exploits. These crutches belong corporeally in a life built out of relational, enabling objectifications, of coming into being through meldings with the physicality of the wheelchair, the bed, the cast, the crutches, all of which produced a vital, living, achieving sportswriter.

Bob Bowie's Denver *Post* cartoon of Frank Haraway arriving for Bears baseball spring training in the 1950s. From Haraway family archives.

Aided by his crutches, Dad developed a sense of balance that sustained him without the "sticks," as he called them, while standing and taking tiny steps using his partly flexible knees. That way, with unreturnable serves—in later years, mostly made illegal—and enviable timing, he won three straight Colorado State Table Tennis Championships in the 1930s.[7] If you've ever watched table tennis, you know it's a sport that requires covering a lot of ground with your legs, which was exactly what my father could not do. He won because of hand–eye coordination, balance, guts, upper-body strength, mind–body inventiveness, and desire—and because of his living in relationship to his own physicality in a way that never for a minute considered either denial or immobility (i.e., living outside the body) as a viable option.

To be in a companion-species relationship was the viable way of life. He was lucky to have a concatenated series of partners, including the wheelchair, the crutches, and the attention and resources of his parents

Frank Haraway and his younger brother, Jack, playing baseball about 1929. From Haraway family archives.

Frank Haraway playing table tennis in the 1930s. From Haraway family archives.

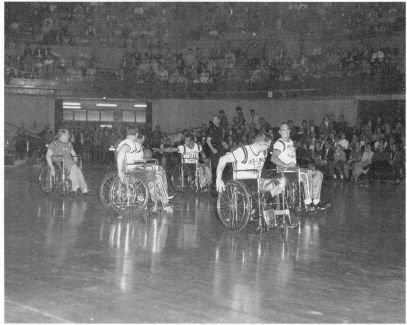

Frank Haraway and other men playing wheelchair basketball during halftime at a professional basketball game that Haraway was covering for the Denver *Post* about 1960. From Haraway family archives.

and friends.[8] The vitality came from living with regard to all those partners. Another photo that spilled out of Dad's files, one we put near his casket at the mortuary, eloquently makes this point. The photographer caught Dad unawares from behind in the late afternoon during batting practice before the game. Dad is in the third-base coaching box, looking toward the pitcher's mound. It's hard to be sure, but he looks to be about forty years old, and he's wearing a his typical checkered sports shirt. At first, it just seems he's standing relaxed on crutches in a slightly A-frame position. Then you see that he has his knees bent at a ninety-degree angle, with the soles of his shoes facing the camera. He is standing relaxed on his crutches all right, still and calm and utterly airborne.

My father lived his adult life, with his crutches, at speed. What I remember as a little girl was running down the block to keep up, not

Figure 17. Frank Haraway watching batting practice at Bears Stadium, 1960s. From Haraway family archives.

walking with someone less abled. Still, I need to return to walking for a while to understand better how modifying bodies work. Early on, I noticed that my two brothers, both my older brother, Bill, and my younger brother, Rick, neither of whom had hip disorders of any kind, walked a lot like my father. They still do, if you know what to look for. They literally embodied the gait of this man. This fact was not much remarked in the family; after all, it was normal for sons to be like their father, wasn't it? Theirs was a mimetic looping through the storied, masculine bodies of fathers and sons, which at no point was regarded as mimicking disability or any sort of oddity. The term *disability* didn't enter the family, not because there was denial about the need for crutches, but because these objects were normal parts of paternal equipment, all meanings intended. Certainly, they were part of the reproductive apparatus that shaped the bodies of my brothers.

This shared gait was about coming into cognizance of, in regard to, our father's body in a life-shaping way. In a sense, Dad's crutches symbiotically infused the bodies of all the family. My brothers and I would, naturally, borrow his crutches to try them out and see how fast we could go. We all did things like that, but only my brothers literally walked my father's walk. I did not have my father's gait; I had his way with language. My brothers did too, actually—Bill, as a financial adviser, in the idiom and lineage of our businessman grandfather; and Rick, as a social worker and peace and justice worker, in the vulgate of our mother, Dorothy Maguire, which was influenced by her Catholic formation and in which what later came to be called the "preference for the poor" was both doctrine and life-affirming bread. Trembling when she had to give her much-practiced treasurer's reports to the PTA, Mom shunned verbal public performance, but she knew the word was made flesh in taking people's needs and pain to her own heart. Laughing, she and I played with Latin words when I pestered her with my worries that it might be a sin to use sacred language in an overly serious, speculative child's fantasies. She was eloquent with good advice for me, even though I knew her own mind–body, in the vice grip of belief, was blasted by the minefields of Catholic contradiction and unspeakable yearning in the teeth of doctrine. She had the more speculative, self-analytical consciousness in our family but not the tools for expression. In 1960 she died of a heart attack, on a Monday morning in October after we had all left for school and work. I think my father never had any idea about her entrapment, but he did know her gift. I also think the physicality through which I came into relationship with my father, through which I won his regard, was through the sensuality of words and the acts of writing. We talked about, punned on, played with, and ate words for dinner; they were our food, too, even while we ate from my mother's mind–body, in her cooking and in her loneliness and barely acknowledged physical vulnerability.

In his eighties, Dad needed his crutches more and more for getting around, even in the house. Then, he started falling. He fell hard in January 2005 and broke his hip. Because of the extensive scarifying calcification from the childhood tuberculosis, there was no way to use a pin, or an external stabilization device, or anything else to hold the separated bones together so that they could heal well enough to give him half a chance to walk or even stand again. So, out of bed for decades, he lived his last eight months mostly back in bed, again in poorly relieved pain, relearning how to be mobile without legs. His bone-deep regard for people did not fail him. He flirted mercilessly with the nurses, Claudia and Lori, and the massage therapist, Tracy, with the same cheerful heterosexual self-confidence that plagued my feminist soul and roused my latent envy. He also formed gentle, trusting bonds with male caretakers—John, the blond Denver kid, and Lucky, the immigrant from Ghana—unaided by the specular and verbal devices of flirtation and across gulfs of race, class, and intimate bodily dependency. I thought the women who cared for him became his friends in spite of, not because of, his flirting; they knew that another kind of regard was operating even more powerfully, if less articulately. They still call my family, the men and the women call, to see how we are doing.

In the last months, Dad acquired a talented cyborg wheelchair that was radically different from the 1920s chariot I see in the old photos. The ad brochure promised everything but flight. Dad developed an affectionate, joking relationship with Drew, the kind and able wheelchair salesman. The physical therapist, Shawna, set up orange traffic cones in a line for him in the hallway of the rehab center, the one we called Rocky Road, so that he could practice navigating without taking down fellow dubiously ambulatory residents. It didn't take us long to up the limits on his liability insurance. Semi-recumbent, he had to pass Shawna's driving test with this chip-implanted, overachieving chair, which he never for a minute trusted but of which he was rather proud, even though he couldn't get into it or out of it on his own. This chair never quite became a beloved significant other. This partner was overwhelmingly about loss from which there would be no exit. It was a much fancier chair than the one of his youth, but it no longer signified getting well and going to the games. This chair, this transaction between wary companion species, was about the practice of dying. Even so, the chair assisted this process with companions of many species, both the apparatuses and the people, in a way that continued to stimulate a sportswriter's eye for the vitality of movement in the world.

The apparatus of companion species included satellite installations and a new television set to watch the games, as well as phone calls and visits with friends and colleagues to continue his professional relationship with, and lifelong pleasure in, sports. Brother Rick and his wife, Roberta, even got him into a van and to a baseball game once, to the National League press box named for him; but it was too hard, too painful, to do again. His partners of many species included all the means that he and we could imagine for staying in the game as long as he could.

And then he couldn't. He came down with pneumonia and decided not to treat it. He decided to go, because he judged that in any meaningful sense, he could stay in the game no longer. His game story was filed. Indeed, on his desk we found a stickie with the logo of the "morning fish wrapper," that is, the *Rocky Mountain News*, the rival newspaper, stuck in a plastic photo cube, on which he had penciled his last game story for us to savor: "When the good Lord decides I can no longer go to the games I love so much, I just want to be remembered as a happy man who loved his family, who loved people, and as a sports fan who got paid for writing what he saw." We worried for a while that we should have cremated his crutches with his remains; they belonged together; they were one vital body; both should go. Instead, Rick took the crutches home and put them in his living room, where they link us all to our ancestors, those companion species in other kinds of ontic and antic time.

My father was not a particularly self-reflective person; he didn't theorize these matters. As far as I could tell—and to my shame, I never tired of trying to recast him into the mold I wanted him to fit, from praying for his conversion to Catholicism when I was little to trying to get him to read books and analyze everything under the sun when I was older—he didn't reflect on these ramifying mimeses, these looping stories of mind– bodies coming to presence in the world through engaging companion species. I think his relationship to his work and to his life was to write the game stories and to be *in* the game. He never wanted to be a columnist or run the sports department of a big-city newspaper. He certainly never wanted to tell the stories about the commercial, social, and political apparatus that makes professional sports possible. He was not reflective about what it might mean for a man with rigid hips to spend a good part of his adult life whacking the bums of football players in locker rooms, though my first husband earnestly asked him about that more than once. Jaye was gay and extremely interested in homosocial physicality of both sexual and nonsexual kinds. He kept trying to get Dad to think about what the hell was going on and to think through his own multiple bodily relationships with men. These were not Dad's ways of being. These were his children's problems and tasks. He was a man who wrote the game story, and stayed in the game, and whose regard as a father I have not stopped needing.

Because of that need, in respect and with regard to all the players, I end this story, which has taken us through beds, casts, wheelchairs, crutches, and back to chairs, with another game story. As a woman in her fifties, I started playing a demanding sport with a member of another species a few years ago—with a dog, the dog of my heart, Cayenne, a Klingon warrior princess who was bred to be a working Australian shepherd. Her speed and athletic talent are off the scales, but her partner, if eager and fit, is all too weighed down with modest talent and immoderate years. The sport is called agility, a game made up of twenty or so obstacles on a hundred-foot by hundred-foot course, in patterns set out by a diabolical judge, who evaluates the dog–human teams for speed and accuracy of performance.

Playing that sport with Cayenne, now at the Masters level, after thousands of hours of joint work and play, I recognize the looping ontics and antics, the partnerships-in-the-making that transform the bodies of the players in the doing itself. Agility is a team sport; both players make each other up in the flesh. Their principal task is to learn to be in the same

game, to learn to see each other, to move as someone new of whom neither can be alone. To do that with a member of another biological species
is not the same thing as doing it with a cheating, language-wielding, hominid partner. Cayenne and I must communicate throughout our being,
and language in the orthodox linguist's sense is mostly in the way. The
highs that Cayenne and I experience come from focused, trained, responsive, conjoined movement at speed—from coursing together in mind-
body through the patterns for the whole time, when the times in question
range from twenty-five to fifty seconds, depending on the game. Speed
alone is not enough; unfocused by each other's transforming regard, speed
is chaos for us both. You can tell by all the penalties the judge assesses.
The intensity that we both love is finely differentiated from the panic that
destroys us. The "zone" for us is about speed, for sure, but speed organi-
cally braided in a joint, subject-transforming dance that makes the really
good runs "slow"; that is, we see and feel each other, see each other's eyes,
feel each other's moving bodies. Not a wild dash, but trained regard.

From the time we started training for agility competition, true to
my reforming zeal, I tried to get my aged father to be able to see what
this sport is; even after he broke his hip, he got no pass. It's not baseball,
basketball, or football; it's not boxing, hockey, tennis, or golf. It's not
even dog or horse racing. All of those sports he had had to write about
at least once for a living; all of those were legible to a man of his generation, race, and class. No, I insisted, this time you learn agility, the sport
of middle-aged women and their talented dogs, which will someday
occupy the prime-time Monday night TV slot, which is now making
do with that man-breaking sport called football. I showed him diagrams
of international-level Masters courses, explained what's involved technically, played videos of the USDAA (United States Dog Agility Association) Nationals when he was wild with pain and hallucinating on opiates,
and wrote him accounts of Cayenne's and my variously comic and tragic
exploits. He could not die; he was a sportswriter; he was my father.
I wanted his regard; I wanted his approval; I wanted him to get it. I did
not think he was watching or listening, except to murmur cheerful encouragement in a paternal tone, along the lines of "It's nice to have something you enjoy so much." This sport was off the radar for a sportswriter
of his formation.

Then, in the summer of 2005, when he was out of the rehab center, into his own room in an enhanced-care residential facility, and beginning to experience a lot less pain, just for fun I sent him a video of Cayenne and me running some courses at an AKC trial. I said, "This is what we did last weekend; this is what a bunch of the other players did; this is what the game looks like." He wrote me back a game story, crafted with all of his considerable professional skill.[9] He analyzed the runs; he took apart the coherencies and incoherencies. He saw in detail what was at stake, how the canine and human players moved, what worked and did not work. He wrote the game story as if he were a scout for a Major League Baseball team. He not only got it, he got it at the same professional level that he got the events that he was paid for, and he wrote it to me and Cayenne. He gave me—gave us—his regard. It's how he made a living.

TWO CODAS: GRIEF, MEMORY, AND STORY

I. August 25, 2004

> Dear Donnie,
>   Amazing! That was my first reaction upon seeing my (almost) 60-year-old daughter running with her young, high-spirited, lightning-fast pooch in highly-skilled competition. I marveled at the split-second timing required for you and Cayenne to communicate with each other. Yes, I noticed an occasional brief breakdown, quickly remedied as you resumed your run. Honestly, I was impressed. Little did I know when you cuddled up in my arms as a toddler that you would be running a dog in competition at the age of 60! I replayed the video several times and thoroughly enjoyed it.
>   The die is cast. I am working on the Broncos' stats crew Friday night. Wish me luck.
>
> Much love,
> Dad

That game was the last one Dad worked. He died a year later.

When I wrote "A Note of a Sportswriter's Daughter: Companion Species," I remembered this letter as if it had been written in August 2005, not 2004. I remembered more detail on the runs than there was. Only after finishing the paper did I dig the letter out of my files to add quotes from Dad and find the dates for a footnote. Then I understood more than I wanted to know about how grief reworks truth to tell another truth. Fiercely accurate, I remembered the love in this letter. But I redid time, and time chastened me. I learned again that the line between fiction and fact in family stories goes through the living room. The documenting practices of scholarship slice the heart, but they cannot undo the story. "Bodies in the Making: Transgressions and Transformations"—that is what stories chronicle. Stories re-member.

II. After the Game: "Somewhere off Thirty-fourth Street"

Filed by a sportswriter's daughter, December 11, 2005

In the season of recalling miracles on Thirty-fourth Street, Kris Kringle must take a back seat to a marvel that happened closer to home. It happened to Cayenne and me in California's decidedly nonmetropolitan Central Valley. Such a marvel will never happen again. Maybe I dreamed it. I hesitate to tell you in case I wake up. Maybe I'll write again later. No, I must check to see if reality holds. Here goes . . .

Cayenne and I received four perfect qualifying scores out of four runs (ExB Std, ExA JWW) at the Sacramento Dog Training Club's AKC trial at Rancho Murieta Friday and Saturday.

There, I said it. The sun is still shining, and so I'll risk telling you the rest. If the earth shakes, I'll stop.

Only international competitor Sharon Freilich's Rip, among all the Excellent Class dogs of both A and B sections, was faster than we were in three of the runs. In the "Jumpers with Weaves" run on Saturday, we were less than 0.5 seconds behind Sharon and Rip. Oh my. Now I will wake up for sure.

Recklessly, I forge on.

In the remaining run, an ExB Standard, we were fifth, behind a bunch of scruffy big-name border collies, including both of Sharon's dogs (Rip and Cirque). Three seconds separated the second- and fifth-place dogs. If Cayenne had not wanted to discuss the latest scandal of the Bush administration while I was earnestly suggesting a down on the pause table, we might have been first and definitely second. So, we took two first places in our ExA JWW and a second in our other ExB Standard (behind Rip, or did I already mention that?), all with tight turns, serious focus, weaves to use in a teaching video, and blazing times. (I will not mention, although perhaps this is the reason the sun is still shining and the earth not shaking, our less-than-perfect start line holds.)

Am I happy? Is Cayenne a Klingon warrior princess? Oh yes. How do I know? Because the sun is still shining.

7. SPECIES OF FRIENDSHIP

"Species of Friendship" is a collage of e-mails that I sent to my academic colleagues, dogland mentors, agility trainers and fellow players, human family, and a motley of friends between 1999 and 2004. The correspondence is part of "Notes of a Sportswriter's Daughter," which I started in honor of my journalist father, in order to explore some of the excitement, intensity, puzzlement, insight, friendship, competitiveness, love, support, and vulnerability that erupt in the worlds of sports-oriented companion species. The posts range from meditations about dog behavior at an off-leash beach to witnessing the pragmatics of comfort shared between my dying mother-in-law and our dogs. These e-mails are an odd hybrid of field notes, letters, and personal journal entries. They also read like love letters to particular dogs—my agility partners, Roland and Cayenne. Other posts from these "Notes" pepper the chapters of this book. E-mail sociality is a lively scholarly topic these days, and perhaps these posts add to the data, if not to the analysis. However, their scholarly value, or lack of it, is not what motivates their placement in *When Species Meet*. Rather, these posts are traces of the intense beginnings of encounters in dogland, with people and dogs, that have reshaped my heart, mind, and writing. I offer them with trepidation to readers other than those for whom they were first crafted, in the hope that they provoke some of the intensity and puzzlement of being a novice in dogland.

META-RETRIEVERS ON THE BEACH

Vicki Hearne, an accomplished dog trainer and writer, was an e-mail correspondent on CANGEN-L in the late 1990s.

> October 1999
> Dear Vicki,
>
> Now, I see that I lied to you about Roland's "prey drive" and "herding" potential—i.e., his temperament, if I understand your sense of the root *temper*. Watching him with you lurking inside my head over the last week made me remember that such things are multidimensional and situational, and describing a dog's temperament takes more precision than I achieved.
>
> We go to an off-leash, large, cliff-enclosed beach in Santa Cruz almost every day. There are two main classes of dogs there: retrievers and meta-retrievers. Roland is a meta-retriever. (My husband, Rusten, points out there is really a third class of dogs too—the "nons"—not in the game at issue here.) Roland will play ball with us once in a while (or anytime we couple the sport with a liver cookie or two), but his heart's not in it. The activity is not really self-rewarding to him, and his lack of style there shows it. But meta-retrieving is another matter entirely. The retrievers watch whoever is about to throw a ball or stick as if their lives depend on the next few seconds. The meta-retrievers watch the retrievers with an exquisite sensitivity to directional cues and microsecond of spring. These meta dogs do *not* watch the ball or the human; they watch the ruminant-surrogates-in-dog's-clothing.

Roland in metamode looks like an Aussie–border collie mock-up for a lesson in Platonism. His forequarters are lowered, forelegs slightly apart with one in front of the other in hair-trigger balance, his hackles in midrise, his eyes focused, his whole body ready to spring into hard, directed action. When the retrievers sail out after the projectile, the meta-retrievers move out of their intense eye and stalk into heading, heeling, bunching, and cutting their charges with joy and skill. The good meta-retrievers can even handle more than one retriever at a time. The good retrievers can dodge the metas and still make their catch in eye-amazing leaps— or surges into the waves, if things have gone to sea.

Since we have no ducks or other surrogate sheep or cattle on the beach, the retrievers have to do duty for the metas. Some retriever people take exception to this multi-tasking of their dogs (I can hardly blame them), so those of us with metas try to distract our dogs once in a while with some game they inevitably find much less satisfying. I drew a mental Larson cartoon on Thursday watching Roland, an ancient and arthritic Old English sheepdog, a lovely red tricolor Aussie, and a border collie mix of some kind form an intense ring around a shepherd–lab mix, a plethora of motley goldens, and a game pointer who hovered around a human who—liberal individualist to the end—was trying to throw his stick to his dog only. Meanwhile, in the distance, a rescue whippet was eating up sand in roadrunner fashion, pursued by a ponderous, slope-hipped GSD.

It remains true that I can call Roland off of a deer chase on the logging road near our house in Sonoma County most of the time; coursing a deer is not a meta-retrieving task worthy of an Aussie–chow, from his point of view.

There are terriers on the Santa Cruz beach too, and terrier mixes of all sorts. Why don't I *see* what the terrieresque crowd are doing? I am going to listen and watch.

I end with an appealing, neurotic, Airedale–black Lab cross who spends his beach time day after day trying to bury an old Monterey cypress branch, about three feet long and three inches in diameter, in the sand. He digs heroic holes, ignoring the pleas of his human to do *anything* else, but the curly, wire-haired, Labish-looking pooch keeps digging deep holes of small diameter for one end of his giant and recalcitrant stick. Nothing else matters.

Beached in dogland,
Donna

NOVICE PLAY, NOVICE PLAYERS

September 2000
Dear C.A. [Aussie health and genetics activist, dog world mentor, and friend],

Roland was inspiring on Sunday. Most of all, he was patently happy all day (we were at the agility trials for nine hours total, plus four hours of driving). He basked in all the attention, thought his exercise pen (a new experience for him) was a fine place to rest and watch all the dogs between walks and runs, regarded the brace of barking Jack Russell terriers next door to us with detachment, and met the performance demands on and around the course with very few signs of stress (a few yawns was all) and lots of evidence of enjoyment. His runs were solid and bode well for his getting his novice titles without too much fuss in the not-so-distant future (or so I dream).

We did not get a qualifying leg in the Standard course because we missed the entry to the weave poles, entering at the second pole on each try. In the Novice Class in the USDAA rules, you get to retry the weave poles as often as you need to get the *#*!* things properly negotiated, but after the third try for a correct entry I just let him weave and went on with the course. We'll just get more practice on weave entries at home and in class. He wasn't fast overall, but still within allowed time, and he stayed with me mentally. I have a tendency to get physically ahead of him, partly because working with Cayenne is so different and partly because I am a border collie at heart myself, but I am learning to pay better attention to Roland's rhythms. He sticks too close to me, and we need to do some more distance targeting exercises over two or three jumps in succession to get him running out with more drive.

His jumpers run was very good, marred only a little by his losing momentum at the first pinwheel after the wing jump and needing some strong pushing to get over the next jump, foiling my plans for a clean backcross and fast pivot. I need to remember who *he* is and keep us a team. I think I confused him at the wing jump right before the first pinwheel jump and slowed him down at just the wrong point. The last two-thirds of the jumper course was a real high for both of us. He was much faster and sailed through the second pinwheel and the hurdles, with a fun, fast finish

Roland jumping at a Bay Team agility trial in 2001. Courtesy of Tien Tran Photography.

over a double jump. We were both excited by the end and that made us more accurate and clean.

A couple of friends from local Aussie rescue stayed almost two hours after their runs just to watch Roland's last run (our class was the last event of the whole day), and that felt really good. Susan Caudill (Willem the Pyr's person, who now lives on our land) filmed the runs, along with several others, on her videocamera; so it was useful to look at the runs afterward to see what we all did. Our next event is the AKC Sir Francis Drake trials on September 16. I think I am getting hooked on agility!

Cayenne will have her first birthday before long—how can a year have gone by? Watching her entice Roland into playing with her this morning was a stitch. She just kept squeaking her toy in his face and running off until he gave in and chased her and then played tug-of-war with the toy. She runs circles around him and is uncatchable unless she lets herself be caught. I have the impression that just to keep him in the game she deliberately gets herself into parts of the yard where Roland has some advantage because of his weight and strength and so can pin her momentarily against a fence or into a gully. If she just keeps beating him to toys or runs too fast and pivots too abruptly, he loses interest. If she gets him into a really playful state of mind, he'll go belly up for her and wrestle with her for a long time, handicapping himself by staying in a down position and chewing gently on her proferred parts while she assaults him with abandon from above. With her Pyr buddy Willem, she hangs on to the base of his feathery tail and gets dragged across his yard; then she lets go and circles him furiously, herding him where she wants. It's hard to be grumpy myself in the morning watching this kind of joyful doggish beginning! Of course, coffee also helps . . .

Learning to be a novice,
Donna

BABY WEAVES

February 2001

Dear friends,

News bulletin for the agility addicted and their long-suffering mentors: Yesterday in our back yard, Ms Cayenne Pepper graduated to twelve in-line weave poles, moving up from a six one-inch staggered and six in-line channel weave setting. She shoots through in-line accurately with *speed*. Her entrances need work—she can run by the entrance and then not know how to get in. We'll work on that, using some of the ideas Kirstin Cole gave me. But yesterday afternoon, she did the twelve poles perfectly about eight times, four from each end. Then she was able to take a jump at a forty-five-degree angle after the weave pole exit and keep driving without any problem. Treats all around!

Cayenne weaving at a Bay Team agility trial in 2003. Courtesy of Tien Tran Photography.

I also had her jump (sixteen-inch practice height), turn forty-five degrees and enter correctly into the right side of the poles, weave twelve poles, turn ninety degrees to a box-and-inclined-plywood sheet that I used for target/touch practice, stop correctly (two feet on, two feet off), and then get treated. She did it!

We have the elementary right and left commands now, and I am looking forward to seeing if they are functional on some serpentines outside our backyard. Her swing and around commands are working well, and she will do sequenced obstacles when I am up to about ten to twelve feet away from her, driving her from behind. (She, of course, is hardly being driven; but the notion feeds my sense of having something to do out there! She's racing!) Sometimes she will do the weave poles as a send-away (one-inch offset in channel weave setup), and she's gotten reliable at send-aways into the tunnel (until she ate the child play tunnel last week) or over one or two jumps (not three unless I bait a touch plate at the end of the sequence). We haven't done any real obstacle discrimination work.

Her *very* mouthy "herding" pestering of other dogs at the dog park is a sight to see. Folks at the park regard her as a kind of playground director. Trouble is, she's getting too committed to this project! We need to get her to obey call-offs better when she gets too pesky and in-the-face of other dogs, especially retrievers trying to do their job. She provoked another young Aussie into a fight yesterday that we had to break up. We'll start putting her on leash and going to another area of the park if she disobeys settle-down commands and keeps bothering other dogs. Sound right? Other ideas for controlling this nuisance behavior? There's a fine line here between play that all the dogs like and Ms Cayenne fomenting a riot.

Roland is interesting to watch in relation to Cayenne's park behavior. He monitors the goings-on from some distance, not letting the youngsters interfere with his

collecting more human members for his growing park fan
club, who might be prevailed upon for a tasty treat or due
adulation. But when the goings-on among the chasing and
playing dogs get rowdy, he switches from his people-focused
"aren't I the softest dog you've ever seen?" friend-and-treat
scavenging mode into an all "alpha dog who was a wolf only
yesterday" (coat hair partially lofted, hacked-off tail raised as
high as he can get it, head up, eyes bright, muscles shining
through, and a fast, prancing gait), whose only concern is
other canines. Looking about six inches taller than he is, he
runs between the rowdy dogs, not infrequently hip-bumping
the dog Cayenne is playing with out of the way. He can stop
rowdy behavior cold and split dogs off from each other like a
champion shedding sheep. (He can also join in and become
part of the bumptious scene, but not in the same way as
Cayenne, because he doesn't have the utterly hard-wired,
in-your-face need to bark, chase, head off, turn, and nip until
the other dog morphs into the tough cow Cayenne [aka
daughter of Slash V] always knew s/he was underneath the
dog-park disguise.)

Weaving in line,
Donna

HOME STUDY

March 19, 2001
Dear friends,

Catherine de la Cruz roped me into doing a home
assessment in Santa Cruz for Great Pyrenees rescue this
week, if you can imagine! I think she figured that our Willem
fence-building exploits qualified me—especially since she
doesn't have any real Pyrish person in Santa Cruz and wants
a report about a woman who wants one of the dogs whom
Catherine is responsible for. I consulted with my brother
Rick about how he does adoption home studies for human

rescues. Rick is director of Catholic Family Services in Raleigh, and he does a lot of assessments prior to rehoming children. He reinforced my sense that the job is to be the adoptee's advocate while remaining the soul of tact. Why am I quaking in my boots?! I don't even have a novice leg in fence engineering! (Good fences seem to be nonnegotiable for placing a rescue Pyr!)

Speaking of novice legs, Roland and I did not get any in Madera Saturday at the USDAA trials. We did make interesting mistakes. I think that means we might be able to learn from them. Carefully timing her remarks to make an impact without damaging the novice handler's fragile self-esteem, our teacher Gail Frazier tactfully said that the reason Roland and I did not do well in our Standard course was that I neglected to give Roland any information during the run! That sounds pretty basic, I must say. She was, alas, quite correct. We missed getting our Gamblers run by 0.25 seconds, but we got our points and then all the required obstacles in sequence, which have to be worked at a (tiny, i.e., novice) distance. We were overtime because I set Roland up badly for the run at the jump to tunnel opener into the Gamble, and so he came back from the tunnel entrance to discuss the rule book with me before he agreed to go into the tunnel. Our discussion took several seconds. Next time I'll discuss all the fine print with him before our run! The good part is that he *did* go into the tunnel and finish the Gamble sequence correctly.

I talked with Dad yesterday on the phone and waxed all analytical about our agility runs in Madera, thinking he, as a sportswriter, would want a blow-by-blow account. He interrupted me to tell a baseball story. Donna, he said, you remember Andy Cohen, who used to manage the Denver Bears when you were a kid? Sure, I said, that's when the Bears were a Yankee farm club. Right, says Dad. Well, he reminisces, Andy was watching a hitter at batting practice at spring training one time. Now this hitter, a center fielder, was supposed to be the Bears' best hope for the season, but he was swinging at pitch after pitch and hitting nothing but air. He starts analyzing what he's doing wrong, and it just gets worse. Andy gets fed up and tells the guy to get out of the batter's box. The manager steps in, sets his stance, lines up his bat, and gets ready to clobber the ball into the stratosphere. The pitch comes in; Andy swings and misses, the air hissing in the bat's wake. This sorry picture is repeated about ten times, as Andy swings and misses. Then he steps out of the batter's box, aims a spray of tobacco juice at a passing ground beetle, gives the bat back to the hapless hitter, wipes his hands on his pants, and says, "There, now do you see what you are doing?"

As the bumper sticker says, "Shut up and train,"
Donna

ENFORCER

April 8, 2001
Dear friends,

Nice thing at the dog beach this afternoon: Roland the HufflePuff Enforcer was looking like he might get into a fight with a couple of big-balled big males, and some sparring was already under way. Rusten and I were nearby, and I said firmly, "Leave It, Come, Sit!" Miracle of miracles, he left it, came, and sat. I was thanking my lucky stars, and remembering Pyr alpha bitch Catherine de la Cruz's and Linda Weisser's daunting stories of breaking up fights among large dogs, knowing I could not have measured up. Rusten looked grateful to some sort of deity too, even though he is braver than I am, or perhaps just more committed to not letting anyone in this world get hurt.

Then what to my wondering ears should I hear but the patter of my fellow dog beach humans, saying, "My, my, did you see that! That dog just walked out of a fight and came and sat! How do they get him to do that?" Good question. "Liver cookie" seems such a mundane answer. But then, I never did rise above the level of popular religion—at least not since I retired from wannabe Jesuit.

As the masthead on *The Bark* says, "Dog is my co-pilot."

Reverently grateful,
Donna

KLINGON WARRIOR PRINCESS

May 30, 2001
Dear Friends,

Ms Cayenne Pepper has shown her true species being at last. She's a female Klingon in heat. Now, you may not watch much TV or be a years' long fan of the Star Trek universe like I am, but I'll bet the news that Klingon females are formidable sexual beings, whose tastes run to the ferocious, has reached everyone. The Pyr on our land, the intact twenty-month-old Willem, has been Cayenne's playmate since they were both puppies, beginning at about four months. Cayenne was spayed when she was six and a half months old. She's always happily humped her way down Willem's soft and inviting backside, starting at his head end with her nose pointed to his tail, while he lies on the ground trying to chew her leg or lick a rapidly passing genital area. But during our Memorial weekend's brief stay on the Healdsburg land things have heated up, put mildly. Willem is a randy, gentle, utterly inexperienced adolescent male soul (and Susan makes very sure he stays inexperienced and properly fenced!). Cayenne does not have an estrus hormone in her body (but let us not forget those very much present adrenal cortices pumping out aldosterone and other so-called androgens that get lots of the credit for juicing up mammalian desire in males and females). But she is one turned on little bitch with Willem, and he is INTERESTED.

She does not do this with any other dog, "intact" or not.
None of their sexual play has anything to do with remotely
functional heterosexual mating behavior—no efforts of
Willem to mount, no presenting of an attractive female
backside, not much genital sniffing, no whining and pacing,
none of all that "reproductive" stuff. No, here we have pure
polymorphous perversity that is so dear to the hearts of all
of us who came of age in the 1960s reading Norman O.
Brown. Willem lies down with a bright look in his eye.
Cayenne looks positively crazed as she straddles her genital
area on the top of his head, her nose pointed toward his tail
end, and presses down and wags her backside vigorously. I
mean hard and fast. He is trying for all he's worth to get his
tongue on her genitals, which inevitably dislodges her from
the top of his head. Looks a bit like the rodeo, with her
riding a bronco and staying on as long as possible. They have
slightly different goals in this game, but both are committed
to the activity. Sure looks like eros to me. Definitely not
agape. They keep this up for about five minutes to the
exclusion of any other activity. Then they go back to it for
another round. And another. Susan's and my laughing,
whether raucous or discreet, does not merit their attention.
Cayenne growls like a female Klingon during the activity,
teeth bared. She's playing, but oh my, what a game. Willem is
earnestly intent. He is not a Klingon, but what we would call
a considerate lover.

Have you seen anything like this with a spayed female
and an intact male? Or any other combination, for that matter?
Their youth and vitality seem to have made a mockery of
reproductive heterosexual hegemony, as well as of abstinence-
promoting gonadectomies. Now, I, of all people, who have
written all-too-infamous books about how we Western
humans project our social orders and desires onto animals
without scruple, should know better than to see confirmation
of Norman O. Brown's *Love's Body* in my spayed Aussie
dynamo and Susan's talented landscape guardian dog with

that big, sloppy, velvety tongue. Still, what do you think is going on? (Hint: This is not a game of fetch or chase.)

Should I tell the writers of the Star Trek world anything about the real Klingon on earth?

Time to get to real work!
Donna

SKUNKED

September 3, 2001
Dear friends,

Roland got his third qualifying leg in Novice Standard at USDAA this weekend, and so is now officially a titled mutt: Agility Dog!

To celebrate, Rusten and I bought a big steak for Roland, Cayenne, and all the dogs who owned the people who had a barbecue at Gail Frazier's RV on Saturday after the runs.

Then Roland, AD, promptly got skunked, literally. Hardly seems fair, but at the motel while he was doing his last duties of the day, he got sprayed full in the face. Rusten made an 11 p.m. dash for a twenty-four-hour drug store somewhere in Hayward to get hydrogen peroxide, baking soda, and Tecnu® (works on the same principle as it does for poison oak—pulls the oil out and then washes away with soap and water). I held the reeking, titled victor in the parking lot until Rusten got back with the supplies. We then escorted him into the tiled motel bathroom, where I stripped, got in the tub with him, and Rusten and I began the always edifying process of getting skunk perfume off the face and neck of a dog at midnight. The best that can be said is that his odor was socially acceptable (humanly speaking) Sunday morning, and the Vagabond Inn in Hayward is still accepting dogs. I wish they'd evict their resident skunks.

So many ways to be humiliated in agility—a regular school for moral growth!

Cayenne didn't get any qualifying Standard runs in three tries, but our mistakes were interesting (read: hours of training and a lot of luck will fix this!). Best of all, she had a dynamite run Monday afternoon in Jumpers. Clean run; fifth place. Her pace was blindingly fast, but she cannot be said to have taken the shortest path to very many of the jumps. Never have I seen such wide turns without a wrong course resulting! She was joyful, and we had a ball for 28.74 harrowing seconds.

My injured Achilles tendons did not pop. I ran wrapped in layers of neoprene, a material I owe either to the space race or to money-drenched professional football. Rusten ordered ice and more ibuprofen after all the runs. I'm only limping a little tonight. It's nice to have a resident trainer—almost as good as intact connective tissue itself.

Off to Gail's for our next lesson tomorrow. We work on tight turns to get that fifth place to first!

Pam Richards and I are going to do Novice Pairs together at the USDAA meet in Madera in October—she with Cappuccino, I with Cayenne. (Capp and Cayenne are littermates, born 9/24/99, both red merles, both half masks, both flashy, fast dogs. Besides Capp's being the tallest dog from that litter and Cayenne the shortest, the main difference is Pam and Cappuccino are seriously well-trained national competitors! Oh, I forgot the sexual difference, but, as usual, that hardly signifies.) Stay tuned.

Cheers,
Donna

WOBBLIES

April 1, 2002
Dear indulgent dog friends,

Cayenne Warrior Princess got her Novice Agility certificate in the North American Dog Agility Council

[NADAC] on Saturday! We worked hard for that one. She's a crowd pleaser whether we run accurately or not—speed and athleticism are *both* in her lexicon. I, of course, like the runs when we are both doing the same course and not indulging in independent course design, each without regard for the judge's version, or in casual jump bar demolition or tunnel hopping. Sunday, I was convinced Cayenne is really a Wobblie organizing an anarchist strike against accurate performance of the contact obstacles. No sooner had we started running at the Open level than she popped every contact, maybe hitting one or two by accident, but surely not by her devious intention.

Speaking of tunnel hopping, Saturday we also got a clean run Q and fourth place in "Tunnelers," a new NADAC game. That fourth place was in relation to all the twenty-inch category dogs, even the Elite crowd. We were fast, and she was on with her "lefts" and "rights." Thrilling, to tell the truth.

I remain firmly in love with this canine demon. Good thing.

Next agility stop is Power Paws Camp, May 6–10. It's fortunate I can call all this research for publishing "Notes of a Sportswriter's Daughter." I hope the IRS agrees . . .

As they wisely say, "Shut up and train!"
Donna

DIVA

May 28, 2002
Hi Gail,

I'll see you in the morning, but got the urge to tap out an entry for "Notes of a Sportswriter's Daughter" first. The occasion is recovery from the NADAC meet at Elk Grove over the Memorial Day weekend. I think I'll need at least twelve steps and a higher power.

Ms C. Pepper needs a new name; and a temperamental, hypertalented, flagrantly unpredictable opera star comes to mind. Diva Dog. Saturday morning, she burned through an Open Gamblers course with seventy-one points, a Q, and first place. We would have had eighty-one points if she hadn't popped poles in her weaves. There was time to spare before the whistle blew, but we were in position. She made her ten-point optional last obstacle in the Gamble after the required two, four, six, eight. She also did a sizzling Tunnelers, earning a second place, a Q, and her Novice Tunnelers title. She and the first-place dog (a border collie, I am forced to say) got the fastest two scores out of all the dogs of all classes and sizes in the Tunnelers event—about a hundred dogs.

But then Sunday, Cayenne was in her own zone, flying to the beat of some unknown canine devil. She held her stays at the start line with a wild look in her eye and every muscle taut. There were no breaks before the "all right" at the start line no matter how far I led out, but we had precious little control after she flew over the first obstacles. She was either rigid with anticipation on the start line or flying in some personal gravity-free space all day. It was all wide turns and failure to touch any part of the contact obstacles—up, down, or top! Some of this was flawed handling, some inconsistent training, and some was something else. She was just plain wild and unfocused. I was nervous and telegraphed that to her. I left the rings muttering that I'd consider taking bids on a certain young agility prospect; I savored the fantasy of turning down the million dollar figures for Cayenne that would be forthcoming! Frank Butera was very calming, reminding me of the wild ride he and Cayenne's brother Roca (same parents, earlier breeding) had a couple of years ago. Rusten propped up my despairing soul.

Monday, I had signed up to run only with Roland. What a different dog! He got a fourth place in Novice Jumpers, but didn't Q because he had a 1.8 second time fault, consequent on his checking out a human pole setter on his way round the hurdles. He got a solid fourth place and Q on his Novice Touch 'n Go. He missed his Gamble after a nice but unspectacular thirty-three-point opening (he got six Gamble points). Only one dog got the Gamble in the novice twenty-inch class. Renzo, Cayenne's brother and Paul Kirk's new dog from the Oxfords' last breeding of Randy and Bud, got the top score in that Gamblers run, but no Q either. Roland got a rock-solid but not fast Q in his Tunnelers run. Finally, he was solid and within time in his Standard run. Running with Roland felt very nice, very calming. He was a rock-solid partner dog. All the mistakes were obvious handler errors, and he gave me plenty of time to think on the course. Cayenne looked utterly unbelieving that Roland was getting all the attention, and she was left waiting in her crate. I was unsympathetic.

Trouble is, I am in love with Cayenne and want to be good for and with her. Really good. Desire is a devil in a red merle coat.

See you in the morning,
Donna

TALES FROM THE CRYPT

Tuesday, September 17, 2002
Dear Gail,

Roland was great Sunday, and Cayenne was worse by far. Roland got his second Open Standard qualifying run (and a second place), and so he only needs one more Q for his Open title. Because I've been concentrating on Cayenne, he's only run in two Standard events in Open—one last February and one Sunday. I am very proud of the boy—and he was proud of himself. At least, he definitely knew he was doing well. His fur was shining and his body was round and beautiful. His face was wide, eyes alert, and whole self attuned to me as his team member. We were, in short, communicating, on and off the course.

Now to "tales from the Crypt"!

Saturday, Cayenne popped the A-frame contact in her otherwise fairly good Novice Standard. She did a correct dog walk contact (including waiting for the release), but did not hold the teeter as long as she should have—and I did not give her clear information about what I wanted there. I left the course with her after the teeter, and gave her quiet, definite, standing-still "wrongs" at the A-frame and dog walk, bringing her back before we went on. But she was in high stress mode—very squirrelly.

At home, I can't get her to miss two-on, two-off (or four-on for the teeter); and she waits for the release command, even if I climb the roof and throw hamburgers (well, you see what I mean). In class, she is consistent at making the contacts correctly, but will break her position before the release if I move oddly or ask her to stay too long and she is excited. In the trials, she is, at this point, almost never making the A-frame contacts at all, and she pops the dog walk about 50 percent of the time. Help!!!!

Sunday, she was simply wild—a Klingon Warrior Princess in her own world. She popped contacts all over her Standard run and had poor attention in her Jumpers event. She seemed stressed out and unresponsive, something she has done before when Roland is also there. I think I need to take her and Roland separately, at least for now.

Thanks for promising to think with me tomorrow about how we can make some headway on the contact problem.

We have a trial in Dixon this weekend. Stay tuned!

I ought to be doing my real work!

Cayenne's inconsistent trainer and your abject student, Donna

SMITTEN

January 2003

Dear long-suffering dog friends,

So now I indulge in the pleasurably embarrassing custom of "the brag" . . .

Ms Cayenne Pepper was truly lovely this weekend at a Haute Dawgs NADAC trial at Starfleet. We ran in the Open class for all events.

Miracle of miracles, I saw four paws on each and every contact zone; and three-quarters of the time (actual count) she held two-on, two-off like she had superglue on her feet. I know that's not 100 percent, and my character and her future are a ruin for running after such failures; but we did run on after I stated emphatically, "Oops! Sit!"

The last event of the weekend was the best. The Jumpers setup was three rows of four jumps, equally spaced in ranks, with two U-shaped tunnels set up outside the rectangle of jumps at one end. It was like the setup Pam showed us at Gail's in December. In Elite, both tunnels were traps; in Open one tunnel was a trap and the other was a judge-approved boomerang launching device. The path was really a big X hooked together with U-turns and serpentines (and in Elite, an extra little loop thrown in).

Xo and Chris did a fabulous job in the Elite version; they flowed like a graceful, fast river populated by a Doberman bitch and a human man. Cayenne was an accurate blur in the Open version, which opened with a diagonal across four jumps, a U-turn and straight run over three jumps, another U-turn and straight down the second line of three jumps, into a three-jump serpentine, ending with a layered fling into the yawning mouth of a tunnel, whereby the dog was catapulted into the final diagonal run across four jumps.

Cayenne's first place was a 17.83-second run (9 seconds under Standard course time and 6 seconds ahead of a nice, fast Aussie who dogged our heels all weekend). I watched and cheered, occasionally waving my hands, probably in a jerky fashion and blessedly outside her range of vision, to tell her what to do. I guess my feet and shoulders were in the right places at the right times, and I must have run too because I was out of breath. Cayenne had apparently analyzed the course correctly, because she did not make so much as a false twitch. I think I said, "Go!" once or twice. No time for "Over!" and who needed it anyway? What else could she do?

Cayenne contributed to breed science this weekend too, in the form of cheek cells for a UC Davis gene analysis project on ivermectin and related drug metabolism. The researcher wielding the cotton swabs said the samples would be stored permanently for possible other future research.

Back to real work, alas.

Smitten in Santa Cruz,
Donna

PERSONALS COLUMN

December 29, 2003
Dear dog friends,

Ms C. Pepper did very well on Sunday at TRACS [Two Rivers Agility Club of Sacramento]. We missed Qs in both Excellent A Standard and JWW because of one refusal in each, both caused by my ambiguous cueing. She was twelve seconds under Ex A Standard course time in JWW, but I caused a refusal ON THE LAST JUMP. That was painful! A tiny, little, minuscule hesitation, but at the wrong place and the judge was, alas, looking. I'm sure perfection is in my future, just not sure when!

Meanwhile, I read a troubling ad in the personals column of the local newspaper: "Olympic quality dog seeks adequate handler. Inquire discreetly at—our phone number!" She wouldn't do that, would she?

Threatened with abandonment,
Donna

TOUCHING COMFORT

Rusten's mother, troubled by advancing dementia, lived with us for four years until she died in late 2004. Below are two stories of companion species, the first addressed to Karen McNally, my UCSC colleague in earth sciences who gave us Roland as a two-year-old in 1997, the second addressed to agility friends.

March 26, 2002
Dear Karen,

You would have warmed to the sight of Roland this morning. I was watching out of the corner of my eye from the kitchen sink. Roland heard Rusten's mom stirring above and beginning to come down the stairs in her determined but shaky step. Roland quietly went to the bottom of the stairs and sat, with his ears held gently back in happy mode, his whole body collected and smooth, and his rounded puff tail swishing back and forth in eager but controlled anticipation. Katharine breached the door between the up- and downstairs, and the two friends made eye contact. She and Roland gazed softly at each other for several seconds. A long time. Then she came down the last couple of stairs, holding on to the banister for support. Roland waited calmly as she accomplished the last step over to him and put her soft hands around his receptive face. She massaged his face for several seconds; he just sat very still and smooth, with a face so soft it brought tears to my eyes. Then she walked by him and said good morning to me as I held out her pretty Italian ceramic cup full of oily, aromatic coffee. Companion species, indeed.

Donna

October 27, 2004
Dear agility friends,

Rusten's mother, Katharine, sometimes gets quite crazy and paranoid, usually about finances. Because her memory is so fragmentary, she produces continuity in other ways, often by narrating experiences that are totally real to her but that simply did not happen in the material world. Those experiences can be more real to her than even her cherished memories from her childhood. Sometimes these hyperreal experiences are very nice, like long trips to Alaska, full of details that never happened. Or her certainty that she has already seen a film we go to, and remembers the people she saw the film with, even though it was only released to theaters that day. Other times the crafted memories are fierce and hurtful, full of terror at her not being in control and feeling duped or injured by someone. She screamed at Rusten yesterday, saying he was calling her a liar. He went on to tennis anyway, not rising to the bait and knowing that getting caught in a loop of explanations of the "real" world (in this case a bill from the dentist that he had already gone over with her many times) would only make her more agitated. No matter what, R remains incredibly gentle. Not simple, these aged and needy parents!

After R left for tennis, K was quiet for a while, then came downstairs in tears, almost hysterical, thinking she had said something terrible to Rusten, but not knowing what it was. It took a long time to comfort her, holding her and rocking and telling her she did not say anything awful, and even if she had been mad at him, everyone has a right to lose it sometimes and freak with anger. I kept telling her about all the positive things she does all the time and how much R and I want her and feel blessed that she wants to live with us. That's true, if not the whole truth! But who needs the whole truth anyway. She calmed down, needed lots of hugs, and then went to do the dishes, which comforted her some more.

The most interesting thing, though, was not what she and I were doing, but what she and the dogs were doing the whole time she was crying and desperate for comfort and relief from feelings of guilt, shame, and bewilderment. She was on the couch, and I was kneeling below her, my hands on her knees and hugging her periodically. Cayenne slipped her body between us (she would NOT be denied) and snuggled onto K's lap, with her head pressed hard against K's breasts. C's face was tilted up to K's head. Every chance C got, she licked K's face, then pressed her head against K's breasts again. Her spot in K's lap was nonnegotiable. She would not budge until K was calm. Roland, meanwhile, had his head inserted between me and K's lap, putting his head on her knees along with my hands and pressing firmly against her body with all his weight. He also would not budge until K was calm. K's hands the whole time were kneading the dogs' bodies, first one, then the other. She did not know what she was doing consciously, but the touch comfort among K, R, and C was stunning. Toward the end, the dogs made K laugh at *their* need for comfort, as well as their ability to give comfort. That laughter was the last step in her letting go of her grief and loss that afternoon.

From dogland,
Donna

8. TRAINING IN THE CONTACT ZONE
Power, Play, and Invention in the Sport of Agility

He enriches my ignorance.
—Ian Wedde, "Walking the Dog," in *Making Ends Meet*

PAYING ATTENTION

Vincent the Rhodesian ridgeback was not an agility dog. He was the walking and running companion of New Zealand/Aotearoa writer and dog lover, Ian Wedde. Wedde and Vincent have taught me much that I need to say about the sport of agility, a game that I play with my fast herding dog, Cayenne. She enriches my ignorance. Playing agility with Cayenne helps me understand a controversial, modern relationship between people and dogs: training to a high standard of performance for a competitive sport. Training together, a particular woman and a particular dog, not Man and Animal in the abstract, is a historically located, multispecies, subject-shaping encounter in a contact zone fraught with power, knowledge and technique, moral questions—and the chance for joint, cross-species invention that is simultaneously work and play. Writing this chapter with Cayenne is not a literary conceit but a condition of work. She is, legally, a research dog in the University of California, just as I am a research human; this status is required of both of us if we are to occupy an office in the History of Consciousness Department on the campus of the University of

California at Santa Cruz. I did not originally seek this status for Cayenne; I would have liked her company in the office simply as my companion. But dogs who are merely friends are banned from UCSC for obscure reasons having something to do with a dog's murdering a donkey thirty-odd years ago near the old barn on campus, but really having more to do with the remarkable problem-solving strategies among bureaucrats running things in the world. If there is a difficulty involving some individuals (unsupervised dogs and clueless humans?), then ban all members of the class rather than solve the problem (retrain the campus community?). Only the dogs, of course, not the clueless humans, were actually banned. That, however, is a story for another day. The material–semiotic exchange between Cayenne and me over training is the subject of this chapter; it is not a one-sided affair. The chief campus animal control officer recognized her as a knowledge worker. After careful temperament testing (of Cayenne; I was given a pass although my impulse control is more fragile than hers) and practical interviews assessing both of us for skills in following orders, the officer filled out papers to legalize Cayenne's presence. The box checked was "research."

Many critical thinkers who are concerned with the subjugation of animals to the purposes of people regard the domestication of other sentient organisms as an ancient historical disaster that has only grown worse with time. Taking themselves to be the only actors, people reduce other organisms to the lived status of being merely raw material or tools. The domestication of animals is, within this analysis, a kind of original sin separating human beings from nature, ending in atrocities like the meat–industrial complex of transnational factory farming and the frivolities of pet animals as indulged but unfree fashion accessories in a boundless commodity culture. Or, if not fashion accessories, pets are taken to be living engines for churning out unconditional love—affectional slaves, in short. One being becomes means to the purposes of the other, and the human assumes rights in the instrument that the animal never has in "it"self. One can be somebody only if someone else is something. To be animal is exactly not to be human and vice versa.

Grammatically, this matter shows up in editing policies of major reference books and newspapers. Animals are not allowed personal pronouns such as *who*, but must be designated by *which*, *that*, or *it*. Some contemporary reference manuals allow an exception to this: if a particular animal has a name and sex, the animal can be an honorary person designated by personal pronouns; in that case, the animal is a kind of lesser human by courtesy of sexualization and naming.[1] Thus, pets can have names in the newspapers because they are personalized and familialized but not because they are somebody in their own right, much less in their *difference* from human personhood and families. Within this frame, only wild animals in the conventional Western sense, as separate as possible from subjugation to human domination, can be themselves. Only wild animals can be somebody, ends not means. This position is exactly the opposite of the grammar reference books' granting derivative personhood only to those animals most incorporated into (Western) humanlike sexuality and kinship.

There are other ways to think about domestication that are both more historically accurate and also more powerful for addressing past and present brutalities and for nurturing better ways to live in multispecies sociality.[2] Tracking only a few threads in a densely complex fabric, this chapter examines the case of people and dogs working to excel in an international competitive sport that is also part of globalized middle-class consumer cultures that can afford the considerable time and money dedicated to the game. Training together puts the participants inside the complexities of instrumental relations and structures of power. How can dogs and people in this kind of relationship be means and ends for each other in ways that call for reshaping our ideas about and practices of domestication?

Redefining domestication, the Belgian philosopher and psychologist Vinciane Despret introduces the notion of "anthropo-zoo-genetic practice," which constructs both animals and humans in historically situated interrelationships. Emphasizing that articulating bodies to each other is always a political question about collective lives, Despret studies those practices in which animals and people become available to each other, become attuned to each other, in such a way that both parties become more interesting to each other, more open to surprises, smarter, more "polite," more inventive. The kind of "domestication" that Despret explores adds new identities; partners learn to be "affected"; they become "available to events"; they engage in a relationship that "discloses perplexity."[3] The personal pronoun *who*, which is necessary in this situation, has nothing to do with derivative, Western, ethnocentric, humanist personhood for either people or animals, but rather has to do with the query proper to serious relationships among significant others, or, as I called them elsewhere, companion species, *cum panis*, messmates at table together, breaking bread.[4] The question between animals and humans here is, Who are you? and so, Who are we?

Who is not a relative pronoun in the co-constitutive relationships called training; it is an interrogative one. All the parties query and are queried if anything interesting, anything new, is to happen. In addition, *who* refers to partners-in-the-making through the active relations of coshaping, not to possessive human or animal individuals whose boundaries and natures are set in advance of the entanglements of becoming together. So, how *do* dogs and people learn to pay attention to each other in a way that changes who and what they become together?[5] I will not try to answer that question in the large; instead, I will try to figure out how Cayenne and I learned to play agility together well enough to earn a modest certificate, if one that we found demanded our laughter, tears, work, and play for thousands of hours over several years: the Masters Agility Dog title in the United States Dog Agility Association. Our championship eludes us; she enriches my ignorance.

THE GAME'S AFOOT

What is the sport of agility?[6] Picture a grassy field or dirt-covered horse arena about one hundred by one hundred feet square. Fill it with fifteen to twenty obstacles arranged in patterns according to a judge's plan. The sequence of the obstacles and difficulty of the patterns depend on the level of play from novice to masters. Obstacles include single, double, or triple bar jumps; panel jumps; broad jumps; open and closed tunnels of various lengths; weave poles, consisting of six to twelve in-line poles through which the dog slaloms; pause tables; and contact obstacles called teeter-totters, A-frames (between 5.5 and 6.5 feet high, depending on the organization), and dog walks. These last are called contact obstacles because the dog must put at least a toenail in a painted zone at the up and down ends of the obstacle. Leaping over the contact zone earns a "failure to perform" the obstacle, which is a high-point penalty. Dogs jump at a height determined by their own height at their shoulders or withers. Many of the jump patterns derive from those used in horse-jumping events, and indeed horse events are among the sporting parents of dog agility.

Human handlers are allowed to walk through the course for about ten to fifteen minutes before the dog and human run it; the dog does not see the course beforehand at all. The human is responsible for knowing the sequence of obstacles and for figuring out a plan for human and dog to move fast, accurately, and smoothly through the course. The dog takes the jumps and navigates the obstacles, but the human has to be in the right position at the right time to give good information. Advanced courses are full of trap obstacles to tempt the untimely or the misinformed; novice runs test fundamental knowledge for getting through a course accurately and safely with nothing fancy required. In a well-trained team, both human and dog know their jobs, but any knowledgeable observer will see that the overwhelming number of errors on a course are caused by bad handling on the human's part. The errors might be bad timing, overhandling, inattention, ambiguous cues, bad positioning, failure to understand how the course looks from the point of view of the dog, or failure to train basics well beforehand. I know all of these disasters from all-too-much personal experience! Qualifying runs in the higher levels of the sport require perfect scores within a demanding time limit. Teams are ranked by accuracy and speed, and runs can be decided by hundredths of seconds. Thus, working for tight turns and efficient paths around the course is important.

Agility began in 1978 at Crufts in the United Kingdom when a trainer of working trial dogs, Peter Meanwell, was asked to design a dog-jumping event to entertain spectators waiting for the main action at the classy dog show. In 1979, agility returned to Crufts as a regular competitive event. After about 1983, agility spread from the United Kingdom to Holland, Belgium, Sweden, Norway, and France, and it has since continued to spread across Europe as well as to North America, Asia, Australia and New Zealand, and Latin America. The United States Dog Agility Association was founded in 1986, followed by other organizations in the United States and Canada. In 2000 the International Federation of

Cynological Sports (IFCS) was founded on the initiative of Russia and Ukraine to unite dog sport organizations in many countries and hold international competitions.[7] The first IFCS world championship was held in 2002.[8] The growth in participation in the sport has been explosive, with thousands of competitors in many organizations, all with somewhat different rules and games.

Workshops, training camps, and seminars abound. Successful competitors frequently hang out their shingle as agility teachers, but only a few can actually make a living that way. California is one of the hot spots of agility, and in that state on any given weekend year-round, several agility trials will occur, each with two hundred to three hundred or so dogs and their people competing. Most dog–human teams I know train formally at least once a week and informally all the time. The year I kept count, I spent about four thousand dollars on everything it took to train, travel, and compete; that is considerably less than many humans spend on the sport. In the United States, white women about forty to sixty-five years old dominate the sport numerically, but people of several hues, genders, and ages play, from preteens to folks in their seventies. In my experience, lots of human players hold professional jobs to pay for their habit or are retired from such jobs and have some disposable income. Many people also play who make very little money and have hard working-class jobs.[9]

Many breeds and mixed-ancestry dogs compete, but the most competitive dogs in their respective height classes tend to be border collies, Australian shepherds, shelties, and Parson Jack Russell terriers. High-drive, focused, athletic dogs and high-drive, calm, athletic people tend to excel and find themselves in the agility news. But agility is a sport of amateurs in which most teams can have a great time and earn qualifying runs and titles, if they work and play together with serious intent, lots of training, recognition that the dogs' needs come first, a sense of humor, and a willingness to make interesting mistakes—or, better, make mistakes interesting.

Positive training methods, offspring of behaviorist operant conditioning, are the dominant approaches used in agility. Anyone training by other methods will be the subject of disapproving gossip, if not dismissed from the course by a judge who is on the lookout for any human's harsh correction of a dog. Dogs get precious little more leeway if they are harsh with their humans or other dogs! Beginning her training career with marine mammals in 1963 at Hawaii's Sea Life Park, Karen Pryor is the most important single person for teaching and explaining positive methods to the amateur and professional dog-training communities, as well as many other human–animal communities. Her blend of science and practical demonstration has had a major impact.[10] So, what is positive training?

In the simplest terms, positive training methods are standard behaviorist approaches that work by marking desired actions called behaviors and delivering an appropriate reward to the behaving organism with a timing that will make a difference. That's positive reinforcement. Reinforcement in behaviorism is defined as anything that occurs in conjunction with an act and has a tendency to change that act's probability. That bit about "in conjunction with an act" is crucial. Timing is all; tomorrow, or even five seconds after the interesting behavior, is way too late to get or give good information in training. A behavior is not something just out there in the world waiting for discovery; a behavior is an inventive construction, a generative fact–fiction, put together by an intra-acting crowd of players that include people, organisms, and apparatuses all coming together in the history of animal psychology. From the flow of bodies moving in time, bits are carved out and solicited to become more or less frequent as part of building other patterns of motion through time. A behavior is a natural–technical entity that travels from the lab to the agility training session.

If the organism does something that is not wanted, ignore it and the behavior will "extinguish" itself for lack of reinforcement (unless the undesired behavior is self-rewarding; then, good luck). Withholding social recognition by not noticing what each other is doing can be a powerful negative reinforcement for dogs and people. Supposedly mild negative reinforcers like "time outs" are popular in agility training and human schools in the United States. Restraint, coercion, and punishment—such as ear pinching—are actively discouraged in agility training in any situation I have experienced or heard about. Strong negative words like "no!"— emitted in moments of great frustration, broken-down communication, and loss of human calm—are rationed severely, kept for dangerous situations and emergencies, and not used as training tools. In the hands of unskilled but aspiring lay trainers like me, using strong negative reinforcers and punishments is foolish as well as unnecessary, in no small part because we get it wrong and do more harm than good. Just watch a dog shut down in the face of a tense or negative human and hesitate to offer anything interesting with which to build great runs. Positive reinforcement, properly done, sets off a cascade of happy anticipation and inventive spontaneous offerings for testing how interesting the world can be. Positive reinforcement improperly done just reduces the stock of liver cookies, chew toys, and popular confidence in behavioral science.[11]

The devil, of course, is in the details. Some of these demons are:

- learning how to mark what one thinks one is marking (say, with a click of a little tin cricket or, less accurately, a word like "yes!")
- timing (i.e., knowing how long after a mark one has to deliver a reward and delivering it in that window; otherwise whatever just last happened is what's being rewarded)
- working and playing in such a way that dogs (and people) offer interesting things that can be positively reinforced (Luring can help show what's wanted in early training of something new, but luring does not reinforce and quickly gets in the way.)
- knowing what is really rewarding and interesting to one's partner
- correctly seeing what actually just happened
- understanding what one's partner is in fact paying attention to
- learning how to break complex patterns down into technical bits or behaviors that can be marked and rewarded
- knowing how to link behaviors into chains that add up to something useful
- knowing how to teach chains of behavior from the last part to the first (backchaining), by using bits of a behavior chain that a dog already understands as a reward for a bit that comes right before
- knowing how many repetitions are informative and effective and how many shut everybody down with stress and boredom
- knowing how to identify and reward approximations to the end-goal behavior (Trying to teach left and right turns? Start by marking and rewarding spontaneous glances in the desired direction, don't rush over steps, don't go so slow that your dog dies of old age or boredom.)

+ knowing when—and how—to stop if something is not working
+ knowing how and when to back up to something that is easier and already known by one's partner if something harder isn't working
+ keeping accurate count of the actual frequency of correct responses in a given task instead of imagining what they are, whether one is in an inflationary or deflationary mood
+ keeping learning situations fun and cognitively interesting for one's partner
+ evaluating whether or not the dog, the human, and the team actually do know how to do something in all of the circumstances in which they will need to perform the "behavior" (Chances are high that the relevant variable in a real agility trial was left out of training, and so what was the variable that caused a dog who knew her job, or so one thought, to blow an obstacle? or caused the human to become unreadable? Go back and train.)
+ avoiding tripping on one's dog or the equipment
+ perceiving the difference between a lure, a reward, and a tug rope crashing into one's unsuspecting dog's head because the handler can't throw accurately
+ not dropping food treats and clickers all over the practice field
+ figuring out how to reward oneself and one's partner when everything seems to be falling apart

Obviously, one would hope, it is essential for a human being to understand that one's partner is an adult (or puppy) member of another species, with his or her own exacting species interests and individual quirks, and not a furry child, a character in *Call of the Wild*, or an extension of one's intentions or fantasies. People fail this recognition test depressingly often. Training together is all extremely prosaic; that is why training with a member of another biological species is so interesting, hard, full of situated difference, and moving.[12] My field notes from classes and competitions repeatedly record agility people's remarks that they are learning about themselves and their companions, human and dog, in ways they had not experienced before. For a middle-aged or older woman, learning a new competitive sport played seriously with a member of another species provokes strong and unexpected emotions and preconception-breaking thinking about power, status, failure, skill, achievement, shame, risk, injury, control, companionship, body, memory, joy, and much else. Men who play the sport are almost always in the marked minority, and they feel it. It is hard to escape the subject-changing conjunction of gender, age, and species against a background of seemingly taken-for-granted (if not always empirically accurate) race, sexuality, and class.[13]

The human being actually has to know something about one's partner, oneself, and the world at the end of each training day that she or he did not know at the beginning. The devil is in the details, and so is the deity. "Dog is my co-pilot," says the masthead on the magazine *Bark*, a motto I repeated like a mantra in e-mail posts with my agility friends. In my experience, very few undertakings in life set such a high and worthwhile standard of knowledge and comportment. The dog, in turn, becomes shockingly good at learning to learn, fulfilling the highest obligation of a good scientist. The dogs earn their papers.

THE CONTACT ZONE
Blood on the Path

August 26, 2003
Dear friends,

Cayenne earned her Advanced Agility Dog title in the United States Dog Agility Association on Sunday, and so now we run in the Masters ring! She got a fast, clean, first-place run to earn her title; she made me very proud. We also ran fast and accurately in the qualifying round of the Steeplechase, placing eighth in a field of thirty-seven serious national champions and other masters and advanced twenty-two-inch class dogs. The top ten got to run in the final round.

We bombed the final round because I took her off the course when she failed to wait for my release word from the A-frame contact, my method these days for training this too consistent glitch. It was really HARD to leave the course before finishing the run, because we had a real chance to place and literally everybody at the meet was watching this featured event of the day. But we did leave, to the relief of my teacher and mentors. It was harder still to put Cayenne back in her crate with no word of encouragement, food treat, or even glance. My blood was a thick smear from the place we left the ring to her crate. However, our reward was three perfect A-frame contacts in our Snooker game immediately afterward. String cheese to Cayenne and self-knowledge to me! She glowed and towed me back to her crate, as if in the Iditarod, for heaps of treats and face-to-face smiles.

I learn such basic things about honesty in this game, things I should have learned as a child (or before tenure in academia) but never did, things about the actual consequences of fudging on fundamentals. I become less showy and more honest in this game than in any other part of my life. It's bracing, if not always fun. Meanwhile, my over-the-top love for Cayenne has required my body to build a bigger heart with more depths and tones for tenderness. Maybe that is what makes me need to be honest; maybe this kind of love makes one need to see what is really happening because the loved one deserves it. This is nothing like the unconditional love that people ascribe to their dogs! Odd and wonderful.

Celebrating in Healdsburg,
Donna

Let us return to the approximately two-foot-long yellow contact zone painted onto the up and down ends of teeter-totters, dog walks, and A-frames.[14] Then, let's forget dog walks and teeter-totters, because Cayenne and I found their rigors intuitively obvious; the goddess alone knows why. However, at least one murder mystery I know features the A-frame as the instrument of death.[15] I understand that plot very well; Cayenne and I came close to killing each other in this contact zone. The problem was simple: we did not understand each other. We were not communicating; we did not yet *have* a contact zone entangling each other. The result was that she regularly leapt over the down contact, not touching the yellow area with so much as a toepad before she raced to the next part of the course, much less holding the lovely two-rear-feet on the zone, two-front-feet on the ground until I gave the agreed-on release words (*all right*) for her to go on to the next obstacle in the run. I could not figure out what she did not understand; she could not figure out what my ambiguous and ever-changing cues and criteria of performance meant. Faced with my incoherence, she leapt gracefully over the charged area as if it were electrified. It was; it repelled us both. Then, we rejoined each other in a coherent team, but our qualifying run was in the trash can. We performed our contacts correctly in practice, but we failed miserably at trials. Furthermore, we were far from alone in this common dilemma for dogs and people training together in agility. That paint strip is where Cayenne and I learned our hardest lessons about power, knowledge, and the meaningful material details of entanglements.

Indeed, I remembered tardily, seven years before Cayenne was born I already knew that about contact zones from colonial and postcolonial studies in my political and academic life. In *Imperial Eyes*, Mary Pratt coined the term *contact zone*, which she adapted "from its use in linguistics, where the term 'contact language' refers to improvised languages that develop among speakers of different native languages who need to communicate with each other consistently. . . . I aim to foreground the interactive, improvisational dimensions of colonial encounters so easily ignored or suppressed by diffusionist accounts of conquest and domination. A 'contact' perspective emphasizes how subjects are constituted in and by their relations to each other. . . . It treats the relations . . . in terms of co-presence, interaction, interlocking understandings and practices, often within radically asymmetrical relations of power."[16] I find something eerily apt in Pratt's discussion for dog–human doings at the bottom of the A-frame. Cayenne and I definitely have different native languages, and much as I reject overdoing the analogy of colonization to domestication, I know very well how much control of Cayenne's life and death I hold in my inept hands.

My colleague Jim Clifford enriched my understanding of contact zones through his nuanced readings of articulations and entanglements across borders and among cultures. He eloquently demonstrated how "the new paradigms begin with historical contact, with entanglement at intersecting regional, national, and transnational levels. Contact approaches presuppose not sociocultural wholes subsequently brought into relationship, but rather systems already constituted relationally, entering new relations through historical processes of displacement."[17] I merely add naturalcultural and multispecies matters to Clifford's open net bag.

I learned much of what I know about contact zones from science fiction, in which aliens meet up in bars off-planet and redo one another molecule by molecule. The most interesting encounters happen when Star Trek's universal translator is on the blink, and communication takes unexpected, prosaic turns. My feminist sf reading prepared me to think about dog–human communication dilemmas and (polymorphously perverse) joys more flexibly than the more hard-boiled imperialist fantasies found in sf. I remember especially Naomi Mitchison's *Memoirs of a Space-woman*, in which the human communications officer on space explorations had to figure out how to make "noninterfering" contact with quite an array of sentient critters; several curious progeny resulted. Suzette Haden Elgin's pan-species linguist sf, starting with *Native Tongue*, also prepared me for training with dogs. There was no universal translator for Elgin, only the hard work of species' crafting workable languages. And if shape-shifting skill in the contact zone is the goal, no one should forget Samuel R. Delany's *Babel 17*, in which intriguing data-flow interruptions seem the order of the day.[18]

Even more tardily in my agility training dilemmas, I remembered that contact zones called ecotones, with their edge effects, are where assemblages of biological species form outside their comfort zones. These interdigitating edges are the richest places to look for ecological, evolutionary, and historical diversity. I live in north-central coastal California where, on the large geological scale of things, the great ancient northern and southern species assemblages intermix, producing extraordinary complexity. Our house is along a creek in a steep valley, where walking up from the creek on either northern- or southern-facing hillsides puts one dramatically into changing ecologically mixed-species assemblages. Naturalcultural histories are written on the land, such that the former plum orchards, sheep pastures, and logging patterns vie with geological soil types and humidity changes to shape today's human and nonhuman inhabitants of the land.[19]

Furthermore, as Juanita Sundberg analyzes for the cultural politics of conservation encounters in the Maya Biosphere Preserve, conservation projects have become important zones of encounter and contact shaped by distant and near actors.[20] Such contact zones are full of the complexities of different kinds of unequal power that do not always go in expected directions. In her beautiful book *Friction*, anthropologist Anna Tsing explores the people and organisms enmeshed in conservation and justice struggles in Indonesia in recent decades. Her chapter on "weediness" is a moving, incisive analysis of the wealth and species diversity of nature-cultures shaped by swidden agriculture into so-called secondary forests, which are being replaced by legal and illegal logging and industrial-scale monocropping in a violent reshaping of landscapes and ways of life. She lovingly documents the threatened collecting and naming practices of her elder friend and informant Uma Adang. The contact zones of species assemblages, both human and nonhuman, are the core reality in her ethnography. As Tsing puts it in an essay that tracks mushrooms in order to form a sense of the webs of world history, "Species interdependence is a well known fact—except when it comes to humans. Human exceptionalism blinds us." Riveted on stories either praising or damning human control of nature, people so blinkered assume that human nature, no matter how culturally various in detail, is essentially—often stated as "biologically"—constant, whereas human beings reshape others, from molecule to ecosystem. Rethinking "domestication" that closely knots human beings with other organisms, including plants, animals, and microbes, Tsing asks, "What if we imagined a human nature that shifted historically together with varied webs of interspecies dependence?" Tsing calls her webs of interdependence "unruly edges." She continues, "*Human nature is an interspecies relationship.*"[21] With Tsing's approval, I would add that the same is true of dogs, and it is the human–dog entanglement that rules my thinking about contact zones and fertile unruly edges in this chapter.

In a sibling spirit, anthropologist Eduardo Kohn explores multispecies contact zones in Ecuador's Upper Amazon region. Doing ethnography among the Quechua-speaking Runa and the various animals with whom they craft their lives, Kohn tracks naturalcultural, political, ecological, and semiotic entanglements in species assemblages in which dogs are central actors. He writes, "Amazonian personhood, very much the product of interaction with nonhuman semiotic selves, is also the product of a certain kind of colonial subjection.... This essay looks particularly to certain techniques of shamanistic metamorphosis (itself a product of interacting, and in the process blurring, with all kinds of nonhuman selves) and how this changes the terms of subjection (bodies are very different kinds of entities in this part of the world) and delineates certain spaces of political possibility."[22] Cayenne and I have no access to shamanistic metamorphoses, but reworking form to make a kind of one out of two is the sort of metaplasmic rearrangement we sought.

Thinking about metamorphosis and suffering in a state of arrested development with Cayenne in the yellow-paint swatch of the A-frame, I comforted myself with the reassurance that most of the transformative things in life happen in contact zones. And so I turned for insight to the phenomena of reciprocal induction studied in developmental biology. As a graduate student in Yale's Biology Department in the 1960s, I studied morphogenetic interactions through which cells and tissues of a developing embryo reciprocally shape each other through cascades of chemical–tactile communications. The techniques to track these complex interactions and the imagination to build better theoretical concepts have become very powerful over the last twenty years. Scott Gilbert's several editions of *Developmental Biology*, starting in 1985, are a wonderful site to track a growing grasp of the centrality of reciprocal induction, through which organisms are structured by the mutual coshaping of the fates of cells.[23] The point is that contact zones are where the action is, and current interactions change interactions to follow. Probabilities alter; topologies morph; development is canalized by the fruits of reciprocal induction.[24] Contact zones change the subject—all the subjects—in surprising ways.

Interactions among taxonomically distinct organisms, in which structures in one organism do not develop normally without properly timed interactions with other associated organisms, are at the heart of a recent theoretical and experimental synthesis in biology called ecological developmental biology, in which Gilbert has been a key player.[25] For example, Margaret McFall-Ngai has shown that the sacs housing luminescent *Vibrio* bacteria on the adult squid *Euprymna scolopes* do not develop unless juvenile squid acquire an infection from the bacteria, resulting in a cascade of developmental events producing the final receptacles for the symbionts.[26] Similarly, human gut tissue cannot develop normally without colonization by its bacterial flora. Earth's beings are prehensile, opportunistic, ready to yoke unlikely partners into something new, something symbiogenetic. Co-constitutive companion species and coevolution are the rule, not the exception. Ecological and evolutionary developmental biology are fields that could form a rich contact zone with feminist philosophers, theoretical physicists, and science studies scholars Karen Barad, with her framework of agential realism and intra-action, and Astrid Schrader, with her approach to intra- and interspecies ontologies.[27]

Perhaps my problems in the contact zones of agility have neurotically induced too large a deviation into other kinds of unruly edges to reassure me that something good comes from repeated failures to communicate across asymmetrical difference. Nonetheless, all the elements for retraining Cayenne's and my contact zones are now assembled.

First, let us consider the question of relations of authority in the reciprocal inductions of training. Agility is a human-designed sport; it is not spontaneous play, although this chapter will return to play soon. I think I have good reasons for judging that Cayenne loves to do agility; she plants her bum in front of the gate to the practice yard with fierce intent until I let her in to work patterns with me. On the mornings when we are driving to a trial, she tracks the gear and stays by the car with command in her eye. It's not just the pleasure of an excursion or access to a play space. We do nothing else in the agility yard but work on the obstacle patterns; that is the yard she wants access to. Spectators comment on the joy Cayenne's runs make them feel because they feel her whole self thrown into the skilled inventiveness of her course. This dog is easily annoyed by food rewards, for example, when given during her intense sit–stay at the start line before the release word to begin the run, when what she wants is to fly over the course. The run is her chief positive reinforcement. She is a working dog with great focus; her whole mind–body changes when she gains access to her scene of work. However, I would be a liar to claim that agility is a utopia of equality and spontaneous nature. The rules are arbitrary for both species; that is what a sport is; namely, a rule-bound, skilled, comparatively evaluated performance. The dog and the human are ruled by standards that they must submit to but that are not of their own choosing. The courses are designed by human beings; people fill out the entry forms and enter classes. The human decides for the dog what the acceptable criteria of performance will be.

But there is a hitch: The human must respond to the authority of the dog's actual performance. The dog has already responded to the human's incoherence. The real dog—not the fantasy projection of self— is mundanely present; the invitation to response has been tendered. Fixed by the specter of yellow paint, the human must finally learn to ask a fundamental ontological question, one that puts human and dog together in what philosophers in the Heideggerian tradition called "the open": Who are you, and so who are we? Here we are, and so what are we to become?[28]

Early casualties of taking this question seriously became some of my favorite stories about freedom and nature. These were stories I wanted Cayenne and me to inhabit for life but turned out to produce painful incoherence in our intra-actions, especially for her. Criteria of performance

SEE? RIGHT HERE!..."THE DOG AND HANDLER FORM A TEAM." A TEAM!!!

Cartoon by James Liddle from *Agility Trials and Tribulations.* Reprinted with permission of the publisher, Howln Moon Press.

on an A-frame are not natural to either dogs or people but are achievements dependent on invented as well as inherited naturalcultural possibilities. I could think that playing agility just makes space for a dog's natural
abilities when she sails over jumps (that turned out not to be precisely
true either), but fixing mistakes on the A-frame forced me to confront the
pedagogical apparatuses of training, including their relations of freedom
and authority. Some radical animal people are critical of any human training "of" another critter. (I insist "with" is possible.) What I see as polite
manners and beautiful skill acquired by the dogs I know best, they regard
as strong evidence of excessive human control and a sign of the degradation of domestic animals. Wolves, say the critics of trained animals, are
more noble (natural) than dogs precisely because they are more indifferent to the doings of people; to bring animals into close interaction with
human beings infringes their freedom. From this point of view, training is
antinatural domination made palatable by liver cookies.

Behaviorists are notoriously cavalier about what constitutes natural
(biologically meaningful) behavior in an organism (human or not); they
leave that preserve to the ethologists and their descendants. For behaviorists, if the probability of an action can be changed, no matter how
meaningless the bit of action may be to the organism or anybody else,
then that action is fodder for the technologies of operant conditioning.
Partly because of this agnosticism deep in the history of behaviorism
about both functionality (related to adaptation and so evolutionary theory) and meaning to the animal (tied to the question of interiority),
Karen Pryor and other trainers of so-called wild animals in captivity, such
as dolphins and tigers, have been accused either of ruining them by introducing nonnaturalistic behaviors or of making critters into robots by
treating them as stimulus-response machines. Pryor and other positive
trainers answer that their work improves the lives of captive animals and
should become part of normal management and environmental enrichment.[29] Engaging in training (education) is interesting for animals, just as
it is for people, whether or not a just-so story about contributing to reproductive fitness can be made to fit the curriculum.

I rather like the idea that training with an animal, whether the critter is named wild or domestic, can be part of disengaging from the semiotics and technologies of compulsory reproductive biopolitics. That's a

project I like to see in human schools too. Functionless knowing can come very close to the grace of play and a poiesis of love. I would, of course, be aghast at the idea that behaviorism has a corner on potentially playful pedagogical approaches for any critters, including people. From this point of view, an irony infusing the life-interest-enhancing and management work of behaviorist trainers in zoos and other captive animal facilities is that one of the few remaining powerful justifications offered for these places is that they are essential to keep the individuals and species in their care from extinction in their vanishing habitats. Animals in zoos, for all their dabbling in the rewards of behaviorism, have never been more enmeshed in compulsory reproductive biopolitics than they are in the twenty-first century!

I must admit, however, that the ironies of queer politics are not the reason I train seriously with Cayenne for daily life and for sport. Or maybe queer politics, if not all the ironies, are at the heart of agility training: The coming into being of something unexpected, something new and free, something outside the rules of function and calculation, something not ruled by the logic of the reproduction of the same, *is* what training with each other is about.[30] That, I believe, is one of the meanings of *natural* that the trained people and dogs I know practice. Training requires calculation, method, discipline, science, but training is for opening up what is not known to be possible, but might be, for all the intra-acting partners. Training is, or can be, about differences not tamed by taxonomy.

Throughout my academic life, whether as a biologist or a scholar in the humanities and social sciences, I had looked down on behaviorism as a vapid science at best, hardly real biology at all, and an ideological, determinist discourse at heart. All of a sudden, Cayenne and I needed what skilled behaviorists could teach us. I became subject to a knowledge practice I had despised. I had to understand that behaviorism is not my caricature of a mechanistic pseudoscience fueled by niche-marketed food treats, but a flawed, historically situated, and fruitful approach to material–semiotic questions in the fleshly world. This science has addressed my questions, and I think also Cayenne's. I needed not only behaviorism but also ethology and the more recent cognitive sciences. I had to comprehend that comparative cognitive ethologists do not operate with a cartoon of animal machinic nonminds whipped into computational shape with math and computers.

Preoccupied with the baleful effects that the *denial* of human control and power in training relationships has on dogs, I have understressed so far another aspect of the human obligation to respond to the authority of the dog's actual performance. A skilled human competitor in agility, not to mention a decent life companion, must learn to recognize when *trust* is what the human owes the dog. Dogs generally recognize very well when the human being has earned trust; the human beings I know, starting with myself, are less good at reciprocal trust. I lose Cayenne and me many qualifying scores because, in the sport's idiom, I "overhandle" her performance. For example, because I am not confident, I do not see that *she* has mastered the difficult correct entries into weave poles at speed and that I do not need to rush to do a front cross, thereby, as often as not, blocking her path. Indeed, when I trust Cayenne I do not ever need to rush, no matter the pattern or obstacle. I do not need to be as fast as she is (good thing!); I merely need to be as honest. In one difficult run in an Excellent Standard class at an AKC trial in which most high-level competitors ahead of us were missing their weave pole entry, I failed my obligation to recognize and respond to Cayenne's earned authority, and I imposed my bent-over, anxious, controlling self in her path about two feet from the first pole. Laughing and chiding me afterward, my friends described what she did to get me out of the way and save our qualifying score. According to our observers, Cayenne saw me coming, clipped her smoothly curving stride slightly, and dodged around me, all but shouting, "Get out of my way!" while she slipped magically between poles one and two and wove very fast without break in rhythm through the twelve poles. In my mind's ear, I heard my agility teacher Gail Frazier telling me over and over, "Trust your dog!"

Honesty and response to the dog's authority take many forms. True, I do not need to be as fast as she is, but I do need to stay in as good physical condition as I can, practice patterning my body at speed (thus, all those choreographed aerobics classes at the gym!), cross train (I do a lot more balanced exercise of all kinds than I would if I did not owe bodily coherence to Cayenne), be willing to learn to make moves on the field that give her better information even if those moves are hard for me to master, and treat her like a full adult by not bending over and hovering at difficult parts of a course. I hear my astute instructor Lauri Plummer in last week's class tell me that once again I was bent over playing nursemaid in a section of the course that sapped my confidence but not Cayenne's. "Stand up straight!" is a mantra that agility teachers repeat endlessly to their recalcitrant human students. I believe this chant is necessary because we do not actually recognize our dogs' authority but, in spite of our best intentions, treat them too often like athletic toddlers in fur coats. It is hard not to do that when dog culture in America, even in agility, relentlessly refers to human partners as "mom" or "dad." "Handler" is only a little better; that word makes me think that human agility partners imagine they have their controlling hands on the helm of nature in the body of our dogs. Humans in agility are not handlers (nor are they guardians); they are members of a cross-species team of skilled adults. With an ear to the tones of asymmetrical but often directionally surprising authority in contact zones, I like "partner" much better.

The mixed practices of training require savvy travels in sciences and stories about how animals actually feel and think as well as behave.

Cartoon by James Liddle from *Agility Trials and Tribulations.* Reprinted with permission of the publisher, HowIn Moon Press.

Trainers can't forbid themselves the judgment that they can communicate meaningfully with their partners. The philosophic and literary conceit that all we have is representations and no access to what animals think and feel is wrong. Human beings do, or can, know more than we used to know, and the right to gauge that knowledge is rooted in historical, flawed, generative cross-species practices. Of course, we are not the "other" and so do not know in that fantastic way (body snatching? ventriloquism? channeling?). In addition, through patient practices in biology, psychology, and the human sciences, we have learned that we are not the "self" or "transparently present to the self" either, and so we should expect no transcendent knowledge from that source. Disarmed of the fantasy of climbing into heads, one's own or others', to get the full story from the inside, we can make some multispecies semiotic progress. To claim not to be able to communicate with and to know one another and other critters, however imperfectly, is a denial of mortal entanglements (the open) for which we are responsible and in which we respond. Technique, calculation, method—all are indispensable and exacting. But they are not

Cayenne and I at an agility trial in 2006. Copyright Richard Todd Photographer. Published with permission.

response, which is irreducible to calculation. Response is comprehending that subject-making connection is real. Response is face-to-face in the contact zone of an entangled relationship. Response is in the open. Companion species know this.

So, I learned to be at ease with the artificiality, the naturalcultural art, of training for a sport with a dog. But surely, I imagined, she could be free off the course, free to roam the woods and visit the off-leash parks. I had taught her an obligatory recall that authorized that freedom, and I was as nasty as any novice trainer feeling her oats about people who have no idea how to teach a good recall and whose clueless dogs give a bad name to freedom and an unfair fright to fleeing deer.[31] I watched how my fellow agility competitor and friend Pam Richards trained with Cayenne's littermate brother, Cappuccino, and I was secretly critical of how relentlessly she worked with Capp to fix his attention on her and hers on him in the activities of daily life. I knew Capp was aglow with pleasure in his doings, but I thought Cayenne had the greater animal happiness.[32] I knew Pam and Capp were achieving things in agility out of our reach, and I was proud of them. Then, Pam took pity on us. Taking the risk to judge that I actually wanted to become less incoherent with Cayenne, she offered to show me in detail what we did not know. I became subject to Pam so that Cayenne could become free and lucid in ways not admitted by my existing stock of freedom stories.[33]

Pam is nothing if not thorough. She backed us up, forbidding me to put Cayenne on the A-frame in competition until she and I knew our jobs. She showed me that I had not "proofed" the obstacle performance in about a dozen fundamental ways. And so I set about actually teaching what the release word meant instead of fantasizing that Cayenne was a native English speaker. I started thinking practically about adding distractions to make the "two-on, two-off" performance that I had chosen for us more certain in circumstances approximating the intense world of trials. I learned to send her over the A-frame to the bottom and the magic two-on, two-off paw position, no matter where I was, no matter if I was moving or still, no matter if toys and food were flying through the air and complicitous friends of various species were jumping up and down crazily. Pam watched us and then sent us back again with the mordant comment that Cayenne did not yet know her job because I had not yet taught it.

Finally, she said I was sufficiently coherent and Cayenne sufficiently knowledgeable that we could do the A-frame in competition—if I held the same standard of performance there that had become normal in training. Consequences, that sledge hammer of behaviorism, were the point. If, by letting Cayenne go on to the next obstacle, I rewarded a legally adequate performance in the contact zone, but one that did not match our hard-won criterion, I was condemning her and me to a lifetime of frustration and loss of confidence in each other. If Cayenne did not hold two-on, two-off and wait for release, I was to walk her calmly off the course without comment or glance and zip her into her crate without reward and stroll away. If I did not do that, I had less respect for Cayenne than for my fantasies.

For more than two years, we had not advanced out of novice competition levels because of the A-frame contact zone. Subject to Pam's narratives of freedom and authority, after Cayenne and I had retrained each other more honestly I walked her off the course at a real trial once and was given a year of perfect contacts after that. My friends cheered us over the finish line in our last novice event as if we had won the World Cup. "All" we had done was achieve a little coherence. The occasional breakdowns in that contact zone that still happen are quickly fixed, and Cayenne sails through this performance with a gleam in her eye and pleasure written all over her coursing body. Among other competitors, she is known for great contacts. A random reinforcement schedule doesn't hurt, but Cayenne's love of the game—love of work—is our real salvation.

But what about Cayenne's independent animal happiness off the course compared with the bond of attention between Pam and Capp? Here, I think Pam and I have changed each other's narratives and practices of freedom and joy. I had to face the need for many more "I pay attention to you; you pay attention to me" games to fill Cayenne's and my not-so-leisure hours. I had to deal with my sense of paradise lost when Cayenne became steadily and vastly more interested in me than in other dogs.[34] The price of the intensifying bond between us was, well, a bond. I still notice this; it still feels like a loss as well as an achievement of large spiritual and physical joy for both Cayenne and me. Ours is not an innocent, unconditional love; the love that ties us is a naturalcultural practice that has redone us molecule by molecule. Reciprocal induction is the name of the game.

Pam, for her part, tells me she admires the sheer fun in Cayenne's and my doings. She knows that can exact a price on performance criteria. The gods regularly laugh when Pam and I take Cayenne and Cappuccino out to a grassy field and urge them to play with each other and ignore us. Pam's partner, Janet, will even leave a riveting women's basketball game on TV to revel in the unmatchable joy when Cayenne and Cappuccino play together. All too frequently, Cayenne can't get Capp to play; he has eyes only for Pam's throwing arm and the ball she has hidden away. But when they do play, when Cayenne solicits her littermate long and hard enough, with all the metacommunicative skill at her command, they increase the stock of beauty in the world. Then, three human women and two dogs are in the open.

Thinking about how animals and human beings who train together become "available to events," Vinciane Despret suggests that "the whole matter is a matter of faith, of trust, and this is the way we should construe the role of expectations, the role of authority, the role of events that authorize and make things become."[35] She describes what has been found in studies of skilled human riders and educated horses. The French ethologist Jean-Claude Barrey's detailed analysis of "unintentional movements" in skilled riding show that homologous muscles fire and contract in both horse and human at precisely the same time. The term for this phenomenon is *isopraxis.* Horses and riders are attuned to each other. "Talented riders behave and move like horses. . . . Human bodies have been transformed by and into a horse's body. Who influences and who is influenced, in this story, are questions that can no longer receive a clear answer. Both, human and horse, are cause and effect of each other's movements. Both induce and are induced, affect and are affected. Both embody each other's mind."[36] Reciprocal induction; intra-action; companion species.[37] A good run in agility has very similar properties. Mimetic matching of muscle groups is not usually the point, although I am sure it occurs in some agility patterns, because the dog and the human are coperforming a course spatially apart from each other in differently choreographed and emergent patternings. The nonmimetic attunement of each to each resonates with the molecular scores of mind and flesh and makes someone out of them both who was not there before. Training in the contact zone, indeed.

Daemon Tear

April 2, 2006

Dear Agility Friends,

In practice a couple of weeks ago with Rob near Watsonville, Cayenne and I had an interesting experience that I suspect you can relate to. The class is at night, 8–9:30, and has a dozen teams in it; in short, the class is big and sometimes a bit chaotic, and many of us are bone tired by then anyway. Many nights, my concentration is iffy, but that night both Cayenne and I were glued to each other's souls and did not make a mistake over several runs with difficult sequences and discriminations. Then at 9:25, we had our last run, one with only ten obstacles, albeit with a couple of challenging discriminations, one of the themes of the night. None of these had given us any trouble. We did fine until the last discrimination in the last run. In a nanosecond, we came apart, literally, and each went a different way. We each stopped instantly, no longer on the same course, and looked at each other with a blatantly confused look on her dog and my human face, eyes questioning, each body–mind bereft of its partner. I swear I heard a sound like Velcro ripping when we came apart. We were no longer "whole." I turned on time, in the right spot, and had all my parts technically correct; Cayenne turned well and correctly too. Then, we just lost each other. Period. It was not a "technical" mistake for either of us, I swear. Rob saw nothing wrong and did not know what happened. I swear Cayenne and I both heard the Velcro ripping when our cross-species conjoined mind–body, which we are when we run well, came apart. I've experienced losing her mentally before, of course, as she has me. Almost always, the actual literal error of a course—usually a tiny but fatal glitch in timing—is a symptom of such a loss of each other. But this was different—much more intense—maybe because we were both tired and we had been unconsciously but strongly linked all night. She looked abandoned, and I felt abandoned. I experienced the confused look we gave each other to be full of loss and yearning, and I truly think that was what her expressive canine being was screaming too. I think the communication between us was as unambiguous as a play bow would be in its context. Just as a play bow binds responding partners to take the risk of playing, somehow we unbound each other from the game. Something severed us. All of this happened in much less than a second.

Have you read the Philip Pullman series, *Golden Compass, Subtle Knife,* and *Amber Spyglass,* in which a human–daemon link is a main part of the fictional world? The daemon is an animal familiar essential to the human, and vice versa, and the link is so strong and necessary to being whole that its deliberate severing is the violent crime driving the plot. At one point, the narrator says, "Will, too, felt the pain where his daemon had been, a scalded place of acute tenderness that each breath tore at with cold hooks" (*Amber Spyglass,* 384). Earlier, the narrator described the crime of severing daemon and human: "While there is a connection, of course, the link remains. Then the blade is brought down between them, severing the link at once. They are then separate entities" (*Golden Compass,* 273).[38]

Surely, I am dramatizing the rip between Cayenne and me over a little agility discrimination—tire or jump?—late on a rainy Wednesday night in March in a central California horse arena. Yet, this tiny tear in the fabric of being told me something precious about the weave of the whole-selves commitment that can bind companion species in a game of conjoined living, in which each is more than one but less than two. We trained hard—for years, actually—to develop this kind of link; but both its coming into being and its coming apart are only made possible by that discipline, not made by it.

Does all that make any sense?

Coming apart in Sonoma County,
Donna

PLAYING WITH STRANGERS

Agility is a sport and a kind of game that is built on the tie of cross-species work and play. I have said a lot about work so far but too little about play. It is rare to meet a puppy who does not know how to play; such a youngster would be seriously disturbed. Most, but not all, adult dogs know very well how to play too, and they choose doggish or other play partners selectively throughout their lives if they have the opportunity. Agility people know that they need to learn to play with their dogs. Most want to play with their canine partners if for no other reason than to take advantage of the tremendous tool that play is in positive-training practices. Play builds powerful affectional and cognitive bonds between partners, and permission to play is a hugely valuable reward for correctly following cues for both dogs and people. Most agility people want to cavort with their dogs for the sheer joy of it too. Nonetheless, astonishingly, a great many agility people have no idea how to play with a dog; they require remedial instruction, beginning with learning how to respond to real-life dogs rather than fantasy children in fur coats or humanoid partners in doubles tennis.[39] Better at understanding what someone is actually doing than people are, dogs can be pretty good teachers in this regard. But discouraged dogs who have given up on their people's ability to learn to play with them politely and creatively are not rare. People have to learn how to pay attention and to communicate meaningfully, or they are shut out of the new worlds that play proposes. Not so oddly, without the skills of play, adults of both the canine and hominid persuasion are developmentally arrested, deprived of key practices of ontological and semiotic invention. In the language of developmental biology, they become very bad at reciprocal induction. Their contact zones degenerate into impoverishing border wars.

I suggest people must learn to meet dogs as strangers first in order to unlearn the crazy assumptions and stories we all inherit about who dogs are. Respect for dogs demands at least that much. So, how do strangers learn to play with each other? First, a story.

"Safi taught Wister to jaw wrestle, like a dog, and she even convinced him to carry a stick around in his mouth, although he never seemed to have a clue what to do with it. Wister enticed Safi into high-speed chases, and they'd disappear over the hills together, looking for all the world like a wolf hunting her prey. Occasionally, apparently accidentally, he knocked her with a hoof, and she would cry out in pain. Whenever this occurred, Wister would become completely immobile, allowing Safi to leap up and whack him several times on the snout with her head. This seemed to be Safi's way of saying, 'You hurt me!' and Wister's way of saying, 'I didn't mean it.' Then they would resume playing. After they tired of racing, Safi often rolled over on her back under Wister, exposing her vulnerable belly to his lethal hooves in an astonishing display of trust. He nuzzled her tummy and used his enormous incisors to nibble her favorite scratching spot, just above the base of her tail, which made Safi close her eyes in bliss."[40]

Safi was bioanthropologist Barbara Smuts's eighty-pound German shepherd–Belgian sheepdog mix, and Wister was a neighbor's donkey. Meeting in a remote part of Wyoming, dog and donkey lived near each other for five months. Wister was no fool; he knew his ancestors were lunch for Safi's ancestors. Around other dogs, Wister took precautions, braying loudly and kicking threateningly. He certainly did not invite them into predator chases for fun. When he first saw Safi, he charged her and kicked. But, Smuts relates, Safi had a long history of befriending critters from cats and ferrets to squirrels, and she set to work on Wister, her first large herbivore buddy, soliciting and inviting, skillfully and repeatedly, until he took the great leap to risk an off-category friendship.

Of course, the kind of predators dogs are know how to read in detail the kind of prey donkeys are and vice versa. Evolutionary history makes that plain. The panorama of pastoral economies in human–animal histories also testifies to this fact; dogs have herded sheep and other chlorophyll-chomping species in a wide range of naturalcultural ecologies.[41] The whole process would not work if sheep did not know how to understand dogs as well as dogs know how to interpret them. Herbivores and canines have also learned to work together in other ways that depend not on predator–prey semiotics but on the sharable meanings and practices of social bonding and territory identification. Livestock guardian dogs and their herbivorous charges and companions testify to this skill. But the fully adult Safi and Wister played together by raiding their predator–prey repertoire, disaggregating it, recombining it, changing the order of action patterns, adopting each other's behavioral bits, and generally making things happen that did not fit anybody's idea of function, practice for past or future lives, or work. Dog and donkey weren't precisely strangers at the start, but they were hardly conspecific littermates or cross-species partners given to inhabiting one member's fantasy of unconditional love. Dog and donkey had to craft atypical ways to interpret each other's specific fluencies and to reinvent their own repertoires through affective semiotic intra-action.

I contorted sentences into knots in the last few paragraphs to avoid using the word *language* for what is happening in play. Too much weight has been loaded on to questions and idioms of language in considering the doings of the great variety of animals and people alike.[42] Especially for thinking about world making and intelligent intra-action among beings like dogs and donkeys, to ask if their cognitive, communicative skills do or do not qualify for the imprimatur of language is to fall into a dangerous trap. People always end up better at language than animals, no matter how latitudinarian the framework for thinking about the matter. The history of philosophy and of science is crisscrossed with lines drawn between Human and Animal on the basis of what counts as language. Also, the history of training in agility is littered with the dire consequences of people thinking dogs mean the same thing by words and their combinations that human beings do.

I am not uninterested in the lively theoretical work and empirical research going on these days in regard to questions about language touching human and nonhuman animals. There is no doubt that many animals across a wide range of species, including rodents, primates, canids, and birds, do things few scientists expected them to be able to do (or had figured out *how* to recognize, partly because hardly anyone expected anything interesting to show up, at least not in testable, data-rich ways).[43] These recently documented talents fuel conversations and arguments in several sciences as well as popular culture about what counts as language. When even Noam Chomsky, long famous for his touching faith that the hard science of linguistics proves that people do it and animals don't, becomes the object of his still pure colleagues' ire for selling out, or at least reconsidering the matter from another point of view and in the company of odd new colleagues, we know something big is happening in evolutionary comparative cognitive sciences, and language is on the menu. In particular, MIT's Chomsky and his Harvard colleagues, Marc Hauser and W. Tecumseh Fitch, said in print, "However, we argue that the available data suggest a much stronger continuity between animals and humans with respect to speech than previously believed. We argue that the continuity hypothesis thus deserves the status of a null hypothesis, which must be rejected by comparative work before any claims of uniqueness can be validated. For now, this null hypothesis of no truly novel traits in the speech domain appears to stand."[44] That nicely turns the tables on what has to be proved!

Let us stay with the word *continuity* for a moment, because I think it misrepresents the strength and radicalism of Chomsky, Hauser, and Fitch's resetting of what counts as the null hypothesis. Because the odd singular words *human* and *animal* are so lamentably common in scientific and popular idioms and so rooted in Western philosophical premises and hierarchical chains of being, *continuity* easily implies that just one continuum is replacing one chasm of difference. Hauser and his colleagues, however, belong to a tribe of comparative cognitive scientists and neurobiologists who have thoroughly demolished that lame figure of difference. They disaggregate singulars into fields of rich difference, with many geometries of system and subsystem architecture and junctions and disjunctions of properties and capacities, whether at scales of different species or of brain organization in a particular critter. It is no longer possible scientifically to compare something like "consciousness" or "language" among human and nonhuman animals as if there were a singular axis of calibration.[45] Part of the radicalism of these powerful recent scientific comparative evolutionary interdisciplines is that they do not invalidate asking about consciousness and language. Rather, inquiry becomes inextricably rich and detailed in the flesh of complexity and nonlinear difference and its required semiotic figures. Encounters among human beings and other animals change in this web. Not least, people can stop looking for some single defining difference between them and everybody else and understand that they are in rich and largely uncharted, material–semiotic, flesh-to-flesh, and face-to-face connection with a host of significant others. That requires retraining in the contact zone.

Similar to the question of language is the wrangling over whether critters other than people have a "theory of mind," that is, know that other beings have the same or similar sorts of motives and ideas that oneself has. Stanley Coren argues that "dogs . . . do seem to understand that other creatures have their own points of view and mental processes."[46] Coren insists that this ability is highly advantageous for social species and for predator–prey associates, and its development is likely to be greatly favored by natural selection. He and others provide numerous descriptions and accounts in which it seems both appropriate to acknowledge this capacity in many other species, including dogs, to recognize different points of view and also intellectually anorexic, indicating extreme epistemological fasting and narrative regurgitation, to assume the opposite.

Nonetheless, exacting, comparative, experimental testing is, in my opinion, extremely important, with the null hypothesis in force that the lack of the capacity is generally what has to be shown to a high degree of statistical significance if folks are expected to believe their dogs have no "minds" and no ability to take account of the "minds" of others. Precisely specified similarities ought to be the position that has to be refuted, rather than the opposite. What might possibly be meant by "mind" and by "recognizing another's point of view," of course, is at least as much at stake for people these days as for pooches. No single axis of difference, and so no single postulate of continuity, does justice to the motley of communicating critters, including people and dogs. "Minds" are not all of the human sort, to say the least. Figuring out how to do the needed sorts of experimental work, in which heterogeneous material–semiotic entanglements are the norm, should be great fun and scientifically very creative.[47] That such acute work largely remains to be done gives a pretty good idea about how abstemious, if not frightened of otherness, researching and philosophizing humans in Western traditions have been.

Among beings who recognize one another, who respond to the presence of a significant other, something delicious is at stake. Or, as Barbara Smuts put it after decades of careful scientific field studies of baboons and chimps, cetaceans, and dogs, copresence "is something we taste rather than something we use. In mutuality, we sense that inside this other body, there is 'someone home,' someone so like ourselves that we can co-create a shared reality as equals."[48] In the contact zones I inhabit in agility, I am not so sure about "equals"; I dread the consequences for significant others of pretending not to exercise power and control that shape relationships despite any denials. But I am sure about the taste of copresence and the shared building of other worlds.

Still, the figures of language and mind do not take me to the kind of inventiveness Cayenne and I experience in our game. Play is the practice that makes us new, that makes us into something that is neither one nor two, that brings us into the open where purposes and functions are given a rest. Strangers in mindful hominid and canid flesh, we play with each other and become significant others to each other. The power of language is purported to be its potentially infinite inventiveness. True enough in a technical sense ("discrete infinity"); however, the inventive potency of play redoes beings in ways that should not be called language but that deserve their own names. Besides, it is not potentially *infinite* expressiveness that is interesting for play partners but, rather, unexpected and nonteleological inventions that can take mortal shape only within the finite and dissimilar naturalcultural repertoires of companion species. Another name for those sorts of inventions is joy. Ask Safi and Wister.

Gregory Bateson did not know that fine dog and donkey, but he did have a human daughter with whom he engaged in the risky practice of play. Play is not outside the asymmetries of power, and both Mary Catherine and Gregory felt that force field in their father–daughter contact zone in "Metalogue: About Games and Being Serious."[49] They learned to play in that force field, not in some Eden outside it. Their play was linguistic, but what they had to say tracks what Cayenne and I learned to do, even if Wister and Safi remain undisputed masters of the art. Here's how this metalogue starts (14):

> DAUGHTER: Daddy, are these conversations serious?
> FATHER: Certainly they are.
> D: They're not a sort of game that you play with me?
> F: God forbid . . . but they are a sort of game that we play together.
> D: Then they're *not* serious!

Then ensues their noninnocent playful investigation into what is play and what is serious and how they require each other for their reinvention of the world and for the grace of joy. Loosening the iron bit of logic, with all of its utterly functional ability to follow single tracks to their proper ends, is the first step. Father says hopefully, "I think that we get some ideas straight, and I think that the muddles help." He says, "If we both spoke logically all the time we would never get anywhere" (15). If you want to understand something new, you "have to break up all our ready-made ideas and shuffle the pieces" (16).

F and D are playing a game, but a game is not play. Games have rules. Agility has rules. Play breaks rules to make something else happen. Play needs rules but is not rule-defined. You can't play a game unless you inhabit this muddle. D ponders aloud, "I am wondering about our muddles. Do we have to keep the little pieces of our thought in some sort of order—to keep from going mad?" F agrees, then adds, "But I don't know *what* sort of order" (16). D complains that the rules are always changing when she plays with F. I know Cayenne and I have felt that way about each other. D: "The way you confuse everything—it's sort of cheating." F objects, "No, absolutely not" (17). D worries, "But is it a *game*, Daddy? Do you play *against* me?" Drawing on how a child and a parent play together with colored blocks, F aims for some sort of coherence: "No. I think of it as you and I playing against the building blocks" (17). Is this Safi and Wister's playing against the rules of their species heritages? Is it Cayenne's and my playing in the arbitrary swatch of yellow paint that is our contact zone? F elaborates, "The blocks themselves make a sort of rules. They will balance in certain positions, and they will not balance in other positions" (18). No glue allowed; that *is* cheating. Play is in the open, not in the glue pot.

Just when I thought I had it, F paraphrases D: "'What sort of order should we cling to so that when we get into a muddle, we do not go mad?'" F answers his paraphrase, "It seems to me that the 'rules' of the game is only another name for that sort of order." D thinks that she now has the answer, "Yes—and cheating is what gets us into muddles." No rest for the wicked is F's motto: "Except that the whole point of the game is that we do get into muddles, and we do come out on the other side" (19). Is that what the playful practice of making mistakes interesting in agility training helps us understand? Making mistakes is inevitable and not particularly illuminating; making mistakes interesting is what makes the world new. Cayenne and I have experienced that in rare and precious moments. We play with our mistakes; they give us that possibility. It all happens very fast. F owns up, "Yes, it is I who make the rules—after all, I do not want us to go mad." D is undeterred, "Is it *you* that makes the rules, Daddy? Is that fair?" F is unrepentant, "Yes, daughter, I change them constantly. Not all of them, but some of them." D: "I wish you'd tell me when you're going to change them!" F: "I wish I could [he doesn't really]. But it isn't like that . . . certainly it is not like chess or canasta. It's more like what kittens and puppies do. Perhaps. I don't know" (19–20).

D jumps at this: "Daddy, why do kittens and puppies play?" Comprehending that play is not *for* a purpose, F unapologetically, and I suspect triumphantly, brings this metalogue to a close: "I don't know—I don't know" (20). Or, as Ian Wedde said of Vincent, "He enriches my ignorance." And, as Wister said of Safi: "I'll give this dog a chance. Her constant bowing might mean I am not lunch. I'd better not be mistaken, and she had better see that I have accepted her invitation. Otherwise, she is one dead dog, and I am one savaged donkey."

So, we reach another point to which Bateson takes us: metacommunication, communication about communication, the sine qua non of play. Language cannot engineer this delicate matter; rather, language relies on this other semiotic process, on this gestural, never literal, always implicit, corporeal invitation to risk copresence, to risk another level of communication. Back to another metalogue. D: "Daddy, why cannot people just *say* 'I am not cross at you' and let it go at that?" F: "Ah, now we are getting to the real problem. The point is that messages we exchange in gestures are really not the same as any translations of these gestures into words."[50]

Bateson also studied other mammals, including monkeys and dolphins, for their play and their practices of metacommunication.[51] He was not looking for denotative messages, no matter how expressive; he was looking for semiotic signs that said other signs do not mean what they otherwise mean (as in a play gesture indicating that the following bit is *not* aggression). These are among the kinds of signs that make relationships possible, and "preverbal" mammalian communication for Bateson was mostly about "the rules and contingencies of relationship."[52] In studying play, he was looking for things like a ritual bow followed by "fighting" that is not fighting and is known not to be fighting by the participants (and by human observers who bother to learn something about the critters they are privileged to watch). Play can occur only among those willing to risk letting go of the literal.[53] That is a big risk, at least for adults like Cayenne and me; those wonderful, joy-enticing signals like play bows and feints usher us over the threshold into the world of meanings that do not mean what they seem to mean. That is not the linguist's "discrete infinity," nor is it the comparative neurobiologist's "continuity." Rather, the world of meanings loosed from their functions is the game of copresence in the contact zone. Not about reproducing the sacred image of the same, this game is nonmimetic and full of difference. Dogs are extremely good at this game; people can learn.

Biologist Marc Bekoff has spent countless hours studying the play of canids, including dogs. Granting that play might sometimes serve a functional purpose either at the time or later in life, Bekoff argues that that interpretation does not account for play or lead one even to recognize its occurrence. Instead, Bekoff and his colleague J. A. Byers offer a definition of play that encompasses "all motor activity performed postnatally that appears to be purposeless, in which motor patterns from other contexts may often be used in modified forms and altered temporal sequencing."[54] Like language, play rearranges elements into new sequences to make new meanings. But play also requires something not explicit in Bekoff and Byer's definition in the 1980s, namely, *joy* in the sheer doing.[55] I think that is what one means by "purposeless." If "desire" in the psychoanalytic sense is proper only to human language–constituted subjects, then sensuous "joy" is what play-constituted beings experience. Like copresence, joy is something we taste, not something we know denotatively or use instrumentally. Play makes an opening. Play proposes.

I want to stay with altered temporal sequencing for a moment. Functional patterns put a pretty tight constraint on the sequence of actions in time: first stalk; then run to outflank; then head, bunch, and cut out the selected prey; then lunge; then bite and kill; then dissect and tug. The sequences in a serious conspecific fight or in any other of the important action patterns for making a living are different but no less sequentially disciplined. Play is not making a living; it discloses living. Time opens up. Play, like Christian grace, can allow the last to become first, with joyful results. Ian Wedde's reflections on his walks with Vincent the ridgeback tell me something about the temporal open that I and, I think, Cayenne experience when we play together, whether choreographing the more structured forms of an agility run, with its dance of rule and invention in the kinesthetic matching of two swiftly moving bodies, or the looser play patterns we do with chase, wrestle, and tug. "I'm unsure about the therianthropism involved in pondering a dog's sense of time—what I know is a degree of reciprocity in our shared experience of it. For me it came to involve pace, space and focal length, as well as duration and memory. My sense of the present became more vivid; concurrently, Vincent's perceptual pace altered if he was required to share my speed. Our combined time contained my enhanced sense and his altered pace; we were both fixed in vivid temporal foregrounds."[56]

In Cayenne's and my experience of playing together, this play of strangers, both partners experience Wedde's kind of altered temporal sense. Inside that jointly altered but still unidentical sense, time in the sense of sequencing also opens up. Unexpected conjunctions and coordinations of creatively moving partners in play take hold of both and put them into an open that feels something like an eternal present or suspension of time, a high of "getting it" together in action, or what I am calling joy. No liver cookie can compete with that! Agility people often joke with one another about their "addiction" to playing agility with their dogs. How can they possibly justify the thousands of hours, thousands of dollars, constant experiences of failure, public exposure of one's foolishness, and repeated injuries? And what of their *dogs'* addiction? How can their dogs possibly be so intensely ready *all the time* to hear their human utter the release word at the start line that frees them to fly in coordinated flow with this two-legged sf alien across a field of unknown obstacles? There is, after all, a lot that is not fun about the discipline of training for people or for dogs, not to mention the rigors of travel and the erosions of confined boredom while waiting for one's runs at an event. Yet, the dogs and the people seem to egg each other on to the next run, the next experience of what play proposes.

Besides, joy is not the same thing as fun. I don't think very many people and dogs would keep doing agility just for the fun; fun together is both unreliable in agility and more easily had elsewhere. I ask how Cayenne can possibly know the difference between a good run and a mediocre one, such that her entire bodily being glows as if in the phosphorescent ocean after we have flown well together? She prances; she shines from inside out; by contagion, she *causes* joy all around her. So do other dogs, other teams, when they flame into being in a "good run." Cayenne is pleased enough with a mediocre run. She has a good time; after all, she still gets string cheese and lots of affirming attention. Mediocre runs or not, I have a good time too. I've made valued human friends in agility; I get to admire a great motley of dogs; and the days are uncluttered and pleasant. But Cayenne and I both know the difference when we have tasted the open. We both know the tear in the fabric of our joined becoming when we rip apart into merely functional time and separate movement after the joy of inventive isopraxis. The taste of "becoming with" in play lures its apprentice stoics of both species back into the open of a vivid sensory present. That's why we do it. That's the answer to my question, Who are you, and so who are we?

Good players (watch any adept dog or reread Mary Catherine and Gregory Bateson in their metalogue) have a sizable repertoire for inviting and sustaining their partners' interest and engagement in the activity and for calming any worries the partner may develop about lapses into the literal meaning of alarming elements and sequences. Bekoff suggests that these animal abilities to initiate, facilitate, and sustain joint "fair" play, where partners can take risks to propose something even more over-the-top and out-of-order than the players have yet ventured together, underlie the evolution of justice, cooperation, forgiveness, and morality.[57] Remember Wister's letting Safi whack him with her snout when the donkey had accidentally caught the dog's head with an overly exuberant hoof. I remember also how many times in training with Cayenne, when I am incoherent and hurtful instead of inviting and responsive, that I describe what I feel from her as her forgiveness and her readiness to engage again. I experience that same forgiveness in play with her outside formal training when I misinterpret her invitations, preferences, or alarms. I know perfectly well that I am "anthropomorphizing" (as well as theriomorphizing) in this way of saying things, but *not* to say them in this manner seems worse, in the sense of being both inaccurate and impolite.[58] Bekoff is directing our attention to the astonishing and world-changing naturalcultural evolution of what we call trust. For myself, I am also partial to the idea that the experience of sensual joy in the nonliteral open of play might underlie the possibility of morality and responsibility for and to one another in all of our undertakings at whatever webbed scales of time and space.

So, at the end of "Training in the Contact Zone," I return to Isabelle Stengers, whom we met in chapter 3, "Sharing Suffering," in her introduction of the idea of cosmopolitics, which requires copresence. I need Stengers here for her reading of Whitehead's notion of a proposition. In her paper titled "Whitehead's Account of the Sixth Day," Stengers writes, "Propositions are members of the short metaphysical list of what can be said to exist, what is required by the description of actual entities as such. . . . The coming into existence of new propositions may need, and does need, a social environment, but it will not be explained in social terms. The event of this coming into existence marks the opening of a full range of new diverging possibilities for becoming, and as such generally signifies a break in continuity, what can be called a social upheaval."[59] I risk this excursion into speculative process philosophy and Whitehead's vocabulary, this other playing with strangers, in the same spirit that I approach training with my partners in the contact zones of agility. Stengers says that the conceptual role of Whitehead's technical terms lies in "the imaginative jump produced by their articulation. . . . their meaning cannot be elucidated right away, just as an animal cannot be approached right away. In both cases you need some slowing down and learning what they demand and how they behave" (1). It is a case of conceptual politesse, of cosmopolitics, this learning to play with strangers.

I said that "play proposes," and I argued that people must learn to meet dogs as strangers, as significant others, so that both can learn the corporeal semiosis of cross-species trust and enter the open of risking something new. Agility is an ordinary sport or a game, in which the syncopated dance of rule and invention is the choreography that reshapes players. I know that Whitehead did not have dog–human agility runs in mind when he elaborated his sense of a proposition, but Stengers is more promisingly promiscuous in her love of the speculative work and play of propositions. Emboldened by Stengers, I suggest that a "good run" in agility is a "mode of coherence," a "concrescence of prehensions," and an event of "profound disclosure"—all in Whitehead's terms.

For Whitehead, coherence means interpreting together what had been seen only in mutually contradicting terms. Stengers quotes Whitehead, "In the becoming of an actual entity, the potential unity of many entities in disjunctive diversity acquires the real unity of an actual entity"

(12).[60] An achieved actual entity is outside time; it exceeds time in something I will call the sheer joy of that coming together of different bodies in coshaping motion, that "getting it," which makes each partner more than one but less than two. An actual entity increases the multiplicity of the world: "The many have become one, and are increased by one" (23). This is ordinary reciprocal induction. "Becoming is not to be demonstrated; it is a matter of sheer disclosure. In contrast, the question of '*how* an entity becomes' is the one for which a demand for coherence may be positively put to work" (13). Reasons, experiments, training hard, making mistakes interesting, objectivity, causes, method, sociology and psychology, consequences: here is where these things come into their own. Human beings (and other organisms) need the fleshly practice of reason, need reasons, need technique, but, unless they are delusional, and many are, what people (and other organisms) do not have (except in a very special sense in mathematical and logical proof) is transcendent sufficient reasons.

The open beckons; the next speculative proposition lures; the world is not finished; the mind–body is not a giant computational exercise but a risk in play. That's what I learned as a biologist; that's what I learn again in the contact zones of agility. People must not explain away by tautology—just-so stories of relentless function—what needs to be understood, that is, disclosed. I think Stengers agrees with me that the same thing applies across species.

If we appreciate the foolishness of human exceptionalism, then we know that becoming is always becoming *with*—in a contact zone where the outcome, where who is in the world, is at stake. "For Whitehead, the experiences which come to matter on the sixth day are those which may be associated with the intense feeling of alternative, unrealized possibilities" (16). Stengers insists that philosophy aims at transformative disclosure and that the efficacy of propositions is not limited to human beings. "Propositions should not be confused with linguistic sentences. . . . The efficacy of propositions is not restricted to creatures of the sixth day. . . . Propositions are needed in order to give their irreducible reasons . . . for the possibility of the kind of disruption of social continuity we may observe when even oysters or trees seem to forget about survival" (18). A proposition is about something that is not yet. A proposition is a social adventure, lured by unrealized ideals (called "abstractions") and enabled by the risk of what Stengers and Whitehead call "wandering," what Bateson named a "muddle," and what Wedde and I suggest is the risk of play. This is queer theory, indeed, outside reproductive teleology and off-category—that is, off-topic, out of *topos* (proper place), into *tropos* (swerving and so making meaning new).

God is definitely not queer. The sixth day of creation in Genesis 1:24–31 is when God, helpfully speaking English, said, "'Let the earth bring forth living creatures according to their kinds.' . . . And God made the beasts of the earth according to their kinds and the cattle according to their kinds, and everything that creeps upon the ground according to its kind. And God saw that it was good." A little overfocused on keeping kinds distinct, God then got to making man (male and female) in his own image and giving them all too much dominion, as well as the command to multiply out of all bounds of sharing the earth. I think the sixth day is where the problem of joint mundane creaturely kinship versus human exceptionalism is sharply posed right in the first chapter of Jewish and Christian monotheism. Islam did no better on this point. We have plurals of kind but singularity of relationship, namely, human dominion under God's dominion. Everything is food for man; man is food only for himself and his God. In this feast, there are no companion species, no cross-category messmates at table. There is no salutary indigestion, only licensed cultivation and husbandry of all the earth as stock for human use. The posthumanities—I think this is another word for "after monotheism"—require another kind of open. Pay attention. It's about time.

ENDING IN A CONTACT ZONE: THE DEVIL IS IN THE DETAILS

August 28, 2001
Dear Agility Friends,

Up until now, I would not have said Ms Cayenne Pepper was drawn to the pause table. This morning, however, while Rusten was putting the last coat of lurid yellow paint on the rough sandy surface of the new pause table he made me for my birthday (along with a very professional A-frame, broad jump, and teeter-totter),

Cayenne made known her great, if newfound, love for jumping onto this contact obstacle. Splat into the wet, bright paint she leapt, blithely ignoring my strongly worded suggestion that, in fulfillment of her normal morning obligations, she leave early and speed the newspaper to Caudill's mailbox in exchange for a tasty vitamin pill.

As my teacher Gail Frazier will attest, it is not unheard of for Cayenne in training and at trials to bounce off the pause table before the magic of the release cue. Not this time. She held her ground with conviction; no two-point penalties for her. Belly to the paint, Cayenne was telling me that we now have that automatic down on the table for which we had worked so hard. Timing is all.

Decorated for play at this weekend's USDAA trials,
Donna

III. TANGLED SPECIES

9. CRITTERCAM
Compounding Eyes in Naturecultures

In this interconnection of embodied being and environing world, what happens in the interface is what is important.
—Don Ihde, *Bodies in Technology*

Fingery eyes literally plunge the viewer into materialized perceptions.
—Eva Shawn Hayward, "Envisioning Invertebrates: Immersion, Inhabitation, and Intimacy as Modes of Encounter in Marine TechnoArt"

Anything can happen when an animal is your cameraman.
—Crittercam advertisement

INFOLDINGS AND JUDGE'S CHAMBERS

Don Ihde and I share a basic commitment. As Ihde puts it, "Insofar as I use or employ a technology, I am used by and employed by that technology as well. . . . We are bodies in technologies."[1] Therefore, technologies are not mediations, something in between us and another bit of the world. Rather, technologies are organs, full partners, in what Merleau-Ponty called "infoldings of the flesh." I like the word *infolding* better than *interface* to suggest the dance of world-making encounters. What happens in the folds is what is important. Infoldings of the flesh *are* worldly embodiment. The word makes me see the highly magnified surfaces of cells shown by scanning electron microscopes. In those pictures, we experience in optic–haptic touch the high mountains and valleys, entwined organelles and visiting bacteria, and multiform interdigitations of surfaces we can never again imagine as smooth interfaces. Interfaces are made out of interacting grappling devices. Further, syntactically and materially, worldly embodiment is always a verb, or at least a gerund. Always in formation, embodiment is ongoing, dynamic, situated, and historical. No matter what the chemical score for the dance—carbon, silicon, or something else—the partners in infoldings of the flesh are heterogeneous. That is, the infolding of *others to one another* is what makes up the knots we call beings or, perhaps better, following Bruno Latour, things.[2] Things are material, specific, non-self-identical, and semiotically active. In the realm of the living, critter is another name for thing. Critters are what this chapter is about.

Never purely themselves, things are compound; they are made up of combinations of other things coordinated to magnify power, to make something happen, to engage the world, to risk fleshly acts of interpretation. Technologies are always compound. They are composed of diverse agents of interpretation, agents of recording, and agents for directing and multiplying relational action. These agents can be human beings or parts of human beings, other organisms in part or whole, machines of many kinds, or other sorts of entrained things made to work in the technological compound of conjoined forces. Remember also, one of the meanings of *compound* is "an enclosure, within which there is a residence or a factory"—or, perhaps, a prison or temple. Finally, a compound animal in zoological terminology refers to a composite of individual organisms, an enclosure of zoons, a company of critters infolded into one. Connected by Crittercam's stolon—that is, the circulatory apparatus of its compounded visualizing practices—zoons are technologies, and technologies are zoons.

So, a compound is both a composite and an enclosure. In "Crittercam: Compounding Eyes in Naturecultures," I am interested in querying both of these aspects of the early twenty-first-century composition made up of nonhuman marine animals, human marine scientists, a series of cameras, a motley of associated equipment, the National Geographic Society, a popular television nature show, its associated Web site, and sober publications in ocean science journals.

At first glance, strapped to the body of critters such as green turtles in Shark Bay, off Western Australia, humpback whales in the waters off southeast Alaska, and emperor penguins in Antarctica, a nifty miniature video camera is the central protagonist. Since the first overwrought seventeenth-century European discussions about the camera lucida and camera obscura, within technoculture the camera (the technological eye) seems to be the central object of both philosophical pretension and self-certainty, on the one hand, and cultural skepticism and the authenticity-destroying powers of the artificial, on the other hand. The camera—that vault or arched chamber, that judge's chamber—moved from elite Latin to the vulgar, democratic idiom in the nineteenth century only as a consequence of a new technology called photography, or "light-writing." A camera became a black box with which to register pictures of the outside world in a representational, mentalist, and sunny semiotic economy, an analogy to the seeing eye in brainy, knowing man, for whom body and mind are suspicious strangers, if also near neighbors in the head. Nonetheless, no matter how gussied up with digitalized optical powers, the camera has never lost its job to function as a judge's chamber, in camera, within which the facts of the world—indeed, the critters of the world—are assayed by the standard of the visually convincing and, at least as important, the visually new and exciting.

At second glance, however, Crittercam, the up-to-the minute photographic judge's chamber packed by the likes of dugongs and nurse sharks, entrains us, compounds us, within heterogeneous infoldings of the flesh that require a much more interesting dramaturgy than that possible for any self-reporting, central protagonist, no matter how visually well endowed. This second glance will occupy most of this chapter, but first we have to plough through some very predictable semiotic road blocks that try to limit us to a cartoonish epistemology about visual self-evidence and the lifeworlds of human–animal–technology compounds.

FIRST SIGHT

In 2004, the National Geographic Channel launched a series of TV shows called Crittercam.[3] The announcements and framing narratives for the show present an easy target for a chortling ideology critique with a superiority complex.[4] The animals who carry the attached cameras into their watery worlds are presented as makers of home movies that report on the actual state of things without human interference or even human presence. As the American Association for the Advancement of Science online Science Update put it in 1998, we will learn "why one marine scientist started handing out camcorders directly to the sea creatures he wanted to study. The result: Some very unique home movies." Crittercam, we are told in the voice-over of the 2004 television series, "can reveal hidden lives." The camera is a "National Geographic high-tech scientific video tool worn by species on the edge." The reports come from that sacred–secular place of endangerment, of threatened extinction, where beings are needy of both physical and epistemological rescue. Reports from such edges have special power. "Anything can happen when an animal is your cameraman," declaimed a brochure for the series that I picked up at the Hearst Castle gift shop on the California coast in February 2004.

National Geographic Channel's Web site whetted the audience's appetite for dis- and reembodiment through identification: "Meet our camera crews—they're all animals! . . . Sit back and imagine you are taking a ride on the back of the world's greatest mammal, or seeing life from the point of view of a penguin. The new Crittercam series takes you as close as you can get to the animal world." The camera is both physical "high technology" and immaterial channel to the interior reaches of another. Through the camera's eye glued, literally, to the body of the other, we are promised the full sensory experience of the critters themselves, without the curse of having to remain human: "Sense water rushing past, hear the thunderous roar of the wind and experience the thrill of the hunt. . . . Dive, swim, hunt, and burrow in animal habitats where humans can never go." Addressing children, the February 6, 2004, on-line *Crittercam Chronicles* asked, "Have you ever wondered what it would be like to BE a wild animal? . . . You can experience their life the way they do." Speaking to adults, National Geographic tells us that the Crittercam is rapidly changing science fiction into reality by "eliminating human presence and allowing us entry into otherwise virtually inaccessible habitats."

Immediate experience of otherness, inhabitation of the other as a new self, sensation and truth in one package without the pollution of interfering or interacting: these are the lure of *Crittercam*, the TV show, and Crittercam, the instrument. Reading these promises, I felt as if I were back in some versions of consciousness-raising groups and film projects of the early 1970s women's liberation movement, in which self-reporting on unmediated experience seemed attainable, especially if women had cameras and turned them on themselves. Become self by seeing self through the eyes of self. The only change is that National Geographic's *Crittercam* promises that self becomes other's self. Now, that's point of view!

SECOND SIGHT

The National Geographic Web site tells a little parable about the origin of the Crittercams themselves. In 1986 in the waters off Belize, a big shark approached a diving biology graduate student and filmmaker, Greg Marshall, and swam away with three quick strokes of its powerful tail. Marshall looked longingly after the disappearing shark and spotted a small sucker fish, a remora, an unobtrusive witness to sharky reality, clinging to the big predator. "Envying the remora its intimate knowledge of shark life, Marshall conceived a mechanical equivalent: a video camera, sheltered by waterproof housing, attached to a marine animal." Now our origin story is getting more interesting; we are no longer inside a cartoon ideology of immediacy and stolen selves. Instead Marshall longed for, and built, *the remora's* intimate view of shark life.[5] Some body-snatching is still going on here, but becoming-remora is much more promising in an entangled-species world. Endowed with second sight, we can now enter the compounded world of infoldings of the flesh, because we have left the garden of self-identity and risked the embodied longings and points of view of surrogates, substitutes, and sidekicks. At last, we get to grow up— or, in another idiom, get real. Neither cynical nor naive, we can become savvy about reality engines.[6] We are, in Ihde's words, bodies in technologies, in fold after fold, with no unwrinkled place to stop.

If we take the remora seriously as the analogue for Crittercam, then we have to think about just what the relationships of human beings are to the animals swimming about with sucker cameras on their hides. Clearly, the swimming sharks and loggerhead turtles are not in a "companion animal" relationship to the people, on the model of herding dogs or other critters with whom people have worked out elaborate and more-or-less acknowledged cohabitations.[7] The camera and the remora are more about accompanying than companioning, more about "riding along with" rather than "*cum panis,*" that is, "eating bread with." Remoras and Crittercams are not messmates to either people or sharks; they are commensals, neither benefactors nor parasites but devices with their own ends who/which hitch a ride. So, this chapter turns out to be about a commensal techno-logical lifeworld. Same housing, not the same dinner. Same compound; distinct ends. Together for a while, welded by vacuum-generating suckers or good glue. Thanks to their remora-like technological surrogates, in spite of narratives to the contrary, *Crittercam*'s people are decidedly *not* absent from the doings of the animals they are interested in; technologi-cally active humans get to ride along, holding on as best they can.

At this point, the scholar of science and technology studies starts asking about how the Crittercams are designed and built; how that design changes for each of the forty-odd species who had their techno-remoras fitted by 2004; what things look like from the attached cameras, some of which seem to be at very odd angles; what the devices' technical and social history is over time; how well they hold on; how the join is broken and data collected and read; how audiences (scientific and popular, child and adult) learn the needed semiotic skills to watch animal home vid-eos and have any idea of what they are seeing; what kinds of data besides the visual the devices can collect; how those data integrate with data col-lected in other ways; how the National Geographic Crittercam projects attach themselves to established, ongoing research projects on the animals; whether those collegial attachments are parasitic, cooperative, or com-mensal; and whose (animal and human) labor, play, and resources make all this possible. Once one gets beyond the numbing narratives of diving with/as the gods and feeling the divine wind in the abducted face, it turns out that all of these questions can be addressed from the TV shows them-selves and their associated Web site.

It is impossible to watch *Crittercam* shows and not be exhausted and exhilarated by the scenes of athletic, skillful human beings lustily infold-ing their flesh and their cameras' flesh with the bodies of critter after crit-ter. The sheer *physicality* of all that is Crittercam dominates the television screen. How could a mentalistic "camera's eye" narrative ever take hold in the face of such immersion in boats, sea spray, waves, immense whales and slippery dugongs, speed and diving, piloting challenges, team inter-actions, and the materialities of engineering and using the plethora of cameras and other data-collecting devices that are Crittercam? Indeed, the visual structuring of the TV episodes emphasizes bodies, things, parts, substances, sensory experience, timing, emotions—everything that is the thick stuff of Crittercam's lifeworld. The cuts are fast; the visual fields, littered; the size scales of things and critters in relation to the human body, rapidly switched so that the viewer never feels comfortable with the illusion that anything much can be physically taken for granted in relation to oneself. Part bodies of organisms and technologies predominate over whole-body shots. But never is *Crittercam*'s audience allowed to imagine *visually* or *haptically* the absence of physicality and crowded presences, no matter what the voice-over says. The word may not be made flesh here, but everything else is.

Consider first the boats, the people in them, and the animals pursued by them. The TV show audience learns quickly that each *Crittercam* project requires fast boats; expert pilots; and agile, jocular, well-muscled scientist–divers ready to jump off a moving boat and embrace a large swimming critter who is presumably not especially longing to hug a human. In the episode about green turtles and loggerhead turtles off Western Australia, the host Mike Heithaus tells the audience that "chasing after turtles is kind of like being a stunt driver." Of course, first the crews have to find the animals to whom they want to attach their sort of commensal remora. Looking for leatherback turtles off Costa Rica, Crittercam people worked with former poachers–turned–tour guides to find these biggest—and, naturally, acutely endangered—marine reptiles on earth, who make a living eating jellyfish. Crittercam scientists and entertainment producers also have to consider that some critters can't wear the current generation of videocams safely; too much drag could lead to the animal's early demise. Thus, we learn, imperial turtles will have to wait for more miniaturization for their remora-like accompaniments.

In the waters of Shark Bay, where the National Geographic Remote Imaging Team and television crew were looking for dugongs, local Aboriginals worked on the boats as sea trackers.[8] Implicit in that labor practice are the complex metamorphoses of these particular Aboriginal people from hunters of dugongs to their conservationists and comanagers of research permits and ecotourism. Plant-eating mammals that spend all of their lives in the sea, dugongs are marine relatives of elephants, who shared their last common ancestor about twenty-five million years ago. TV show host Heithaus, himself a PhD scientist who studies predator–

prey interactions among marine animals, with a special taste for sharks, never fails to remind the viewer of the conservation message in all Crittercam projects. Such messages include reassurances that special permits were obtained to harass endangered animals with research boats, that interference was kept to a minimum and never pursued to the point of exhausting the animals, and that all of the operations are part of saving organisms and habitats on the edge of extinction.

That has always been the argument of natural history extravaganzas, whether colonial or postcolonial. It might even be true. It takes believing that, under current conditions, knowledge saves; or at least, if not a sufficient condition for enduring and flourishing, finite secular knowledge called science is definitely a necessary condition. Sign me on to that religion. Still, I do long for an idiom that considers multispecies flourishing outside the idiom and apparatus of "Saving the Endangered [fill in the blank]." Rooted in a commitment to the mortal mundane, rather than to either Sacred or Secular Salvation, my longing has to do with the heterogeneous actors necessary to Isabelle Stengers's cosmopolitics.

Not all Crittercams are attached with a hug. Besides considering whether a barnacle-crusted hide will accept sucker cups, be better off with epoxy glue, or need some other attachment technique, Crittercam people have to solve, *physically*, how to get the videocam packages onto beings as different from one another as dugongs, humpback whales, nurse sharks, and emperor penguins. Take the humpback whales off southeast Alaska. Computer simulations helped remote imaging engineers design special suction cups for these critters. We hear on TV that "technology, teamwork, and a federal permit were required to get this close to the whales." Many weeks of unsuccessful attempts to attach a camera to a whale (almost a whole research season) were reduced to a couple of minutes of TV time showing one failed attempt after another to plant a camera hanging off a long pole onto a giant moving whale from a boat. Sixteen Crittercams (each worth about ten thousand dollars) were finally successfully deployed. Retrieving those cameras after they came off the whales is an epic tale in itself; witness the ninety miles traveled and the seven hours in a helicopter, following elusive VHF signals, that lead engineer Mehdi Bakhtiari logged to get one camera back from the sea. Thankfully, the remoras on the whales got an eyeful, but more of that later.

Crittercam units are assembled on the TV screen. Attachment devices (sucker, fin clamp, or adhesive mount), integrated video camcorder and data-logging system, microphone, pressure and temperature gauges, headlights, the tracking system for cameras (both those that are still attached and those that have been released from the animals), and the remote release button are all given screen time. However, the technology is put together so quickly in a burst of fast visual cuts from component to component that the viewer is dazed more than informed. Still, it would be impossible to get the visual impression that the camera is a mentalistic, dematerializing black box.

In a more relaxed mood, the interested viewer has easy Internet access to technical descriptions and time lines for the Crittercam packages. We learn that in 2004 the cameras record on Hi-8 or digital video tape; that housings are modified for different conditions, with titanium-encased units equipped with visual intensification capability that can record at two thousand meters or more; that field reprogrammability of key elements is facilitated by onsite personal computers; that other sorts of data are logged by sensors for salinity, depth, speed, light level, audio, and more; and that data and imaging sampling can be segregated for different time-scheduling demands corresponding to the research questions being asked. We learn about time-sampling schedules and capacities of the data-collecting devices. Three hours of color recording by 2004 is pretty impressive, especially when those hours can be parsed to acquire, say, twenty seconds every three minutes.

On the Internet, we learn about the progressive miniaturization and greater powers of Crittercams from the first model in 1987, when outer diameters were 7 inches or more, to outer diameters of 2.5 inches with increased data-collecting capabilities in 2004. Sneaked into the Web site narrative is the information that most of Crittercam's complex body is proprietary but was initially built on the basis of existing systems from Sony and JVC. Property matters; by definition, it is about access; Crittercam is about access. We are told about Greg Marshall's early unsuccessful hunt for both funding and scientific credibility and his eventual success with the backing of the National Geographic Society. That took the savvy instincts of a National Geographic television producer, John Bredar. Development grants followed, with the first successful deployments on free-swimming sharks and sea turtles in 1992. Now Greg Marshall heads up National Geographic's Remote Imaging Program, which is engaged in worldwide scientific collaborations. Finally, we aren't allowed to forget the dreams for the future: Someday Crittercam packages will tell us about physiological parameters such as EKG and stomach temperature. Then, there is the two-inch camera in the near-term imagination of the engineers. These are home movies with a future twist.

The TV screen itself in *Crittercam* episodes deserves close attention. Especially in scenes featuring Crittercam footage, the viewer is invited to adopt the persona of a videogame player by the semiotic design of the screen. Blocking any naturalistic illusions, the screen is literally outlined like a game space, and the shots from the heads of the critters give forward-pointing motion like that of a videogame avatar. We get the point of view that searchers, eaters, and predators might have of their habitat.

But perhaps most striking of all is the small amount of actual Crittercam footage amid all the other underwater photography of the animals and their environments that fills the episodes. Actual Crittercam footage is, in fact, usually pretty boring and hard to interpret, somewhat like an ultrasound recording of a fetus. Footage without narration is more like an acid trip than a peephole to reality. Cameras might be askew on the head of the critter or pointed down, so that we see lots of muck and lots of water, along with bits of other organisms that make precious little sense without a lot of other visual and narrative work. Or the videocams might be positioned just fine, but nothing much happens during most of the sampling time. Viewer excitement over Crittercam imagery is a highly produced effect. Home movies might be the right analogy after all.

The most visually interesting—and by far the largest amount of—underwater photography in the episodes is given no technical discussion on the TV programs at all. We learn nothing about who took this plentiful non-Crittercam footage, what their cameras were like, or how the animals and camera people interacted. Reading the credits doesn't help much. On the other hand, these genres of footage are familiar to anyone who watches much marine natural-history film and TV. Familiarity in no way diminishes potency. Focused by Eva Shawn Hayward's lens in her analysis of the 1965 film *The Love Life of the Octopus* (*Les amours de la pieuvre*), by Jean Painlevé and Genevieve Hamon, I experience in

Crittercam's "conventional" footage some of the same pleasures of intimacies at surfaces, fast changes in scale, ranges of magnification, and the immersive optics of refraction across varying media.[9] Painlevé and Hamon's films are aesthetically much more self-conscious and skilled than *Crittercam*'s assemblages, but once one learns how the dance of magnifications and scales shapes the join of touch and vision to produce Hayward's "fingery eyes," enabled by the biological art-film work, one seeks—and finds—that kind of vision much more widely. In addition, the haptic-visual symphony of *Crittercam* is helped immeasurably by the intense watery physicality of the whole package. For that, I will watch a lot of odd-angle shots of sea bottoms taken from the hides of critters equipped with techno-remoras.

Crittercam episodes promise something else too: scientific knowledge. What is learned about the animals' lives matters a great deal. Without this dimension, the whole edifice would come tumbling down. Visual–haptic pleasures in part objects and voyeuristic revels in the athletic maneuvers of vigorous young people and other critters in surging waters would not hold me or, I suspect, much of anyone else. In this matter, I am no cynic, even if my eye is firmly on the culturally located technosocial apparatus of knowledge production. Folks in technoculture need their juicy epistemophilic endorphin surge as much as they need sorts of sensory engagement. The brain is, after all, a chemically avid sensory organ.

All the episodes of *Crittercam* emphasize that the remote imaging people from National Geographic hooked up with marine zoologists doing long-term research. In each case, the *Crittercam* folks thought their apparatus could help resolve an interesting and ecologically consequential question that was not easily addressable, if at all, by other technological means. The long-term projects provided nearly all the information about habitats, animals, research questions, and grounds for worries about habitat degradation and depleted populations. For example, before *Crittercam* came on the scene, more than 650 sea turtles caught and tagged over five years had yielded information crucial to understanding the shark–turtle, predator–prey ecologies of Shark Bay off Western Australia. But the *Crittercam* people offered a means to go with the animals into places humans otherwise could not go to see things that changed what we know *and how we must act as a consequence,* if we have learned to care about the well-being of the entangled animals and people in those ecologies.

Probably because I work and play with herding dogs in real life, the humpback whale collaboration is my favorite one to illustrate these points. Fifteen years of research about how humpbacks live and hunt in the waters off southwest Alaska preceded the arrival of the Crittercam.[10] The scientists knew each whale individually by his or her calls and tail-fluke markings. The biologists developed strong ideas about the whales' collaborative hunting after watching them collect giant mouthfuls of herring. But researchers could not prove that collaborative hunting was indeed what the whales were doing, with each whale taking its place in a choreographed division of labor, like that of pairs of expert border collies gathering the sheep on the Lancashire countryside. Whale scientists suspected that individually known humpbacks had been knowledgeably working together for decades to harvest their fishery, but the limits of humans diving with the giant cetaceans stopped them from obtaining crucial visual evidence. Being crushed is no way to secure good data. The Crittercam gave questing humans a way to accompany the whales as if the people were merely commensal sucker fishes along for the ride—and the photo op. In the idiom of Bruno Latour's science and technology studies, the scientists and the natural history entertainment jocks "delegated" parts of their work to the Crittercam multitasking package and to the animals who bore the devices into their worlds.[11]

We have already seen how hard it was to secure the cameras to the whale hides and then recover them afterward. The sixteen successfully deployed Crittercams from near the end of the season were precious. The scientists wanted to test their hypothesis that certain whales deliberately blew bubbles from below to surround and trap herring that had been herded into tight congregations by other whales, forming a kind of net around the prey. Then, in unison the whales surged upward with their mouths gaping to collect their teaming dinner. People could see the bubbles from the surface, but they could not see how or where or by whom they were produced. Humans could not really tell if the whales were dividing their labor and hunting socially.

Footage from the first fifteen Crittercams did not show what the biologists needed. Suspense on television mounted, and, I like to think, suspense and worry were also rife in the non-TV labs, where people were trying to make sense of the often confusing, vertigo-inducing pictures the videocams brought back. Then, with the sixteenth videotape, shot by a Crittercam-bearing member of the pod, came a clear view, just a few seconds long, of a whale going below the gathered herring that were surrounded by other whales and blowing a bubble net. Callers, bubble blowers, and herders were all accounted for. Bits of footage put together from several cameras gave a reconstructed, visually supported narrative of the border collie–like whales gathering their fish-sheep, penning them flawlessly, and eating them enthusiastically. Good border collies don't do that part, but their cousins and ancestors, the socially hunting wolves, do.

A knowledge bonus also came from the Crittercam in the humpback whale social hunting story. Bits of whale skin adhered to the detached suction cups once the videocam packages were released, and so DNA analyses could be done of individually known (and named) whales who had taken attributable pictures of one another and their habitat. The result: the discovery that whales in the social hunting groups were not close kin. The close teamwork over years would have to be explained, ecologically and evolutionarily, in some other way. I know I should suppress my pleasure in this result, but I raise my California wine glass to the extrafamilial social worlds of working whale colleagues. My endorphins are at high tide.

THIRD SIGHT

So, the compound eyes of the colonial organism called Crittercam are full of articulated lenses from many kinds of coordinated, agential zoons— that is, the machinic, human, and animal beings whose historically situated infoldings are the flesh of contemporary naturecultures. Fugal accompaniment is the theme, not humans abstemiously staying away to let the animals tell an unmediated truth by making pictures of themselves. That much seems clear. But something is missing from my story so far, something we need to be at home in the hermeneutic web that is Crittercam. The question I have been deferring is simple to ask and the devil to answer: What is the semiotic agency of the animals in the hermeneutic labor of Crittercam?

Are they just objects for the data-gathering subjects called people and (by delegation) machines, just "resistance" or "raw material" to the potency and action of intentional others? Well, it shouldn't take recounting twenty-five years of feminist theory and science studies to determine the answer there: no. Okay, but are the animals then completely symmetrical actors whose agency and intentionality are just cosmetically morphed variants of the unmarked kind called human? The same twenty-five years of feminist theory and science studies shout the same reply: no.

It's easy to pile on the negatives. In the Crittercam assemblage, the hermeneutic agency of the animals is not voluntary, not that of the first-person cameraman, not intentional, not like that of coworking or companion animals (my border collie analogy notwithstanding), not a weaker version of the always strong human hermeneutic game. It's harder to specify the positive content of the animals' hermeneutic labor in Crittercam's particular naturalcultural encounter.

But it is not impossible to get started. First, there is no way even to think about the issue outside the relentlessly fleshly entanglements of this particular techno-organic world. There is no general answer to the question of animals' agential engagement in meanings, any more than there is a general account of human meaning making. Don Ihde insisted that in the human–technology hermeneutic relation, the technology adapts to the humans and vice versa. Human bodies and technologies cohabit each other in relation to particular projects or lifeworlds. "In so far as I use a technology, I am also used by a technology."[12]

Surely the same insight applies to the animal–human–technology hermeneutic relation. Hermeneutic potency is a relational matter; it's not about who "has" hermeneutic agency, as if it were a nominal substance instead of a verbal infolding. Insofar as I (and my machines) use an animal, I am used by an animal (with its attached machine). I must adapt to the specific animals even as I work for years to learn to induce them to adapt to me and my artifacts in particular kinds of knowledge projects. Specific sorts of animals in specific ecologies and histories make me adapt to them even as their life doings become the meaning-making generator of my work. If those animals are wearing something of my making, our mutual but unidentical coadaptation will be different. The animals, humans, and machines are all enmeshed in hermeneutic labor (and play) by the material–semiotic requirements of getting on together in specific lifeworlds. They touch; therefore they are. It's about the action in contact zones.

That's the kind of insight that makes us know that situated human beings have epistemological–ethical obligations to the animals. Specifically, we have to learn who they are in all their nonunitary otherness in order to have a conversation on the basis of carefully constructed, multisensory, compounded languages. The animals make demands on the humans and their technologies to precisely the same degree that the humans make demands on the animals. Otherwise, the cameras fall off and other bad things happen to waste everybody's time and resources. That part is "symmetrical," but the contents of the demands are not symmetrical at all. That asymmetry matters a great deal. Nothing is passive to the action of another, but all the infoldings can occur only in the fleshly detail of situated, material–semiotic beings. The privilege of people accompanying animals depends on getting these asymmetrical relationships right.[13] Compound eyes use different refractive indices, different materials, different fluids, to get something in focus. There is no better place to learn such things than in the immersive depths of the earth's oceans.

10. CHICKEN

ROOSTER: *Ego dixi: Coccadoodul du.*
CHICKENS: *Gallus magnifice incendens exclamat. Nunc venit agricola.*
—GRUNT, PIGORIAN CHANT FROM SNOUTO DOMOINKO DE SILO

Chicken is no coward. Indeed, this warrior bird has plied his trade as a fighting cock around the world since the earliest days such fowl consented to work for people, somewhere in South and Southeast Asia.[1]

Anxious if brave, Chicken Little has long worried that the sky is falling. He has a good vantage point from which to assess this matter; for Chicken, right along with his overreaching companion, *Homo sapiens,* has been witness to and participant in all the big events of Civilization. Chicken labored on the Egyptian pyramids, when barley-pinching pharaohs started the world's first mass egg industry to feed the avians' co-conscripted human workers. Much later—a bit after the Egyptians replaced their barley exchange system with proper coins, thus acting like the progressive capitalists their exchange partners always seem to want in that part of the world—Julius Caesar brought the Pax Romana, along with the "ancient English" chicken breed, the Dorking, to Britain. Chicken Little knows all about the shock and awe of History, and he is a master at tracking the routes of Globalizations, old and new. Technoscience is no stranger either. Add to that,

Chicken knows a lot about Biodiversity and Cultural Diversity, whether one thinks about the startling variety of chickenkind for the five thousand years of their domestic arrangements with humanity or considers the "improved breeds" accompanying capitalist class formations from the nineteenth century to now. No county fair is complete without its gorgeous "purebred" chickens, who know a lot about the history of eugenics. It is hard to sort out shock from awe in chickenland. Whether the firmament takes a calamitous tumble or not, Chicken holds up a good half of the sky.

In 2004 C.E., Chicken Little donned his spurs once more and entered the war on words thrust on him by Current Events.[2] Ever a gender bender, Chicken joined the LGBT Brigade and outdid himself as a postcolonial, transnational, pissed-off spent hen and mad feminist.[3] Chicken admitted that s/he was inspired by the all (human) girl underground fight clubs that s/he found out about on www.extremechickfights.com. Ignoring the sexism of *chick*, extreme or not, and the porn industry and pedophilic scene that vilifies the name of chicken, our Bird raptured those fighting girls right out of History and into his trannie sf world, fit to confront the Eagles of War and the Captains of Industry. S/he felt this rapturous power because s/he recalled not just the exploits of Cousin Phoenix but also the years when s/he too was a figure of Jesus Resurrected, promising the faithful that they would rise from the ashes of History's barbecues.

Barbecue. An unkind reminder of where Chicken Little had best concentrate her attention. For, at the end of a millennium, in 2000, ten billion chickens were slaughtered in the United States alone. Worldwide, five billion hens—75 percent in cramped, multioccupancy quarters called battery cages—were laying eggs, with Chinese flocks leading the way, followed by those in the United States and Europe.[4] Thai chicken exports topped $1.5 billion in value in an industry supplying Japanese and E.U. markets and employing hundreds of thousands of Thai citizens. World chicken production was 65.6 million tons, and the whole operation was growing at 4 percent per year. Captains of Industry, indeed. Chicken could conclude that a major avian vocation seems to be breakfast and dinner while the world burns.[5]

Contrary to the views of her pesky friends in the transnational animal rights movement, our Opportunistic Bird is not against surrendering a pound of flesh in exchange for pecking rights in the naturalcultural contractual arrangements that domesticated both bipedal hominids and winged gallinaceous avians. But something is seriously foul in current versions of multispecies global contract theory.[6]

One way to tell the trouble (one detail among myriads) is that a three-year study in Tulsa, Oklahoma—a center of factory chicken production—showed that half the water supply was dangerously polluted by poultry waste. Go ahead, microwave sponges in your kitchens as often as the clean food cops advise; inventive bacteria will outwit you with their fowl alliances.

Well, one more detail. Manipulated genetically since the 1950s to rapidly grow megabreasts, chickens given a choice choose food laced with painkillers. "Unsustainable growth rates" are supposed to be about dotcom fantasies and inflationary stock markets. In Chicken's world, however, that term designates the daily immolation of forced maturation and disproportionate tissue development that produces tasty (enough) young birds who are often enough unable to walk, flap their wings, or even stand up. Muscles linked in evolutionary history and religious symbolism to flight, sexual display, and transcendence instead pump iron for transnational growth industries. Not satisfied, some agribusiness scientists look to post genomics research for even more buffed white meat.[7]

Since chickens were the first farm animals to be permanently confined indoors and made to labor in automated systems based on Technoscience's finest genetic technologies, research on feed-conversion efficiency, and miracle drugs (not painkillers but antibiotics and hormones),[8] Chicken might be excused for being unimpressed by the McDonald Corporation's grudging agreement in 2000 to require that its suppliers give 50 percent more space per bird destined to be Chicken McNuggets and Eggs McMuffin. Still, McDonald's was the first corporation in the world to admit that pain and suffering are concepts familiar to underrated bird brains. Chicken's ingratitude is no wonder, when few "humane" slaughter laws in the United States or Canada to this day apply to chickens.[9]

In 1999 the European Union did manage to ban battery cages, beginning in 2012. That should allow for a smooth transition. Perhaps more sensitized to ever-ready Holocaust analogies, the Germans will make those cages illegal in 2007. In the market-besotted United States,

Chicken's hope seems to be in designer eggs for the omega-3 fatty acid–conscious and free-range certified organic chickens for the conscience-stricken and pure of diet.[10] The up-to-the-minute ethically fastidious might procure their chicken fix like the citizens in *Oryx and Crake*, Margaret Atwood's sf, especially in the sense of speculative fiction, novel (published in 2003). There, "ChickenNobs"—tasty organs without organisms, especially without annoying heads that register pain and perhaps have ideas about what constitutes a proper domestic bird's life—are on the menu. Genetically engineered muscles-without-animals illustrate exactly what Sarah Franklin means by designer ethics, which aim to bypass cultural struggle with just-in-time, "high technology" breakthroughs.[11] Design away the controversy, and all those free-range anarchists will have to go home. But remember, Chicken squawks even when his head has been cut off.

The law cannot be counted on. After all, even human laborers in the chicken industry are superexploited. Thinking of battery cages for laying hens reminds Chicken Little of how many illegal immigrants, ununionized women and men, people of color, and former prisoners process chickens in Georgia, Arkansas, and Ohio. It's no wonder that at least one U.S. soldier who tortured Iraqi prisoners was a chicken processor in her civilian life.

It's enough to make a sensitive Bird sick, as much from the virus of transnational politics as from the other kind. An avian flu outbreak in seven Asian nations shocked the world in the winter of 2004 and fear of a global pandemic remains lively in 2007. Luckily, by mid-2006 only about 130 humans had died, unlike the tens of millions who succumbed in 1918–19. Mass culling remains the officially recommended response to every appearance of the disease in domestic flocks, and sporadic threats to kill migrating birds are not empty.[12] Chicken Little could not find figures for total estimated bird deaths worldwide, from the disease and from culling. But before the end of 2004, about twenty million chickens were prophylactically slaughtered in Thailand alone. Global TV news showed unprotected human workers stuffing innumerable birds into sacks, tossing them undead into mass graves, and sprinkling on lime. In Thailand, 99 percent of chicken operations are, in Global Speak, "small" (fewer than one thousand birds, since it takes more than eighty thousand to be "large") and could not afford biosecurity—for people or birds. Newscasters waxed eloquent about a threatened transnational industry but spoke nary a word about farmers' and chickens' lives. Meanwhile, Indonesian government spokespeople in 2003 denied any avian flu in those salubrious quarters, even while Indonesian veterinary associations argued that millions of birds showed signs of avian flu as early as October of that year. And then came Indonesia's unpleasant number-one world rank for human deaths in 2006.

Perhaps the Bangkok *Post* on January 27, 2004, got the war of worlds, words, and images right with a cartoon showing migratory birds from the north dropping bombs—bird shit full of avian flu strain H5N1—on the geobody of the Thai nation.[13] This postcolonial joke on transborder bioterrorism is a nice reversal of U.S. and European fears of immigrants of all species from the global south. After all, prototypes for

Peace Chicken. Copyright Dan Piraro. Reprinted with permission. All rights reserved.

technoscientific, export-oriented, epidemic friendly chicken industries were big on the Peace Corps agenda (a theme picked up later by the General Agreement on Tariffs and Trade), right along with artificial milk for infants. Proud progenitor of such meaty progress, the United States had high hopes for winning the Cold War in Asia with standardized broilers and layers carrying democratic values. In Eugene Burdick and William J. Lederer's 1958 novel, *The Ugly American*, set in a fictional Southeast Asian nation called Sarkan, Iowa chicken farmer and agricultural teacher Tom Knox was about the only decent U.S. guy. Neither Knox nor subsequent Development Experts seem to have cared much for the varied chicken–human livelihoods thriving for a few thousand years throughout Asia. In 2006, it seemed, the TV news showed unstandardized chickens living in close contact with ordinary people only to illustrate backwardness and public health failures, except for occasionally advertising tasty free-range birds living in the European Union and North America and destined for transnational affluent niche markets. Even those birds have to go indoors when H5N1 comes calling.

Sub-Saharan Africa entered the story in the most abject way, seemingly naturally once again; postcolonial tropes, not to mention postcolonial injustice, demand it.[14] In February 2006, the H5N1 strain of bird flu was confirmed on three farms in northern Nigeria, initiating large-scale culls. Making public health control measures especially difficult, customary poultry husbandry, in which people and birds associate closely, exists cheek by jowl with a fledgling agribusiness chicken industry that would make Iowa's Tom Knox proud. By August 2006, human cases of bird flu were confirmed, tens of thousands of birds had died, poultry markets were closing down, and the World Health Organization had approved fifty million dollars to try to stem the trouble.

Two suspects, both signifying transborder crossings outside the reach of the law, emerged for spreading the virus to Nigeria—migrating birds and illegally imported baby chicks. Closer scrutiny of the geographical pattern of affected farms indicated that migrating birds were insignificant compared with that staple of global neoliberalism: illegal trade involving the world's poorest populations tied to the most economically entrepreneurial configurations.[15] Without reliable climate-controlled hatchery facilities, Nigerians sought to cash in on the lucrative global poultry trade through obtaining extralegal chicks from China. Smuggling of all sorts between Africa and China is not news; comprehending that a global pandemic coupled to ordinary African farmers' further immiseration might be one of its fruits did open a few eyes.[16] But never enough eyes.

How many good citizens of the above-ground world would be surprised by the news that an illegal trade in chicken parts makes more money than even weapons trafficking in another abjected, war-riddled geopolitical zone, namely, the borderlands joining Moldavia, Trans-Dniestria, and Ukraine in the former Soviet Union? Spicing this particular story is the name locals give to the trafficked chicken hind quarters: "Bush legs," a moniker tracing to George senior's program to ship U.S. poultry to the Soviet Union in the early 1990s.[17] Worldwide, the illegal animal trade of all sorts is second in total value only to illegal drugs.

Chicken is, of course, no virgin to debates about political orders. Our fowl was the darling of savants' disputes about the nature of mind and instincts, and the "philosopher's chick" was a staple of European nineteenth-century learned idioms. Translated into the only proper global language, famous experiments in comparative psychology gave the world the term *pecking order* in the 1920s. Chicken Little remembers that this research by the Norwegian Thorleif Schjelderup-Ebbe, a serious lover and student of chickens, described complex social arrangements worthy of fowl, not the wooden dominance hierarchies in biopolitics that gained such a hold on cultural imaginations.[18] Behavioral sciences of both human and nonhuman varieties continue to find anything but dominance and subordination hard to think about. Chicken knows that producing better accounts of animal doings, with one another and with humans, can play an important role in reclaiming livable politics. But first came the hard years for chickens, whose subjection to the scientific, commercial, and political dreams of aspiring communities, entrepreneurs, and nation builders alike is not yet over.

In the 1920s, seeking to escape urban poverty, several hundred Jewish families—idealists, secularists, socialists, Jews from the shtetls of Eastern Europe and the sweatshops of New York's Lower East Side—got the word that they could make a living in the "Chicken Basket of the World," the little town of Petaluma in California.[19] Economic crises and unbridgeable debates about Israel or the Soviet Union all but tore the once-thriving community apart after World War II, but not before Chicken had brought the Petaluma Jewish Folk Chorus together with Paul Robeson in concert. Chicken fared less well; Petaluma was a major center of the industrialization of animal life, and neither socialism nor communism of that period had any strategies to offer laboring bodies who were not human. Perhaps partly because of that gap in the visions of those who most knew how to work toward communitarian freedom, the hyperexploited laboring bodies of both chickens and humans are joined in a terrifying global industry by the early twenty-first century.

The hopeful and tragic politics of Jewish chicken farmers turns up one more time in Chicken Little's research, this time joined to the fowl's reading pursuits in science fiction. From the first decades of the twentieth century, Rutgers, the state university of New Jersey, like other U.S. land-grant colleges, was a leader in poultry science linked to the industrialization of the chicken in American and world agriculture. After World War II, multitudes of veterans looked to poultry farming as a way to prosperity. Among the avid students studying at Rutgers's Poultry Science Department in the late 1940s was a young woman with a job in wartime army photo intelligence behind her (and ahead of her, a role in the development of the CIA from 1952 to 1955 as well as a PhD in experimental psychology earned in 1967). This chicken science student would become known to the sf world in the late 1960s as a reclusive male writer named James Tiptree Jr. But in the 1940s she was Alice Sheldon, who, with her husband Col. Huntington Sheldon, ran a small chicken farm in New Jersey from 1946 to 1952. Tiptree's biographer records Alice and Huntington's love of the Rutgers scene, all of it, including the science, the business, and the comradeship. "Most of their fellow students were veterans like them, though several were on their way to Palestine to lend their farming skills to the proposed new state of Israel."[20]

Whether publishing as James Tiptree Jr., Alice Sheldon, or Racoona Sheldon, this category bender worthy of Chicken Little wrote science fiction that toyed mercilessly with species, alternation of generations, reproduction, infection, gender, genre, and many kinds of genocide. Did those chickens inspire some of her quirky sf imagination and unsettling feminist thought experiments? Tiptree "once told [fellow sf writer] Vonda McIntyre she was sketching out a plot about 'a chicken hatchery set in the asteroids, run by women in competition with a huge processed-foods corporation.'"[21] Were Tiptree's chickens ever free-ranging fowl pecking at insects, or were they hatched in incubators for the developing post-war animal–industrial complex? Did Racoona Sheldon resonate with that greatest threat to outdoor chickens in the United States, the wily raccoon? Did the luxuriating brutalities of industrial chicken production that took off in the 1950s fuel any of Tiptree's many dark alien biological stories?[22]

Laying hens and fertile eggs dominate Chicken Little's closing thoughts. Perversely, s/he finds there the stuff of still possible freedom projects and renewed awe. The British claymation film *Chicken Run* (2000) stars 1950s Yorkshire hens facing a life of forced toil. The appearance of Rocky, the Rhode Island red, catalyzes a liberation drama that gives no comfort either to "deep animal rights" imaginations of a time before cospecies domestication or to millennial nation builders and free traders in chicken flesh. Pecking hens have other biopolitical tricks tucked under their wings.

Perhaps the Rare Breeds Survival Trust (RBST) and its sibling organizations around the world are incubating what socialists, communists, Zionists, Asian industrial tigers, nationalists in the Caucasus, transnational poultry scientists, and Iowa Democrats failed to imagine: ongoing chicken–human lives that are attentive to complex histories of animal–human entanglements, fully contemporary *and* committed to a future of multispecies naturalcultural flourishing in both wild and domestic domains.[23] RBST works against the premises and practices of factory farming on many levels, none of them reducible to keeping animals as museum specimens of a lost past or as wards in a permanent guardianship, in which utilitarian relations between animals and people, including eating meat, are always defined as abuse. RBST maintains a database of breeds of poultry threatened with disappearance through industrial standardization; plans in advance how to protect rare-breed flocks from extermination by culling in bird flu and other epidemic disasters; supports husbandry conducive to whole-organism well-being of both animals and people; analyzes breeds for their most economical and productive uses, including new ones; and demands effective action for animal well-being in transport, slaughter, and marketing. None of this is innocent, nor is the success of such approaches guaranteed. That is what "becoming with" as a worldly practice means.

Chicken Little returns in the end to the egg—fertile eggs in school biology labs that once gave millions of young hominids the privilege to see the shocking beauty of the developing chick embryo, with its dynamic architectural intricacies.[24] These cracked-open eggs did not offer an innocent beauty, but neither did they give warrant to colonial or postcolonial arrogances about Development. The contact zone of the chick embryo can renew the meaning of awe in a world in which laying hens know more about the alliances it will take to survive and flourish in multispecies, multicultural, multiordered associations than do all the secondary Bushes in Florida and Washington. Follow the chicken and find the world.

The sky has not fallen, not yet.

11. BECOMING COMPANION SPECIES IN TECHNOCULTURE

BECOMING FERAL: CATS IN TWENTY-FIRST-CENTURY RURAL SONOMA COUNTY

October 4, 2002, e-mail to fellow dog agility enthusiasts

Hi there, friends,

Rusten and I have been in a catless relation to the world since the death five years ago of twenty-one-year-old, former-feral-cat-turned-couch-mistress, Moses, but no more. A bone-thin, feral, gray tabby female had a litter of four near the barn this spring and then, sadly, got run over by a car on Mill Creek Road. We had been supplementing her food for a while by then, and we adopted her five-week-old kittens for the proud job of barn cats. Our cars parked by the old barn regularly became home to enterprising mice, who seemed to be building thriving murine communities in the warm engine compartments. Plastic wrapping on the cars' electrical wires must have provided needed trace nutrients; in any case, the rodents had a relish for munching colorful synthetics. We hoped for a little predator control assistance from felines.

All four kittens are flourishing and still very much feral. One of the little black guys (now known to be a male and bearing the name of all-black-clad Spike from *Buffy the Vampire Slayer*) will let me pick him up and stroke him, but the others are satisfied with service from humans in the form of food and water. They otherwise much prefer the company of each other and a barn full of rodents. Spike, the tame one—also the runt of the litter—might find himself a traveling house cat in Santa Cruz come winter quarter, if he will agree to the transition. And if I can get Cayenne to agree to share her couch with a feline. . . . Right now she alternates between terror of cats (instilled by her godhuman's cat, Sugar) and considering them lunch.

When they were about six months old, we trapped the kittens, one at a time, with the help of Forgotten Felines in Sonoma County, and got them sterilized and vaccinated for rabies and distemper. The agreement with Forgotten Felines if they help with trap and release is that the humans promise to feed the feral cats for the duration of their lives—expected to be about eight to nine years, compared with one to two years for a feral cat not fed regularly by humans and fifteen to twenty years for a well-cared-for pet who comes indoors regularly at night. Word from the cooperating vet and the farm feed store that rents the traps is that there are probably thousands of supplemented, sterilized feral cats in Sonoma County. Insisting on our using the traps, the vet would not let us bring the cats to him in a regular cat crate because of a history of serious scratch and bite wounds from feral cats in getting them ready for surgery.

Our hope is that the cats will have a fine life keeping the rodents in check so that we can park by the barn again without providing warm, low-cost, tract housing in our air ducts for reproducing mice. Our felines are also supposed to keep further feral cats from settling in nearby. I hope they understand this contract! Meanwhile, bearing names from the *Buffy* and *Dark Angel* TV series, they are fat, sassy, and beautiful. Come up soon and check out Spike (black male), Giles (black male), Willow (dark gray tabby female), and Max (light gray tabby female). You will notice that one of the striped tabbies bears the name of bar code–marked Max from *Dark Angel*.

We'd change Willow's name if you could come up with another bar code–marked TV character. Any ideas?

Landmate Susan Caudill and Rusten decided that our cats have undergone the defining experience of alien abduction—lifted out of one's home without warning by strange-looking giants of unknown origin, held in dark isolation for a period, brought to a chrome- and light-filled medical facility and subjected to penetration with needles and forced reproductive alterations, returned to one's original location and released as if nothing had happened, and expected to carry on until the next abduction at some unknown future time.

As beings who have undergone surgery and vaccination and therefore been interpellated into the modern biopolitical state, these cats have earned names to go with their historical identities and subject status. Just think, when else and where else in hominid–feline cohistories would the offspring of a dead feral cat

1. be taken up by a household of overeducated, scientifically trained, middle-aged war resisters;
2. be aided by an animal welfare volunteer organization with a quasi-wilderness ideology and a soft spot for animal-rights speak;
3. become the recipient of the donated time and services of a vet trained at a post–Civil War, land grant, science-based university and his technical staff;

4. be caught with a trap-and-release technology designed to get rid of vermin without the moral blot of killing them (the same technology designed to relocate wildlife in national parks and such);

5. receive serums tied to the history of immunology and to Pasteur in particular;

6. be fed MaxCat specially formulated kitten food certified by a national standards organization and regulated by food-labeling laws;

7. be named for a teenage vampire killer and genetically engineered characters on U.S. television;

8. and still have the status of wild animals?

Is this what Muir meant? In wilderness is our hope . . .

Much love,
Donna

p.s.: a philosophical postscript

Interpellation is taken from French post-structuralist, Marxist, philosopher Louis Althusser's theory for how subjects are constituted from concrete individuals by being "hailed" through ideology into their subject positions in the modern state. Early in the twentieth century, the French rescued the word from obsolescence (before 1700 in English and French, *to interpellate* had meant "to interrupt or break in on speech") to refer to calling on a minister in the legislative chamber to explain the policies of the ruling government. Today, through our ideologically loaded narratives of their lives, animals "hail" us animal people to account for the regimes in which they and we must live. We "hail" them into our constructs of nature and culture, with major consequences of life and death, health and illness, longevity and extinction. We also live with each other in the flesh in ways not exhausted by our ideologies. In that is our hope . . .

p.p.s.: an update from December 2006

Life-table statistics have a way of coming true with a vengeance, and the category called "feral" has a way of making claims on those fated to live and die there. Always the most tame and the first to enjoy morning scratch and ankle-twining sessions with provident humans at the food bowl, Spike was run over by a car when he was two years old. We were lucky a neighbor found his body in a drainage ditch and asked if he was ours. We found Willow dead one morning with her front leg torn off, presumably by a raccoon from the crowd of animals whom we did not intend to provision but who had their own ideas about resources and power. Raiding the cats' food arrangements with aplomb, Steller's jays by day and raccoons by night engaged in what can only be called an arms race with us and the felines, as we tested various organisms' (including our own) abilities to solve lock-and-key problems in a practice that would have made the fathers of comparative psychology proud. Our loyalty seemed due the cats and not the jays and raccoons, because we had produced the food competition and invited—really engineered—the cats into semidependence on us.

Giles and Max are still alive in December 2006, but they have each sustained serious abdominal and leg wounds from fights, from which they have healed, though not completely. They are burdened with tapeworms and probably other parasites; we can see the dried tape segments near their anuses. Their lives are palpably fragile. They are not pets; they do not get the care of a middle-class pet. They and we have rituals of expectation and affectionate touch enacted on a daily basis. Waiting for us from safe lookouts, or for our landmate Susan when Rusten and I are in Santa Cruz, the cats take dust baths in the gravel with enthusiasm when we appear, progressing to twining their bodies around hominid ankles and soliciting food and grooming in communicative gestures familiar to all cat people. Max's belly wound from this summer is still draining. Giles's rear leg seems healed from last year's long rip and subsequent circulatory insufficiency and persistent ulceration. They are wild enough that the process of getting them to a vet would probably have caused them worse injuries. And then what? Can cats raised feral become traveling, middle-class, academic pets in two different territories, one urban and one rural? What obligations ensue from the experience of entangled lives once touch has been initiated?

Their fur is shiny and eyes bright. Their high-end kibble diet is scientifically formulated and is probably why they can resist infection so well. The lamb protein in that diet is derived from industrial sheep-raising and slaughtering systems that should not exist, and the rice is hardly full of multispecies justice and well-being either, as anyone living off the water politics of California agribusiness knows. Meanwhile, we affluent humans won't buy and eat that particular (cheap) meat for ourselves, and we try to buy organic grains from sustainable agroecological farms. Who is fooling whom? Or is my wry indigestion a prick to trying to do better as companion species, individually and collectively, even while committed to permanent reexamination about what is better? The cats hunt avidly, and they still play with each other, even with their life scars. I don't care when I see Steller's jay feathers littering their hunting grounds; those avian populations are not threatened by domestic cats around here. I do remember the statistics of songbird kills by even well-provisioned pet cats in many places—enough to destabilize populations and add to the threat to already threatened species. I wish I knew the score in my region, but I do not. Would I kill our feral cats if I learned they were a problem for the local quail or other birds?

As for the contract we put out on rodents (I will leave unexamined the implicit category of vermin that fuels my unstably funny tone), our cats seem more into ranching than predator control. I am convinced they only crop surplus adolescent male rodents and carefully husband the pregnant females, finding them nice nests in our cars' innards. At least, the barn's various rodent populations seem to thrive in their presence. Would I know if our dusky-footed wood rat or deer mice populations were in trouble? Does provisioning feral cats carry obligations to follow through on questions of species diversity and ecological balances in microregions?

Nothing about the multispecies relationships I am sketching is emotionally, operationally, intellectually, or ethically simple for the people or clearly good or bad for the other critters. Everything about these specific, situated relationships is shaped from inside middle-class, rural or suburban, animal welfare– and rights–inflected, techno-scientific cultures. One thing seems clear to me after four years of living out—and imposing—face-to-face mutually opportunistic and affectionate relationships with critters who are no more and no less alien presences on this land than my human household and who would otherwise have died four years ago outside our ken: becoming feral demands—and invites—becoming worldly just as much as any other species entanglements do. "Feral" is another name for contingent "becoming with" for all the actors.

BECOMING EDUCATED: TEACHING U.S. HISTORY IN A COMMUNITY COLLEGE IN SONOMA COUNTY

What do feral cats have to do with community college students, besides having numbers assigned to them for tracking purposes and being required to get vaccinations? The short answer is that both classes of beings are "educated" through their intra-actions within historically situated technology. *When Species Meet* is about the entanglements of beings in technoculture that work through reciprocal inductions to shape companion species. Certain domestic animals have played the starring roles in this book, but it should be clear by now that many categories of beings, including technological assemblages and college students, count as "species" enmeshed in the practice of learning how to be worldly, how to respond, how to practice respect. In the spring of 2006, Evan Selinger, a science and technology studies colleague from philosophy, asked me to participate in a book he was coediting that posed a series of five questions to various scholars generously classed as philosophers.[1] The little essay below is adapted from my reply to one of Selinger's questions, namely, "If the history of ideas were to be narrated in such a way as to emphasize technological issues, how would that narrative differ from traditional accounts?"

"Ideas" are themselves technologies for pursuing inquiries. It's not just that ideas are embedded in practices; they *are* technical practices of situated kinds. That said, there is another way to approach this question. Several years ago I took a freshman course on American history offered at night at our local community college in Healdsburg, California, in order to add to the enrollment figures so that the instructor, my husband, Rusten Hogness, could give me an F and thus have the freedom to give better grades to the real students, since the History Department insisted on grading to a strict curve. Among other pursuits, Rusten is a software engineer who then was working at a little Hewlett-Packard branch office with fellow engineer friends. They all took the course for failing grades too, so that Rusten and his students could forget the curve and concentrate on learning. A couple years before, Rusten had taken this course himself from our housemate and friend, Jaye Miller, so that he could take an F and free up the curve for Jaye's students. It was easy to sign up for community college courses without supplying complete transcripts from previous education and without leaving much of a trail into further education or professional paths.

Without giving away our identities or purposes to the other students, who were of varying ages and experiences, all of us rogue enrollees actually worked pretty hard and joined in discussions all the time. Rusten taught the whole course through the history of technology, focusing on things such as the shoe lasts, guns, surgeries, and potted meat of the Civil War; the railroads, ranches, and mines of the Rocky Mountain West; the calorimeters of food science in land grant colleges and their relation to labor struggles; and P. T. Barnum's populist testing of the mental acumen of visitors to his displays (were they a hoax? were they real? I seem to recall that to be a famous philosophical query). Throughout the class, a wide-ranging set of questions in philosophy, politics, and cultural history came together to think better about possible shapes of science and technology. The idea that technology is relational practice that shapes living and dying was not an abstraction but a vivid presence. The history of a nation, as well as the history of ideas, had the shape of technology. Old and important books such as Sigfried Giedion's 1947 *Mechanization Takes Command* and Lewis Mumford's 1934 *Technics and Civilization* helped us through the course's conventional required textbook. The real students, as well as the faux failures, loved the course and knew a great deal more about "the history of ideas," including things like information and thermodynamics, as well as work, land rights, war, and justice, at the end of the term than at the beginning.

Rusten loves to teach, and he is fiercely committed to democratic scientific and technical competence and literacy. He has always taught with as much of a hands-on approach as possible and with a bright eye on the history of popular science and struggles for a more democratic society. We met in the 1970s in the History of Science Department at Johns Hopkins, where he was a graduate student studying nineteenth-century French and American popular science, among other things. He was also teaching the natural sciences and mathematics, as well as history and social studies, at the Baltimore Experimental High School. There, he constantly had his students hanging out in labs, hospitals, factories, and technology museums, and he taught politics, history, science, and technology as an integral part of Baltimore's story as an industrial port city with a fraught racial, sexual, and class history. He turned our kitchen into a chemistry lab, literally, and persuaded the students to think about industrial chemistry as well as the science and technology of cooking as a way to nurture both the pleasure of the science and a better sense of how divisions of labor and status work in science and technology.

Years before, Rusten, a war resister and pacifist in the Vietnam era, had done two years of alternative service in the Muslim southern Philippines, teaching mathematics and philosophy in a little fisheries college to students who were mostly dead a few years later from the repression of both separatist and revolutionary movements by the U.S.-supported regime in Manila. Questions about technologies of globalization and of "antiterrorism" are indelibly written onto his optic tectum and in intimate contact with whatever signals are working their way through the cerebrum.

Rusten's paternal grandfather, Thorfin Hogness, had headed the physical chemistry division of the Manhattan Project and then partici-pated in civilian scientists' struggles over the control of nuclear science and technology after the war. Perhaps as a result, most of Rusten's siblings and cousins are directly engaged in their working lives and their com-munity presence in "the history of ideas from a technological perspective" and vice versa. I tell this family story to foreground the knot of public and intimate worlds tying together what we call technology and what we might mean by philosophical perspectives. I am not sure if this way of approaching the question is traditional or not; it depends on what tradition one focuses on. But I am sure that I learned more U.S. history and more history of philosophy, as well as history of technology, in the one course in my life that I failed than in a great pile of those others marked with A's.

12. PARTING BITES
Nourishing Indigestion

Knowing is a direct material engagement, a practice of intra-acting with
the world as part of the world in its dynamic material configuring, its
ongoing articulation. . . . Ethics is about mattering, about taking account
of the entangled materializations of which we are a part, including new
configurations, new subjectivities, new possibilities—even the smallest
cuts matter.
—KAREN BARAD, MEETING THE UNIVERSE HALFWAY

One never eats entirely on one's own: this constitutes the rule
underlying the statement, "One must eat well." . . . I repeat,
responsibility is excessive or it is not a responsibility.
—JACQUES DERRIDA, "EATING WELL, OR THE CALCULATION
OF THE SUBJECT"

Consider a northern hairy-nosed wombat, sometimes called the bulldozer of the bush, as she burrows intently in the dry woodland floor of the Ebbing Forest National Park in central Queensland, Australia. Keeping the dirt out, the female's backward-facing pouch shelters a young joey attached to a teat on her belly. Including perhaps only twenty-five breeding females in the early years of the twenty-first century, with adults weighing between fifty-five and ninety pounds, these roguish but vulnerable marsupials are among the world's rarest large mammals.[1] Consider also the cobbled together microscopic critter, *Mixotricha paradoxa*, literally, "the paradoxical one with mixed up hairs." At about five hundred microns in diameter, the motley of critters going by the name *Mixotricha paradoxa* can just be discerned by the naked human eye. Not among the charismatic macrofauna in anybody's national park but nonetheless critical to recycling nutrients in forests, these hard-working, cellulose-processing protists live in the hind gut of a south Australian termite named *Mastotermes darwiniensis*.[2] So much in Australia carries Darwin's name and legacy.

It might seem tragically easy to count the Queensland wombats, if only these nocturnal and crepuscular, generally solitary, and secretive critters would show themselves to the census takers.[3] Accounting for *Mixotricha* raises another kind of numerical dilemma. *Mixotricha*, incited by a scanning electron microscope, visibly bristles with its resistance to enumeration. The bristles—mistaken, at lower magnifications, for cilia on a comprehensible single cell—show themselves under the EM to be hundreds of thousands of hairlike *Treponema* spirochetes, whose motion propels their cohabiting messmates through life, steered by four flagella poking out of the cone-shaped anterior end of the protist. Made up of a nucleated cell and four sorts of bacterial microbes (whose different kinds number from about 200 to 250,000 cells), with its five entangled genomes, "*Mixotricha paradoxa* is an extreme example of how all plants and animals—including ourselves—have evolved to contain multitudes."[4] Thus, my conclusion begins with companion species nourished in the cavities, crevices, and interdigitations of gestation, ingestion, and digestion among critters indigenous to the southern continent.

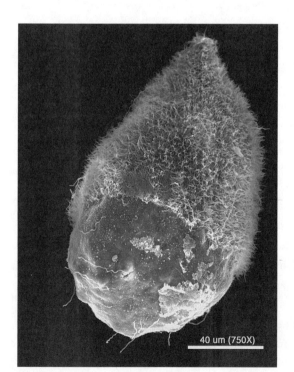

40 um (750X)

Mixotricha paradoxa. Scanning electron micrograph, 750x magnification, by Dean Soulia and Lynn Margulis, University of Massachusetts at Amherst. Courtesy of Lynn Margulis.

Instructed by Eva Hayward's fingery eyes,[5] I remember that "becoming with" is "becoming worldly." *When Species Meet* strives to build attachment sites and tie sticky knots to bind intra-acting critters, including people, together in the kinds of response and regard that change the subject—and the object. Encounterings do not produce harmonious wholes, and smoothly preconstituted entities do not ever meet in the first place. Such things cannot touch, much less attach; there is no first place; and species, neither singular nor plural, demand another practice of reckoning.[6] In the fashion of turtles (with their epibionts) on turtles all the way down, meetings make us who and what we are in the avid contact zones that are the world. Once "we" have met, we can never be "the same" again. Propelled by the tasty but risky obligation of curiosity among companion species, once we know, we cannot not know. If we know well, searching with fingery eyes, we care. That is how responsibility grows.

Lynn Margulis and Dorion Sagan suggested that the myriads of living organisms owe their evolved diversity and complexity to acts of symbiogenesis, through which promiscuous genomes and living consortia are the potent progeny of ingestion and subsequent indigestion among messmates at table, when everyone is on the menu. Sex, infection, and eating are old relatives, hardly deterred by the niceties of immune discrimination, whose material and syntactic intra-actions make the cuts that birth kin and kind. Let me suggest, then, parting bites that might nourish mortal companion species who cannot and must not assimilate one another but who must learn to eat well, or at least well enough that care, respect, and difference can flourish in the open.

The first bite returns us to the hairy-nosed wombat, this time with some unexpected companions. Melbourne-based artist Patricia Piccinini has fabulated plausible companion species—her term—to protect the southern continent's endangered species, including the northern hairy-nosed wombat. She is suspiciously inquisitive rather than sanguine about her introduced critters, even if their principal habitat is the art exhibition, Web site, and catalog.[7] Alerting viewers to both danger and possibility, her drawings, installations, and sculptures palpably argue that she has fallen in love with her sf-like progeny; she has certainly made me do so. Piccinini remembers Australia's and Aotearoa New Zealand's naturalcultural history of introduced species, human and nonhuman alike, with modern examples such as the South and Central American cane toad, shipped from Hawaii to northern Queensland in 1935 to munch repressively on the cane beetle that eats the sugar cane that gobbles up laboring people, who need the money from sugar to feed their children.[8] She remembers the exterminist consequences of well-intentioned introductions of companion species—in this example, for the unintended meal, that is, the endemic amphibians gobbled up by voracious, prolific, mobile cane toads. She knows that the African buffel grass planted for European cattle in the white settler colony outcompetes the native grasses on which the hairy-nosed wombats depend and that the threatened wombats contend for food and habitat with cattle, sheep, and rabbits. These marsupials also endure predation by dingoes, mammals dating from much earlier introductions, who have achieved ecological charismatic macrofauna status today after a long career as vermin to Europeans and a longer history as companion species to Aboriginals. Yet the modern rehabilitated nationalist dingoes, even after the cattle have been evicted and the buffel grass discouraged in the work of ecological restoration, have to be fenced out of the patch of Queensland's semiarid grassland and woodland that is the only place left for northern hairy-nosed wombats to burrow and dine.

But then, Piccinini knows, living beings in knotted and dynamic ecologies are opportunistic, not idealistic, and it is not surprising to find many native species flourishing in both new and old places because of the resources provided by interlopers from other lands and waters. Think of the kookaburras, displaced from their own former ranges, eating introduced pest snails and slugs alongside European starlings. Piccinini knows, in short, that introducing species (from another watershed, another continent, or another imagination) is often a world-destroying cut, as well as sometimes an opening to healing or even to new kinds of flourishing.[9] Piccinini's fabulated companion species to endangered species may be one more handy newcomer, among many, rather than a destructive invader, among many, or they may be both, the more usual course of things. The crucial question is not, Are they original and pure (natural in that sense)? but rather has to be, What do they contribute to the flourishing and health of the land and its critters (naturalcultural in that sense)? That question does not invite a disengaged "liberal" ethics or politics but requires examined lives that take risks to help the flourishing of some ways of getting on together and *not* others. Generally positive to animals Europeans have disparagingly called "feral," Australian Aboriginal peoples have tended to evaluate what Westerners call "species assemblages," new and old, in terms of what sustains the human and nonhuman, storied, changing, cared-for, and lived world called "country," as Anglophones hear the word.[10] As Barad put it for ears tuned to Western philosophy and science: "Embodiment is a matter not of being specifically situated in the world, but rather of being of the world in its dynamic specificity. . . . Ethics is therefore not about right response to a radically exterior/ized other, but about responsibility and accountability for the lively relationalities of becoming of which we are a part."[11] Curiosity should nourish situated knowledges and their ramifying obligations in that sense.[12]

Piccinini is also working explicitly in response to and in dialogue with technoculture and its biotechnologies. Her series called Nature's Little Helpers queries the tangled naturalcultural life forms central to conservation practices and to assisted reproductive practices. Both of these technocultural apparatuses have been central to *When Species Meet*, in which the categories of "endangered species" have repeatedly overflowed with the pain and hopes of their ill-contained actors, even when the vulnerable ones are "merely" kinds of dogs and their multispecies, historically dynamic, situated ways of life.

Made of silicone, fiberglass, hair, leather, and the goddess knows what else, a fabulated critter titled *Surrogate (for the Northern Hairy-Nosed Wombat), 2004* is one of Nature's Little Helpers. In the drawing *James (sitting), 2006*, a surrogate and a human baby sit face-to-face.[13] Intensely curious and just maybe slightly apprehensive, little James looks ready to reach out (left-handed). I know that babies often hurt the animals they grab. I trained with my dogs and children on loan from my graduate students, so that the canids might tolerate such exploratory excesses by badly coordinated, unaccountable, tiny hominids unwisely endowed too early in their development with grasping hands. Is the surrogate also well instructed? Why should s/he be? Surrogate and baby are close, maybe too close for a human child and an alien guardian species, who looks vaguely benign or maybe just pensive; who can read such a half-seen countenance? The appealing, full-frontal surrogate in color on the cover of the exhibition catalog *In Another World* does not answer my doubts or Piccinini's. The creature's ventral surface *does* sport a proper navel, indicating some kind of mammalian kinship, however reconfigured in technochimeras and however foreign to the gestational needs of marsupial wombats. The surrogate was not fabulated to be a protector of *Homo sapiens*, after all, but of *Lasiorhinus kreftii*, whose habitats and associates have been blasted by the very species introduced by James's kin. I am not sure what Queensland's indigenous peoples call or called northern hairy-nosed wombats, although "Yaminon" is an Aboriginal name (whose?) for these animals, a name that appears in conservation contexts today without discussion of the human or nonhuman historical naturecultures that generated it. I am even less sure what names different Aboriginal peoples might give the dorsally armored surrogate.[14] But whatever the proper names, the surrogate could reasonably decide that James and his kin do not fall under her (his?) writ of protection.

Handsome dorsal plates are the least of the interesting structures rippling down the backside of the surrogate. Three pairs of gestational

Patricia Piccinini, *James (sitting)*, 2006. Graphite on paper. Courtesy of the artist.

pouches run down the spine of the protector companion species, nurturing three stages of wombat development. Aligned with that of other marsupials such as the red kangaroo, surrogate wombat reproduction seems to be run on "just-in-time" principles for stocking embryos on the gestating body. Just out of the birth canal (whose?) and barely able to crawl up the surrogate's fur to wait its turn to finish making a wombat, a barely formed embryo surely inhabits the top pouch. Attached to a teat? Does the surrogate have teats in those odd sphincter-ringed, draw-string pouches? How not? Normal northern hairy-nosed wombats have only two teats in their single, backward-facing pouch, so they can't handle three young out of the body at once, and they give birth to only one young at a time, once a year. Joeys stay in the pouch eight to nine months. But if they are like kangaroos, these wombats could have arrested embryos ready to speed up their life course if the senior joey dies—or is disappeared by aliens. Northern hairy-nosed wombats like to have their babies in the rainy season, and getting a replacement joey into the pouch too late, when the succulent grasses are drying out, would not bode well for that reproductive cycle anyway. Maybe the surrogates take just-emerged joeys from wombat females and put them in their own pouches, thus forcing the wombats to birth another embryo from their body sooner and multiplying the number of young who can be raised in a season. This would not be the first time that forced reproduction was employed as an evolutionary and ecological rescue technology! Ask any tiger in a Species Survival Plan database. No wonder Piccinini is suspicious as well as open to another world.

The middle rung of surrogate pouches houses more developed but still hairless baby wombats; they are far from ready to explore the outside world. A teat, a pouch, and a vigilant surrogate's armored spine are all that are required for now. The third rung of pouches holds mature furry baby wombats, and one is crawling out of the pocket to begin its risky encounters in a wider world. For a few months, this joey can leap back into the pouch when things get too scary and supplement grass with milk, but even the best wombs or pouches, alien or native, give time-limited protection.

Again, I wonder if the surrogate is a male or female maternal creature; my imperializing gender categories will not let the matter rest. Of course, this query is rooted in my historically situated neurosis (and its biological and reproductive discourses), not the surrogate's. I am reminded that only about twenty-five breeding female northern hairy-nosed wombats live on planet Earth to gestate the young of their species. Being female in such a world never comes without paying the price of value. No wonder Piccinini felt called on to introduce her surrogates. I'd love to call the surrogate "queer" and let it go with a celebratory frisson that comes so cost-free to those usually identified as heterosexual, but I am sure Piccinini would withdraw her permission to use her image if I tried to get away with that. The surrogate remains a creature that nourishes indigestion, that is, a kind of dyspepsia with regard to proper place and function that queer theory is really all about. The surrogate is nothing if not the mutter/matter of gestation out of place, a necessary if not sufficient cut into the female-defining function called reproduction. To be out of place is often to be in danger and sometimes also to be free, in the open, not yet nailed by value and purpose.

There is no fourth rung of guarded gestation. James may be facing the surrogate, but I wager that the baby wombat and the baby human will find each other quickly in this narrative tableau. Then, what the world of companion species might become is open. The past has not laid enough ground for optimism for relations between white settler humans and wombats. Yet the past is far from absent or lacking in rich offerings for reworlding. Katie King offers a theoretical tool she calls pastpresents to think about the work of reenactment. She writes, "I think of pastpresents as quite palpable evidences that the past and the present cannot be purified each from the other; they confront me with interruptions, obstacles, new/old forms of organization, bridges, shifts in direction, spinning dynamics."[15] With this kind of material–semiotic tool as companion, the past, present, and future are all very much knotted into one another, full of what we need for the work and play of habitat restoration, less deadly curiosity, materially entangled ethics and politics, and openness to alien and native kinds symbiogenetically linked. In Barad's terms, we have here the world-making processes of intra-action and agential realism.

Nibbling on the material–semiotic joint linking gestation and indigestion—a connection well known to any marsupial, mammalian, or extraterrestrial critter of whatever gender who has ever been pregnant or just sympathetic—I offer a second parting bite. In 1980 I applied for a tenured position in feminist theory in the History of Consciousness program at the University of California at Santa Cruz. Actually, Nancy Hartsock and I applied to share the job, but Nancy withdrew to stay in Baltimore, and I pressed on, avid for the job. For years, people assumed Nancy and I were lovers because we took action to share a job; that way of surmising sexuality is surely interesting! But lamentably, it is outside the scope of this already too promiscuous book. The day of my job talk, I was picked up at the airport and delivered to the Dream Inn (where else?) by two HistCon graduate students, Katie King and Mischa Adams. They were in a hurry to get to a birth celebration in the Santa Cruz Mountains. A feminist lay midwife had assisted the birth, and there was to be a feast to share a meal of the placenta. Coming from The Johns Hopkins University and its technoscientific and biomedical excesses, I was enthralled, altogether ready to celebrate the bloody materiality of community affirmation in welcoming a baby human. Then I learned that the husband (of the placenta? of the mother? kin relations blurred) was to cook the placenta before serving it. This seemed to bring the feast into a yuppie orbit somehow, away from the mortal sacrament my Catholic formation respected. Would there be a tangy sauce? Things were out of kilter, at least in my East Coast prepped imagination. But I did not have time to worry; the job talk was pressing. Katie and Mischa took off for the feminist, anarchist, pagan cyberwitch mountains, whose waters fed the history of consciousness in those years.[16]

After the talk, my hosts took me out to dinner, and Katie and Mischa joined us from their previous meal. As everybody savored an elaborately eclectic ensemble of colorful, geographically fabulated foods at India Joze, no one discussed my passionately crafted lecture and its images. All attention, including mine, was focused on deciding who could, should, must, or must not eat the placenta. No one agreed; everyone made worlds grow from their figure of the meal. Philosophy, the history of religion, folklore, science, politics, popular dietary doctrines, aesthetics: all were in play. One person insisted that proteins were proteins, and it did not matter what the source was; the placenta was just biochemical food. Someone asked if Catholics before Vatican II could eat the placenta on Friday. The protein reductionist found herself in deep water fast. Those who cited an ancient matriarchy or some indigenous oneness with nature as warrant for eating afterbirth material got repressive looks from those attentive to the primitivizing moves of well-intentioned descendants of white settler colonies.

Katie and Mischa reported a solemn, rather than festive, sharing of bits of placenta—cooked with onions—in which friends shared nutrients needed by mother and baby at this moment of beginnings. That's my idea of a terran sacramental feast. Our informants reported the event as a potluck, eaten separately from the placental ceremony. The world here was not yuppie but hippie. Katie had brought soy milk that she had made in her kitchen. Health-conscious vegetarians at India Joze had some trouble with the low-fiber fare of the placenta, but the radical feminist vegan at table decided that the only people who *must* eat the placenta were fellow vegans, because they sought meals from life and not from death. In that sense, the placenta was not food from killed or exploited animals. Some worried whether accumulated toxins were especially high in human placentas, especially if the mother were known to eat high on the food chain. No one suggested placental zoonoses as a danger, because somehow no one saw cross-species connection in eating this flesh that controls the relations between self and other in pregnancy's commerce between mother and infant. Fresh from Marxist–feminist Baltimore habitats and sated on structuralism, I was still having trouble with the class play between the raw and the cooked.

One thing was clear: I had found my nourishing community at last, even as its members began to look a little green around the gills while they contemplated their comestibles. This community was composed of people who used their considerable intellectual skill and privilege to play, to tell serious jokes, to refuse to assimilate to each other even as they drew nourishment from one another, to riff on attachment sites, and to explore the obligations of emergent worlds where untidy species meet. These people let me join them, and my stomach has never settled.

There is a third and last parting bite necessary to explore how to proceed when species meet. No community works without food, without eating *together*. This is not a moral point, but a factual, semiotic, and material one that has consequences. As Derrida put it, "One never eats entirely on one's own."[17] That is a deeply unsettling fact if one wants a pure diet. Driven by such a fantastic desire, a diner's only permitted food would be oneself, ingesting, digesting, and gestating the same without end. Maybe God can have a solitary meal, but terran critters cannot. In eating we are most inside the differential relationalities that make us who and what we are and that materialize what we must do if response and regard are to have any meaning personally and politically. There is no way to eat and not to kill, no way to eat and not to become with other mortal beings to whom we are accountable, no way to pretend innocence and transcendence or a final peace. Because eating and killing cannot be hygienically separated does *not* mean that just any way of eating and killing is fine, merely a matter of taste and culture. Multispecies human and nonhuman ways of living and dying are at stake in practices of eating. As Barad said about world-making relationalities, "Even the smallest cuts matter."[18] Derrida argued that any real responsibility must be excessive. The practice of regard and response has no preset limits, but giving up human exceptionalism has consequences that require one to know more at the end of the day than at the beginning and to cast oneself with some ways of life and not others in the never settled biopolitics of entangled species. Further, one must actively cast oneself with some ways of life and not others *without* making any of three tempting moves: (1) being self-certain; (2) relegating those who eat differently to a subclass of vermin, the underprivileged, or the unenlightened; and (3) giving up on knowing more, including scientifically, and feeling more, including scientifically, about how to eat well—together.

In reference to the necessary, hard, ethical and political questions posed by those deeply committed to joint human and nonhuman animal well-being, among whom I number animal rights workers, I have touched in this book on the struggle for a viable modern agropastoralism and against the meat–industrial complex. Much of my conversation takes place in the intertextual play between writing above and below the line, between endnotes and foretext. But I have had too little to say about contemporary hunting in technocultural societies, an activity in which killing and eating are especially close. This is a huge and complicated topic, and I do not intend to enter it deeply. But I do want to recall a meal in my own academic community in order to say why every time I am confronted by passionate positions that configure opponents as benighted, I find practices of truth in the supposedly benighted camp, practices that I need, that we need. This is a biographical fact that has become more than that; this fact is why I experience becoming worldly as a process of nurturing attachment sites and sticky knots that emerge from the mundane and the ordinary. In my story here, the ordinary takes the form of our annual departmental party for faculty and graduate students. Fittingly, dogs come back into the picture in this story as agents of multispecies kinship formation as well as hunting companions, friends, and sports partners.

My colleague and friend Gary Lease is a religion studies scholar with exemplary allergies to dogmatic theologies of all kinds, even in tiny doses. Lease also has a keen scholarly knowledge of the history of ritual in the fleshly details of various practices of animal sacrifice, which intersect in a Venn diagram with hunting practices but are not the same thing. Understanding the aggregations and disaggregations of animal sacrifice and hunting is important for many reasons, including gaining some distance from assertions of identity made by both opponents and supporters, even philosophically sophisticated ones such as a number of ecofeminists, a community long dear to my heart, and Derrida, a more recent messmate. Histories are complex and dynamic in the human–nonhuman animal relations called hunting and do not lend themselves to typological reduction, except for purposes of hostile polemic, dogmatic purity, and hackneyed origin stories, usually of the Man-the-Hunter genre. That does not mean we are reduced to the god trick of an easy relativism about situated hunting practices, any more than an easy relativism about any other practice in the quest to eat well together, to refuse to make classes of beings killable, and to inhabit the consequences of what we know and do, including killing. To repeat myself, outside Eden, eating means also killing, directly or indirectly, and killing well is an obligation akin to eating well. This applies to a vegan as much as to a human carnivore. The devil is, as usual, in the details.

Lease is a consummate hunter, cook, host, and environmentalist with enviable public and private credentials of acting on his knowledgeable, affective commitments. He knows a great deal about those he kills, how they live and die, and what threatens their kind and their resources. His approach is resolutely tuned to ecological discourses, and he seems tone deaf to the demands individual animals might make as ventriloquized in rights idioms. My sleep is more haunted by these murmurings. But Lease is far from deaf to the profoundly (and diversely) emotional and cognitive demands individual animals and hunters make on each other. Lease acknowledges and cares about nonhuman animals as sentient beings in the ordinary sense of that term, even if technical knowledge of sentience remains hotly contested. He certainly understands that the kinds of animals he hunts feel pain and have rich emotions. He hunts all over the world; he hunts regionally as often as he can; his home is full of what he kills; and his generous table never offers industrially produced meat. Small wonder that his practices would generate orgies of both pleasure and indigestion at our annual departmental feasts!

I will focus on a whole feral pig roasting in Lease's back yard in Santa Cruz, California, one spring evening a few years ago. Too easy, my reader might cry; feral pigs are pests, known environmental thugs ripping up the hillsides where proper native organisms ought to be living. People regularly call feral pigs "rototillers"; if burrowing wombats were as numerous (and as alien?), their moniker of "bulldozers of the bush" might win them fewer fans in the ecological community. Feral pigs are "introduced species," politely put, and invaders deserving what they get, in the xenophobic idiom of the immigration shy. I tracked some of that in a popular Web site article called "Alien Invaders."[19] Feral pigs lack sufficient predatory pressure that needs to be supplied by human hunters, even if extermination is not the goal. All true.[20]

But feral pigs are not an easy case. They are a highly intelligent, opportunistic, socially adept, well armed, and emotionally talented lot, who have demonstrably strong feelings about one another and about their hunters, both human and canine. Would you kill and eat a feral dog or a pet pooch eating more than his or her share of the world's resources? Who determines such shares? Pigs have just as much claim on life as a dog (and what about humans?), if social, emotional, and cognitive complexity is the criterion. Derrida got it right: There is no rational or natural dividing line that will settle the life-and-death relations between human and nonhuman animals; such lines are alibis if they are imagined to settle the matter "technically."

Whether posed in idioms of ecology or animal rights, right-to-life discourses are not going to solve the questions posed by that savory dead pig in Lease's yard. Pigs do less damage to hillsides, watersheds, and species diversity than the industrial California wine industry, much less the real estate industry. The factory-farmed pork industry treats pigs (and people) like calculable production units. That industry is infamous for polluting whole watersheds and damaging literally thousands of species as a result, including people. Adept hunters such as Lease treat pigs like wily animals with lives of their own. Lease has excellent ecological warrant for hunting pigs, but he hunts lots of other kinds of animals who are not considered raving environmental serial killers. However, he hunts only in accord with strict conservation practices (often in relation to projects that provide local, sustainable, skilled jobs for "endangered" people as well) and with testable, revisable, fallible knowledge. He is fierce about killing with as little terror and pain as his skill makes possible, certainly much less than any raccoon I have witnessed pulling a cat apart or any cougar I envision killing a pig. Nonetheless, most people do not have to eat meat, and felines generally do; more peaceful alternatives exist for people. But the calculus of suffering and choice won't solve the dilemma of the departmental party either, and not only because all the alternatives carry their own burden of assigning who lives and who dies and how. The crisis the party faced was a cosmopolitical one, where neither human exceptionalism nor the oneness of all things could come to the rescue. *Reasons* were well developed on all sides; *commitments* to very different ways of living and dying were what needed to be examined together, without any god tricks and with consequences.

Hunting, killing, cooking, serving, and eating (or not) a pig is a very intimate personal and public act at every stage of the process, with major consequences for a community that cannot be—and should not be—composed along the lines of organic holism. Several diners in Lease's yard that spring not only refused to eat the succulent pork he served but also argued passionately that he was out of line to serve hunted meat. They argued that his kind of hospitality was an act of aggression not only to the animals but also to the students and faculty. The department should adopt a vegan practice, they maintained, or at least a practice that did not include the community's facing the body of a whole animal for collective consumption. But feral pigs, hunters, eaters, and resisters are companion species, entangled in a messy meal with no sweet dessert to settle everybody's digestion. In any case, sugar hardly seems the proper histori-cal antacid to hunting! What is to be done, if neither liberal relativism nor the fiat of the self-certain of any stripe is a legitimate option?

What actually happened is that Lease did not again hunt and cook a pig for the department. We all avoided conflict. Sliced deli meats seemed tolerable, if barely, and no real collective engagement on the ways of life and death at stake took place. Obligatory "good manners" foreclosed cos-mopolitics, with its kind of polite meetings. I think that was a great loss, much worse than ongoing acid indigestion, because the different approaches could not all be assimilated, even while they all made truth claims that could not be evaded. Or at least I felt them all pulling at my innards, and I was not alone. Remembering the dinner at India Joze, I longed for the kind of serious play that the cooked placenta evoked. But the placenta was in the mountains, confronted by others, and the pig was in Lease's yard, confronted by the departmental diners. Besides, there aren't many emotionally demanding, sentient placentas in the hills stalked by hunters.

I think cosmopolitical questions arise when people respond to seri-ously different, felt and known, finite truths and must cohabit well with-out a final peace. If one knows hunting is theologically right or wrong, or that animal rights positions are dogmatically correct or incorrect, then there is no cosmopolitical engagement. Perhaps I project too much from my own personal and political experience in these areas, and I am too easily swayed by friendships and, face-to-face (or book-to-book), getting how the world is to someone else. But these qualities are among those that define the talents of social animals like us, and I think we ought to make more, not less, use of them when species meet. In the sense I have tried to develop in this book, I respect Lease's hunting practices in my bones, and I eat his food with gratitude. In the same sense, I respect friends and colleagues such as Carol Adams, Lynda Birke, and Marc Bekoff, all of whom are scholars and activists whose love of animals leads them to oppose meat eating and hunting of all sorts, not just factory farming.[21] Bekoff, a behavioral biologist and tireless animal advocate, acknowledges that some hunters, like Lease, experience and practice love for the animals they kill, and he remarks that he is very glad such hunters do not love him. It *is* hard to imagine. But Lease and Bekoff are messmates in too many ways for that to be the last word. They are both deeply knowledgeable and active animal advocates, both alert to the nonanthropomorphic competences of many kinds of animals, both environmentalists with solid credentials in the world, both open to play and work with nonhuman animals, both committed to knowing well and eating well. That I feel them both in my gut is not relativism, I insist, but the kind of pain that simultaneously true and unharmonizable things cause. Dialectics is a powerful tool for addressing contradictions, but Bekoff and Lease do not embody contradictions. Rather, they embody finite, demanding, affective, and cognitive claims on me and the world, both sets of which require action and respect without resolution. That's my idea of nourishing indigestion, a necessary physiological state for eating well together.

It's late afternoon in December, time for my canine and human household to go running together and come home to cook dinner. It's time to return to the ordinary knots of daily multispecies living in a particular place and time. If I ignore this simple fact, a determined dog's paws will be on my keyboard typing strange codes I may not know how to delete. Throughout this book, I have tried to ask how taking such things seriously draws us into the world, makes us care, and opens up political imaginations and commitments. Almost eight years ago, I found myself in unexpected and out-of-bounds love with a hot red dog I named Cayenne. It is not surprising that she acted as a kin maker in a middle-class U.S. home in the early twenty-first century, but it has been an awakening to track how many sorts of kin and kind this love has materialized, how many sorts of consequences flow from her kiss. The sticky threads proliferating from this woman–dog tangle have led to Israeli settler ranches on the Golan Heights in Syria, French bulldogs in Paris, prison projects in the midwestern United States, investment analyses of canine commodity culture on the Internet, mouse labs and gene research projects, baseball and agility sports fields, departmental dinners, camera-toting whales off Alaska, industrial chicken-processing plants, history classrooms in a community college, art exhibitions in Wellington, and farm-supply participants in a feral cat trap-and-release program. Official and demotic philosophers, biologists of many kinds, photographers, cartoonists, cultural theorists, dog trainers, activists in technoculture, journalists, human family, students, friends, colleagues, anthropologists, literary scholars, and historians all enable me to track the consequences of love and play between Cayenne and me. Like Ian Wedde's Vincent, she enriches my ignorance.[22]

When Species Meet works by making connections, by trying to respond where curiosity and sometimes unexpected caring lead. No chapter has a bottom line, but they all have barely contained traffic between the lines and between the foretext and endnotes in an attempt to engage a cosmopolitical conversation. Animals are everywhere full partners in worlding, in becoming with. Human and nonhuman animals are companion species, messmates at table, eating together, whether we know how to eat well or not. Many pithy slogans might urge us on in trying to learn more about how to flourish together in difference without the telos of a final peace. A rough one from the dog world might be, "Shut up and train!" But I prefer to end with a longing that it might be said of me someday what good agility players say of those whose runs they admire, "She has met her dog."

NOTES

1. WHEN SPECIES MEET

1. Beatriz Preciado, who teaches about technologies of gender at the Museum of Contemporary Art in Barcelona and about queer theory, prosthetic technologies, and gender in Paris, introduced me both to nuances of the terms *alter-globalisation* and *autre-mondialisation* and to the cosmopolitan pooch Pepa, who walks the cities of Europe in the French lesbian canine traditions, marking a kind of worldliness of her own. Of course, *autre-mondialisation* has many lives, some of which can be tracked on the Internet, but the versions Preciado gave me animate this book. In a manuscript she sent me in August 2006, Preciado wrote: "Fabricated at the end of the nineteenth-century, French bulldogs and lesbians co-evolve from being marginal monsters into becoming media creatures and bodies of pop and chic consumption. Together, they invent a way of surviving and create an aesthetics of human–animal life. Slowly moving from red-light districts to artistic boroughs all the way to television, they have ascended the species pile together. This is a history of mutual recognition, mutation, travel and queer love. . . . The history of the French bulldog and that of the working queer woman are tied to the transformations brought on by the industrial revolution and the emergence of modern sexualities. . . . Soon, the so-called French bulldog became the beloved companion of the 'Belles de nuit,' being depicted by

artists such as Toulouse Lautrec and Degas in Parisian brothels and cafes. [The dog's] ugly face, according to conventional beauty standards, echoes the lesbian refusal of the heterosexual canon of female beauty; its muscular and strong body and its small size made of the *molosse* the ideal companion of the urban *flâneuse*, the nomad woman writer and the prostitute. [By] the end of the nineteenth century, together with the cigar, the suit or even writing [itself], the bulldog became an identity accessory, a gender and political marker and a privileged survival companion for the manly woman, the lesbian, the prostitute and the gender reveler [in] the growing European cities.... The French bulldog's survival opportunity really began in 1880, when a group of Parisian Frenchy breeders and fans began to organize regular weekly meetings. One of the first members of the French bulldog owners club was Madame Palmyre, the proprietor of the club 'La Souris' located in the lower reaches of Paris in the area of 'Mont Martre' and 'Moulin Rouge.' This was a gathering place for butchers, coachmen, rag traders, café owners, barrow boys, writers, painters, lesbians and hookers. Lesbian writers Renée Vivien and Natalie Clifford Barney and Colette, as well as modernist writers such as Catulle Mendes, Coppée, Henry Cantel, Albert Mérat and Léon Cladel gathered together with bulldogs at La Souris. Toulouse Lautrec immortalized 'bouboule,' Palmyre's French bulldogs, walking with hookers or eating at their tables. Representing the so-called dangerous classes, the scrunched-up faces of the bulldog, as those of the manly lesbians, were part of the modern aesthetic turn. Moreover, French writer Colette, friend of Palmyre and customer of La Souris, would be one of the first writers and political actors to be always portrayed with her French bulldogs, and most specially her beloved 'Toby-Le-Chien.' By the early 1920s, the French bulldog had become a biocultural companion of the liberated woman and writer in literature, painting, and the emerging media."

2. For a larger discussion of contact zones, see chapter 8, "Training in the Contact Zone."

3. Thanks to History of Consciousness graduate student Eben Kirksey for that reference and for his organizing the "Multispecies Salon" in November 2006, at UC Santa Cruz.

4. *Fingery eyes* is Eva Hayward's term for the haptic–optic join of camera with marine critters, especially invertebrates, at the multiple interfaces of water, air, glass, and other media through which visual touch occurs in art and science. See Eva Hayward, "Fingery-Eyes: What I Learned from *Balanophyllia elegans*," for the *Encyclopedia of Human–Animal Relationships*, ed. Marc Bekoff (Westport, Conn.: Greenwood Publishing Group, forthcoming).

5. *Intra-action* is Karen Barad's term. By my borrowing, I also touch her in Jim's dog. Karen Barad, *Meeting the Universe Halfway: Quantum Physics and the Entanglement of Matter and Meaning* (Durham, N.C.: Duke University Press, 2007).

6. Paul Rabinow, *Essays on the Anthropology of Reason* (Princeton, N.J.: Princeton University Press, 1996), argues for the virtue of curiosity, a difficult and often corrosive practice that is not much honored in U.S. culture, no matter my views about obligation and pleasure.

7. A. N. Whitehead, *Science and the Modern World*, Lowell Lectures, 1925 (New York: Mentor Books, 1948). Whitehead writes: "An event is the grasping into unity of a pattern of aspects. The effectiveness of an event beyond itself arises from the aspects of itself which go to form the prehended unities of other events" (111).

8. I discuss these kinds of technocultural images in Donna Haraway, *Modest_Witness@Second_Millennium* (New York: Routledge, 1997), 131–72, 173–212, 293–309.

9. My alliance with Bruno Latour in *Politics of Nature: How to Bring the Sciences into Democracy* (Cambridge, Mass.: Harvard University Press, 2004) and in *We Have Never Been Modern*, trans. Catherine Porter (Cambridge, Mass.: Harvard University Press, 1993) is obvious here and often in my explorations of how "we have never been human." That suggestive title has also been used to allied effect by Eduardo Mendieta, "We Have Never Been Human or, How We Lost Our Humanity: Derrida and Habermas on Cloning," *Philosophy Today*, SPEP Supplement (2003): 168–75; and Brian Gareau, "We Have Never Been Human: Agential Nature, ANT, and Marxist Political Ecology," *Capitalism, Nature, Socialism* 16, no. 4 (December 2005): 127–40. I am indebted also to Don Ihde, *Bodies in Technology* (Minneapolis: University of Minnesota Press, 2002), for his readings of Merleau-Ponty's "infoldings of the flesh" and much else.

10. See Bruno Latour and Peter Weibel, eds., *Making Things Public: Atmospheres of Democracy* (Karlsruhe: ZKM Center for Arts and Media; and Cambridge, Mass.: MIT Press, 2005) for a wealth of worlds no longer beholden to the Great Divides.

11. All of these words, *technology, nature, organic,* and more generate protean webs of meaning that have to be addressed in intimate historical detail. But here, I want to foreground the still readily heard oppositions and assumed transparencies of meanings in still current idioms.

12. Jacques Derrida, "And Say the Animal Responded?" trans. David Wills, in *Zoontologies: The Question of the Animal,* ed. Cary Wolfe (Minneapolis:

University of Minnesota Press, 2003), 121–46, 138. In an e-mail dated September 1, 2006, Isabelle Stengers reminded me that Freud was conducting an exclusionary propaganda war for his own theory of the unconscious by means of his apparatus of narcissistic wounds and their treatment. Human exceptionalism has not been the only Western tradition, much less a universal cultural approach. Stengers was most annoyed by the third wound, in which Freud seems to address Descartes and Cie, "but which also entails blanket judgment about traditional soul healing crafts, which get assimilated to sheer suggestion." Derrida does not address this matter because the orthodox Cartesian tradition is his target. The pity is that this tradition stands for the West *tout court* in so much philosophy and critical theory, a fault of which I have been as guilty as anyone. For a crucial corrective, see Erica Fudge, *Brutal Reasoning: Animals, Rationality, and Humanity in Early Modern England* (Ithaca, N.Y.: Cornell University Press, 2006). The question Derrida takes on is how "to break with the Cartesian tradition of the animal–machine that exists without language and without the ability to respond," but only to react (121). To do that, it is not enough to "subvert" the subject; the topography of the Great Divide that maps the animal *in general* and the human *in general* has to be left behind in favor of "the whole differentiated field of experience and of life-forms" (128). Derrida argues that the truly philosophically scandalous (and psychoanalytically revealing) move in positing human exceptionalism, and so dominion, is *less* refusing "the animal" a long list of powers ("speech, reason, experience of death, pretense of pretense, covering of tracks, gift, laughter, tears, respect, and so on—the list is necessarily without limit") and *more* "what calls itself human" rigorously attributing to man, to himself, such self-constituting attributes (137). "Traces erase (themselves), like everything else, but the structure of the trace is such that it cannot be in anyone's *power* to erase it. . . . The distinction might appear subtle and fragile but its fragility renders fragile all the solid oppositions that we are in the process of tracking down" (138).

13. A useful analysis of the nonteleological heart of Darwinism can be found in Elizabeth Grosz, *The Nick of Time: Politics, Evolution, and the Untimely* (Durham, N.C.: Duke University Press, 2004).

14. Yudhijit Bhattarcharjee, "Evolution Trumps Intelligent Design in Kansas Vote," *Science* 313 (August 11, 2006): 743.

15. In a 2005 survey of adults in thirty-two European nations and the United States and a similar 2001 query of the Japanese, only people in Turkey expressed more doubts about evolution than U.S. Americans, whereas 85 percent of Icelanders were comfortable with the idea that "human beings, as we

know them, developed from earlier species of animals." About 60 percent of U.S. adults surveyed either did not "believe" in evolution or expressed doubts. Over the last twenty years, the percentage of adults in the United States accepting evolution has declined from 45 percent to 40 percent. The percentage of adults not sure of their position increased from 7 percent in 1985 to 21 percent in 2005. See Jon Miller, Eugenie Scott, and Shinji Okamoto, "Public Acceptance of Evolution," *Science* 313 (August 11, 2006): 765–66; *New York Times*, Tuesday, August 15, 2006, D2. I do not find it strange that these doubts about the histories of human evolution go along with hypertrophied faith in certain kinds of engineering and in war-making and profit-extraction technologies. Science is not one.

16. With little feet growing from its ventral surface for moving from salty seas to dry land in the great evolutionary adventure, the Darwin fish is a symbol generally understood to be a parodic reply to the Christian Jesus fish (no feet) on car bumpers and refrigerator doors of fellow citizens. Check out www .darwinfish.com; the opportunity to market a commodity is never missed. One can also purchase a fish design with *gefilte* inscribed in it. As Wikipedia (http://en.wikipedia.org/wiki/Parodies_of_the_ichthys_symbol) tells us, "The Darwin fish has led to a minor arms race in bumper stickers. A design was made with a larger 'Jesus fish' eating the Darwin fish. Sometimes, the larger fish contains letters that spell the word 'TRUTH.' A further step shows two fish, one with legs labeled 'I evolved,' the other without legs labeled 'You didn't.'"

17. John Paul Scott and John L. Fuller, *Genetics and Social Behavior of the Dog* (Chicago: University of Chicago Press, 1965). For a discussion of this research project in biological, political, and cultural contexts, see Donna Haraway, "For the Love of a Good Dog," in *Genetic Nature/Culture*, ed. Alan Goodman, Deborah Heath, and M. Susan Lindee (Berkeley and Los Angeles: University of California Press, 2003), 111–31. In my account I drew heavily on Diane Paul, "The Rockefeller Foundation and the Origin of Behavior Genetics," in *The Politics of Heredity* (Albany: State University of New York Press, 1998). On August 27, 1999, Faye Ginsburg e-mailed me, "Paul Scott was like an uncle to me, and my dad has spent a good part of his life studying the evolution of canine behavior as a social process. [I] played with [my father's] wolves as a kid, not to mention the coy-dog and other unfortunate creatures. . . . I should dig out the December 3, 1963 issue of *Look* magazine with me romping with the wolves and playing with super aggressive inbred rabbits!!!" The lab also had dingoes. Faye did dig out the article, complete with great pictures of wolf and girl in proper face-to-face greeting and in play. For the photos and more, see "Nurturing the Genome: Benson Ginsburg Festschrift," June 28–29, 2002, http://ginsburgfest

.uconn.edu/. Faye Ginsburg studies Indigenous digital media production and consumption, as well as disability and public culture. See Faye Ginsburg, "Screen Memories: Resignifying the Traditional in Indigenous Media," in *Media Worlds: Anthropology on New Terrain*, ed. Faye Ginsburg, Lila AbuLughod, and Brian Larkin (Berkeley and Los Angeles: University of California Press, 2002).

18. This passage is taken from Donna Haraway, *The Companion Species Manifesto: Dogs, People and Significant Otherness* (Chicago: Prickly Paradigm Press, 2003), 1–3.

19. I adapt the term *becoming with* from Vinciane Despret, "The Body We Care For: Figures of Anthropo-zoo-genesis," *Body and Society* 10, no. 2 (2004): 111–34. She refigured the story of Konrad Lorenz with his jackdaws: "I suggest that Lorenz became a 'jackdaw-with-human' as much as the jackdaw became in some ways a 'human-with-jackdaw.' . . . This is a new articulation of 'with-ness,' an undetermined articulation of 'being with.' . . . He learns to be affected. . . . Learning how to address the creatures being studied is not the *result* of scientific theoretical understanding[;] it is the *condition* of this understanding" (131). For a feminist extension of "becoming with," see Maria Puig de la Bellacasa, "Thinking with Care," paper delivered at the meetings of the Society for Social Studies of Science, Vancouver, B.C., November 2–4, 2006.

20. Foundational theorists of intersectionality have been U.S. feminists of color, including Kimberle Crenshaw, "Demarginalizing the Intersection of Race and Sex," in *Feminist Legal Theory: Foundations*, ed. D. Kelly Weisberg (Philadelphia: Temple University Press, 1993), 383–98; Angela Davis, *Women, Race and Class* (New York: Random House, 1981); Chéla Sandoval, *Methodology of the Oppressed* (Minneapolis: University of Minnesota Press, 2000); Gloria Anzaldùa, *Borderlands/La Frontera* (San Francisco: Aunt Lute Books, 1987); and many others. For a primer, see "Intersectionality: A Tool for Gender and Economic Justice," *Women's Rights and Economic Change* 9 (August 2004), www.awid.org/ publications/primers/intersectionality_en.pdf.

21. For trenchant analysis, see Katherine Hayles, *How We Became Posthuman: Virtual Bodies in Cybernetics, Literature, and Informatics* (Chicago: University of Chicago Press, 1999); and Cary Wolfe, *Animal Rites: American Culture, the Discourse of Species, and Posthumanist Theory* (Chicago: University of Chicago Press, 2003). The "posthumanities," however, seems to me a useful notion for tracking scholarly conversations. On "conversation" (versus "debate") as political practice see Katie King, *Theory in Its Feminist Travels* (Bloomington: Indiana University Press, 1994). King's new book, *Network Reenactments: Histories under Globalization* (in preparation), is an indispensable guide to transknowledge makings

and reenactments of many kinds, in and out of the contemporary university. King's notion of pastpresents is particularly useful for thinking about how to inherit histories.

22. See note 20 above for "intersectionality." Carol Adams, *Neither Beast nor Man: Feminism and the Defense of Animals* (New York: Continuum, 1995), 71–84, argues persuasively for an intersectional, not an analogical, approach to the needed allied oppositions to the deadly oppressions and exploitations of animals and of categories of human beings who cannot fully count as "man." Adams writes: "That is, from a humanocentric perspective of oppressed peoples who have been, if not equated with animals, treated like animals, the introduction of animals to resistance politics suggests that, once again, even in resistance humans are being equated with animals. But again this is a result of thinking analogically, of seeing oppression as additive, rather than comprehending the interlocking systems of domination" (84). Sandoval's *Methodology of the Oppressed* has developed a robust theory of oppositional and differential consciousness that should forever prevent hierarchized analogical moves, in which oppressions are both equated and ranked, rather than made to animate another kind of entanglement of becoming with one another that is attentive to the asymmetries of power. For varied ways of dealing with these issues, see also Octavia Butler, *Fledgling* (New York: Seven Stories Press, 2005); Alice Walker, "Am I Blue?" in *Living by the Word* (New York: Harcourt Brace, 1987), 3–8; Angela Davis, "Rape, Racism, and the Myth of the Black Rapist," in *Women, Race and Class*, 172–201; Marcie Griffith, Jennifer Wolch, and Unna Lassiter, "Animal Practices and the Racialization of Filipinas in Los Angeles," *Society and Animals* 10, no. 3 (2002): 222–48; Eduardo Mendieta, "Philosophical Beasts," *Continental Philosophy Review*, under review; and Mendieta, "The Imperial Bestiary of the U.S.," in *Radical Philosophy Today*, vol. 4, ed. Harray van der Linden and Tony Smith (Charlottesville, Va.: Philosophy Documentation Center, 2006), 155–79. In his search for another logic of metamorphosis, Achille Mbembe, *On the Postcolony* (Berkeley and Los Angeles: University of California Press, 2001), tracks the brutalization, bestialization, and colonization of African subjects in philosophy and history. In my experience of writing on the topic, the readiness with which taking animals seriously is heard to be an animalization of people of color is a shocking reminder, if one is needed, of how potent colonial (and humanist) tools of analogy remain, including in discourses intended to be liberatory. Rights discourse struggles with this legacy. My hope for companion species is that we might struggle with different demons from those produced by analogy and hierarchy linking all of fictional man's others.

23. Sha La Bare, writing on sf and religion, Ursula LeGuin, farfetchings, Afro-futurism, Scientology, and the sf mode as historical consciousness, taught me to pay attention to the sf tones of "species." Sha La Bare, "Science Fiction: Theory and Practice," PhD dissertation in progress, History of Consciousness Department, University of California at Santa Cruz.

24. Anna Tsing, "Unruly Edges: Mushrooms as Companion Species," in *Thinking with Donna Haraway*, ed. Sharon Ghamari-Tabrizi (Cambridge, Mass.: MIT Press, forthcoming). See also Anna Tsing, *Friction: An Ethnography of Global Connection* (Princeton, N.J.: Princeton University Press, 2004), especially chapter 5, "A History of Weediness."

25. Jacques Derrida, "The Animal That Therefore I Am (More to Follow)," trans. David Wills, *Critical Inquiry* 28 (Winter 2002): 369–418. Further references to this essay are in parentheses in the main text. This essay is the first part of a ten-hour address Derrida gave at the third Cerisy-la-Salle conference in 1997. See Jacques Derrida, *L'animal autobiographique*, ed. Marie-Louise Mallet (Paris: Galilée, 1999).

26. "Confined within this catch-all concept, within this vast encampment of the animal, in the general singular ... are *all the living things* that man does not recognize as his fellows, his neighbors, or his brothers. ... Animals are my concern. ... I will venture to say that never, on the part of any great philosopher from Plato to Heidegger, or anyone at all who takes on, *as a philosophical question in and of itself*, the question called that of the animal ... have I noticed a protestation *of principle* ... against the general singular that is *the animal*. ... The confusion of all nonhuman living creatures within this general and common category of the animal is not simply a sin against rigorous thinking ... but a crime of the first order against the animals, against animals" (402, 403, 408, 416).

27. I highlight "once its protocol is properly established" to differentiate the kind of question that needs to be asked from the practice of assessing nonhuman animals in relation to human ones by checking the presence or absence of a potentially infinite list of capacities, a process that Derrida so rightly rejected. What is at stake in establishing a different protocol is the never denotatively knowable, for human or nonhuman animals, *relation* of response. Derrida thought Bentham's question avoided the dilemma by pointing not to positive capabilities assessed against one another but to "the non-power at the heart of power" that we share with the other animals in our suffering, vulnerability, and mortality. But I am not satisfied with that solution; it is only part of the needed reformulation. There is an unnamable being/becoming with in copresence that Barbara Smuts, below, will call something we taste rather than something we

know, which is about suffering *and* expressive, relational vitality, in all the vulnerable mortality of both. I am (inadequately) calling that expressive, mortal, world-making vitality "play" or "work," not to designate a fixable capability in relation to which beings can be ranked, but to affirm a kind of "non-power at the heart of power" other than suffering. Maybe a usable word for this is *joy*. "Mortality . . . as the most radical means of thinking the finitude we share with animals" does not reside only in suffering, in my view. (Both quotations come from "The Animal That Therefore I Am," 396.) Capability (play) and incapability (suffering) are *both* all about mortality and finitude. Thinking otherwise comes from the ongoing oddities of dominant Western philosophical conversations, including those Derrida knew best and undid so well most of the time. Some kinds of Buddhist idioms might work better here and be closer to what Derrida meant by establishing a different protocol from Bentham's to ask about suffering, but other idioms offer themselves from many varied and mixed traditions as well, some of which are "Western." I want a different protocol for asking about a lot more than suffering, which at least in U.S. idioms will regularly end in the self-fulfilling search for rights and their denial through abuse. I am more worried than Derrida seems to be here about the way animals become discursive victims and little else when the protocols are *not* properly established for the question, Can animals suffer? Thanks to Cary Wolfe for making me think more about this unsolved problem in this chapter.

28. Emmanuel Lévinas, "The Name of a Dog, or Natural Rights," in *Difficult Freedom: Essays on Judaism*, trans. Sean Hand (Baltimore: Johns Hopkins University Press, 1990), 151–53. Lévinas movingly tells the story of the stray dog called Bobby, who greeted the Jewish prisoners of war as they returned from work each day in a German forced-labor camp, restoring to them knowledge of their humanity. "For him, there was no doubt that we were men. . . . This dog was the last Kantian in Nazi Germany, without the brain needed to universalize maxims and drives" (153). Thus was Bobby left on the other side of a Great Divide, even by a man as sensitive as Lévinas was of the service rendered by this dog's look. My favorite essay in animal studies and philosophy on the question of Bobby and whether an animal has "face" in Lévinas's sense is by H. Peter Steeves, "Lost Dog," in *Figuring the Animal: Essays in Animal Images in Art, Literature, Philosophy, and Popular Culture*, ed. Catherine Rainwater and Mary Pollack (New York: Palgrave Macmillan, 2005), 21–35. See also H. Peter Steeves, *The Things Themselves: Phenomenology and the Return to the Everyday* (Albany: State University of New York Press, 2006). For a full explication of the many ways the dog Bobby "traces and retraces the oppositional limits that configure

the human and the animals," see David L. Clark, "On Being 'the Last Kantian in Nazi Germany': Dwelling with Animals after Lévinas," in *Animal Acts*, ed. Jennifer Ham and Matthew Senior (New York: Routledge, 1997), 41–74, 70. On Derrida and others in the Continental philosophical canon on animals, see Matthew Calarco, *Zoographies: The Question of the Animal from Heidegger to Derrida* (New York: Columbia University Press, forthcoming).

29. The book based on that and subsequent research is Barbara Smuts, *Sex and Friendship in Baboons* (Cambridge, Mass.: Harvard University Press, 1985). I wrote about Smuts in *Primate Visions: Gender, Race, and Nature in the World of Modern Science* (New York: Routledge, 1989), 168–69, 176–79, 371–76. See also Shirley Strum, *Almost Human: A Journey into the World of Baboons* (New York: Random House, 1987). When I wrote *Primate Visions*, I think I failed the obligation of curiosity in much the same way I suggest Derrida did. I was so intent on the consequences of the Western philosophical, literary, and political heritage for writing about animals—especially other primates in the so-called third world in a period of rapid decolonization and gender rearrangements—that I all but missed the radical practice of many of the biologists and anthropologists, women and men both, who helped me with the book, that is, their relentless curiosity about the animals and their tying themselves into knots to find ways to engage *with* these diverse animals as a rigorous scientific practice and not a romantic fantasy. Many of my informants for *Primate Visions* actually cared most about who the animals are; their radical practice was an eloquent refusal of the premise that the proper study of mankind is man. I, too, often mistook the conventional idioms of the philosophy and history of science spoken by most of "my" scientists for a description of what they did. They tended to mistake my grasp of how narrative practice works in science, how fact and fiction coshape each other, to be a reduction of their hard-won science to subjective storytelling. I think we needed each other but had little idea of how to respond. Smuts, as well as such people as Alison Jolly, Linda Fedigan, Shirley Strum, and Thelma Rowell, continued to engage with me then and later with a mode of attention that I call generous suspicion, which I regard as one of the most important epistemological virtues of companion species. Out of the kind of respect I identify as mutual generous suspicion, we have crafted friendships for which I am mightily grateful. See Shirley Strum and Linda Marie Fedigan, eds., *Primate Encounters* (Chicago: University of Chicago Press, 2000). Had I known in 1980 how to cultivate the curiosity I wanted from Derrida, I would have spent much more time at risk at field sites with the scientists and the monkeys and apes, not in the facile illusion that such ethnographic fieldwork would give the truth about

people or animals where interviews and documentary analysis mislead, but as a subject-forming entanglement that requires response one cannot know in advance. I knew I too cared about the actual animals then, but I knew neither how to look back nor that I lacked the habit.

30. Barbara Smuts, "Encounters with Animal Minds," *Journal of Consciousness Studies* 8, nos. 5–7 (2001): 293–309, 295. Further page references are in parentheses in the main text.

31. I did not write "smallest possible units of analysis" because the word *unit* misleads us to think that there is an ultimate atom made up of internal differential relatings, which is a premise of autopoiesis and other theories of organic form, discussed below. I see only prehensile turtles all the way up and down.

32. On the creative force of the prosaic, the propinquity of things in many registers, the concatenation of specific empirical circumstances, the misrecognition of experience by holding to an idea of the experience before having had it, and how different orders of things hold together coevally, see Gillian Goslinga, "The Ethnography of a South Indian God: Virgin Birth, Spirit Possession, and the Prose of the Modern World," PhD dissertation, University of California at Santa Cruz, June 2006.

33. Barbara Smuts, "Embodied Communication in Nonhuman Animals," in *Human Development in the 21st Century: Visionary Policy Ideas from Systems Scientists*, ed. Alan Fogel, Barbara King, and Stuart Shanker (Toronto: publication of the Council on Human Development, forthcoming).

34. When a run goes awry in agility, I hear my fellow dog sport people say of the canine and human persons, "They look like they have never met; she should introduce herself to her dog." A good run can be thought of as a sustained greeting ritual.

35. Gregory Bateson, *Steps to an Ecology of Mind* (Chicago: University of Chicago Press, 1972), 367–70.

36. Gilles Deleuze and Félix Guattari, *A Thousand Plateaus: Capitalism and Schizophrenia*, trans. Brian Massumi (Minneapolis: University of Minnesota Press, 1987), 232–309. Further references are in parentheses in the main text. I am playing with the tones of the vegetable communication of "truck" and Deleuze and Guattari's call-of-the-wild version of a wolf pack. The online word detective (www.word-detective.com/) told me that "the archaic sense of 'truck' means 'dealings, communications, bargaining or commerce,' and is heard today most often in the phrase 'have no truck with,' meaning 'have nothing to do with.' The original form of the English verb 'to truck' appeared in the 13th-century meaning 'to exchange or barter.' One of the surviving uses of this sense of 'truck'

is in the phrase 'truck farm,' meaning 'vegetables produced for market.'" We will see in a minute what production for small markets has to do with setting out a twenty-third bowl and my sense of becoming with significant others.

37. Steve Baker, *The Postmodern Animal* (London: Reaktion Books, 2000), 102–34, has much more appreciation than I do for Deleuze and Guattari's workings of becoming-animal, but Baker too is annoyed by their treatment of pet dogs and cats. Much as I do care about both literary and fleshly dogs and cats, their well-being is not my core worry in reference to D&G's becoming-animal. I think Baker misses the systematic nausea that D&G let loose in their chapter in response to all that is ordinary, especially evident in the figural wolf/dog contrasts but not reducible to them. Multiplicities, metamorphoses, and lines of flight not trapped in Oedipal and capitalist fixities must not be allowed to work that way. Sometimes the herculean efforts needed to dodge various versions of humanism catapult one into empyrean lines of flight proper only to the anomalous gods at their buffed worst. I'd rather own up to the fraught tangle of relatings called "individuals" in idiomatic English, whose sticky threads are knotted in prolific spaces and times with other assemblages, some recognizable as (human and nonhuman) individuals or persons and some very much not. Individuals actually matter, and they are not the only kind of assemblage in play, even in themselves. If one is "accused" of "uncritical humanism" or its animal equivalent every time he or she worries about the suffering or capabilities of actual living beings, then I feel myself in the coercive presence of the One True Faith, postmodern or not, and run for all I am worth. Of course, I am indebted to Deleuze and Guattari, among others, for the ability to think in "assemblages."

38. Unfairly, because D&G could not have known most of these things in the late 1970s in France or elsewhere, I think of trained therapy dogs working to bring autistic children into a social world where even human touch can become less terrifying, or pet dogs visiting the elderly to bring them back to an interest in a bigger life, or dogs accompanying teenagers with severe cerebral palsy in wheelchairs to help both with practical daily tasks like opening doors and even more with social interactions with other humans. I think of all the conversations among humans watching their canine buddies at an ordinary dog park that lead them to a larger civic and artistic world, as well as exchanges about poop bags and dog diets. These are not about becoming-animal, but they are about ordinary, daily becoming-with that does not seem very Oedipal to me. Claims about either bounded individuation or regression are always worth an empirical check; real dogs are ready to oblige. How world-building relations actually develop between a human being and a dog is the subject of ethological and ethnographic

research initiated by Adrian Franklin in Tasmania. See Adrian Franklin, Michael Emmison, Donna Haraway, and Max Travers, "Investigating the Therapeutic Benefits of Companion Animals," *Qualitative Sociology Review* (special issue "Animals and People") 3, no. 1 (2007): 42–58. Franklin is also savvy about how animals, including dogs (in this case, dingoes), feature in disturbing colonial and postcolonial nationalisms. See Adrian Franklin, *Animal Nation: The True Story of Animals and Australia* (New South Wales: New South Wales Press, 2006).

39. The passages on becoming-woman and becoming-child in *A Thousand Plateaus* have been the subject of many commentaries, both for D&G's embrace of the feminine-outside-confinement and the inadequacy of that move. However unintended, the primitivist and racialist tones of the book have not escaped notice either. In my calmer moments, I understand both what D&G accomplish and what this book cannot contribute to a non-Oedipal, antiracist feminism. Rosi Braidotti is my guide to fruitfully learning from Deleuze (who wrote much more than *A Thousand Plateaus*) and, in my view, offers much more toward an autre-mondialisation. See Rosi Braidotti, *Transpositions: On Nomadic Ethics* (Cambridge, U.K.: Polity, 2006). For a wonderful book partly shaped by Deleuze's sensibilities in *Difference and Repetition* (trans. Paul Patton [New York: Columbia University Press, 1995]), see Kathleen Stewart, *Ordinary Affects* (Durham, N.C.: Duke University Press, 2007), which is a subtle backstory of the emergent forces we call things like neoliberalism and advanced consumer capitalism.

40. Lynn Margulis and Dorion Sagan, *Acquiring Genomes: A Theory of the Origins of Species* (New York: Basic Books, 2002). Further references are in parentheses in the main text.

41. Who knows if Lawrence's "becoming-tortoise" referenced in *A Thousand Plateaus* (244) had any relation to the many versions of the "turtles all the way down story"! To track both the positivists' and the interpretivists' approaches to this narrative about nonteleological infinite regress—the world rests on an elephant resting on a turtle resting on turtles all the way down—see http://en .wikipedia.org/wiki/Turtles_all_the_way_down. Stephen Hawking, Clifford Geertz, Gregory Bateson, and Bertrand Russell all got into the act of refashioning this quasi-Hindu tale. In a chapter of that title, Isabelle Stengers tells a "turtles all the way down" story involving William James, Copernicus, and a savvy old lady, in *Power and Invention: Situating Science*, trans. Paul Bains (Minneapolis: University of Minnesota Press, 1981), 61–62. See also Yair Neuman, "Turtles All the Way Down: Outlines for a Dynamic Theory of Epistemology," *Systems Research and Behavioral Science* 20, no. 6 (2002): 521–30, available online. Neuman

summarizes: "The most serious problem facing epistemological research is how to establish solid foundations for epistemology within a recursive system of knowing. The aim of this paper is to respond to this problem by presenting some outlines for a dynamic theory of epistemology. This theory suggests that the most basic unshakeable unit of epistemology is a process of differentiation, which is a self-referential activity. This paper elaborates on this thesis and illustrates its relevance to solving the problem of embodiment in Piaget's genetic epistemology" (521). The self-referential part is the trouble. I want an idiom for both–and: "self-other referential" all the way down.

42. "'Autopoiesis,' literally 'self-making,' refers to the self-maintaining chemistry of living cells. No material object less complex than a cell can sustain itself and its own boundaries with an identity that distinguishes it from the rest of nature. Live autopoietic entities actively maintain their form and often change their form (they 'develop'), but always through the flow of material and energy." Margulis and Sagan, *Acquiring Genomes*, 40. Their target was the notion that a virus, or a gene, is a "unit of life."

43. For his critique of autopoiesis, see Scott F. Gilbert, "The Genome in Its Ecological Context: Philosophical Perspectives on Interspecies Epigenesis," *Annals of the New York Academy of Science* 981 (2002): 202–18. See also Scott Gilbert, John Opitz, and Rudolf Raff, "Resynthesizing Evolutionary and Developmental Biology," *Developmental Biology* 173 (1996): 357–72, 368. For reciprocal induction, see chapter 8, "Training in the Contact Zone."

Lest the reader think "turtles all the way down" is excessively mythological or literary, Gilbert directed me to the Turtle Epibiont Project at Yale, at www.yale.edu/peabody/collections/iz/iz_epibiont.html. Gilbert writes: "Interestingly, the notion that turtles carry the world is a theme found in several cultures. And while they might not support a universe, turtles do support considerable ecosystems on their backs." E-mail from Gilbert to Haraway, August 24, 2006.

For the relevance of this discussion to the phenomena of immunology, see Donna Haraway, "The Biopolitics of Postmodern Bodies: Constitutions of Self in Immune System Discourse," in *Simians, Cyborgs, and Women* (New York: Routledge, 1991), 205–30, 251–54. For an update, see Thomas Pradeu and Edgardo Carosella, "The Self Model and the Conception of Biological Identity in Immunology," *Biology and Philosophy* 21, no. 2 (March 2006): 235–52. Pradeu and Carosella summarize: "The self/non-self model, first proposed by F. M. Burnet, has dominated immunology for 60 years now. According to this model, any foreign element will trigger an immune reaction in an organism, whereas endogenous elements will not, in normal circumstances, induce an immune reaction.

In this paper we show that the self/non-self model is no longer an appropriate explanation of experimental data in immunology, and that this inadequacy may be rooted in an excessively strong metaphysical conception of biological identity. We suggest that another hypothesis, one based on the notion of continuity, gives a better account of immune phenomena. Finally, we underscore the mapping between this metaphysical deflation from self to continuity in immunology and the philosophical debate between substantialism and empiricism about identity" (235).

44. E-mail from Scott Gilbert to Donna Haraway, August 23, 2006.

45. Personal communication, August 23, 2006.

46. Drawing from second-generation cybernetic thinkers such as Humberto Maturana and Francisco Varela, Cary Wolfe reworks autopoiesis so that it cannot mean "self-organizing systems," which is the chief complaint Gilbert and I have. Nothing "self-organizes." Wolfe's development of nonrepresentationalist communication is close to what I mean by companion species engaged in turtling all the way down. The word *autopoiesis* is not the main problem, although I prefer to let it go because I do not think its meanings can be bent enough. What Wolfe and I both insist on is finding an idiom for the paradoxical and indispensable linkages of openness and closure, called by Wolfe "openness from closure" repeated recursively. See Cary Wolfe, "In the Shadow of Wittgenstein's Lion," in *Zootologies*, ed. Cary Wolfe (Minneapolis: University of Minnesota Press, 2003), especially 34–48. My thanks to Wolfe for pushing this question in his e-mail of September 12, 2006. In *Meeting the Universe Halfway* (Durham, N.C.: Duke University Press, 2006), Karen Barad's agential realism, phenomena, and intra-action provide another vital theoretical idiom for this conversation.

47. The Soay are listed with the Rare Breeds Survival Trust in the United Kingdom, and St. Kilda is a "mixed" UNESCO World Heritage Site, designated for both natural and cultural significance. The North American registry and breeder organization can be tracked at www.soaysofamerica.org/. Soay wool fiber enters Internet-mediated spinning and weaving circuits, and Soay meat is valued in agropastoral local and global practices. A tannery sells certified-organic Soay skins, also by Internet. About one thousand Soay sheep on St. Kilda have contributed DNA samples for an important database. Since the 1950s, an "unmanaged," translocated Soay population on the island of Hirta, where people no longer live, has been the subject of extensive ecological, behavioral, genetic, and evolutionary investigation. Archaeologists track the chemical residues of ancient tanneries and collect old Soay DNA from hides. From tourism, through modern agropastoralism and opposition to factory farming, to comparative genomics,

all of this is technoculture in action. See www.soaysheepsociety.org.uk/; www
.kilda.org.uk/; and T. H. Clutton Brock and J. Pemberton, *Soay Sheep* (Cambridge: Cambridge University Press, 2004).

48. Thelma Rowell and C. A. Rowell, "The Social Organization of Feral
Ovis aries Ram Groups in the Pre-rut Period," *Ethology* 95 (1993): 213–32.
These ram groups were not her current beloved Soay but hardy U.S. Texas Barbados critters encountered before she retired from UC Berkeley and returned to
Lancashire. Note the article was published not in a sheep journal but in a major
biobehavioral zoology journal, in which comparisons to monkeys, even if surprising, were normal scientific practice and not evidence for mental disorder. See
Thelma Rowell, "A Few Peculiar Primates," in *Primate Encounters,* ed. Shirley
Strum and Linda Fedigan (Chicago: University of Chicago Press, 2000), 57–70,
for a discussion of the history of studying what Rowell calls the "entertaining,
squabbling species" such as people and many other primates (69). Recent evidence from feral Soay indicates that they might shape their grazing patterns as a
function of the seasonal densities of parasites lying in wait on tall grass tufts. Big
predators aren't the only ones who count in the evolution of behavior. Michael
R. Hutchings, Jos M. Milner, Iain J. Gordon, Ilias Kyriazakis, and Frank Jackson,
"Grazing Decisions of Soay Sheep, *Ovis aries,* on St. Kilda: A Consequence of
Parasite Distribution?" *Oikos* 96, no. 2 (2002): 235.

49. Contending meanings of "the open" in Heideggerian philosophy and
after appear in chapter 8, "Training in the Contact Zone."

50. Vinciane Despret, "Sheep Do Have Opinions," in *Making Things Public,* ed. Latour and Weibel, 363. I am indebted to Despret's interview with Rowell
and her interpretation of the biologist's work in terms of "making available," "the
virtue of politeness," and the role of the twenty-third bowl. Thanks to Maria Puig
de la Bellacasa for bringing the research DVD made by Didier Demorcy and
Vinciane Despret, *Thelma Rowell's Non-sheepish Sheep,* to my graduate seminar
in winter 2006. Despret, Isabelle Stengers, Bruno Latour, Thelma Rowell, and
Sarah Franklin all infuse my writing here and elsewhere. With Sarah Franklin, I
visited Rowell's farm in March 2003 and had the privilege of meeting her sheep
and turkeys and talking with her and Sarah about worlds of animals and people.
For much more on worldly sheep in British and transnational life and technoscience, see Sarah Franklin, *Dolly Mixtures* (Durham, N.C.: Duke University Press,
2007). Stengers's former doctoral student Maria Puig de la Bellacasa was a visiting postdoc at UC Santa Cruz from 2005 to 2007. Maria and other colleagues
and graduate students in our animal studies/science studies/feminist theory
grad seminar in winter 2006 helped shape my thinking about cosmopolitics, the

twenty-third bowl, the open, and companion species. Thanks to all those in my animal studies seminars in the last few years who meet in this book.

51. Thelma Rowell, "Forest Living Baboons in Uganda," *Journal of Zoology* 149 (1966): 344–64. See also Thelma Rowell, *The Social Behaviour of Monkeys* (Middlesex, U.K.: Penguin, 1972). Somewhat to her horror, this little book became very popular among feminists in the 1970s and '80s, including me, who had a grudge against male dominance–hierarchy explanations of all things primate. Haraway, *Primate Visions*, 124, 127, 292–93, 420–21.

52. Running a working farm, Rowell accompanies any decision to kill an animal for food or another reason with arrangements for slaughter on her land, to minimize trauma. Therefore, her animals must remain within informal exchange and cannot be sold commercially. If animals are to be marketed, responsibility includes conditions from breeding to the human meal, shoes, or sweater, including travel and slaughter of the animals. In the context of the work to sustain valuable human–animal lifeways in contemporary terms, the Rare Breed Survival Trust tries, imperfectly, to operationalize these responsibilities in the United Kingdom. Legal changes to allow the sale of meat when the working animal has been slaughtered where he or she lived, and not limit home-slaughtered meat to noncommercial circuits, are crucial to animal and environmental well-being in any meat-eating ecology. In the United States, a movement is growing to develop and legalize mobile slaughter units with certified inspectors. Such practices ought to be mandatory, not just permitted. Two consequences would be no longer limiting such meat to upscale markets but making it the norm for everyone, and therefore greatly reducing meat-eating, since such responsible practices are incompatible with factory-scale slaughtering. The naturalcultural changes inherent in both these points are immense. Currently, a mobile unit can kill about twelve hundred cows per year and serves at best small, niche-market farmers. An industrial slaughtering enterprise kills more than that number of large animals per day, with predictable consequences for human and nonhuman brutalization and environmental degradation. Class, race, and regional well-being are all at stake here for people; living and dying with less suffering are at stake for meat-, hide-, and fiber-producing working animals. For a point of view in Montana, see "Mobile Slaughter Units," *News and Observer*, May 23, 2005, www .mycattle.com/news/dsp_topstories_article.cfm?storyid=17218. On serious work to reform slaughter practices and industrial animal welfare broadly, see Temple Grandin's Web site, www.grandin.com. Her designs of less terrible industrial slaughter systems, with mandatory auditing for actual reduction of animal stress, are well known.

Less well known is her 1989 PhD dissertation at the University of Illinois, focused on the other end of the production process, that is, on environmental enrichment for piglets so that their neural development and behavior can be more normal (www.grandin.com/references/diss.intro.html).

Still "normal" actual conditions for pigs are described and documented at www.sustainabletable.org/issues/animalwelfare/: "Factory farmed pigs are born in small crates that limit the sow's mobility to the point where she cannot turn around. As their mother lays [sic] immobile, unable make a nest or separate herself and her offspring from their feces, piglets are confined in the crate together, prohibited from running, jumping and playing according to their natural tendencies. Once separated from their mother, pigs are confined together in concrete pens with no bedding or soil for them to root in. In such conditions, pigs become restless and often resort to biting other pigs' tails as an expression of stress. Rather than simply giving the pigs straw to play in, many factory farm operators will cut off their pigs' tails in response to this behavior."

Four companies control 64 percent of pork production in the United States. For a soul-chilling analysis of the hog industry, see Dawn Coppin's science-studies and ethnographic PhD dissertation, "Capitalist Pigs: Large-Scale Swine Facilities and the Mutual Construction of Nature and Society," Sociology Department, University of Illinois, Champaign–Urbana, 2002. See Dawn Coppin, "Foucauldian Hog Futures: The Birth of Mega-hog Farms," *Sociological Quarterly* 44, no. 4 (2003): 597–616. Coppin's work is radical in many ways, not least her insistence in bringing the animals into research and analysis as actors. Joining scholarship to work for structural change, Coppin has been the executive director of the Santa Cruz Homeless Garden Project and a visiting scholar at UC Berkeley. In 2006, Arizona voters (64 percent) overwhelmingly passed the Humane Treatment of Farm Animals Act, which prohibits the confinement of calves in veal crates and breeding pigs in gestation crates, both practices that are already banned throughout the European Union but are the norm in the United States.

For the syllabus for my winter 2004 graduate seminar "Animal Studies as Science Studies: We Have Never Been Human," see http://feministstudies .UCSC.edu/facHaraway.html. See also Jonathan Burt, "Conflicts around Slaughter in Modernity," in *Killing Animals*, the Animal Studies Group (Urbana: University of Illinois Press, 2006), 120–44. Then watch Hugh Dorigo's film on factory farming, *Beyond Closed Doors* (Sandgrain Films, 2006).

53. Despret, "Sheep Do Have Opinions," 367.

54. Isabelle Stengers, "The Cosmopolitical Proposal," in *Making Things Public*, ed. Latour and Weibel, 994–1003, 995. See also Stengers, *Cosmopolitiques*,

2 vols. (Paris: La Découverte, 2003; originally in 7 vols., Paris: La Découverte, 1997). Stengers's cosmopolitics is more thoroughly introduced in chapter 3, "Sharing Suffering."

55. On the prosaic and effects through contingent contiguity, see Goslinga, "The Ethnography of a South Indian God."

56. For Dixon's November 7, 2004, article on the wolf–dog hybrids of South Africa, see www.wolfsongalaska.org/Wolves_south_africa_exile.htm.

57. James Bennett, "Hoofbeats and Tank Tracks Share Golan Range," *New York Times*, January 17, 2004, A1, A7. The light tone of this piece is hard to read in 2006, when war upon war upon war tears and threatens to tear everybody and everything apart without end, and it is hard even to imagine what cosmopolitics could look like on this land now. For an unpublished prose poem about three unarmed Arabs who were killed by the Israeli Army when attempting a cattle raid in 1968, see www.janecollins.org/uploads/The%20Golan%20 Heights.doc. For pictures, see "Raising Beef Cattle in Kfar Yehoshua and the Golan Heights," http://geosci.uchicago.edu/~gidon/personal/cattle/cattle.html. See www.bibleplaces.com/golanheights.htm for a story of the biblical presence of cattle on this land; that kind of story shapes today's claims of belonging. For the Zionist notion on "the people of Israel returning to the Golan" (*not* the only position held by Israelis), see www.golan.org.il/civil.html. For hikes on the Golan Heights, see http://galileeguide.com/gguide/etours.html. For a sketch of the complex situation on the Golan Heights after the war in Lebanon in 2006, see Scott Wilson, "Golan Heights Land, Lifestyle Lure Settlers: Lebanon War Revives Dispute over Territory," *Washington Post*, October 30, 2006, A1 (www.washingtonpost.com/wp-dyn/content/article/2006/10/29/AR2006 102900926_pf.html). Annexed in 1981, the Golan Heights supplies about a third of Israel's water. Wilson reports that in 2006, "the population of roughly 7,000 Arabs who remained after the 1967 war has grown to about 20,000. Most of them refused citizenship. Those who accepted are ostracized to this day in the four insular mountain towns where the Druze population is concentrated." (All Web sites accessed on May 4, 2007.)

58. When I first wrote this paragraph, seven-year-old Willem was living with an amputated rear leg from bone cancer, and metastases had recently appeared on his lungs. On that day in early November, he was bright-eyed and energetic, if a little short of breath; and he went on an easy walk with Rusten or me when we finished work for the day. This chapter is for him and his human, Susan. The contiguities of the prosaic, indeed. Willem died just before Thanksgiving, 2006.

59. Check out Food Alliance, founded in 1997, as a collaboration among Washington State University, Oregon State University, and the Washington State Department of Agriculture (www.foodalliance.org/). Explore the "Certified Humane" labeling project (www.certifiedhumane.org), and see "Humane Treatment of Farm Animals Can Improve the Quality of the Meat We Eat," *San Francisco Chronicle*, September 27, 2006. Then go to the Community Food Security Coalition (www.foodsecurity.org/) for a view of race, class, gender, and—in embryonic form—species intersectional analysis and action. Then go to the American Livestock Breeds Conservancy (http://albc-usa.org/) and the networks of the National Campaign for Sustainable Agriculture (www.sustainableagriculture .net/index.php). The California Food and Justice Coalition (www.foodsecurity .org/california/) prominently states in its key principles that "the production, distribution, and preparation of food must be healthy and humane for all humans, animals and ecosystems." Brave words, and a lifetime's work. Not so finally, check out the Intertribal Bison Cooperative, uniting fifty-one American tribes around the restoration of agriculture and the well-being of Indian land, its organisms, and its people (www.intertribalbison.org/). There are also many vegan approaches to food security and justice, for example, track from www.vegan.org/, the Humane Society of the United States, and, of course, People for the Ethical Treatment of Animals. (All Web sites accessed in November 2006.) I end this list, however, not with my sometimes-allied PETA foe but with vegan colleagues-in-struggle—that is, the antiracist, antisexist, justice-oriented, animal-focused vegan Carol Adams, *Neither Man nor Beast*, and her British counterpart, Lynda Birke, *Feminism, Animals, and Science* (Milton Keynes, U.K.: Open University Press, 1994).

60. John Law and Annemarie Mol, "Complexities: An Introduction," in *Complexities: Social Studies of Knowledge Practices*, ed. John Law and Annemarie Mol (Durham, N.C.: Duke University Press, 2002), 20. For a beautiful analysis of the inadequacy of humanist, personalist models for worldly human–animal encounters, see Charis Thompson, "When Elephants Stand for Competing Philosophies of Nature: Amboseli National Park, Kenya," in *Complexities*, 166–90.

61. Perhaps here, in an endnote at the close of introductions, is the place to remember that apparently friendly and curious behavior from wild wolves directed at people is most likely to be an exploration of a possible lupine lunch rather than an affectionate cross-species romp. Companion species, *cum panis*, breaking bread, eating and being eaten, the end of human exceptionalism: this, and not romantic naturalism, is what is at stake in the remembrance. Wildlife expert Valerius Geist explained to hunters in the northern U.S. Rockies that as

wolf population numbers rise well above the levels to which active extermination reduced them and herbivore populations adjust downward from renewed predator pressure, the competent North American opportunistic canids start acting more like Russian wolves than like remnants of a vanishing species set down in the midst of gustatory excess. That is, they start checking out and then stalking and occasionally attacking humans and their animals. Valerius Geist, "An Important Warning about 'Tame' Wolves," *Conservation Connection* (newsletter from the Foundation for North American Wild Sheep) 10 (Summer 2006): 4–5. Thanks to Gary Lease for the article and for many generous conversations about hunting, dogs, and conservation.

2. VALUE-ADDED DOGS AND LIVELY CAPITAL

1. Karl Marx, *Capital*, vol. 1, trans. Ben Fowkes (New York: Vintage Books, 1977), 926.

2. Marx came closest in his sometimes lyrical early work, "Theses on Feuerbach" and "The Economic and Philosophic Manuscripts of 1844," in *The Marx–Engels Reader*, 2nd ed., ed. Robert Tucker (New York: Norton, 1978). He is both at his most "humanist" and at the edge of something else in these works, in which mindful bodies in inter- and intra-action are everywhere. I follow Alexis Shotwell's subtle analysis of Marx's near escape from human exceptionalism implicit in his discussions on how labor power becomes a commodity, sensuousness, aesthetics, and human species being. Alexis Shotwell, "Implicit Understanding and Political Transformation," PhD dissertation, History of Consciousness Department, University of California at Santa Cruz, December 2006, 111–21.

3. An early interdisciplinary effort to write that missing Marxist volume is Sarah Franklin and Margaret Lock, eds., *Remaking Life and Death: Toward an Anthropology of the Biosciences* (Santa Fe, N.M.: School of American Research, 2003). Then came the following abbreviated but crucial list that I take from my winter 2007 graduate seminar called Bio[X]: Wealth, Power, Materiality, and Sociality in the World of Biotechnology: Kaushik Sunder Rajan, *Biocapital: The Constitution of Postgenomic Life* (Durham, N.C.: Duke University Press, 2006); Jerry Mander and Victoria Tauli-Corpuz, eds., *Paradigm Wars: Indigenous People's Resistance to Globalization* (Berkeley and Los Angeles: University of California Press, 2006); Marilyn Strathern, *Kinship, Law and the Unexpected: Relatives Are Always a Surprise* (New York: Cambridge University Press, 2005); Catherine Waldby and Robert Mitchell, *Tissue Economies: Blood, Organs, and Cell Lines*

in Late Capitalism (Durham, N.C.: Duke University Press, 2006); Achille Mbembe, *On the Postcolony* (Berkeley and Los Angeles: University of California Press, 2001); Franklin, *Dolly Mixtures*; and Adriana Petryna, Andrew Lakoff, and Arthur Kleinman, eds., *Global Pharmaceuticals: Ethics, Markets, Practices* (Durham, N.C.: Duke University Press, 2006). The course grew partly from thinking about a "figure" in the sense introduced in chapter 1, "When Species Meet: Introductions": Consider a fictional multiple integral equation that is a flawed trope and a serious joke in an effort to picture what an "intersectional" theory might look like in Biopolis. Think of this formalism as the mathematics of sf.

$$\Omega$$
$$\int \text{Bio}\,[X]n = \iiiint \dots \iint \text{Bio}\,(X_1,X_2,X_3,X_4,\dots,X_n,t)\,dX_1\,dX_2\,dX_3\,dX_4\dots dX_n\,dt = \text{Biopolis}$$
$$\alpha$$

X_1 = wealth, X_2 = power, X_3 = sociality, X_4 = materiality, X_n = ??
α (alpha) = Aristotle's & Agamben's bios
Ω (omega) = Zoë (bare life)
t = time

Biopolis is an *n*-dimensional volume, a "niche space," a private foundation committed to "global is local" biocracy (www.biopolis.org/), and an international research and development center for biomedical sciences located in Singapore (http://en.wikipedia.org/wiki/Biopolis). How would one solve such an equation?

4. These are American Pet Products Manufacturers Association figures from the free online teaser taken from their *2005–2006 APPMA National Pet Owners Survey*, available for purchase to non-APPMA members for $595. See www.appma.org. The APPMA annual Global Pet Expo, the industry's largest trade show, is a real eye-opener for any remaining sleeping romantics about pet commodity culture. It is open not to the general public but only to retailers, distributors, mass-market buyers, and "other qualified professionals." By not shelling out $595 for the pet owners survey, I lost my chance to get the lowdown on such things as details on where U.S. pet dogs are kept in the day and at night, groomer visits and methods of grooming used, methods used to secure dogs in the car, types of food and size of kibble purchased, number of treats given, types of leashes or harnesses used, type of food bowls used, information sources consulted and books and videos owned, dog-care items purchased in the last twelve

months, pet-themed gifts purchased, holiday parties given for dogs, expressed feeling about benefits and drawbacks of dog ownership, and much more—all duplicated for every common species of pet. Not much in the practice of capital accumulation through the lives of companion animals is left to chance.

5. "The US Pet Food and Supplies Market," April 2004, www.Mind Branch.com.

6. www.appma.org/press_industrytrends.asp (accessed May 4, 2007).

7. "The World Market for Dog and Cat Food for Retail Sale: A 2005 Global Trade Perspective," ICON Group International, February 2004, www .MindBranch.com. A brief, free, pdf-format summary is available online from MindBranch, Inc. To learn more, you have to pay. Obtaining my limited commercial facts for this chapter cost only my phone number inscribed on an online form, followed by an advertising call or two—much more easily resisted than the new liver cookies at Trader Joe's. I am indebted to Joe Dumit for thinking about the right (or obligation) to health and food as drugs.

8. Mary Battiata, "Whose Life Is It, Anyway?" (*Washington Post*, August 2, 2004) tells us that a four-year vet education in the United States costs about two hundred thousand dollars. Setting up a small vet practice starts at about five hundred thousand dollars. Battiata cites the 1998 study of vet fee structures and lagging salaries by the consulting firm KPMG.

9. See www.pjbpubs.com/cms.asp?pageid=1490, November 24, 2003.

10. Charis Thompson, *Making Parents: The Ontological Choreography of Reproductive Technologies* (Cambridge, Mass.: MIT Press, 2005). See also Haraway, *The Companion Species Manifesto.*

11. See, for example, Ruth La Feria, "Woman's Best Friend, or Accessory?" *New York Times,* December 7, 2006, E4, 7.

12. Justin Berton, "Hotels for the Canine Carriage Trade," *San Francisco Chronicle,* November 13, 2006, A1, 6. The marketing in all of the examples discussed was entirely directed to affluent human beings' ideas/fantasies and paid scant heed to anything like biobehavioral assessments of how dogs and other boarded species would do best in unfamiliar surroundings. Paying for a "training vacation" might go a long way to increasing civil peace, say, compared with paying for suites appointed with color-coordinated humanesque furniture and Animal Planet TV shows.

13. Brian Lavery, "For Dogs in New York, a Glossy Look at Life," *New York Times,* August 16, 2004.

14. Margaret E. Derry, *Bred for Perfection: Shorthorn Cattle, Collies, and Arabian Horses since 1800* (Baltimore: Johns Hopkins University Press, 2003).

15. For their place in complex nationalisms and ethnic identity discourses, consider the Karelian bear dog, the Suomen-pystyykorva (Finnish spitz dog), the Norsk elghund grå (Norwegian elkhound), the Kelef K'naani (Israeli Canaan dog), the Australian dingo (an Eora Aboriginal word), the Islandsk farehond (Iceland sheepdog), the Korean Jindo dog, and the Japanese Shiba inu, Hokkaido inu, Shikoku inu, Kai inu, and Kishu inu—and I have hardly started. Comparing the fascinating histories, discourses, and naturalcultural politics in which Canaan dogs and dingoes figure would require another book. Both kinds of dogs scavenge and hunt in the so-called pariah or primitive dog categories, made over for globalized breed club standardization. Reconstituted or reinvented dogs of the hunting elites of European feudalism also are a fascinating contemporary story. Check out the Irish wolfhound in this regard, complete with the breed's first-century B.C.E. Celtic origin story, along with the details of the dog's nineteenth-century "recovery" enabled by the Scottish captain George Augustus Graham's breeding of dogs called Irish wolfhounds, who still remained in Ireland with Borzoi, Scottish deerhounds, and Great Danes. The popularly recited details of the Great Rescuer's craft seem never to pollute the pure-origin story of ancient nobility or disturb the keepers of the closed stud books in the breed clubs. *Value-added* seems the right term for these breeding operations!

Probably the most important collection in the world of Southwest Indian art, including weaving, pottery, Kachina figures, and much else, is housed at the School of American Research in Santa Fe, New Mexico, in exquisite adobe buildings commissioned by two transplanted, wealthy, eccentric, New York women, Elizabeth and Martha Root White. The sisters also raised many of the most famous Irish wolfhounds of that breed's early period in the United States, between the 1920s and World War II, on this rugged and beautiful property. The land and buildings now serve as a major anthropological research and conference center. Rathmullan Kennel's Irish wolfhounds are buried in a little graveyard on the grounds, marking the value-added encounter of wealth, gender, aestheticized and reinvented tradition in dogs and human beings, white people's collection of indigenous artifacts on a grand scale, philanthropy, activism in support of Pueblo Indian land rights and health, patronage of the arts of Europe, the United States, and Indian nations, as well as scholarship of a kind that reaches across generations, nurturing some of the best twentieth- and twenty-first-century anthropology in all subfields. When I visited the dogs' graves at the School of American Research in 2000 after writing the first versions of "Cloning Mutts, Saving Tigers" for Sarah Franklin and Margaret Lock's workshop "New Ways of Living and Dying," the bones of the Whites' Irish wolfhounds seemed like fleshly, fantasy-laden, Euro-American ancestors in this complex colonial and national tangle. See Gregor Stark and E. Catherine Rayne, *El Delirio: The Santa Fe World of Elizabeth White* (Santa Fe, N.M.: School of American Research, 1998). For photographs of people, grounds, and dogs (including a re-creation by the White sisters of a sixteenth-century hunting party with Irish wolfhounds for a Santa Fe festival) and for a detailed description of the myriad practices that sustained these upper-class show dogs, see Arthur F. Jones, "Erin's Famous Hounds Finding Greater Glory at Rathmullan," *American Kennel Gazette* 5, no. 5 (1934), online at www.irishwolfhounds.org/jones.htm.

16. Franklin, *Dolly Mixtures*.

17. Donna Haraway, "Cloning Mutts, Saving Tigers: Ethical Emergents in Technocultural Dog Worlds," in *Remaking Life and Death: Towards an Anthropology of the Biosciences*, ed. Sarah Franklin and Margaret Lock (Santa Fe, N.M.: School of American Research Press, 2003), 293–327; also discussed in chapter 5, "Cloning Mutts, Saving Tigers," in this volume. Genetic Savings and Clone, Inc., the private corporate labs in which the never-successful Missyplicity Project came to rest after the researchers at Texas A&M lost heart, went out of business in October 2006, leaving its frozen companion-animal tissue bank to the livestock-cloning firm ViaGen. Genetic Savings and Clone did announce the live birth of two cloned cats in 2004 and mounted its Nine Lives Extravaganza, the world's first commercial cloning service for cats, with an advertised price of twenty-three thousand dollars plus sales tax in February 2006. CopyCat, one of the 2004 kittens, cost fifty thousand dollars. No sequel called Cheaper by the Dozen followed. The president of the Humane Society of the United States could only have been called ecstatic at hearing of Genetic Savings and Clone's departure; he was quoted by Reuters news service on October 13, 2006, calling the business failure a welcome "spectacular flop" in light of the resources needed for addressing pet overpopulation. Truth be told, that is my reaction too. I just read my newspaper's monthly list of shelter dogs and cats needing homes in my small town.

18. Hwang W.-S. et al., "Dogs Cloned from Adult Somatic Cells," *Nature* 436, no. 7051 (August 4, 2005): 641. Somatic cell nuclear transfer—the Dolly technique—was the technology employed. In view of the faked data on human embryonic stem cell (hESC) clones, Snuppy's authenticity was doubted, but he was pronounced a definite clone of Tel, the DNA donor, and a major advance for stem cell research by independent investigators in January 2006. See http://en .wikipedia.org/wiki/Snuppy to get started on this story. Over a thousand dog embryos were transferred into 123 different bitches to produce three pregnancies

and one living dog. The special difficulties involved in cloning dogs compared with other animals are detailed in Gina Kolata, "Beating Hurdles, Scientists Clone a Dog for a First," *New York Times*, August 4, 2005. On the hESC controversy, Hwang still has supporters in South Korea, and many scientists elsewhere acknowledge the extraordinary international competitive pressures at play in the whole field.

19. From McCaig's posting on CANGEN-L, the Canine Genetics Discussion Group Listserv, around 2000. To understand the work of border collies and the way they are regarded by their people, see Donald McCaig: *Nop's Trials* (Guilford, Conn.: Lyons Press, 1992; orig. 1984); *Nop's Hope* (Guilford, Conn.: Lyons Press, 1998); *Eminent Dogs, Dangerous Men* (Guilford, Conn.: Lyons Press, 1998).

20. Edmund Russell, "The Garden in the Machine: Toward an Evolutionary History of Technology," in *Industrializing Organisms: Introducing Evolutionary History*, ed. Susan R. Schrepfer and Philip Scranton (New York: Routledge, 2004), 1–16.

21. Ibid., 1.

22. Track the show through www.dogswithjobs.com/.

23. For the history of dogs as subjects for behavioral genetics research, see Scott and Fuller, *Genetics and the Social Behavior of the Dog*; Paul, "The Rockefeller Foundation and the Origin of Behavior Genetics"; Haraway, "For the Love of a Good Dog: Webs of Action in the World of Dog Genetics." The early hopes for the first U.S. Canine Genome Project, which was led by Jasper Rine and Elaine Ostrander, included connecting dog genes and behaviors, using crosses of purebred dogs identified for different behavioral specializations, such as Newfoundlands and border collies. Some of the talented fruits of those odd crosses play agility at the same trials that Cayenne and I frequent. The ideas about behavioral genetics in some of the early pronouncements of the Canine Genome Project were the butt of joking among dog people and also other biologists for simplistic formulations of what different kinds of dogs do and how "genes" might "code for" "behaviors," formulations that are rarer in postgenomic discourse. Check out "Finding the Genes That Determine Canine Behavior," www .bordercollie.org/k9genome.html (accessed May 4, 2007), for an explanation to dog people of what the Canine Genome Project was about. Research into behavioral genetics is not necessarily simplistic or unimportant for people or other species. However, old-fashioned ideology dressed up as research plays a big role in the history—and probably future—of this field. Ostrander mainly concentrated on comparative cancer genomics in dogs and humans at the Fred Hutchinson

Cancer Research Center, in Seattle. In 2004, the National Human Genome Research Institute (NHGRI) named her as the new chief of its Cancer Genetics Branch, one of the seven research branches in the Division of Intramural Research. Related to psychopharmacogenetics, comparative behavioral genetics remains a long-term research commitment in the NHGRI.

24. Kerstin Lindblad-Toh et al., "Genome Sequence, Comparative Analysis, and Haplotype Structure of the Domestic Dog," *Nature* 438 (2005): 803–19. Elaine Ostrander was one of many prominent (and not so prominent) coauthors on this paper. Several international labs also had canine genetic mapping projects of various kinds dating from the 1990s.

25. Stephen Pemberton, "Canine Technologies, Model Patients: The Historical Production of Hemophiliac Dogs in American Biomedicine," in *Industrializing Organisms*, ed. Schrepfer and Scranton, 191–213.

26. Ibid., 205.

27. Peter Kramer, *Listening to Prozac* (New York: Penquin, 1993).

28. See Andrew Pollack, "In Trials for New Cancer Drugs, Family Pets Are Benefiting, Too," *New York Times*, November 24, 2006.

29. This awful story can be tracked from the Southern Poverty Law Center, Intelligence Report in 2001, "Aryan Brotherhood: Woman's Death Exposes Seamy Prison Scam," www.splcenter.org/intel/intelreport/article.jsp?aid=203 (accessed May 5, 2007). In the year of the mauling death of Diane Whipple by two large mastiff-type dogs in a San Francisco apartment building, the incidence and severity of dog bites in San Francisco in all public places were significantly lower as a result of effective public education programs. That did not stop the public demand to remove dogs from public areas or greatly restrict their freedom in the wake of the mauling. About twenty dog-bite related human deaths occur in the United States per year in a dog population of over seventy million. Those statistics do not justify any of the deaths, but they do give a sense of the size of the problem. See Janie Bradley, "Dog Bites: Problems and Solutions," Animals and Society Institute, Baltimore, Md., November 2006. This policy paper is available through the Society and Animals Forum, http://plus7.safe-order.net/psyeta/catalogue/product_info.php?products_id=41 (accessed May 4, 2007).

30. For the 2004 series, see www.imdb.com/title/tt0395048/.

31. See also Andrea Neal, "Trained Dogs Transforming Lives: A Service Program to Benefit People with Disabilities Is Also Helping U.S. Prison Inmates Develop a Purpose for Their Lives," *Saturday Evening Post*, 277, no. 5 (September 1, 2005). Go to www.pathwaystohope.org/prison.htm for the Prison Dog Project (accessed May 5, 2007). Canine Support Teams is the project at the

California Institute for Women. The Pocahontas Correctional Unit in Chester-field, Virginia, is a women's facility that trains inmates in dog grooming. Gender assumptions seem well groomed here. The Second Chance Prison Canine Program in Tucson, Arizona, is "a group of advocates for people with disabilities, prison inmates, and animal welfare in Arizona [who] coordinate a prison pet partnership program to address issues common to these three groups" (www .secondchanceprisoncanine.org/, accessed May 5, 2007). Go to www.coyote communications.com/dogs/prisondogs.html (accessed May 5, 2007) for a partial list of active prison dog-training programs, which include institutions with projects for training stray dogs and cats as well as dogs for people with disabilities. See T. Harbolt and T. H. Ward, "Teaming Incarcerated Youth with Shelter Dogs for a Second Chance," *Society and Animals* 9, no. 2 (2001): 177–82. Canada and Australia also have programs. Animal Planet TV shows analyzed in this chapter were first aired in 2004.

32. Thompson, *Making Parents*, figure 8.1.

33. For example, besides the texts already cited in note 3, see Cori Hayden, *When Nature Goes Public: The Making and Unmaking of Bioprospecting in Mexico* (Princeton, N.J.: Princeton University Press, 2003); Stefan Helmreich, "Trees and Seas of Information: Alien Kinship and the Biopolitics of Gene Transfer in Marine Biology and Biotechnology," *American Ethnologist* 30, no. 3 (2003): 341–59; Kimberly TallBear, "Native American DNA," PhD dissertation, University of California at Santa Cruz, December 2005; Eric Hirsch and Marilyn Strathern, eds., *Transactions and Creations: Property Debates and the Stimulus of Melanesia* (Oxford, U.K.: Berghahn, 2005). I use the idiomatic term *critter* to mean a motley crowd of lively beings including microbes, fungi, humans, plants, animals, cyborgs, and aliens. Critters are always relationally entangled rather than taxonomically neat. I pray that all residual tones of *creation* have been silenced in the demotic *critter*. It would not do for entangled "turtles all the way down" to be burdened with origin and telos in a father god.

3. SHARING SUFFERING

1. Nancy Farmer, *A Girl Named Disaster* (New York: Orchard Books, 1996), 239. Rejecting medical treatment of any kind for themselves, the Vapostoris adhere to an independent African Christian church founded in 1932 by Johane Maranke. In 2006, besides other mammals, about three hundred thousand to five hundred thousand people in sub-Saharan Africa are infected with sleeping sickness, and about forty thousand human beings die every year. The

current epidemic dates from 1970, after screening and surveillance effective against previous outbreaks were relaxed. See http://en.wikipedia.org/wiki/Sleeping_sickness.

2. See Rebecca M. Herzig, *Suffering for Science: Reason and Sacrifice in Modern America* (New Brunswick, N.J.: Rutgers University Press, 2005).

3. The classic exposition is C. B. Macpherson, *The Political Theory of Possessive Individualism* (London: Oxford University Press, 1962).

4. Karen Barad, *Meeting the Universe Halfway: Quantum Physics and the Entanglement of Matter and Meaning* (Durham, N.C.: Duke University Press, 2007), has, over many years and in several publications, crafted the powerful feminist theory of intra-action and agential realism. She and I are in firm solidarity that this theory richly applies to animals entangled in relations of scientific practice.

5. My thinking about what sharing suffering might mean was worked out partly in an extended e-mail dialogue in July 2006 with Thom van Dooren, an Australian scholar and writer on the worlds of seeds in technoscientific agriculture. On July 3, 2006, van Dooren wrote: "Some suffering appears to benefit only very specific groups in very superficial ways. Seeing how this all happens requires that we inhabit the kinds of shared spaces that you're talking about. But this is all 'epistemological sharing,' and I have no idea how we might share in a more concrete, messy, and I think meaningful, way. This is also important, I think, in getting at what's going on in global human relationships in which we are all very definitely implicated in the suffering of countless humans (e.g., in the way in which our lifestyles are made possible by theirs), and also in factory farming. These 'critters' (to borrow another of your terms) all suffer for us too—in one way or another. How might we actually inhabit a shared space of suffering with them, and to what end? Especially, when so much of this suffering seems completely unjustified and preventable. In short, I'm not sure that I really do get it. . . . I'm not sure what solidarity and sharing amount to unless I'm willing to take their place. Which prompts a whole lot of questions about why I can't switch places with them, why, for example, some creatures (even some humans) are 'allowed' to suffer and others are not."

6. See Schrepfer and Scranton, eds., *Industrializing Organisms*. Karen Rader, *Making Mice: Standardizing Animals for American Biomedical Research, 1900–1955* (Princeton, N.J.: Princeton University Press, 2004), is indispensable for understanding how economic, scientific, cultural, and institutional meanings of *natural* and *man-made* are negotiated in shaping keystone experimental organisms.

7. In the 1970s and '80s, Marxist feminists faced a partly analogous task in foregrounding what differently situated women do that could not count as labor in classical Marxist analysis, in which the figure of the male worker and his family recalls the structural relation of human beings and their animals. The question was transfigured fundamentally in Nancy Hartsock, "The Feminist Standpoint: Developing the Ground for a Specifically Feminist Historical Materialism," in *Discovering Reality*, ed. Sandra Harding and Merill Hintikka (Dordrecht, The Netherlands: Reidel, 1983), 283–310. Taking the sensuous labor of differently situated animals seriously might come more easily to feminists now because of this history.

8. Val Plumwood, *Feminism and the Mastery of Nature* (London: Routledge, 1993); Greta Gaard, ed., *Ecofeminism: Women, Animals, Nature* (Philadelphia: Temple University Press, 1993). Feminists have also argued early, often, and well for caring in all its senses as a core needed practice. For twenty-first-century young feminists' writing on care, see Maria Puig de la Bellacasa on "thinking with care" in the context of the European feminist group "Nextgenderation." See www.nextgenderation.net/writings.html and www.nextgenderation.net/belgium/soul/care/html. (Both Web sites accessed May 5, 2007.) See also chapter 1, n. 19, in this volume.

9. Of many examples, consider the sensitive treatment by Eileen Crist of the ways that language molds writers', including scientific writers', understanding of and relations with animals. Her work is crucial to seeing how the ascription of mindful action only to humans and mindless behavior to animals works. Eileen Crist, *Images of Animals: Anthropomorphism and Animal Mind* (Philadelphia: Temple University Press, 1999). Always attuned to dogs in flesh and print, I think the new book by Alice Kuzniar, *Melancholia's Dog* (Chicago: University of Chicago Press, 2006), is extraordinary. *Melancholia's Dog* is a risky and improper book; that is, Kuzniar gives us an acutely intelligent work, intellectually and emotionally, that actually takes seriously what goes on affectively between dogs and people. Attuned to the sadness of unavowed and repudiated attachment across species difference, Kuzniar addresses us, human beings, who refuse to understand that it is we who must learn to comprehend—or even just to notice—the depth, difficulty, and urgency of canine–human relations, so that we might learn at last to speak properly about such matters as pet loss and death, shared vulnerability, and resonating empathic shame. *Melancholia's Dog* lovingly inhabits works of visual and literary art in order to make palpable the urgent need to nurture the practice of articulate respect for the complexities of our attachments across the bounds of species difference. Drawing on literature,

philosophy, psychoanalysis, and film, Erica Fudge makes us fundamentally re-think what relating with animals is and might be. Erica Fudge, *Animal* (London: Reaktion Books, 2002). The entire Reaktion Books series on animals (*Dog, Cockroach, Crow, Oyster, Rat,* and more), under the editorship of Jonathan Burt, is full of remarkable insights, materials, and analyses.

10. Indispensable work includes: Carol Adams and Josephine Donovan, eds., *Animals and Women: Feminist Theoretical Explorations* (Durham, N.C.: Duke University Press, 1995); Adams, *Neither Man nor Beast;* Lynda Birke, *Feminism, Animals, and Science: The Naming of the Shrew* (Buckingham, U.K.: Open University Press, 1994); and Mette Bryld and Nina Lykke, *Cosmodolphins: Feminist Cultural Studies of Technology, Animals, and the Sacred* (London: Zed Books, 2000). Adams has paid particular attention to questions of racism and the blocks in the way of needed solidarity for effective antiracist, proanimal, feminist work. See also Linda Hogan, *Power* (New York: W. W. Norton, 1998); Ursula LeGuin, *Buffalo Gals and Other Animal Presences* (New York: New American Library, 1988); and Alice Walker, "Am I Blue?" in *Living by the Word* (New York: Harcourt Brace, 1987).

11. As Katie King, fellow lover of Nancy Farmer, wrote me about Baba Joseph, "I am also interested in what it means to be willing to be wicked because it matters." E-mail, July 11, 2006.

12. Baba Joseph is not a leading scientist but an animal caretaker and research assistant. His position in the scientific hierarchy is similar to the most frequent one between animals and people in biomedical research labs today. Writing about the affective–cognitive tension between the suffering of lab animals and of people living with HIV/AIDS, Eric Stanley reminded me that low-waged lab technicians with few degrees of freedom in their work practice are the humans most often "in the presence of" suffering animals in mechanized industries of drug testing and other major technoscientific investigations. What might nonmimetic sharing of suffering mean if this chapter were to stress the division of scientific labor affecting animals that is on a scale foreign to the hier-archical, but still face-to-face, scenes in Nancy Farmer's book? See Eric Stanley, "Affective Remains," qualifying essay in progress, History of Consciousness Department, University of California at Santa Cruz. Jennifer Watanabe, history of consciousness graduate student, has also emphasized these matters in seminar papers based on her work as a lab technician in a California primate research facility.

13. Donna J. Haraway, "FemaleMan©_Meets_OncoMouse™," in *Modest _Witness@Second_Millennium,* 49–118, 79.

14. Smuts, "Encounters with Animal Minds."

15. Jacques Derrida (with Jean-Luc Nancy), "'Eating Well,' or the Calculation of the Subject: An Interview with Jacques Derrida," in *Who Comes after the Subject?* ed. Eduardo Cadava, Peter Connor, and Jean-Luc Nancy (New York: Routledge, 1991), 96–119. *Sacrifice* is a common word with many meanings, not all contained in Derrida's analyses, but his treatment of the logic of sacrifice in Jewish and Christian lineages, including their secular heirs and siblings in the history of philosophy, is important. For critical disappointment in Derrida's efforts in "Eating Well," see David Wood, "Comment ne pas manger—Deconstruction and Humanism," in *Animal Others: On Ethics, Ontology and Animal Life,* ed. H. Peter Steeves (Albany: State University of New York Press, 1999), 15–35. For detailed and astute readings and extensions of Derrida's extraordinary writings on animal matters in philosophy, see Wolfe, *Animal Rites,* especially his chapter on the failure of rights discourses, "Old Orders for New: Ecology, Animal Rights, and the Poverty of Humanism," and his essay on Derrida and Lévinas (among others), "In the Shadow of Wittgenstein's Lion: Language, Ethics, and the Question of the Animal." For another strongly argued insistence on the irreducible multiplicity of animals and the historically contingent relationships humans have with animals, see Barbara Herrnstein Smith, "Animal Relatives, Difficult Relations," *differences* 15, no. 1 (spring 2004): 1–23. Unfortunately, philosophers like Derrida are unlikely to read, cite, or recognize as philosophy the large feminist literatures indicated in my notes, above. I blame that less on the "philosopheme" of the Animal and more on that of the Man and his cyclopean-like, incurious citation practices! The feminist work was often both first and also less entrammeled in the traps of misrecognizing animals as singular, even if we have been just as caught in the nets of humanism and are in need of the kind of thinking Derrida and Gayatri Spivak do.

16. This kind of "open" is elucidated in Agamben's reading of Heidegger. Agamben is very good at explicating how the "anthropological machine" in philosophy works. In my view, bare life (*zoë*) notwithstanding, he is no help at all for figuring out how to get to another kind of opening, the kind feminists and others who never had Heidegger's starting point for *Dasein* of profound boredom can discern. Giorgio Agamben, *The Open: Man and Animal,* trans. Kevin Attel (Stanford, Calif.: Stanford University Press, 2004), 49–77.

17. Derrida, "The Animal That Therefore I Am (More to Follow)," 417. See also Derrida, "And Say the Animal Responded?"

18. Derrida, "The Animal That Therefore I Am (More to Follow)," 394–95. For vivid graphic art on just these matters, see Sue Coe, *Pit's Letter* (New

York: Four Walls Eight Windows, 2000), and www.graphicwitness.org/coe/coebio.htm (accessed May 5, 2007). Coe works within a framework of animal rights and uncompromising critical prohibition against eating or experimenting on animals. Her witness is radical. I find her visual work compelling but the political and philosophical formulations much less so. Extended to the critique of speciesism, the logic of humanism and rights is everywhere, and the substance of moral action is denunciation, prohibition, and rescue, such that inside instrumental relations, animals can only be victims. Still, her images have the force of William Blake's and Pieter Breugel's visions, and I need her flaming eyes to burnish my knowledge of hell—an inferno for which my world, including myself, is responsible.

19. The statistics for animals killed worldwide by people for use in almost every aspect of human lives are truly staggering (easily obtainable—check the Internet), and the growth of that killing in the last century is, literally, unthinkable, if not uncountable. The staggering growth of the human population in that same period is part of the reason but not a sufficient explanation for the scale of animal killing. The advertisements for an important new book state simply that killing is the most common form of human interaction with animals. See the Animal Studies Group, *Killing Animals* (Urbana: University of Illinois Press, 2006). Anyone watching the destruction of chickens and other birds to fend off the threat of bird flu's spreading to people can have no doubt about such claims. Not to take all this killing seriously is not to be a serious person in the world. *How* to take it seriously is far from obvious.

20. That Jesus was a sacrifice is intrinsic to the holy scandal of the Good News. Unlike the first Isaac, for whom an animal substitute was provided in the nick of time, the Son of Man brought about his own sacrifice, and it was sweet to his Father. The nice thing about Christians who take this Story seriously is that they understand that, all of a sudden, Man is subject to a killing that is not murder. Jesus is a scapegoat to beat all other surrogates, and this meal has been a feast for a couple thousand years already. This is indeed big trouble for the law. No wonder secularism never satisfies the consumers of this category-breaking and endlessly repeated sacrifice. My feminist pagan soul coupled with my multispecies work ethic thinks we can do better than either the fleshly Son of Man or his more ethereal secular siblings.

21. Derrida, "The Animal That Therefore I Am (More to Follow)," 408.

22. Ibid., 377.

23. J. M. Coetzee, *Disgrace* (New York: Viking, 1999); J. M. Coetzee, *The Lives of Animals* (Princeton, N.J.: Princeton University Press, 2001). Barbara

Smuts made a similar complaint against the absence of real critters in *The Lives of Animals*. See Barbara Smuts, "Reflections," in *The Lives of Animals*, 107–20. Cary Wolfe writes about David Lurie and Elizabeth Costello in "Exposures," Introduction to *Philosophy and Animal Life* (New York: Columbia University Press, forthcoming). The fictional character Elizabeth Costello has a much more complex relation with the adequacy of the discourse of rights and reason in J. M. Coetzee, *Elizabeth Costello* (New York: Viking, 2003), when she faces language's breakdown of the kind that reaches inside and rearranges one's innards. Nonetheless, the Tanner Lectures represent a common, powerful, and in my view powerfully wrong approach to the knots of animal and human killing and killability. It is not that the Nazi killings of the Jews and others and mass animal slaughter in the meat industry have no relation; it is that analogy culminating in equation can blunt our alertness to irreducible difference and multiplicity and their demands. Different atrocities deserve their own languages, even if there are no words for what we do.

24. Pemberton, "Canine Technologies, Model Patients."

25. Haraway, *Modest_Witness@Second_Millennium*, 110–12.

26. Stengers, "The Cosmopolitical Proposal." See also her two-volume *Cosmopolitiques*. Stengers is in long and rich conversation with Bruno Latour on cosmopolitics. See Latour, *Politics of Nature*.

27. Training animals of a huge range of species, from octopuses to gorillas, to cooperate actively with people in scientific protocols and husbandry, as well as training human caregivers to provide innovative behavioral enrichment for the animals in their charge, is a growing practice. Trained animals are subject to less coercion of either physical or pharmaceutical kinds. Such animals are calmer, more interested in things, more capable of trying something new in their lives, more responsive. Previous scientific research, as well as a bit of finally listening to people who work well with animals in entertainment and sport, has produced new knowledge that in turn changes moral possibilities and obligations in instrumental relationships such as those in experimental animal laboratories. Experimental animal science, in this case behaviorist and comparative psychology, has produced knowledge crucial to changing the conditions of work for people and animals in experimental animal science. To respond also means to learn to know more; to learn to learn is not something that just the animals in operant conditioning do. Learning to learn takes figuring out how to cohabit a multispecies world shaped by cascades of earned trust. Training involves an asymmetrical relationship between responsive partners. Getting each other's attention is the core of the relationship. The Animal Behavioral Management

Alliance, founded in 2000, is the professional association focused solely on training animals, mostly so-called exotics living in human-structured worlds, to improve the lives of the critters. A good journalistic account of how people learn to improve the lives of mostly "nondomestic" animals who work in a variety of jobs, in everything from zoo display, TV and film, to research labs, is Amy Sutherland, *Kicked, Bitten, and Scratched: Life and Lessons at the World's Premier School for Exotic Animal Trainers* (New York: Viking, 2006).

Experimental lab scientists get the point eventually. On September 23, 2006, an article by Andy Coghlan titled "Animal Welfare: See Things from Their Perspective," *New Scientist* 2570 (September 2006): 6–7, reported on a conference at the Royal Society in London focusing on the ways animals interpret the world, including the implications for treatment of animals working in scientific research. Coghlan writes that "the Institute for Laboratory Animal Research is carrying out the country's [the United Kingdom's] first in-depth investigation into stress and distress in laboratory animals." The goal is to develop a set of objective measures of distress and well-being for various species, so that care can be more appropriate and uncoupled from common narratives and assumptions unchecked by data. The Royal Society was the scene of Robert Boyle's reports on the gas laws in seventeenth-century England; maybe we can expect a similar revolutionizing impact from the 2006 reports. How does one know if a dog or a mouse is in pain? An objective answer to that sort of question can actually be found if one (a) is curious and (b) also cares. Ordinary, fallible instruments such as psychometric assessments in the context of comparative medicine are handy twenty-first-century air pumps, bypassing the theologies of debates about animal sentience and confronting the evacuation of the heart and mind in current animal industrial practices in science and elsewhere. For a good example of the still flawed but nonetheless better attention to canine experimental subjects' well-being, see Robert Hubrecht, "Comfortable Quarters for Dogs in Research Institutions," University Federation for Animal Welfare, U.K., www.awionline.org/pubs/cq02/ca-dogs.html (accessed May 5, 2007). For an exposé of at least some actual conditions for research dogs, those unlucky enough to be in the jaws of the Beagle Unit at Huntington Life Sciences in the United Kingdom, at least between 1996 and 2006, see "Inside HLS," www.shac.net/MISC/Inside_HLS_Full_Report.html (accessed May 5, 2007). The footage from this exposé aired on Britain's channel 4 in 2005, sparking a major antivivisection campaign. Hubrecht works hard to eliminate practices like those at HLS. He won the 2004 GlaxoSmithKline Laboratory Animal Welfare Prize. If only my skepticism about the mercies of big pharma could be put to rest . . . But the extent and power of Hubrecht's and others' raising standards of care are real and important. For a medical research organization (RDS) approach to animals in experimental practice, see www.rds-online.org.uk/ (accessed May 5, 2007). RDS reports that there were about three million scientific procedures using animals in the United Kingdom in 2005.

28. Despret, "The Body We Care For."

29. Hélène Cixous, "Stigmata, or Job the Dog," in *Stigmata, Escaping Texts* (New York: Routledge, 1998), 243–61. I am grateful to Adam Reed for giving me Cixous's essay and for his evident pain and care in reading it.

30. Indiana University literary scholar, writer, and lawyer for animal well-being Alyce Miller organized the Kindred Spirits conference (in Bloomington, Indiana, September 7–9, 2006) to bring diverse scholars, artists, and activists together outside the setup of animal rights versus animal welfare. The excellent presentations, as well as thoughtful and principled presence of the participants, continue to work on my mind and heart. See www.indiana.edu/~kspirits/index .htm.

31. E-mail from Sharon Ghamari-Tabrizi to Donna Haraway, July 15, 2006.

32. Susan Harding, "Get Religion," in ms., 2006.

33. Thompson, *Making Parents.*

34. A rough measure of this increased use of rodents is the importance of mice carrying knockout genes. Comparative genomics is the name of the game. Several nations have large new projects to produce tens of thousands of knockouts, that is, mice strains with disabled genes. For example, the U.S. National Institutes of Health announced the Knockout Mouse Project to make ten thousand new mutants; Europe and Canada are after another thirty thousand. China aims to produce one hundred thousand different mutants in twenty thousand lines of mice, each with a different knockout gene. *Science* magazine estimates the size of the international effort to be the largest since the Human Genome Project. The goal is to have knockouts for every mouse gene and make them available publicly. Mass-produced mutant mice are the machine tools for the comparative study of gene function. Cataloging, distribution, and intellectual property are only some of the matters being fully aired. See David Grimm, "A Mouse for Every Gene," *Science* 312 (June 30, 2006): 1862–66. Mouse well-being warrants no mention. How could it, when their status as animals is lost in rhetoric like the following? "As a group, the knockout projects are trying to create something akin to the international superstore IKEA, where in a single trip, customers can buy a houseful of easy-to-assemble furniture at reasonable prices.... Some assembly

would be required: turning those frozen embryos into live mice. . . . Such a resource would be a far cry from today's mouse trade, which is more like buying furniture from neighbors" (1863). I do not oppose carefully considered invasive research with mice. My question is not that but how to engage in such practices face-to-face, inside the mortal knot of becoming with other animals. I find it collectively psychotic, and highly functional, to deal in rhetorical and other research practices as if the mice were only tools or products and not also sentient fellow critters. The both/and is very hard to hold on to. Losing a grip on the both/and means toppling into the unbridgeable chasm between self-satisfied instrumental rationality, on the one hand, and perhaps equally self-satisfied right-to-life discourse, on the other hand. The problem for companion species, I argue, is not how to be satisfied but how to handle indigestion. The same issue of *Science*, a couple pages before the story on knockout mice, carried an animal-behavior item titled "Signs of Empathy in Mice" (1860). The question might better be whether very many people show such signs in their dealings with mice. Perhaps human genes to support such capacities were knocked out by alien cat researchers in an earlier era. See also Lynda Birke, "Who—or What—Is the Laboratory Rat (and Mouse)?" *Society and Animals* 11, no. 3 (2003): 207–24.

35. Pearse is a researcher at the Institute of Marine Sciences, University of California at Santa Cruz, editor of the renowned journal *Invertebrate Biology*, and coauthor of the classic text *Animals without Backbones: An Introduction to the Invertebrates*, by Ralph Buchsbaum, Mildred Buchsbaum, John Pearse, and Vicki Pearse, 3rd ed. (Chicago: University of Chicago Press, 1987). See www.iode .org/oceanexpert/viewMemberRecord.php?&memberID=1623 (accessed May 5, 2007). Pearse generously helps History of Consciousness science studies grad students with the marine zoology aspects of their dissertations. See Eva Shawn Hayward, "Envisioning Invertebrates: Immersion, Inhabitation, and Intimacy as Modes of Encounter in Marine TechnoArt," qualifying essay, History of Consciousness Department, University of California at Santa Cruz, December 2003.

36. Michael Hadfield, e-mail to Donna Haraway, August 2, 2006. On the snail research see, M. G. Hadfield, B. S. Holland, and K. J. Olival, "Contributions of *ex situ* Propagation and Molecular Genetics to Conservation of Hawaiian Tree Snails," in *Experimental Approaches to Conservation Biology*, ed. M. Gordon and S. Bartol (Berkeley and Los Angeles: University of California Press, 2002). See also www.kewalo.hawaii.edu/labs/hadfield/ and www.hawaii.edu/eecb/ FacultyPgs/michaelhadfield.html (both Web sites accessed May 5, 2007).

37. Scott Gilbert, e-mail to Donna Haraway, August 9, 2006.

38. Isabelle Stengers, *Penser avec Whitehead* (Paris: Gallimard, 2002). See www.ensmp.fr/~latour/articles/article/93-STENGERS.html (accessed May 5, 2007) for Bruno Latour's review of *Penser*. Alfred North Whitehead: *Science and the Modern World; Process and Reality,* corrected ed. (New York: Free Press, 1979); *Modes of Thought* (New York: Macmillan, 1938).

4. EXAMINED LIVES

1. The joke is perhaps too precious, but paraphilias, or sidewinding loves, are just about every kind of libidinally invested connection known to psychoanalysis and sexology since Havelock Ellis, and I would be disappointed if dog love were not in there somewhere. A matter of interest for feminists, epistemophilia, or the love of knowledge, is all about scooping and scoping out the mother's body in the subject's perverse lust to know its origins. Nothing innocent in that! Curiosity is right in there with other sorts of digging in mud and scoping out—spelunking, really—in tubes and caves. Curiosity is not a nice virtue, but it does have the power to defeat one's favorite self-certainties.

2. For a long-range view of the emergence of working dogs of all kinds, see Raymond Coppinger and Richard Schneider, "Evolution of Working Dogs," in *The Domestic Dog: Its Evolution, Behaviour, and Interactions with People,* ed. James Serpell (Cambridge: Cambridge University Press, 1995), 21–47. For the emergence of working animals broadly, see Juliet Clutton-Brock, *A Natural History of Domesticated Mammals* (Cambridge: Cambridge University Press, 1999). For a study of the strength and antiquity of human–dog affectional and social bonds suggested by the worldwide distribution of ancient dog burial sites, ties that the author sees as defining dogs as a species, see Darcy F. Morey, "Burying Key Evidence: The Social Bond between Dogs and People," *Journal of Archaeological Science* 33 (2006): 158–75. On Native working, pet, food, and other dogs in the Americas before the arrival of European canine kinds, see Marion Schwartz, *A History of Dogs in the Early Americas* (New Haven, Conn.: Yale University Press, 1997). On the importance of animals in imperial settler colonies, see Virginia Anderson, *Creatures of Empire* (New York: Oxford University Press, 2006).

3. Linda Rorem, "Australian Shepherd History," www.glassportal.com/herding/shepherd.htm (accessed May 5, 2007). The recently reissued classic on the ten-thousand-year interaction of sheep and human beings is M. L. Ryder, *Sheep and Man* (London: Duckworth, 2007). Ryder published extensively from his base in the Agricultural Research Council's Animal Breeding Research

Organization in Edinburgh. Sarah Franklin, my friend and colleague who herds me mercilessly into sheep–human–dog naturalcultural ecologies, gives a gold mine of information in *Dolly Mixtures*.

4. Molecular genetic studies do not show the mitochondrial- or nuclear-DNA segments in living U.S. dogs that would be expected from the offspring of preconquest dogs, who seem to have been massively killed off or to have died off or both with the arrival of European dogs and their fierce people and destructive domestic food animals. I do not know if Navajo dogs have been specifically examined with this question in mind. But see Mark Derr, *Dog's Best Friend* (New York: Holt, 1997), 12, 168–75, for the opinion that some Navajo dogs closely resemble specific sorts of preconquest American dogs and for a discussion of their flock-guarding behavior under Navajo systems of pastoralism.

5. From "The Navajo Sheep Project," www.recursos.org/sheepislife/dine.html. See also www.ansi.okstate.edu/breeds/sheep/navajochurro/index.htm and www.navajo-churrosheep.com/. (Web sites accessed on May 5, 2007.) For a good introduction to the history of Navajo textiles, see Eulalie H. Bonar, ed., *Woven by the Grandmothers: Nineteenth-Century Navajo Textiles from the National Museum of the American Indian* (Washington, D.C.: Smithsonian Institution Press, 1996). For astute, engaged, and moving arguments for needed countermodernities in Australian worlds and elsewhere, see Deborah Bird Rose, *Reports from a Wild Country: Ethics for Decolonisation* (Sydney: University of New South Wales Press, 2004).

6. From "Sheep Is Life," www.recursos.org/sheepislife/dine.html (accessed May 5, 2007).

7. I adopt the locution "more-than-human" from Australian anthropologist, philosopher, and science studies scholar Thom van Dooren, in his PhD dissertation, "Seeding Property: Nature, Human/Plant Relations and the Production of Wealth," Australian National University, 2007.

8. Different breeds of meat and fiber sheep in international trade have long been important in the history of capital, and Australia is a key player. Never pretty for the sheep, the trade has only become more brutal with factory farming and has technoscientifically enabled reduction of animals to little more than bioproducers of money. Only one example is the many millions of live sheep shipped annually by countries such as Australia and Uruguay to the Middle East and Asia for Ramadan; the death rate of these sheep in transit has become an international scandal. For a global trade advertisement, see www.alibaba.com/catalog/11156166/Sheep_For_Ramadan.html (accessed May 5, 2007). U.K.-export sheep go mainly to northern Europe, especially France. For a view from

ovine hell, see Sue Coe and Judith Brody, *Sheep of Fools* (Seattle, Wash.: Fantagraphics Books, 2005).

9. Franklin, *Animal Nation,* 157, notes that the immigrant dingo, with its four-thousand-year history on the island continent, is held responsible not only for the extermination of the Australian marsupial thylacines on mainland Australia but also more recently for depredations on the white settler colony's pastoral economy, resulting in a ten-thousand-kilometer fence from Queensland to South Australia. Franklin tells of the still more recent econationalist rehabilitation of the dingo into a symbol of native wild nature in important vacation and tourist sites such as Fraser Island. The American Kennel Club gave dingoes its imprimatur in 1993, designating them an Australian dog breed. The dingo has even achieved the mixed grace of becoming officially endangered as a result of its unblessed interbreeding with ordinary feral dogs. U.S. wolves have followed a similar route from vermin and killers, deemed worthy of soul-chillingly effective and brutal extermination campaigns and bounty hunters, to members of the ecoelite of the super-Native charismatic macrofauna. See Jody Emel, "Are You Man Enough, Big and Bad Enough? Wolf Eradication in the U.S.," in *Animal Geographies,* ed. Jennifer Wolch and Jody Emel (London: Verso, 1998), 91–118. Post–Captain Cook extirpation campaigns against dingoes contributed strongly to the extinction of sixteen other Australian species of mammals by removing their top predator, freeing introduced European predators such as foxes to feast unmolested on the southern continent's ground-dwelling species such as the eastern hare-wallaby. See *New Scientist* (November 11, 2006): 17. For an extraordinary ethnography that centers the importance of dingoes to Aboriginal people of the Northern Territory, see Deborah Bird Rose, *Dingo Makes Us Human* (Cambridge: Cambridge University Press, 1992).

10. Good breed history of the Australian shepherd, complete with great pictures of the old-style ranch dogs and the modified ideal "versatile" Aussies of the post-1970s, can be found in two Australian Shepherd Club of America yearbooks: *Twenty Years of Progress: 1957–1977* and *Proving Versatility: 1978–82.* That Roland, Rusten's and my Aussie–chow cross, looks like the old-style herding Aussies goes a long way in explaining why he was given an "Indefinite Listing Privilege" from the American Kennel Club as an Australian shepherd when I sent in his picture. I told what I knew for sure of his ancestry—namely, that his unregistered, undeniably Aussie dam worked sheep and cattle in California's Central Valley—and neglected to mention the chowish coats and purple tongues of his littermate sisters. Since the whole litter had had their tails mutilated Aussie-style, and he was castrated and so blocked from genetic pollution of more

high-born Aussie lines, our sable-merle Roland had a chance. Sable merle is a disqualifying, but formerly not uncommon, color and coat pattern for kennel-club Aussies in the show ring. Besides, Roland did very well in the American Herding Breeds Association herding-aptitude field test, earning a qualifying certificate as well as a respectful look and encouragement to continue his stock training from some serious herding-trial people. I requested AKC breed registration for three reasons: (1) to run with him in AKC agility, (2) to buffer him from "dangerous breed" paranoia about chow chows if he ever gets into trouble, and (3) to indulge my feelings about the incongruence of institutionally closed gene pools and herding talent. Besides, I am somewhat more positive than I used to be about the role of kennel clubs in keeping the valuable legacy of kinds of dogs alive. There are other ways, biologically and socially, to nurture kinds of dogs into the future, but kennel clubs are generally what we have to work from in the industrial world now. Besides, many of the people working for dogs in these clubs utterly dashed my prejudices. I write about Roland's papers now because this abidingly sweet dog is too old to get into much trouble, even if he wants to. Besides, paternity is never certain, a matter of some historical importance. This is the doubt that fueled wars of succession where human bastardy was at issue, and in today's technoscientific times such uncertainty drives kennel clubs to demand the registration of DNA parentage verification for litters. Biotech companies in dogland have sprouted up to provide the tests for a nice little profit. Blood and genes make a heady mixture, as every antiracist feminist theorist knows, whether thinking about human or nonhuman animals.

11. Long before positive training methods became popular, Sisler trained with hotcakes and praise; he never taught dogs on lead. He and his brother looked for, worked with, and bred good working dogs. His and his dogs' acts became famous in the United States and Canada, and his "blue dogs" played in the Disney movies *Run Appaloosa Run* and *The Best Cow Dog in the West*. Sisler died in 1995. For more information, see http://worknaussies.tripod.com/ and www.workingaussiesource.com/stockdoglib/scott_sisler_article.htm (Web sites accessed May 5, 2007). The Sisler Ranch was on the Farm Tour of the Idaho Organic Exchange in 2004; this cattle ranch practices no-till seeding, rotational grazing, biological weed control, riparian management, and use of settling ponds and filter strips. See *Idaho Organic Alliance Newsletter* (Winter 2004): 5.

12. See Vicki Hearne, *Adam's Task: Calling Animals by Name* (New York: Knopf, 1986), and her novel, *The White German Shepherd* (New York: Atlantic Monthly Press, 1988). To her death, Hearne remained acerbic about "positive

training" methods and food treats. In that particular, Hearn would not have approved of the hotcake-dispensing Sisler! I think she was both fixed in her opinions, come hell or high water—or evidence—and an educated genius with and about animals and their relations with people. Hearne insisted on dogs' right and need to work and to be respected for their judgment and ability and therefore on their entitlement to an education with real criteria and consequences. All of that meant that Hearne considered dogs to be sentient, conscious beings with minds that are not human. Her best philosophical work, in my opinion, lays out the grounds in her cross-species practice and that of other dog people for that view. For working dog-handler arguments in a science studies idiom for dogs' intentionality and ability to engage in creative, coordinated performances with human beings and other dogs (in their case, field gun dog work and sheep herding in both trial and farm conditions), see Graham Cox and Tony Ashford, "Riddle Me This: The Craft and Concept of Animal Mind," *Science, Technology, and Human Values* 23, no. 4 (1998): 425–38. Cox and Ashford correctly emphasize that "domestic" animal behavior and abilities have received much less research attention than animal behavior in both "the wild" and "the laboratory" (429). It is impossible to take "domestic" animals seriously, especially dogs, given their evolutionary history with people, without paying attention to human–animal co-constituted behavior. I am more sympathetic than Hearne or Cox and Ashford to the usefulness in many situations of technical training approaches derived from behaviorism as part of the education of dogs and people, but I agree that without a vivid sense of working with *someone*, not *something*, and therefore a practical commitment to nonhuman embodied cognitive competence, nothing very interesting can happen together, because the human being won't be prepared to respond. Theorizing and building on cross-species achievements in the context of tested practice are knowledge-producing activities that ought to be called what they are—science (*Wissenschaft*).

13. Committed to working stock dogs, herding trial people are fractious, demanding, and proud, for good reason. The subject of a rich oral culture, well-known competitive lines of working Aussies are the result of extensive culling as well as training. For a fascinating view of quite different approaches to the working herders, track the Web sites of Hangin' Tree Working Australian Shepherds (www.adastrafarm.com/AustralianShepherds/HanginTreeWorkingAustralian Shepherds/tabid/70/Default.aspx), Slash V dogs (http://users.htcomp.net/ slashv/home.htm), and Oxford dogs (www.promedia.net/users/ox4ranch/). See also www.stockdog.com/breeders/aussie.htm. (All Web sites accessed May 5, 2007.)

That a kennel could continue to use the name "Hangin' Tree" in 2006 without comment says something ugly about race and class in Salmon, Idaho, where this working Aussie line was developed—and well beyond, right into the body of my whole multispecies nation, where, alas, "hangin' tree" appears throughout the pedigree. I assume the various breeders' proud continuation of the name today, and probably its initial use by those who developed the line, carries no conscious connection to rough "justice" in the West for Chinese, white, black, and Indian people or to the lynching of African Americans in the South and elsewhere. However, hearing the tones of "hangin' tree" comes with touching my dog and the dogs of my friends seriously. My kin include Hangin' Tree dogs. Memory—and inheriting its consequences—surges through touch. I hear again Billy Holiday's 1939 recording of "Strange Fruit," and I see the indelible photographs of scenes of lynching across the United States, even as I fall in love with a beautiful, talented puppy newly coming into my extended kin group in agility. Maybe it is just as well that the formal name "Hangin' Tree" remains in the written pedigrees of thousands of serious working dogs, whose ancestors really were part of the Anglo conquest of the West. Forgetting is not a route to response. Holiday sang,

> Here is the fruit for the crows to pluck
> For the rain to gather, for the wind to suck
> For the sun to rot, for the tree to drop
> Here is a strange and bitter crop.

For a summary and a picture, see http://en.wikipedia.org/wiki/Strange_Fruit. For crucial analysis, see Angela Davis, *Blues Legacy and Black Feminism* (New York: Vintage, 1999).

The serious working and trialing kennels place their dogs in suburban sports homes (and even pet homes) but with considerable demands about what the dogs will do in agility or whatever (often written into the sales contracts) and great reservations about where these dogs would belong if only there were enough real herding jobs. Ad Astra Farm is a good example of a working-herder kennel that also breeds special sheep and ducks for the sport of trialing. The well-being of the other partners to the dogs and humans in the sport—the sheep, cattle, and ducks—is not an optional question for serious companion species. Is the sport okay for the noncarnivores? The answer should not be automatic as a function of one's preexisting ideology but should be a provocation to research and response in the context of changing histories. That approach is essential to my sense of "worldliness."

14. Harriet Ritvo, *The Animal Estate* (Cambridge, Mass.: Harvard University Press, 1987), is the first place to go to understand how the animal-show culture and breeding for show are technologies of human class, nation, and gender formation.

15. Carol Adams, *The Pornography of Meat* (New York: Continuum, 2004), makes a compelling case for veganism in the context of a sophisticated, intersectional critique of the connection of the meat industry's brutality toward animals and toward people, especially women and even more especially women of color. "Ordinary" meat eating is not just complicity, in Adam's view, but both inexcusable direct violence against animals and participation in the violent oppression of classes of people. To track what becomes food for technocultural people and some of the needed response, see Michael Pollan, *Omnivore's Dilemma: A Natural History of Four Meals* (New York: Penguin, 2006).

16. Stengers, "The Cosmopolitical Proposal," 995.

17. Thanks to Sharp for two extensive formal interviews, Fresno, Calif., March 14, 1999, and November 7, 2005, and for permission to quote. Since the fall of 1998, Sharp has generously shared her Aussie knowledge and work with me in e-mails, on the CANGEN-L site for discussion of dog population genetic diversity and depletion, at agility trials to which she came to see Cayenne and me run, over dinners in California's Central Valley, in comparing notes on the course we both took online in dog genetics from the Cornell University vet school, through her work on the Web site of the Australian Shepherd Health and Genetics Institute, and through her publications and manuscripts (including some great love stories sold under a pseudonym to magazines of nondog women). I serve as a reader for chapters of Sharp's book-in-progress on dog genetics and health for breeders. Sharp helped me find Cayenne's breeder when I wanted a puppy who would likely grow up to enjoy and excel at agility. Such a dog would be more likely to come into the world in the stock dog culture than the show conformation culture. Many mutts can also become dynamite agility dogs, but the high-drive herding dogs prevail.

Sharp has also been an informal genetic counselor for me and Cayenne, referring us to the merle gene researcher Sheila Schmutz. See http://homepage .usask.ca/~schmutz/merle.html and http://homepage.usask.ca/~schmutz/dog colors.html (Web sites accessed May 5, 2007). As expected (because I knew a great many of her relatives and had extensive communication with her scrupulous, nonsecretive breeders), Cayenne's cheek swab–derived DNA showed her to be heterozygous, not homozygous, for merle (a coat pigment-distribution pattern). Merle is an autosomal dominant gene that has recently been mapped and characterized at a molecular level. In homozygous form, merle results in a nearly 100 percent incidence of neural deafness or visual defects or both. In its heterozygous form, merle is not known to predispose any sensory impairment. Cayenne is unilaterally neurologically deaf, a highly unusual condition for a heterozygote. Merle is a popular coat pattern in Aussies and several other breeds. Breeding merle to merle produces on average 25 percent homozygotes for M, and so such breedings are widely regarded by Aussie people as unethical.

18. C. A. Sharp, "The Biggest Problem," *Double Helix Network News* (Summer 2000): 2. Before going further, it is important to note that mutts and street dogs have genetic diseases too. Indeed, large mixed populations will show the whole gamut of such conditions at various frequencies. The special issue for purebreds is that they are a kind of institutionally produced Galápagos Islands of the dog world, in which populations are cut off from out-crossing, and so only a subset of canine gene-linked disorders is likely to appear in any one breed. However, if lots of inbreeding—including the common practice of line breeding to concentrate the genetic contribution from highly valued dogs—is the norm, over the generations (and it can happen fast), specific disease-linked genes will occur much more commonly in the homozygous state. Further, if particular male dogs with highly prized appearance or behavior sire large numbers of puppies (the "popular sire syndrome"), those dogs' alleles will become more and more frequent, with consequences for undesirable traits as well as for the ones sought. Females cannot parent anything like the number of puppies that males potentially can, but overuse of a dam also matters. Overall, breed genetic diversity will be reduced as too few dogs contribute their genes to the next generations, and in addition to a higher incidence of specific genetic diseases, reduced vitality from excessive homozygosity can take many forms, probably especially immune dysfunction. All of this means that a major form of breed health activism concerns both learning to avoid doubling up on undesirable genes and learning to breed to enhance genetic diversity or at least maintain rather than deplete it. Each breed will have different diseases of special interest, but the shape of the problem and the response of health activists in technoculture are the same. Activists in different breeds share information and strategy with one another. The links on the Australian Shepherd Health and Genetics Institute Web site to other breeds' health and genetics groups illustrate this networking (www.ashgi.org/). Much breed genetic activism runs up against deeply held beliefs inherited from nineteenth-century doctrines of blood and excellence that are built into the face-to-face mentoring practices that reproduce breeders. A vivid account of how these idioms of pedigree operate in horse-breeding worlds is Rebecca Cassidy, *The*

Sport of Kings: Kinship, Class, and Thoroughbred Breeding in Newmarket (Cambridge: Cambridge University Press, 2002).

19. Founded in 1966 with a focus on canine hip dysplasia, the OFA maintains searchable databases on numerous orthopedic and genetic diseases. Participation is voluntary, and information remains confidential unless the dog's owner specifically releases it into the public domain. Breed clubs and the AKC could require such participation in order for anyone to register his or her dogs, but that kind of obligatory standard is not yet acceptable in the United States, where black helicopters in the sky are seen to accompany any infringement on individual and commercial interests (unless one is labeled a terrorist, in which case any kind of infringement seems to be okay). See www.offa.org/. Developing open databases in which all breeding dogs and their close relatives are included has been a major goal of dog health activists. CHIC, the Canine Health Information Center (www.caninehealthinfo.org/), is a centralized database jointly sponsored by the AKC's Canine Health Foundation and the OFA. CHIC goals are "1) to work with parent clubs in the identification of health issues for which a central information system should be established; 2) to establish and maintain a central health information system in a manner that will support research into canine disease and provide health information to owners and breeders; 3) to establish scientifically valid diagnostic criteria for the acceptance of information into the database; and 4) to base the availability of information on individually identified dogs at the consent of the owner." Since each breed has different health concerns, CHIC works with parent clubs to set up breed-specific standards for becoming a CHIC-enrolled breed. For example, for Australian shepherds, required tests are OFA evaluations for hip and elbow dysplasia and Canine Eye Registry Foundation evaluation for eyes. Optional tests are recommended for collie eye anomaly, autoimmune thyroiditis, and multiple drug resistance. The current inability to test for the genetic background of epilepsy is a major issue in the breed.

Establishing the norm of appropriate universal participation is the elusive key. Even the best intentioned become confused in the face of ever-increasing lists of testable genetic disorders, and many high-priority screening tests have not yet been developed; also, multiplying gene tests is no more a panacea for responsible canine parenthood than it is for human beings setting out to make babies. Which tests, in which circumstances, and at what cost are the stuff of technocultural cosmopolitics for researchers as well as for breeders and other dog people. The commercialization of the genome, especially in diagnostics and as fast as possible in therapeutic vet pharma, is as evident and problematic in affluent canine worlds as it is in human ones. Cancer is a hot spot in these companion-species biopolitics. The "gene for X" functions as a powerful fetish.

20. Sharp, "The Biggest Problem," 2.

21. Starting with a genetic eye disease is overdetermined in my companion-species tale. Sharp has a progressive genetic condition that has robbed her of a large portion of her vision, which stops her precious little from robust participation in online culture and extensive travel and speaking on behalf of canine genetic-health research and action, but vision loss did put an end to her breeding Aussies for show.

22. Because the Internet now plays such a dominant role in dog genetic health communication and education, mail subscriptions in 2006 numbered about one hundred. Many of Sharp's key articles are on the ASHGI Web site. She has won three coveted awards for her dog health writing: two awards in 1999 from the Dog Writers Association of America for the article "The Price of Popularity" and for the *DHNN* itself, and the AKC's first annual Golden Paw Award in 2003 for "The Rising Storm: What Breeders Need to Know about the Immune System."

23. Quotations not otherwise documented come from my recorded interviews with Sharp in 1999 and 2005.

24. C. A. Sharp, "CEA and I," www.workingdogs.com/doc0183.htm, linked through the Canine Diversity Project, www.canine-genetics.com/ (Web sites accessed May 5, 2007).

25. For principles of test breeding and CEA pedigree analysis, see *DHNN* (Summer–Spring 1993).

26. L. F. B. Rubin, *Inherited Eye Disease in Purebred Dogs* (Baltimore: Williams and Wilkins, 1998).

27. Lionel Rubin, Betty Nelson, and C. A. Sharp, "Collie Eye Anomaly in Australian Shepherd Dogs," *Progress in Veterinary and Comparative Ophthalmology* 1, no. 2 (1991): 105–8.

28. George A. Padgett, *Control of Canine Genetic Diseases* (New York: Howell Book House, 1998), 194, 239.

29. Bruno Latour, *Science in Action* (Cambridge, Mass.: Harvard University Press, 1987); Donna Haraway, "Situated Knowledges: The Science Question in Feminism as a Site of Discourse on the Privilege of Partial Perspective," *Feminist Studies* 14, no. 3 (1988): 575–99.

30. Sharp, "CEA and I."

31. "The CEA 'support group,' always informal, does not really exist anymore. Over the years folks have wandered out of the breed or on to other things,

but it was helpful at the time." C. A. Sharp, e-mail communication, April 13, 1999.

32. Paul Rabinow, "Artificiality and Enlightenment: From Sociobiology to Biosociality," in *Incorporations*, ed. J. Crary and S. Kwinter (New York: Zone Books, 1992), 234–52.

33. With about 1 percent of Aussies affected with CEA, CERF reports from the late 1990s indicate that the gene frequency was fairly steady, with 10–15 percent of Aussies being likely carriers. Sharp, e-mail communication, April 13, 1999.

34. See www.optigen.com/opt9_about.html (accessed May 5, 2007). The CEA test in 2006 cost $180, with discounts for litters and for online purchase. In 2005, the online dog magazine published a report (www.dogplace.com/library/Ed_DNA_litmus_test_0508.htm, accessed May 5, 2007) of how a researcher at Cornell's Baker Institute for Animal Health, who was seeking blood samples from dogs to investigate the genetic background to cryptorchidism, treated the head of a dog media organization asking for more information about the study before promoting it on its Web site, which the organization anticipated doing. The scientist's complete failure to address any of the dog organization's intelligently phrased (to my eye) questions illustrates an important aspect of dealing with some scientist–entrepreneurs, a matter that can shape participation—or lack of it—in research. Without telling me names or companies, Sharp described various experiences of being ignored and subjected to overt or unconscious disrespect, despite her credentials and history. Even practicing vets with clients' dogs who might be sampled are ignored by some unnamable scientists, despite their business plans and ambitious biotech companies. This kind of fact explains why dog health activists, in general, and Sharp, in particular, work so hard to build links between bench scientists and ordinary dog people. Sharp also gave me several accounts of thick cooperation and collaboration between investigators and dog people. Her long-term relation with Sheila Schmutz is one such example. On her Web site (http://homepage.usask.ca/~schmutz/merle.html, accessed May 5, 2007), Schmutz credits Sharp for helping her obtain samples for her research, and in the *DHNN* Sharp explains and promotes Schmutz's research among Aussie people. See also S. Schmutz, T. G. Berryere, and C. A. Sharp, "KITLG Mapping to CFA15 and Exclusion as a Candidate Gene for Merle," *Animal Genetics* 34, no. 1 (February 2003): 75–76. In 2006 Keith Murphy's group at Texas A&M reported that a retrotransposon insertion in a gene called SILV is responsible for the merle pattern.

35. Sharp is frequently invited to give genetics and health presentations to

various Aussie organizations, and she asks only for direct travel expenses and a donation to ASHGI. Dog medical genetics might be fully commercialized in companies such as OptiGen, VetGen, and others, but the health activists support their work for dogs largely out of their own funds. The same pattern has been the subject of study in human health support systems and activist organizations, for example, in the stunning amount of volunteer time and expertise required of the parents of autistic children. This combination of well-capitalized, for-profit biomedicine with the extensive, knowledgeable, volunteer labor necessary to the system is typical of contemporary biomedical capitalism across the species divide. See Chloe Silverman, "Interest Groups, Social Movements, or Corporations? Strategies for Collective Action as Biological Citizens," in *Lively Capital*, ed. Kaushik Sunder Rajan (Durham, N.C.: Duke University Press, under review). Biological citizenship is a fundamental concept in science studies scholarship. (See note 52, below.) Sharp is quite savvy about the political economy of genomic and postgenomic research. As she said in our interview on November 7, 2005, "Survival in research used to be 'publish or perish'; now it's 'sell or perish.'" She and other dog activists are also keenly aware of how much of a boost to canine health-centered questions has been given by the publication of the full dog genome in the context of comparative medical genomics, with its utility to scientists interested in human diseases and access to that kind of infrastructure and money. After the National Human Genome Research Institute made the dog genome a priority, progress in sequencing and mapping was rapid. A rough draft based on a poodle was published in 2003, and in 2005 the boxer Tasha was made famous by the publication in a free public database of a 99 percent complete DNA sequence of her genome (with comparisons of sequences in multiple regions to data from ten other dogs). The research dogs came from breed clubs and vet schools. See Kerstin Lindblad-Toh et al., "Genome Sequence, Comparative Analysis, and Haplotype Structure of the Domestic Dog," *Nature* 438 (December 8, 2005): 803–19. Numerous authors and the key institutions of big-time biotech research showed up on the title page, including the Broad Institute, NHGRI, Harvard, and MIT.

36. See C. A. Sharp, "Collie Eye Anomaly in Australian Shepherds," *DHNN* 14, no. 3 (Summer 2006): 2–5. Much of my story is drawn from this essay.

37. In 2007, the Canine Diversity Project Web site was www.canine-genetics.com/. After Armstrong's death, the Listserv became canine-genetics.com on Yahoo. The list is still worthwhile, but the salad days of discussion, when conversion experiences about diversity were the order of the day, were between 1997 and Armstrong's death in August 2001.

38. Unfortunately, the course is no longer offered, but see www.ansci.cor
nell.edu/cat/cg01/cg01.html (accessed May 5, 2007).

39. For example, in Sharp's analyses of pedigrees, identification of dogs
with genetic problems, and assessment of disease risks from a planned mating,
she has never "named names" without the written permission of the owner of the
affected dog or the progenitors of that dog or both. She will not do a pedigree
analysis for a proposed mating unless both parents are owned by the same person, partly to prevent "fishing expeditions" that could cause either deliberate or
inadvertent harm to breeders and partly to protect herself from retribution if
one side of a proposed cross receives worse news than the other. Sharp sent an
e-mail on September 20, 2000, to a small group of her colleagues and friends asking for help in thinking about what risks she could and could not take in sharing
data, when her commitments to openness and her refusal to be bullied put her
in ethical, legal, and financial dilemmas. With information supplied to her by
Aussie owners and breeders and data from open databases when available, she
tracked about two dozen traits and conditions in the breed by 2006 and can track
some of them back more than two decades. Without the statistics produced by
a National Institutes of Health equivalent for dogs (data cost a lot of money and
organization to produce), Sharp does not have a complete picture, but she's got
the best health archives possible for Aussies in current sociotechnical conditions
in dogland. The need for an institutional home for those data is patent.

40. For behavioral genetic research, see http://psych.ucsf.edu/k9behavio
ralgenetics/ (accessed May 5, 2007).

41. C. A. Sharp, "ASHGI: 5 Years of Dedication to Breed Health,"
DHNN 14, no. 2 (Spring 2006): 2–5.

42. Intended to bring together breed health organizations and researchers, the Canine Health Foundation conferences are sponsored by the AKC and
the Nestlé Purina PetCare Company. Because of the *DHNN*, Sharp attended as
a member of the press. She went with what she called her laundry list of activists
and researchers with whom she wanted to talk. In 2005, about three hundred
people attended the conference, in St. Louis, which focused on the canine genome
and cancer. See *DHNN* 13, no. 4 (Fall 2005): 1, 5. Having corresponded for a
couple of years, Sharp and geneticist Sheila Schmutz met in person at the first
CHF conference. Now a friend and collaborator, Schmutz is also a reader for
drafts of Sharp's book manuscript on genetics for breeders. Sharp's contacts with
scientists come about in various ways, including brief e-mail self-introductions
and references to the ASHGI Web site. These introductions frequently go un-
answered, but sometimes productive connections develop. Sharp sees one of her

roles to be educating scientists about purebred-dog people's concerns and cultures so that whole-dog matters, such as grief about genetic disease, make more sense in the lab world.

43. Her kennel Web site is www.foxwoodkennel.com/ (accessed May 5, 2007). Monti breeds rarely and very carefully. The "Ten Steps" pledge is prominent on her Web site. Practicing what she preaches, she lists the numerical scores for a long list of health concerns for a planned breeding. The scores indicate a range of probability that a given difficulty might result from the breeding. Far from suggesting that Foxwood breeds unhealthy dogs, Monti's practice operationalizes honesty and awareness that all biological critters are mortal. No purebred union (and no mutt breeding either) can claim to have no potential for trouble. A breeder's unwillingness to address any problems in the history of his or her dogs with potential buyers is a good indication of an unethical breeder or a puppy mill. Monti's potential puppy buyers can see the probability scores as well as a great deal of other information about the dogs, and they will find a breeder willing to answer their questions openly. No Ostrich Syndrome here! Perusing purebred Web sites on the Internet will quickly show how rare this degree of openness is. Monti also works hard to place her dogs in homes where they will have a real job—search and rescue, agility, herding, or something else.

44. See Kim Monti, "Stylish Footwork: 10-Steps for Health," *DHNN* 13, no. 2 (Spring 2005): 2–5, for an account of the history of Ten Steps.

45. See C. A. Sharp, "The Dirty Dozen Plus a Few: Frequency of Hereditary Disease in Australian Shepherds," *DHNN* 9, no. 3 (Summer 2001): 2–5. The ASHGI Web site gives more detailed information on every condition of interest.

46. C. A. Sharp, "The Road to Hell: Epilepsy and the Australian Shepherd," *Australian Shepherd Journal* 13, no. 4 (July/August 2003), www.ashgi.org/articles/epilepsy_road_hell.htm.

47. C. A. Sharp, "The Biggest Problem," *DHNN* 8, no. 3 (Summer 2000): 2–5, 4.

48. Epilepsy has a long history as a stigmatizing disease among human beings, too, and as a condition whose diagnosis and interpretation are wildly variable. The classic scholarly history up to modern neurology is Oswei Tempkin, *The Falling Sickness* (Baltimore: Johns Hopkins University Press, 1945, rev. ed., 1971). If the reader persists in being interested in *Homo sapiens* in the face of the importance of dogs, see also Fiorella Gurrieri and Romeo Carrozzo, eds., "The Genetics of Epilepsy," *American Journal of Medical Genetics*, Special Issue, 106, no. 2, published online, September 20, 2001. The history of epilepsy among

artists and other exceptional people makes me wonder if there are compensa-
tions for dogs, too, in their terrible experiences of the disease. I also can't help but
wonder what the incidence of epilepsy is among Sharp's Incorrigibles in dogland.
Are they incapable of empathy or too consumed by it?

49. See www.tobysfoundation.org/Ads_Archive.htm (accessed May 5,
2007). The Web site permits the downloading of pdf files of all of the ads from
Toby's Foundation. Pam Douglas and Toby's story is told by Stevens Parr, "The
Face of Epilepsy: How One Pet Owner Is Staring It Down," *Australian Shepherd
Journal*, September/October 2004, available on www.tobysfoundation.org.
Thanks to Douglas for permission to reprint the ad "The Face of Epilepsy."

50. Parr, "The Face of Epilepsy," 17.

51. Some knowledgeable dog people were not so sorry to see VetGen out
of the picture. The company's successful legal attack for patent infringement on
another company that sells DNA diagnostic tests for dogs (GeneSearch) did not
indicate a major commitment to a more open and collaborative medical genetic
culture. The disputed test was for canine von Willebrand disease. My people
worried that VetGen might develop a test first, but its cost and conditions of use
might be far from ideal. VetGen's view was posted on www.vetgen.com/legal
&public_docs.html (accessed November 2006, no longer available on May 5,
2007). The court case in which VetGen defeated GeneSearch was decided on
July 10, 2002, by the U.S. District for the Eastern District of Michigan.

52. Sheila Rothman, "Serendipity in Science: How 3 BRCA Gene Mutations Became Ashkenazi Jewish," paper delivered at the workshop Ethical World
of Stem Cell Medicine, University of California at Berkeley, September 28, 2006;
Gina Kolata, "Using Genetic Tests, Ashkenazi Jews Vanquish a Disease," *New
York Times*, February 18, 2003, http://query.nytimes.com/gst/fullpage.html?
sec=health&res=9F05E0D81E3AF93BA25751C0A9659C8B63. In *Online Science and Technology News* from May 4, 2005, in an article titled "Jewish Sect
Embraces Technology to Save Its Own: The Ashkenazi Jews of New York Have
Turned to Genetic Screening to Save the Lives of Their Children," www
.stnews.org/rlr-438.htm, Deborah Pardo-Kaplan writes: "Through a voluntary,
confidential screening program called Chevra Dor Yeshorim, or 'Association
of an Upright Generation,' unmarried Orthodox Jewish adults worldwide can
be tested to find out if they carry the gene for Tay-Sachs. Each person tested
receives a blood test and an identification number. Before dating, both members
of the potential couple call Chevra Dor Yeshorim's automated hotline and enter
their ID numbers. If both test positive for the Tay-Sachs gene, they are told they
are considered unsuitable marriage partners because of the one-in-four chance

their children will develop the disease." In an e-mail of October 6, 2006, Rayna Rapp, a New York anthropologist who studies genetic citizenship and response to genetic diagnosis, told me, "In the secular programs, one Ashkenazi grandparent 'counts' to strongly recommend Tay-Sachs screening; among the ultra orthodox who use CDY's program (not everyone!!!), direct screening is undertaken on all teens, so that no potentially 'incompatible' matches will be suggested." See Rayna Rapp, *Testing Women, Testing the Fetus: The Social Impact of Amniocentesis in America* (New York: Routledge, 1999).

On genetic citizenship, see Rayna Rapp, "Cell Life and Death, Child Life and Death: Genomic Horizons, Genetic Diseases, Family Stories," in *Remaking Life and Death*, ed. Franklin and Lock, 129–64; Karen-Sue Taussig, "The Molecular Revolution in Medicine: Promise, Reality, and Social Organization," in *Complexities: Anthropological Challenges to Reductive Accounts of Biosocial Life*, ed. S. McKinnon and S. Silverman (Chicago: University of Chicago Press, 2005), 223–47; Deborah Heath, Rayna Rapp, and Karen-Sue Taussig, "Genetic Citizenship," in *A Companion to Political Anthropology*, ed. D. Nugent and J. Vincent (London: Blackwell, 2004), 152–67; and Rayna Rapp, Karen Sue Taussig, and Deborah Heath, "Standing on the Biological Horizon," in progress for *Critique of Anthropology*.

53. Charis Thompson Cussins, "Confessions of a Bioterrorist," in *Playing Dolly: Technocultural Formations, Fantasies, and Fictions of Assisted Reproduction*, ed. E. Ann Kaplan and Susan Squier (New York: Routledge, 1999), 189–219.

54. Susan Conant's many dog sleuth novels, with those beautiful malamutes, are hugely popular in dogland, even with all of our snide remarks about her unshakeable loyalty to the AKC. For her take on puppy millers, genetic disasters, and irresponsible breeding, see Susan Conant, *Evil Breeding* (New York: Bantam, 1999) and *Bloodlines* (New York: Bantam, 1994). See also Laurien Berenson, *A Pedigree to Die For* (New York: Kensington Publishing Corp., 1995).

5. CLONING MUTTS, SAVING TIGERS

A snapshot of a turn-of-the-century moment in a rapidly morphing drama, this chapter, revised in 2006 for *When Species Meet*, was originally written for a workshop in May 2000 at the School of American Research and was first revised in 2002 for inclusion in *Remaking Life and Death*, ed. Franklin and Lock.

1. G. Evelyn Hutchinson, *The Ecological Theater and the Evolutionary Play* (New Haven, Conn.: Yale University Press, 1965); Rabinow, "Artificiality

and Enlightenment"; Latour, *We Have Never Been Modern*; Haraway, *Modest _Witness@Second_Millennium*.

2. Chris Cuomo, *Feminism and Ecological Communities: An Ethic of Flourishing* (New York: Routledge, 1998), 62.

3. Geoff Bowker and Susan Leigh Star, *Sorting Things Out: Classification and Its Consequences* (Cambridge, Mass.: MIT Press, 1999), 27–28.

4. Bruce Fogle, ed., *Interrelations between People and Pets* (Springfield, Ill.: C. C. Thomas, 1981); Aaron Katcher and Allen M. Beck, eds., *New Perspectives on Our Lives with Companion Animals* (Philadelphia: University of Pennsylvania Press, 1983); Anthony Podberscek, Elizabeth S. Paul, and James A. Serpell, eds., *Companion Animals and Us: Exploring the Relationship between People and Pets* (Cambridge: Cambridge University Press, 2000); Victoria Voith and Peter L. Borchert, eds., *Readings in Companion Animal Behavior* (Trenton, N.J.: Veterinary Learning Systems, 1996); Cindy C. Wilson and Dennis C. Turner, eds., *Companion Animals in Human Health* (Thousand Oaks, Calif.: Sage Publications, 1998). For a fuller picture of the literature on companion dogs and human health, see Franklin, Emmison, Haraway, and Travers, "Investigating the Therapeutic Benefits of Companion Animals."

5. I would now demote the language of emergence in favor of reciprocal inductions in order to stress that there is no emergence from a thing in itself, but always a relational knot of intra- and interactions.

6. *The DNA Files II*, Sound Vision Productions, NPR, October 22, 2001.

7. Leslie Pray, "Missyplicity Goes Commercial," *Scientist* 3, no. 1 (2002): 1127, www.the-scientist.com/article/display/20892/. Pray was quoting Lou Hawthorne, the CEO of Genetic Savings and Clone, Inc. John Sperling, the no longer anonymous donor, committed another nine million dollars, and the company relocated to Sausalito, California, from College Station, Texas. Billionaire John Sperling is said to have spent more than nineteen million dollars trying to clone his life partner's dog Missy in the more than seven years the project existed. Sperling is a futurist also involved in the (human) life extension movement and the funding of Biosphere. See http://en.wikipedia.org/wiki/John_Sperling; and http://en.wikipedia.org/wiki/Biosphere. Lou Hawthorne is the son of Joan Hawthorne, Missy's human. When Missy died, Sperling and Joan Hawthorne sought a new dog from dog shelters, which is where Missy came from as well.

8. Sarah Franklin, *Embodied Progress: A Cultural Account of Assisted Conception* (London: Routledge, 1997); Marilyn Strathern, *The Gender of the Gift: Problems with Women and Problems with Society in Melanesia* (Berkeley and Los

Angeles: University of California Press, 1988); Marilyn Strathern, *Reproducing the Future: Anthropology, Kinship and the New Reproductive Technologies* (New York: Routledge, 1992).

9. Michel Foucault, *The Birth of the Clinic: An Archaeology of Medical Perception*, trans. A. M. Sheridan Smith (New York: Pantheon, 1973).

10. I rely on a two-day formal interview with Weisser, December 28–29, 1999, at her home in Olympia, Washington, where I also met her magnificent dogs; three years' of postings on Pyr-L@apple.ease.lsoft.com, a discussion group with about five hundred subscribers in 2001, founded in 1997 and run by Weisser, Catherine de la Cruz, Judy Gustafson, Karen Reiter, and Janet Frashé (the collective computer expertise of these women is not trivial to their dog work); numerous private e-mails; and ongoing personal contacts. I lived for seven years in the same extended household with a Great Pyrenees, Willem deKoonig, who was bred by Weisser. Weisser acts on the ethical commitment to track dogs she breeds throughout their lives and support both them and their people. After a rear leg amputation for bone cancer in June 2006, Willem experienced metastases to his lungs in December; he was euthanized among his human and cat friends. The breeder remained available and vulnerable within this knot of mortal companion species. I also draw on conversations and interviews with Catherine de la Cruz and from the pleasure of meeting some of her dogs. She guided me through the discussion list LGD-L, a rich resource for learning about the several kinds of working livestock guardian dogs on farms, ranches, and hobby suburban properties.

11. Chapter 4, "Examined Lives," tracks the institutional rearrangements and activist struggle for open registries up to 2006.

12. The first U.S. breed open registries for genetic diseases were the PRA Data (started by Georgia Gooch, a Lab retriever breeder, in 1989, to deal with progressive retinal atrophy) and the West Highland Anomaly Task Council (WatcH), which was started in 1989 and registered three diseases by 1997.

13. de la Cruz, Pyr-L@apple.ease.lsoft.com, August 17, 2001.

14. See, for example, *World Conservation Strategy*, IUCN, 1980; the Bruntland Report, *Our Common Future*, WECD, 1987; *Convention on Biodiversity*, 1992; *Valuing Nature's Services*, WorldWatch Institute Report of Progress toward a Sustainable Society, 1997; *Investing in Biological Diversity*, Cairns Conference, OECD, 1997; and *Saving Biological Diversity: Economic Incentives*, OECD, 1996. For a sketch of biodiversity discourses in this period, see E. O. Wilson, ed., *Biodiversity* (Washington, D.C.: National Academy Press, 1988); and E. O. Wilson, *The Diversity of Life* (New York: Norton, 1992).

15. The Canine Diversity Project is at www.canine-genetics.com/ (accessed May 6, 2007). The site was last updated in 2002.

16. See Susan Harding, *The Book of Jerry Falwell* (Princeton, N.J.: Princeton University Press, 1999), for an analysis of how conversion discourse works.

17. In May 2007, clicking on "Species Survival Plan" took one instead to the World Wildlife Fund–Canada page on conservation projects.

18. *SSP* is a North American term. Species Survival Plan® Program is registered by the AZA. See www.aza.org/ConScience/ConScienceSSPFact/ (accessed May 6, 2007). See also European endangered species programs (EESPs) and Australasian species management programs. China, Japan, India, Thailand, Malaysia, and Indonesia have their own equivalents for this global technoscience of indigenous species.

19. See chapter 2, "Value-Added Dogs," for a summary of the nonpet, biomedical dog cloning project in the lab of Hwang Woo-Suk of the Seoul National University. The cloned Afghan hound, Snuppy, was born in 2005 in that project.

20. The site in 2001 was www.missyplicity.com. After Texas A&M researchers and John Sperling's money parted in 2002, the project was continued entirely within Genetics Savings and Clone, Inc., which was founded in February 2000, moved from Texas to California, and closed its doors in October 2006. The Web site www.savingsandclone.com came down by December 2006, and customers for the cryopreservation service were referred to ViaGen at www.viagen.com/our-services/preserving-your-pets/, with the note that "ViaGen has no plans to provide commercial cat or dog cloning services."

21. www.animalcloningsciences.com (accessed spring 2000). Headquartered in Rancho Mirage, California, Animal Cloning Sciences, Inc., in 2006, advertised its research in cloning horses.

22. The Web site address in 2000 was www.lazaron.com. The company became Lazaron Biotechnologies (SA), Ltd., advertising "stem cell expertise for Africa" in a "globally networked center of excellence," www.lazaron.co.za/ (accessed November 2006). The heir of cloning idioms, "regenerative cell technology" was the language of the stem cell world in 2006. The Web site stated that "the company's initial primary business goal is to establish the first human cord blood stem cell bank in Africa." Lazaron has further elaborated on its "bioethical" goal in 2001 of "saving a genetic life." The link to research gave the following profile for the company in 2006:

> Through the company's Animal Bio-cell Division, short to
> medium term projects have already been identified, and are being

further researched and developed at Stellenbosch University in a
research program that ends 2006. It is envisaged that the outcome
of this research will inter alia enable Lazaron to offer regenerative
veterinary cell replacement therapy to the race horse industry
and more specifically aimed at tendon regeneration.

Different assisted reproductive and biotechnology techniques are used to:

1) produce disease-free Cape buffalo calves to replace the diminishing
numbers of this species dying of tuberculosis in our game parks;

2) store genetic material of wildlife and valuable livestock and pet
species for future cloning procedures;

3) produce test tube animal babies where natural breeding of the
species is not possible;

4) collect and store animal stem cells from valuable animals like race-
horses and superior male animals;

5) apply stem cell therapies for the regeneration of torn and damaged
tendons;

6) develop animal models for the study of the therapeutic use of stem
cells in human medicine;

7) investigate alternative methods of somatic and stem cell culture, e.g.
under weightlessness conditions.

23. John Cargill and Susan Thorpe Vargas, "Seeing Double: The Future
of Dog Cloning," *DogWorld* 85, no. 3 (2000): 20–26.

24. www.savingsandclone.com/ethics (accessed 2000–2002).

25. www.missyplicity.com/goals (accessed 2000–2002).

26. www.tamu.edu/researchandgradstudies, 1996 figures (accessed 2000).

27. www.missyplicity.com/team (accessed 2000).

28. www3.cnn.com/EARTH/9509/hartebeast (accessed 2000). Note that
Lazaron Biotechnologies (SA), Ltd., had many of the same goals near the end
of the decade. Instruments such as an SSP and a cryopreservation lab had more
than a little in common as conservation and reproduction strategies in technoculture. Sarah Franklin's *Dolly Mixtures* prepares one to understand such con-
vergences in the details of cross-continental practice.

29. www.tamu.edu/researchandgradstudies/scico98/tamu2.html
(accessed 2000).

30. Thanks to Linda Hogle for an audio tape of the whole event and a
preprint of Hawthorne's presentation, as well as for highlighting the endangered
species remarks.

31. Joseph Dumit, "Playing Truths: Logics of Seeking and the Persistence of the New Age," *Focaal* 37 (2001): 63–75.

32. Lou Hawthorne, "The Ethics of Cloning Companion Animals," preprint for Stanford University's Ethics in Society Program, May 12, 2000. All further quotations of Hawthorne are drawn from this preprint.

6. ABLE BODIES AND COMPANION SPECIES

1. Two of my older brother's children, Mark and Debra, learned Dad's scoring system. Mark said that, across the gulfs of a continent and their own parents' divorce, this way of scoring bound them to a grandfather they barely knew. To be literate in my family means knowing how to code the plays so that a game can be reconstructed in dramatic detail years later. Katie King, *Networked Reenactments* (under review), teaches me how writing technologies make persons. See www.womensstudies.umd.edu/wmstfac/kking/ (accessed May 5, 2007).

2. My reflections on "regard" are in conversation with Wlad Godzich, whose December 20, 2005, e-mail response to my talk at the Bodies in the Making conference was both moving and helpful.

3. See Haraway, *The Companion Species Manifesto*; Tsing, "Unruly Edges"; and Despret, "The Body We Care For." For the join of optics and haptics in species encounters, see Eva Shawn Hayward, "Jellyfish Optics: Immersion in Marine TechnoEcology," paper presented at the October 2004 meetings of the Society for Literature and Science, Durham, N.C.

4. Karen Barad, "Invertebrate Visions: Diffractions, Mutations, Re(con)-figurations, and the Ethics of Mattering," in *Meeting the Universe Halfway*; Astrid Schrader, "Temporal Ecologies and Political Phase–Spaces: Dinoflagellate Temporalities in Intra-action," paper presented at the October 2005 meetings of the Society for Social Studies of Science, Pasadena, California.

5. Thompson, *Making Parents*.

6. My own guess is that Dad fell because TB had already undermined his bones, not that TB was stimulated by falling. Interpretive options of this kind pepper the telling of any story, especially family stories. The line between fiction and fact runs through the living room.

7. For a lively account of the game and its people, see Jerome Charyn, *Sizzling Chops and Devilish Spins: Ping Pong and the Art of Staying Alive* (New York: Four Wall, Eight Windows Press, 2001).

8. For thinking about this sort of thing within actor-network theory in science and technology studies, see Myriam Winance, "Trying Out the

Wheelchair: The Mutual Shaping of People and Devices through Adjustment," *Science, Technology, and Human Values* 31, no. 1 (January 2006): 52–72.

9. I read about some of the secrets of the craft in a book I found in Dad's library after he died: Harry E. Heath, *How to Cover, Write, and Edit Sports* (Ames: Iowa State College Press, 1951). Sports covered: baseball, basketball, football, hockey, boxing, tennis. The baseball scoring system in this book seems much less nimble to me than Dad's. I would be surprised if Dad ever read Heath's tome.

8. TRAINING IN THE CONTACT ZONE

1. Gaëtanelle Gilquin and George M. Jacobs, "Elephants Who Marry Mice Are Very Unusual: The Use of the Relative Pronoun (*Who*) with Nonhuman Animals," *Society and Animals* 14, no. 1 (2006): 79–105.

2. Clutton-Brock, *A Natural History of Domesticated Mammals.* For dogs, see Serpell, ed., *The Domestic Dog;* Raymond and Lorna Coppinger, *Dogs: A Startling New Understanding of Canine Origin, Behavior, and Evolution* (New York: Scribner's, 2001); and Stephen Budiansky, *The Covenant of the Wild: Why Animals Chose Domestication* (New Haven, Conn.: Yale University Press, 1999; original 1992). On evidence from ancient dog burial sites found all over the world for very early emotional bonds and close association between dogs and people, see Morey, "Burying Key Evidence." For a critical historical perspective, see Barbara Noske, *Beyond Boundaries: Humans and Animals* (Montreal: Black Rose Books, 1997). Besides introducing the idea of the "animal–industrial complex," Noske sketches the complexity of human–animal relations in domestication over many thousands of years, defining those relations as humans' alteration of the other animals' seasonal subsistence cycle but also allowing for a more active way in which animals alter human patterns. The ecologies of all the species involved are at the center of attention in this approach to domestication. Noske also insists that we regard animals more like science fictional other worlds and less like mirrors or lesser humans.

3. Despret, "The Body We Care For"; Despret, "Sheep Do Have Opinions."

4. Haraway, *The Companion Species Manifesto.*

5. Biosocial preconditions for paying attention to each other in the kind of training I will discuss are suggested in Brian Harre, Michelle Brown, Christina Williamson, and Michael Tomasello, "The Domestication of Social Cognition in Dogs," *Science* 298 (November 22, 2002): 1634–36, which presents evidence that dogs have genetically stabilized abilities to read the behavior of humans,

abilities that wolves do not have. No one has yet looked for the evidence of human genetically stabilized abilities showing how domestic associates such as dogs and cattle have shaped people, partly because of the dualistic assumption that people change culturally, but animals change only biologically, since they have no culture. Both parts of this assumption are surely wrong, even making allowances for irresolvable fights over what "culture" means among different communities of practice. So far, genetic researchers have looked only for how the history of animal diseases, such as flu, might be written into the human genome by incorporation of all or part the viral genomes. Retroviruses are of special interest, and scientists estimate that about one hundred thousand segments of the human genome (i.e., up to 8 percent of the full human DNA complement) are remarkably similar to retroviruses. See Carl Zimmer, "Old Viruses Resurrected through DNA," *New York Times*, November 7, 2006, D3; and N. de Parseval and Thierry Heidmann, "Human Endogenous Retroviruses: From Infectious Elements to Human Genes," *Cytogenetic Genome Research* 110, nos. 1–4 (2005): 318–32. But the genetic record should be rich with potential for understanding much thicker histories of inter- and intra-action than just viral swapping. Comparative molecular genomics will be a valuable tool in rethinking the history of entanglements called domestic, including behavioral abilities within and across species, such as the behavioral abilities of both dogs and people that allow them to read each other, play with each other, and train with each other.

   6. The Web site www.doggery.org/ has links to introduce agility, as well as the dogs I have trained and played with, Roland and Cayenne. The site has little pictures of the obstacles and links to organizations and descriptions of events. Check www.bayteam.org/index.html and www.cleanrun.com/ for links to a wealth of agility information. The monthly magazine *Clean Run* is a major resource for course designs and analyses, diagrams for practice exercises, training information, equipment descriptions and ads, accounts of the dogs playing the game, interviews with human players all over the world, reports on national and world competitions, sports nutrition information for canine athletes, stress management advice for people and dogs, dog massage instructions, and great agility pictures. Clean Run, Inc., also hosts an online agility discussion group on yahoo.com, and many more Internet discussion groups are dedicated to aspects of the game. Many people build their own equipment for practice, and designs can be found on the Internet. Major agility events are aired on television, and both training videos and videos of major competitions abound (check out www.dogpatch.org/agility/). The Web site www.dogpatch.org/agility/IAL/ial.html is replete with information about agility in countries other than the United States.

(All Web sites accessed May 6, 2007.) The magazine *Dog and Handler* covers all dog sports.

7. One of the fine consequences of the desire of U.S. folks to compete in the IFCS world events is that tail docking and ear cutting of American competition dogs will have to stop. Cayenne, an Australian shepherd, might still have her tail if she had been destined for the world stage. Europeans, unlike their U.S. counterparts, tend not to see black helicopters in the sky when regulations are passed by a transnational agency to control the behavior of kennels and breeders—regulations naming as illegal abuse (which will ban a dog from competition) what the breeder previously saw as only a private matter and club standard. Maybe the pressure will help protect all the other dogs too, but the fight, shamefully, is a big one, and most dogs aren't competitive athletes, nor should they have to be.

8. Brenda Fender, "History of Agility, Part 1," *Clean Run* 10, no. 7 (July 2004): 32–37.

9. For a good sociological study done by researchers who also run with their dogs in agility, see Dair Gillespie, Ann Leffler, and Elinor Lerner, "If It Weren't for My Hobby, I'd Have a Life: Dog Sports, Serious Leisure, and Boundary Negotiations," paper delivered at the American Sociological Association section on Animals and Society, Anaheim, California, 2001. Leffler provided me with her notes from Power Paws agility camp in Placerville, California, in 2000 and 2001. She records for 2000 that 241 human students attended, 146 with their dogs. About 86 percent were women. The camper population was almost all white, but attendees came from as far as England and Japan. Leffler estimated mean and median age to be in the forties. Camp is, as Leffler said, a total immersion experience. Cayenne and I attended the five-day Power Paws camp in 2002 and 2004 and found the experience much as Leffler described it. Going to the camp cost us about a thousand dollars each year, counting everything. Instructors came from about four countries and all over the United States. About a third of the instructors were men, Leffler notes, and the same was true in my years. All the instructors were white, and most were full-time agility instructors. They knew one another from World Team, other camps and workshops, Nationals, and such. Instructors all had very fast dogs such as border collies, working-line Aussies, shelties, and Jack Russell terriers. Leffler, a Rottweiler handler, says acidly in her field notes, "So much for the notion that there's room at the top for amateurs!" Ann Leffler, Liberal Arts and Sciences Program, Utah State University, Logan, Utah 84322.

10. Karen Pryor, *Getting Started: Clicker Training for Dogs* (Waltham,

Mass.: Sunshine Books, 2005), is a good introduction. Karen Pryor's clicker gear store has a Web site: http://clickerpets.stores.yahoo.net/getstarclict4.html (accessed May 6, 2007). For background on Pryor, see http://en.wikipedia.org/wiki/Karen_Pryor. Important books are: Karen Pryor: *Don't Shoot the Dog: The New Art of Teaching and Training* (New York: Bantam, revised 1999; original 1984); *Karen Pryor on Behavior: Chapters and Research* (Waltham, Mass.: Sunshine Books, 1994); and *Lads before the Wind: Diary of a Dolphin Trainer*, rev. ed. (Waltham, Mass.: Sunshine Books, 2004). See also Susan Garrett: *Ruff Love: A Relationship Building Program for You and Your Dog* (Chicopee, Mass.: Clean Run, 2002); and *Shaping Success: The Education of an Unlikely Champion* (Chicopee, Mass.: Clean Run, 2005). Garrett is an internationally known agility competitor and teacher.

11. There are many technical wrinkles on this exceedingly simple description of positive training, but they are not needed for this chapter.

12. I owe my understanding of the prosaic to Gillian Goslinga, "Virgin Birth in South India: Childless Women, Spirit Possession, and the Prose of the Modern World," PhD dissertation, University of California at Santa Cruz, June 2006. I am also indebted to Isabelle Stengers's understanding how the abstractions of science push one to imagine new manifestations, which only make sense in prosaic details.

13. For a long time, because politics, including the politics of race, class, and sexuality, were so inaudible, I thought agility was full of conventional, straight or closeted, conservative, mostly white, middle-class U.S. humans. Used to the flourishing and rarely understated left, antiracist, feminist, lesbian, gay, and trans cultures of Santa Cruz, I misjudged the human social world of agility. To be sure, there were plenty of Bush supporters during the early months of the invasion of Iraq in 2003—made painfully clear by the crop of red, white, and blue flag-waving paraphernalia, from portable chairs to dog collars and even one poor dyed dog, which blossomed in the "war on terror." Also, I have not spent so much time since the mid-1960s in a culture in which it is so difficult to tell who is gay and in which so many of my usually rather savvy guesses have turned out to be wrong. Some of that, I still think, is a reflection of heteronormative worlds in which the "straight" still just is, and conscious and unconscious conformity is taken for granted. On the other hand, I was often wrong because my university culture's usual markers were not informative, and for a great many of the women who play agility, gay or straight, the paucity of men and children is what is really taken for granted most of the time, for better and for worse. I found a revealing joke burned onto a wooden plaque for sale in a booth at one agility meet: "Back

Sunday night. Feed the children." Further, I now think that the interspecies core of the practice of agility actively leads its humans most of the time to protect spaces free of politics-as-usual, in which people who would otherwise fly apart in mutually dismissive judgment can continue to learn from and play with one another and their canine partners. Agility sites are also largely free of any work, whether in the home or on the job, besides the considerable labor that it takes to put on a match. With the exception of paid judges, who are not getting rich on these weekends, almost all of the labor of putting on an agility trial is volunteer and widely shared. Possible germs for a more robust civic culture, these free spaces are rare and precious in U.S. society, where both excess busyness and the search for those we agree with seem to take precedence over actually thinking with someone different from oneself. Little by little, I discovered agility to be a site where many people build friendship networks in which intellectual and political matters are quite lively and openly discussed between runs, sometimes "intersectionally" with people's knowledge and passion about dogs, but more often separately. In addition, it takes a great deal of time in agility worlds to come to know how people make or made their livings and how many people have serious accomplishments—in and out of paid jobs—to their credit besides those in dogs. By now, I am much less sure where the closets are and much more intrigued by the spaces opened up by putting dogs at the center of attention and going very slowly into the other things that make up the lives of agility people. My tennis-playing human life mate, Rusten, thinks this understated, slowly discovered, and very rich quality broadly typifies seriously played, amateur, participant sports outside the American corporate professional sports culture. I now agree.

14. Yellow is not accidental. Dogs see yellow and blue quite well. The red and green of plush holiday dog toys notwithstanding, dogs do not see those colors well at all. See Stanley Coren, *How Dogs Think* (New York: Free Press, 2004), 31–34. If the A-frame is painted green and yellow (which is sometimes the case), dogs have a much harder time distinguishing the contact zone visually than if it is painted blue and yellow. Green looks yellowish to a dog. But the color demarcation is not the most relevant variable in a well-educated dog's contact-obstacle performance.

15. Susan Conant, *Black Ribbon* (New York: Bantam, 1995). The scene of the A-frame murder is a dog sports summer camp. An A-frame falling on a human head has a baleful effect.

16. Mary Louise Pratt, *Imperial Eyes: Travel Writing and Transculturation* (New York: Routledge, 1992), 6–7.

17. James Clifford, *Routes: Travel and Translation in the Late Twentieth Century* (Cambridge, Mass.: Harvard University Press, 1997), 7.

18. Naomi Mitchison, *Memoirs of a Spacewoman* (London: Women's Press, 1985; original 1962); Suzette Haden Elgin, *Native Tongue* (New York: Daw Books, 1984); Samuel R. Delany, *Babel 17* (New York: Ace Books, 1966).

19. See Elna Bakker, *An Island Called California: An Ecological Introduction to Its Natural Communities,* 2nd ed. (Berkeley and Los Angeles: University of California Press, 1984), 97–103, for a discussion of the contemporary mixed assemblages of Arcto-Tertiary and Madro-Tertiary tree species. Ecotones and edge effects are geotemporal as well as niche-spatial processes.

20. Juanita Sundberg, "Conservation Encounters: Transculturation in the 'Contact Zones' of Empire," *Cultural Geography* 13, no. 2 (2006): 239–65.

21. Tsing, "Unruly Edges," ms. 4.

22. Eduardo Kohn, "How Dogs Dream," *American Ethnologist* 34, no. 1 (2007). The quotation is from a personal e-mail communication, November 4, 2005. Kohn is preparing a book titled *Toward an Anthropology of Life: Amazonian Natures and the Politics of Trans-species Engagement.*

23. Scott Gilbert, *Developmental Biology,* 8th ed. (Sunderland, Mass.: Sinauer Associates, 2006).

24. On chreodes as stabilized channels in landscapes of developmental probability and developmental interactions, see C. H. Waddington, *The Evolution of an Evolutionist* (Ithaca, N.Y.: Cornell University Press, 1975). Waddington wrote extensively about "epigenetic landscapes." See Scott F. Gilbert, "Epigenetic Landscaping: C. H. Waddington's Use of Cell Fate Bifurcation Diagrams," *Biology and Philosophy* 6 (1991): 135–54. See also Scott F. Gilbert, "Induction and the Origins of Developmental Genetics," in *A Conceptual History of Modern Embryology,* ed. Scott Gilbert (New York: Plenum, 1991), 181–206; and Scott F. Gilbert and Steven Borish, "How Cells Learn, How Cells Teach: Education within the Body," in *Change and Development: Issues of Theory, Method, and Application,* ed. A. Reninger and E. Amsel (Hillsdale, N.J.: Lawrence Erlbaum, 1997), 61–75. For discussion of Waddington's chreodes and approaches to development in relation to Whitehead's process philosophy, see James Bono, "Perception, Living Matter, Cognitive Systems, Immune Networks: A Whiteheadian Future for Science Studies," forthcoming. For Waddington in the history of embryology, see Donna Haraway, *Crystals, Fabrics, and Fields: Metaphors That Shape Embryos* (Berkeley: North Atlantic Books, 2004; original Yale University Press, 1976).

25. Scott F. Gilbert and Jessica A. Bolker, "Ecological Developmental Biology: Preface to a Symposium," *Evolution and Development* 5, no. 1 (2003): 3–8.

The direct induction of gene expression in a multicellular organism by its microbial symbionts is now considered a normal and crucial developmental mechanism. See Scott F. Gilbert: "Mechanisms for the Environmental Regulation of Gene Expression," *Birth Defects Research (Part C)* 72 (2004); and "Cellular Dialogues during Development," *Gene Regulation and Fetal Development* 30, no. 1 (1996): 1–12.

26. Gilbert, *Developmental Biology,* 808; Margaret McFall-Ngai, "Unseen Forces: The Influence of Bacteria on Animal Development," *Developmental Biology* 242, no. 1 (2002): 1–14.

27. Barad, *Meeting the Universe Halfway.* For a beautiful analysis that joins biologist Joanne Burkholder's studies of the multispecific, multimorphic intra-actions of a polymorphous dinoflagellate, fish, pigs, chickens, and people in the Chesapeake Bay region with philosopher Jacques Derrida's theory of the phantom and its temporality, see Astrid Schrader, "Phantomatic Species Ontologies: Untimely Re/productions of Toxic Dinoflagellates," paper presented at the meetings of the Society for Social Studies of Science, Vancouver, B.C., November 1–5, 2006. To think about contact zones from the ecology of structural chemistry rather than physics or biology, see the remarkable join of dancing, protein structural modeling, haptic–optic–kinesthetic knotting enacted on-screen, and the shaping of scientists in Natasha Myers, "Molecular Embodiments and the Body-Work of Modeling in Protein Crystallography," *Social Studies of Science,* forthcoming. For a view of co-constitutions and contact zones among variously situated salmon and people, see Heather Swanson, "When Hatchery Salmon Go Wild: Population-Making, Genetic Management, and the Endangered Species Act," meetings of the Society for Social Studies of Science, Vancouver, B.C., November 1–5, 2006.

28. Heidegger's notion of the open is quite different from mine. I follow Giorgio Agamben's explication of the importance of "profound boredom" for Heidegger's "open." Agamben, *The Open,* 49–70. Heidegger's open emerges from a radical disengagement from the dross of functionality to acknowledge the awful, essential purposelessness of man, who is defined by no fixed world, no nature, no given place. To achieve this great voiding of illusion, to grasp "negativity," to be free, to understand one's captivity rather than merely to live it as an animal ("awakening *from* its own captivation *to* its own captivation," ibid., 70), a man in Heidegger's story allows the terrible experience of profound boredom to drench his whole self. Nothing need be done, no attachment is necessary, nothing motivates, one need not act. No animal can experience this state (and no woman *qua* "woman"). Yet, only from there can unconcealment, the open,

368 ✦ NOTES TO CHAPTER 8

happen. Only from this great destroying and liberating antiteleological negativity, this perfect indifference, can *Dasein* ("being held suspended in the nothing," ibid., 69), true human being, emerge. Only from this "open" can man grasp the world with passion, not as stock and resource, but in unconcealment and disclosure freed from technique and function. Precisely what differentiates man and animal, what puts them into opposite and unbridgeable singularities, is the possibility of "profound boredom," utter disconnection from function, for man, and the animal's inescapable poverty of world through an unbreakable tie to function and determined attachment. My "open" is quite other, if similarly lustful for nonteleological understanding. It emerges from the shock of "getting it": *This* and *here* are who and where we are? What is to be done? How can respect and response flourish in *this* here and *this* we, even as this *we* is the fruit of the entanglement? At least as wrenching from the busy self-assured life as Heidegger's little scenario, the shock of "getting it" could hardly be further from "profound boredom." Never certain, never guaranteed, the "open" for companion species becomes possible in the contact zones and unruly edges. For ongoing fruitful philosophical engagement with Heidegger's work on *Dasein* but reformatted from a human–animal studies perspective, see Jake Metcalf, "Intimacy without Proximity: Encountering Grizzlies as Companion Species," paper presented at the meetings of the Society for Social Studies of Science, Vancouver, B.C., November 1–5, 2006.

29. See Sutherland, *Kicked, Bitten, and Scratched*, 265.

30. Vicki Hearne believed something similar, but I have left her out of this chapter, because I wanted to inhabit the positive-method training approaches she never stopped despising. Hearne, *Adam's Task*. I mutate Hearne's idiom of animal happiness with gratitude for her extraordinary insights and analyses. See Vicki Hearne, *Animal Happiness* (New York: HarperCollins, 1994). Cary Wolfe's treatment of Hearne is simultaneously sympathetic and sharply critical of her humanist philosophical straitjackets: Wolfe, "Old Orders for New," 48–50. Mary Weaver—a fellow dog enthusiast committed to the good name of pit bulls who understands the knot of surprise, discipline, body, affect, and freedom in such relationships—also shapes my thinking in her writing on human transembodiments. See Mary Weaver, "Affective Materialities and Transgender Embodiments," paper presented at the meetings of the Society for Social Studies of Science, Vancouver, B.C., November 1–5, 2006.

31. Cayenne is neurologically deaf in one ear and so gets no directional or distance information from sound. A rock-solid recall and a no-nonsense "turn and search for me" command are both essential for her to be safe when we walk

in the woods, or anywhere else, for that matter. She also wears a sheep bell so I can track her if she can't find her way back to me. She reliably responded to the "search for me" cue by the time she was twelve weeks old. I think the deer and foxes also appreciate the bell. The snakes, lacking an aural apparatus, cannot hear the bell's tones, but perhaps they take precautions from the vibrations of my dog's footfalls when she courses over the hills above Mill Creek.

32. This is less Vicki Hearne's idea of animal happiness than Ian Wedde's. Respectful of dogs' differences from humans, Wedde ruminated on Epicurus and Seneca when he went with the ridgeback Vincent to an off-leash park on Mount Victoria, in New Zealand. They were together, but it was Vincent's own doggy interests that instructed Wedde, watching without imposing himself. "Epicurus advocated friendship, freedom, and thought as the foundations upon which to build happiness. . . . The Stoics believed that unreasonable expectations are what make us unhappy; some thought is best done in a simple, vivid, sensory present, rather than in the frantic, dystopic realms of desire and over-cooked imagination. I learned to think better as a result of running with Vincent. . . . One of the good things about the dog's utter difference is that he extends the range of what's mysterious in the world; he enriches my ignorance. It's this sense, I think, that many of the Mount Victoria dog-walkers share. . . . The ones who are empathic about their dogs' freedom and social life are humorous . . . they laugh, but without scorn. . . . But the leash-tuggers are seldom humorous . . . and their dogs are often unsocial, anxious, scared, and aggressive. I think it's because they don't understand their need for social freedom. They need to read Epicurus and Seneca, not training manuals." Ian Wedde, "Walking the Dog," in *Making Ends Meet* (Wellington, New Zealand: Victoria University Press, 2005), 357–58. I think we need both those ancients and modern training, not mechanically and anxiously, but skillfully and with joy. From personal correspondence, I know Wedde agrees, and he would never call the many-talented Cappuccino unsocial, anxious, scared, and aggressive, nor Pam a leash tugger!

33. For the sake of a story, I am not telling what I owe, and the detailed practices through which I owe it, to my other trainers—Gail Frazier, Rob Michalski, and Lauri Plummer. They have all labored mightily to teach me moral coherence and technical competence with my fast and demanding dog. I am also shortchanging the particulars of different methods of training contacts and different criteria of performance (running contacts, one rear toe on, etc.). The very differences, coupled with changing approaches in classes as the sport developed, overwhelmed my neophyte self in the early years. I did not yet have the skill to make trustworthy judgments; learning how to make such judgments is one of

the key things my teachers try to nurture. Contact-zone training is a common feature in *Clean Run*; see, for example, the entire vol. 10, no. 11, November 2004 issue, including Karen Pryor on using a clicker to build behavior chains in teaching contacts, Mary Ellen Barry on proofing contacts, and Susan Garrett on the verbal release.

34. Bioanthropologist Barbara Smuts, who now studies dogs after years of studying primates and cetaceans, is resolutely more interested in dog–dog interactions than dog–human ones. She is in the midst of fascinating, labor-intensive biobehavioral analysis of many hours of film of socializing dogs. I draw from Donna Haraway and Barbara Smuts, joint keynote lecture at the meetings of the Society for Literature and Science (SLS), 2004, Durham, N.C. See also Barbara Smuts, "Between Species: Science and Subjectivity," *Configurations*, special section from SLS meeting in 2004, forthcoming.

35. Despret, "The Body We Care For," 121.

36. Ibid., 115.

37. Ian Wedde described how he, his human life-partner, and Vincent were attuned in this way that invents new natures in the world. "We were discussing a TV programme she'd produced and noting how hard it was to guarantee delivery of intended subtlety conveyed by 'tone'—the old problem of telling jokes to strangers. We remembered how hard Vincent had worked, as a pet, to understand our tone. We were both sure he had learned to 'smile' late in life, a heartbreakingly difficult mimicry of what he'd seen us do over many years whenever we met him—not a dog-like showing of teeth, but something like a 'smile,' lower teeth only . . . sad and wonderful" (e-mail to Donna Haraway, August 19, 2004). This is another kind of isopraxis. This story also honors the material–semiotic work pets do.

38. Philip Pullman: *The Golden Compass* (New York: Knopf, 1995); *The Subtle Knife* (New York: Knopf, 1997); *The Amber Spyglass* (New York: Knopf, 2000).

39. Such instruction is readily found in the agility world, for example, expensive workshops by famous trainers to teach people to play with their dogs, magazine articles, demos by friends, and, of course, our dogs' patient forgiveness for repeated human gaffes, such as stuffing a tug toy down a dog's gullet. See Deborah Jones, "Let's Play!" *Clean Run* 10, no. 5 (May 2004): 70–71; Deborah Jones, PhD, and Judy Keller, *In Focus: Developing a Working Relationship with Your Performance Dog* (Chicopee, Mass.: Clean Run, 2004).

40. Smuts, "Encounters with Animal Minds," 293–309, 306.

41. Albion M. Urdank, "The Rationalisation of Rural Sport: British

Sheepdog Trials, 1873–1946," *Rural History* 17, no. 1 (2006): 65–82, explores the interactions of sheep, human beings, and herding dogs in Britain in a period of profound transformation of rural landscapes, work practices, and economies. The skills of dogs rooted in their biological heritage from wolves—such as eyeing prey, stalking, driving, bunching, and cutting—are reshaped not just by the biology of domestic associations with people and herbivores but also by commercial matters and other forces in economic and cultural history. Dogs, people, and sheep are all reshaped in ways that can be read in the changing patterns of sheep trials. "The shepherd's dog became better bred and better trained than ever before, as the shepherd too became better skilled and educated; and so the sheepdog became, fundamentally, the instrument of a revolution in pastoral productivity. But because the sheepdog was a living creature, with an especially high intelligence, his [*sic*] instincts for work were used not just instrumentally, but co-operatively as part of a joint effort, in which dog and shepherd would also create a special bond of affinity" (80). But this is the material semiotics of work, and I am interested in this section in the world-making practices of play. It is worth noting that sheepdog trial people tend to have great disdain for the methods of agility trainers, with their toys, food, and behaviorist idiom. My field notes record sheepdog men praising agility as something nice for dogs who don't have real work. Lots is going on here: gender and rural–suburban tensions, valuations of work and sport, and deeply held beliefs about how dogs learn and what they already know.

42. In a beautiful chapter, "Learning from Temple Grandin, or, Animal Studies, Disability Studies, and Who Comes after the Subject," Cary Wolfe explores ways out of the premises of liberal humanism and its language-sated versions of epistemology, ontology, and ethics that Grandin offers in her explorations of sensory modalities of knowing, including her treatment of the details of her experience as an autistic person of "thinking in pictures." Grandin critiques the denial of an inner life to autistic people on the basis of the implicit assumption and explicit premise that all that is truly thinking must be linguistic. Wolfe notes that this denial "is founded in no small part on the too rapid assimilation of the questions of subjectivity, consciousness, and cognition to the question of language ability" (Wolfe, "Learning from Temple Grandin," in ms., 2006, 2). That assimilation is common, but not unchallenged, in the biobehavioral sciences, but it is ubiquitous and practically mandatory in the social sciences and humanities. If no language, then no subject and no interiority worth the name, no matter the school of thought preferred, from psychoanalysis to linguistics to philosophy of whatever stripe. Putting the so-far ill-crafted alliance of disability studies and animal studies together differently (not Which oppressed group is

more marginalized?—a bankrupt question if ever there was one), Wolfe refigures the relation between assistance dogs and their humans, for example, in work between a service dog and a blind human. He writes, "Wouldn't we do better to imagine this example as an irreducibly different and unique form of subjectivity—neither *Homo sapiens* nor *Canis familiaris*, neither 'disabled' nor 'normal', but something else altogether, a shared trans-species being-in-the-world constituted by complex relations of trust, respect, dependence, and communication (as anyone who has ever trained—or relied upon—a service dog would be the first to tell you)?" (Wolfe, ibid., 13).

43. The overachieving German border collie Rico caused a stir when he proved as able as two-year-old human children to do what linguists call "fast mapping" of new words to objects after only one exposure. Rico knew the labels of over two hundred different items, and he remembered his new words when he was retested four weeks later. It looks like whatever makes fast mapping possible is part of general cognitive abilities that people share with other critters. See Julianne Kaminski, Joseph Call, and Julia Fisher, "Word Learning in a Domestic Dog: Evidence for 'Fast Mapping,'" *Science* 304 (11 June 2004): 1682–83. This news may have been more novel to scientists than to many agility trainers. Cayenne is not exceptional, and I have evidence that she reliably knows about 150 to 250 words or phrases in a great variety of circumstances (but not all circumstances—the power to generalize seems tied to what linguists call the property of "discrete infinity," in which humans definitely excel. My failure to understand the need to teach, one at a time, relevant combinations of circumstances in which a named item or action would appear—what people think of as context but to dogs seems to be the semiotic situation itself—was at the heart of my incoherence in the contact zone). Cayenne learns very quickly and remembers new words (or gestures) for items and actions. Indeed, trainers face the problem of convincing their dogs that some of the item and action names they learned aren't what their people meant for them to learn! Discriminations seem harder to unlearn than to learn.

44. Marc D. Hauser, Noam Chomsky, and W. Tecumseh Fitch, "The Faculty of Language: What Is It, Who Has It, and How Did It Evolve?" *Science* 298 (November 22, 2002): 1569–79, 1574. The orthodox—and carefully supported—position among linguists can be found in Stephen R. Anderson, *Doctor Doolittle's Delusion: Animals and the Uniqueness of Human Language* (New Haven, Conn.: Yale University Press, 2004). For further arguments against their critics, see W. Tecumesh Fitch, Marc D. Hauser, and Noam Chomsky, "The Evolution of the Language Faculty: Clarification and Implications," *Cognition* 97, no. 2

(September 2005): 179–210. The work nurtures interdisciplinary cooperation among evolutionary biologists, anthropologists, psychologists, and neuroscientists. The authors argue that a distinction should be made between functional language in the broad sense (FLB) and language in the narrow sense (FLN). FLB is composed of many interacting subsystems (sensorimotor and computational–intentional) that do not necessarily evolve as a unit. (I would add the need to look at affectional–semiotic–cognitive subsystems.) The only uniquely human component of the language faculty (FLN) is recursion, which is "the capacity to generate an infinite range of expressions from a finite set of elements." This potentially infinite expressive power of language is also called the property of "discrete infinity," the power exercised by humans to "recombine meaningful units into an infinite variety of larger structures, each differing systematically in meaning" (Hauser, Chomsky, and Fitch, "The Faculty of Language," 1576). This is much more than just combining words. But even the kind of computational uniqueness required by FLN becomes subject in a new way to comparative studies; and the authors insist that uniqueness must be a testable hypothesis, not an assumption rooted in premises of human exceptionalism. In addition, the authors argue that such powerful capacities might well have evolved in domains other than communication (such as territory mapping, spatial navigation, and foraging) and then been hijacked for communication in ways uncoupled from tight constraints of function. Language (FLN) may not have come about because it did anything especially useful at first. Language (FLN) may have come into being because it could; and then it got very useful indeed, altogether selectively advantageous, for better and for worse for the planet. The opportunism of evolution is a great boon to the nonteleological thinking of the posthumanities. In addition, once made a seriously testable hypothesis, even FLN is taking hits on the uniqueness of recursion and discrete infinity. It looks like European starlings, if not primate inhabitants of the Bush Whitehouse, "accurately recognize acoustic patterns defined by recursive, self-embedding, context-free grammar. They are also able to classify new patterns defined by the grammar and reliably exclude agrammatical patterns." Timothy Gentner, Kimberly Fenn, Daniel Margoliash, and Howard Nusbaum, "Recursive Syntactic Pattern Learning by Songbirds," *Nature* 440 (April 27, 2006): 1204–7, 1204.

45. Evolutionary zoologists have hardly ever operated with a single axis of biobehavioral difference among animals, no matter what they thought about where humans fit in, but they have not been especially helpful either on questions of language and consciousness, until recent interdisciplines reshaped the topography.

46. Coren, *How Dogs Think*, 310.

47. Marc Hauser, *Wild Minds: What Animals Really Think* (New York: Owl Books, 2001) is a good place to start. This Harvard psychologist and neuroscientist (coauthor with Chomsky, above) argues that organisms possess heterogeneous sets of mental tools, complexly and dynamically put together from genetic, developmental, and learning interactions throughout lives, not unitary interiors that one either has or does not have. For an even more generous view of animals' varied mental and emotional lives, but one similarly insistent on animals' differences and immense variety and one rooted in evolutionary behavioral sciences, see Marc Bekoff, *Minding Animals: Awareness, Emotions, and Heart* (Oxford: Oxford University Press, 2003). For Bekoff, animals are other (nonanthropomorphic) persons, not unlike Barbara Noske's "other worlds" (Noske, *Beyond Boundaries*, xiii). The online bibliography of the Centre for Social Learning and Cognitive Evolution at the University of St. Andrews, in Scotland, is a good place to find references to recent work from one very active research institution.

48. Smuts, "Encounters with Animal Minds," 308.

49. Gregory Bateson, "Metalogue: About Games and Being Serious," in *Steps to an Ecology of Mind*, 14–20. (Further references to this chapter of Bateson's book are in parentheses in the text.) I am indebted to conversations with Katie King about Bateson, and especially about the metalogues. Bateson was one of King's undergraduate teachers in the 1970s at UC Santa Cruz and has been an interlocutor in her transdisciplinary feminist theory ever since. See King, *Networked Reenactments*, under review; and www.womensstudies.umd.edu/wmstfac/kking/ (accessed May 6, 2007).

50. Bateson, *Steps to an Ecology of Mind*, 12.

51. Ibid., 179.

52. Ibid., 367. Exploring the shared dynamics of world building but more interested than I am in this chapter in how communication about something *other* than relationships emerges, Cary Wolfe also cites this passage from Bateson in "In the Shadow of Wittgenstein's Lion," 39. Here, I am more interested in how coshaping happens without language in the linguist's sense of FLN or even in Bateson's sense of "how to be specific about something other than relationship" (*Steps to an Ecology of Mind*, 370; "In the Shadow of Wittgenstein's Lion," 39). Thus, I focus on how we—dogs and people—pay attention to each other and thereby make something new in the world happen. I call that play, invention, and proposition.

53. For another wise person (despite his restricting himself to the study of human beings) who understood how play makes life worth living or, maybe

better, how play makes living creatively possible, see D. W. Winnicott, *Playing and Reality* (London: Tavistock, 1971). Thanks to Sheila Namir for the reference and helpful conversations about play.

54. Marc Bekoff and J. A. Byers, "A Critical Reanalysis of the Ontogeny of Mammalian Social and Locomotor Play: An Ethological Hornet's Nest," in *Behavioural Development: The Bielefeld Interdisciplinary Project*, ed. K. Immelmann, G. W. Barlow, L. Petrinovich, and M. Main (Cambridge: Cambridge University Press, 1981), 296–337. See also Marc Bekoff and J. A. Byers, eds., *Animal Play: Evolutionary, Comparative, and Ecological Approaches* (New York: Cambridge University Press, 1998).

55. For over more than two decades, Bekoff has led the way in paying attention to the emotional aspects of cognition and behavior, including play. See Marc M. Bekoff, *The Emotional Lives of Animals: A Leading Scientist Explores Animal Joy, Sorrow, and Empathy and Why They Matter* (Novato, Calif.: New World Library, 2007). As he told me in an e-mail dated August 6, 2006, "I know joy is the key—just did not include it in 1980." At that time, he probably could not have gotten a scientific paper published that took animal joy seriously. Barbara Smuts was roundly criticized in some primate studies circles when she published a book titled *Sex and Friendship in Baboons* (New York: Aldine, 1985), and primatologist Shirley Strum told me similar stories about severity in publishing standards for using terms such as *friendship* even for nonhuman primates (much less dogs or rats), despite the prevalence of such language in the ordinary idiom among researchers outside the printed word. See Strum, *Almost Human*. This is the same period of time when it seemed perfectly scientific to many to use terms such as *rape* in sober, equation-filled papers to designate forced sex among nonhuman primates and birds. When Jeanne Altmann was the American editor of the prestigious journal *Animal Behaviour* from 1978 to 1983, she negotiated fiercely with authors about whether such terms as *rape* actually describe what the animals are doing. I think that her authoritative, gatekeeping attention to precise description and scientifically defensible sampling techniques in primate field studies is part of the background for beginning to allow terms like *friendship* and to test more carefully terms that sound more scientific (*aggression*) for the invisible work they actually do to shape what scientists know how to see. The point is not that rape or aggression does not happen among animals—far from it. The point is to pay comparable attention to and have testable hypotheses for the full spectrum. Belief that one is protected from anthropomorphism by using a term that is already considered technical would be laughable if it were not so damaging to science. Careful practice of therio-anthropo-morphisms can lead to

much sounder scientific investigation than belief that some idioms are free of figuration and others are polluted with culture. See Haraway, *Primate Visions,* especially 304–16, 368–76, 420–22n7. For a unique collaborative exploration of the coshaping of the thing called "science and society" by field and lab primate biologists, cultural studies scholars, feminist theorists, and science studies scholars (partly overlapping categories), see Strum and Fedigan, eds., *Primate Encounters.*

56. Wedde, "Walking the Dog," 338.

57. Marc Bekoff, "Wild Justice and Fair Play: Cooperation, Forgiveness, and Morality in Animals," *Biology and Philosophy* 19 (2004): 489–520.

58. Writer Ian Wedde's "therianthropism" joins science fiction studies and human-animal studies scholar Istvan Csicsery-Ronay's proposal for an international online journal hosted at DePauw University, for which I offered and he accepted the name *Humanimalia* to signal the reciprocal inductions in play in the emerging interdisciplines of human and nonhuman animal studies, as well as in the historically situated fleshly encounters of people and other animals.

59. Isabelle Stengers, "Whitehead's Account of the Sixth Day," paper delivered at the Stanford University Whitehead Symposium, April 21, 2006, 18. Further references to this paper will occur parenthetically in the main text. My arguments to follow grow from conversations with Stengers and from "The Sixth Day and the Problem of Human Exceptionalism," which is my comment on Stengers's paper, Stanford University Whitehead Symposium, April 21, 2006. See also Stengers, *Penser avec Whitehead.*

60. Whitehead, *Process and Reality,* 104.

9. CRITTERCAM

Note on second epigraph: Tracking the material–semiotic action of multiple luminous refractive bends, Hayward further writes, "I am concerned with how aquatic imaging and hydro-optics cause optics and haptics to slide into each other." Eva Shawn Hayward, "Envisioning Invertebrates: Immersion, Inhabitation, and Intimacy as Modes of Encounter in Marine TechnoArt," qualifying essay, History of Consciousness Department, University of California at Santa Cruz, December 2003.

Note on third epigraph: Text from a 2004 brochure announcing the National Geographic Society's television series *Crittercam,* made up of thirteen half-hour episodes. Twelve featured marine critters, and one tied its cameras to African lions, fruit of a three-year effort to develop Crittercams for land-based studies as well as marine excursions. In this chapter, I will not discuss the interesting land Crittercams, attached so far, predictably, to lions, tigers, and bears. Crittercam research and the TV series are partly funded by the National Science Foundation, described on-screen as "America's investment in the future." The promissory, futuristic, frontier orientations of the show are never out of frame on *Crittercam*; that is the nature of life in the era of Biocapital.

Also predictable, as well as lamentably outside the scope of this chapter, are the miniature TV cameras with transmitters that are attached these days to the foreheads of Northumbrian police dogs. The cameras have infrared lights for filming in dark conditions. Trained to assist during armed sieges and to search sites and relay video information back to human officers, the dogs also deliver mobile phones at the door of premises under siege to facilitate negotiations. See "Dog Cameras to Combat Gun Crime," BBC News, U.K. Division, December 4, 2005, http://news.bbc.co.uk/1/hi/england/4497212.stm (accessed May 5, 2007). Working security camdogs are joined by their pet cousins, who can be fitted with a Japanese-designed miniature digital camera worn around the neck so that the doting human can "finally get a dog's *view* on life" (www.pamperedpuppy.com/puppytrends/archives/2006/02/digital_dog_cam.php, accessed May 5, 2007).

1. Ihde, *Bodies in Technology*, 137.

2. Bruno Latour, "From *Realpolitik* to *Dingpolitik*: An Introduction to Making Things Public," in *Making Things Public*, ed. Latour and Weibel. Available at www.bruno-latour.fr/articles/article/96-dingpolitik2.html (accessed May 5, 2007).

3. Beginning with *National Geographic Explorer* on TBS in 1993, as well as *Great White Shark* in 1995 on NBC, Crittercam images were seen on TV before the 2004 series.

4. Unless otherwise stated, quotations and descriptions throughout this chapter come from various parts of www.nationalgeographic.com/crittercam.

5. Adapted from http://animaldiversity.ummz.umich.edu/site/accounts/information/Remora_remora.html (accessed May 5, 2007), the technical specifications for a remora follow: *Remora remora* is a short, thickset sucking fish with twenty-eight to thirty-seven long slender gillrakers, twenty-one to twenty-seven dorsal fin rays, twenty to twenty-four anal fin rays, and twenty-five to thirty-two pectoral fin rays. The remora has no swim bladder and uses a sucking disk on the top of its head to obtain rides from other animals, such as large sharks and sea turtles. The remora grows to about eighteen inches. Near nothing is known about the remora's breeding habits or larval development. The remora is most often found offshore in the warmer parts of all oceans attached to sharks and

other marine fishes and mammals. The remora are considered to have a commensal relationship with their host, since they do not hurt the host and are just along for the ride. The remora is of unique value to humans. The fish itself is not generally eaten but is instead used as a means of catching large fish and sea turtles. Fishermen in countries around the world use them by attaching a line to their tails and then releasing them. The remora will then swim off and attach itself to a large fish or turtle, which can then be pulled in by a careful fisherman. The remora is not held in high esteem as a food fish, although the Australian Aborigines are said to eat them after using them on fishing trips. On the other hand, Aborigines from the West Indies never ate their "hunting fish" and instead sang songs of praise and reverence to them. The ancient Greeks and Romans had written widely about remoras and had ascribed to them many magical powers such as the ability to cause an abortion if handled in a certain way. Shamans in Madagascar to this day attach portions of the remora's suction disk to the necks of wives to assure faithfulness in their husbands' absence. Following the remoras, Greg Marshall was in good company.

6. I take the term *reality engines* from "The Reality Effect of Technoscience," Julian Bleecker's 2004 PhD dissertation on computer graphics engineering and semiotics and the labor it takes to build and sustain specific material realities (History of Consciousness Department, University of California at Santa Cruz). In this chapter, I use a compound optical device, made up of lenses from a colleague, Don Ihde, and two of my graduate students from different cohorts, Julian Bleecker and Eva Shawn Hayward.

7. See Haraway, *The Companion Species Manifesto*.

8. An area of Aboriginal presence from 20,000 B.C.E. to now, Shark Bay has been a World Heritage Site since 1991. Tourism, endangered species, archaeology sites, indigenous history, colonial first-contact stories and white settlement, an abandoned whaling station, abandoned isolation hospitals for Aboriginals with venereal disease and leprosy, today's native title struggles, natural scientific research, a modern scallop fishery, salt ponds: it's all there, as expected, providing a complex ecology for National Geographic's Crittercam species assemblages. See www.unep-wcmc.org/sites/wh/sharkbay.html. Aboriginal people are involved in cultural revival, political contestation, and site management. On behalf of Malgana Shark Bay people, the Yamatji Marlpa Barna Baba Maaja Aboriginal Corporation filed claims in 1998 with the National Native Title Tribunal. See www.nntt.gov.au/applications/claimant/WC98_17.html. Malgana and Nganda Aboriginal peoples are central to the history of Shark Bay. Records of Aboriginal history in Western Australia, including Shark Bay, can be tracked through

www.sro.wa.gov.au/collection/aboriginalrecords.asp. (All Web sites accessed May 6, 2007.)

9. Hayward, "Inhabited Light: Refracting *The Love Life of the Octopus*," section in Hayward, "Envisioning Invertebrates."

10. In the wake of the 1989 *Exxon Valdez* mega–oil spill in Prince William Sound, the biologically, culturally, and economically crucial Bristol Bay off southwest Alaska was put off limits to oil drilling, first by Congress and then by Bill Clinton's 1998 presidential order. Congress lifted its ban on Bristol Bay drilling in 2003. George W. Bush rescinded the executive order in January 2007. See www.nytimes.com/2007/05/01/washington/01drill.html (accessed May 6, 2007). All five species of Pacific salmon spawn in rivers emptying into Bristol Bay. The area supplies 50 percent of the seafood consumed in the United States. Vulnerable populations of North Pacific right whales, Steller's sea lions, and many other species, as well as fisheries and tourism, are part of the picture. In 2006 the commercial fishing industry was economically depressed, opening the door to renewed action by big oil. Native Alaskan fisheries and protein sources in the region are especially at risk to oil and gas ecological disasters. Local and translocal environmental organizations are major players. Formed under the Alaska Native Claims Settlement Act of December 18, 1971, the Bristol Bay Native Corporation, representing Aleut, Athabascan, and Eskimo peoples, is an important actor in the region as well. See www.bbnc.net/.

11. For the results of the *Crittercam* team–whale biologist collaboration, see Fred Sharpe, Michael Heithaus, Lawrence Dill, Birgit Buhleier, Gregory Marshall, and Pieter Folkiens, "Variability in Foraging Tactics and Estimated Prey Intake by Socially Foraging Humpback Whales in Chatham Strait, Alaska," paper presented at the 15th Biennial Conference on the Biology of Marine Mammals, Greensboro, N.C., 2003.

12. Ihde, *Bodies in Technology*, 137.

13. Don Ihde, "If Phenomenology Is an Albatross, Is Post-phenomenology Possible?" in *Chasing Technoscience*, ed. Don Ihde and Evan Selinger (Bloomington: Indiana University Press, 2003), 131–44. As Ihde puts it, "An asymmetrical but post-phenomenological *relativity* gets its 'ontology' from the *interrelationship of human and non-human*" (143).

10. CHICKEN

Translation note on epigraph: "I said: Cock-a-doodle-do." "The strutting rooster calls. Now comes the farmer." From *Grunt*, Pigorian Chant from Snouto Domoinko de Silo, performed by the Ad Hoc Camerata, discovered, translated, notated, and illuminated by Sandra Boynton (New York: Workman Publishing, 1996), 12.

1. For a serious liberal arts education, read Page Smith and Charles Daniel, *The Chicken Book* (Athens: University of Georgia Press, 2000; original, Boston: Little Brown, 1975). Historian Smith and biologist Daniel collaborated at the University of California Santa Cruz in the 1970s, first, to teach an undergraduate seminar and, then, with their students' research aiding them, to write this unique chicken book, including cultural, historical, religious, biological, agricultural, political, economic, communitarian, and epistemological points of view. Beginning teaching at UCSC in 1980, I inherited the cat's cradle game of chicken that Smith and Daniel played with their students and colleagues.

2. An earlier version of this chapter was published in B. Eekelen, J. Gonzalez, B. Stötzer, and A. Tsing, eds., *Shock and Awe: War on Words* (Santa Cruz: New Pacific Press, 2004), 23–30. A group of friends and student and faculty colleagues at UCSC and beyond collaborated on that little book to try to reposition forces in the war on words launched in the Bush Whitehouse after 9/11. I chose the letter C to see how the world looked from the point of view of Chicken. Susan Squier, a professor at Pennsylvania State University, is doing wonderful research that links biomedical, biological, literary, feminist theoretical, and science studies dimensions of chicken–human relations. See Susan Squier, "Chicken Auguries," *Configurations*, in press for 2007, and keep an eye out for her book in progress, *Poultry Science, Chicken Culture: Practicing AgriCultural Studies*. Located at Te Whare Wananga o Waitaha/University of Canterbury, New Zealand, Annie Potts is writing *Chicken* for the unique Reaktion Books animal series under the general editorship of Jonathan Burt. Potts cofounded Animal Studies Aotearoa.

3. LGBT: Lesbian, Gay, Bisexual, Transgender, not to be confused with BLT (bacon, lettuce, and tomato sandwich). One is a proper fleshly cultural and political formation. The other is too, if you consider the knots of multispecies world making tied up in lettuce, bacon, tomatoes, wheat, yeast, and sugar, as well as the eggs, oil, salt, and citrus juice in mayonnaise. Chicken is no stranger to LGBT or BLT.

4. Ever vigilant—thank all the earth deities—the animal rescue apparatus of modern times has not neglected spent hens, even if there was never a task more fitting for Sisyphus. For a moving story of one rescued spent hen, who lived out her last days in enriched farmyard retirement learning how to be a real chicken, complete with all the elaborate behavior proper to her kind that battery-cage existence had kept her from acquiring, see Patrice Jones, "Funny

Girl: Fanny and Her Friends," *Best Friends* (September/October 2005): 54–55. The chicken and egg industry in Petaluma in 2006 turned spent hens into compost, because the market for animal food and other uses of the tough chicken meat no longer covers the costs of slaughter and processing. Some of the hens have survived gassing with carbon dioxide and burial in the compost piles to stagger into the politics and newspapers of Sonoma County.

5. Figures are from United Poultry Concerns, www.upc-online.org/ (accessed May 6, 2007). See also en.wikipedia.org/wiki/United_Poultry_Concerns.

6. In *Anthropology 2010* (Cambridge, Mass.: MIT Press, forthcoming), Michael Fischer taught me that Michel Serres's notion of contract is rooted in the original Latin meaning, *con-trahere*, or gathering together, as in tightening the rigging of a sailboat. The ropes have to be in reciprocal adjustment for smooth functioning with the wind. Fischer cites the discussion of this meaning of contract in Kerry Whiteside, *Divided Natures: French Contributions to Political Ecology* (Cambridge, Mass.: MIT Press, 2002). That meaning of contract theory would be quite useful in the naturecultures I imagine to be still possible.

7. Myostatin regulates muscle development, and its gene is under intense scrutiny. Commercial interest relates to the world's number-one genetic disease (muscular dystrophies), wasting disorders (including aging and AIDS-related muscle loss), space flight–induced muscle atrophy, sports (watch out, steroid purveyors!), and even faster growing, bigger chicken muscles. See G. N. Scheuermann, S. F. Bilgili, S. Tuzun, and D. R. Mulvaney, "Comparison of Chicken Genotypes: Myofiber Number in Pectoralis Muscle and Myostatin Ontogeny," *Poultry Science* 83, no. 8 (2004): 1404–12.

8. For a hint of the importance of chickens (eggs and broilers) in the economic history of animal–industrial standardization, see Glenn E. Bugos, "Intellectual Property Protection in the American Chicken-Breeding Industry," *Business History Review* 66 (Spring 1992): 127–68; Roger Horowitz, "Making the Chicken of Tomorrow: Reworking Poultry as Commodities and as Creatures, 1945–1990," in *Industrializing Organisms*, ed. S. Schrepfer and P. Scranton (New York: Routledge, 2004), 215–36.

9. I believe that McDonald's was forced to its still shockingly inadequate radical position on living quarters for hens by the much reviled animal rights movement. McDonald's new animal care standards for its suppliers went much further than regulations for poultry legally required. The corporation downplayed the role that People for the Ethical Treatment of Animals (PETA) and the Animal Liberation Front played in its change of heart, but it is hard to deny that their McCruelty to Go campaign attracted the attention of corporate

headquarters. Image control, if not insight into bird lives, is big business. See Rod Smith, Feedstuffs staff editor, "McDonald's Animal Care Guidelines Described as 'Aggressive,' Realistic," *Factory Farming.com: Current Issues*, May 1, 2000, www.factoryfarming.com/mcdonalds.htm. What counts as radical and what as normal is very much at stake in animal–human knots. In reference to slaughter laws, "humane" deserves scare quotes, not only because the laws (much less their application) are too often not humane by any measure, but more fundamentally because the word foregrounds the inappropriate humanist standard applied to killing animals. I think killing deserves deeper thinking if human beings' eating chickens and other animals is to be in the knot of flourishing multispecies living—if that remains possible in the "developed" and globalized neoliberal world as it has become. In 2004, only California, Utah, and North Dakota had laws regulating cruelty in slaughtering birds, and regulating cruelty is not an adequate practice. In that same year, PETA—not my favorite group, to say the least, but not one I can walk totally away from either—obtained underground video footage of extreme overt cruelty (workers stomping on live chickens and hurling them into walls) in a poultry-packaging plant in West Virginia, which produces for Kentucky Fried Chicken. See www.peta.org/feat/moorefield/ (accessed May 6, 2007). These incidents gained considerable attention from the national mainstream media. The damaged and exploited human workers and the brutalized birds cohabit a normal hell that Marx and Engels knew how to describe for factory workers in Manchester in the nineteenth century. The twenty-first century has a full panoply of such profit-maximizing and fantasy-driven worlds, within which sentience is little protection, no matter the species, and a limbic system gets one nowhere at all. The meaningful body becomes mere flesh and so is made killable in the logic of sacrifice. See the discussion of Derrida on that powerful logic in chapter 3, "Sharing Suffering"; and Giorgio Agamben, *Homo Sacer: Sovereign Power and Bare Life*, trans. Daniel Heller-Roazen (Palo Alto, Calif.: Stanford University Press, 1998). See also Charlie LeDuff, "At a Slaughterhouse: Some Things Never Die," in *Zoontologies*, ed. Wolfe, 182–97.

10. Petaluma Farms near me in California is one source for "extra-nutritious DHA Omega-3" (claim on the egg carton) from eggs laid by chickens raised without cages and eating an organic vegetarian diet. The label goes further, calling the operation a "wild hen farm." Called "specialty eggs" in the industry, designer eggs accounted for about 5 percent of U.S. egg sales in 2004. There's lots of room for growth. In 2003, U.S. Americans consumed 74.5 billion eggs, that is, 254 per person. I think operations such as Petaluma Farms deserve my support, but I do experience indigestion at the class and science semiotics (and

realities) of niche marketing. See Carol Ness, "The New Egg," April 7, 2004, www.sfgate.com/cgi-bin/article.cgi?file=/chronicle/archive/2004/04/07/FDGNM5VF9B1.DTL. Thanks to Dawn Coppin for this information. For a Florida agricultural extension service survey of designer eggs available around 2000, see http://edis.ifas.ufl.edu/PS048 (accessed May 6, 2007).

11. Sarah Franklin, "Stem Cells R Us," in *Global Assemblages*, ed. A. Ong and S. Collier (London: Blackwell, 2004), 59–78; Margaret Atwood, *Oryx and Crake* (Toronto: McClelland and Stewart, 2003). Chicken without chickens is not merely a novelist's speculative fiction. For a marvelous reading of *Oryx and Crake* at the intersection of feminism, philosophy, and biology, see Traci Warkentin, "Dis/integrating Animals: Ethical Dimensions of the Genetic Engineering of Animals for Human Consumption," *AI and Society* 20 (2006): 82–102. I would disagree with much of Warkentin's reading of molecular biology as necessarily mechanistic reductionism, but I share her critique of mechanomorphism in vast regions of agribusiness practices, including in what used to be called "pure research." Consider also the pork tissue culture system under scientific development at the University of Utrecht in the labs of Henk Haagsman, using pig stem cells, naturally. See Marianne Heselmans, "Cultivated Meat," www.new-harvest.org/article09102005.htm (accessed May 6, 2007). In 2005, the Dutch government funded the project with two million Euros. Tissue Genesis in Hawaii is another player. Success, defined as developing something edible enough and cheap enough for the market, in about five years is their prediction. See Lakshmi Sandhana, "Test Tube Meat Nears Dinner Table," June 21, 2006, www.wired.com/news/technology/0,71201-0.html?tw=rss.technology. Animals have long been troped as "bioreactors" in technoscientific advertising for drug and agribusiness research. Transgenics and stem cell technologies have increased this kind of figuration markedly. Current research is another instance of the implosion of trope and flesh, as bioreactors stand in for animals "literally." This kind of literalization is one of the things I mean by "material–semiotic," trope and flesh always cohabiting, always co-constituting. For astute ethnographic analysis, see Karen-Sue Taussig, "Bovine Abominations: Genetic Culture and Politics in the Netherlands," *Cultural Anthropology* 19, no. 3 (2004): 305–36.

12. Citing financial constraints, Indonesia had not conducted mass culling in response to its human deaths from bird flu, and probably as a result, this country's total number of recorded human deaths by mid-2006 had surpassed that of Vietnam, which had both culled and vaccinated birds aggressively. Mass culling is immensely unpopular and a political risk, but so is a human pandemic.

Observers estimated that about 9.5 million birds died naturally of bird flu in Indonesia between 2003 and 2005. See www.planetark.com/dailynewsstory.cfm /newsid/31828/story.htm (accessed May 6, 2007). Mass culls have been conducted in many countries, from Canada to Turkey to Egypt to India, that last of which killed about seven hundred thousand birds in February 2006 in response to an outbreak among poultry in Maharashtra. See http://edition.cnn.com/ 2006/HEALTH/conditions/02/20/birdflu.asia.wrap/index.html (accessed May 6, 2007).

13. See Chris Wilbert, "Profit, Plague, and Poultry: The Intra-active Worlds of Highly Pathogenic Avian Flu," *Radical Philosophy* 139 (September/October 2006), www.radicalphilosophy.com/default.asp?channel_id=2187 &editorial_id=22192. Wilbert writes, "In 2006 we awoke, in Europe at least, to the odd situation in which twitchers—obsessive birdwatchers who spend much of their leisure time on the far-flung edges of countries—are being reinvented as the eyes and ears of the state, helping warn of new border incursions. These incursions are posited as taking an avian form that may bring with it very unwelcome pathogens. Everyday avian observations and knowledges of migratory routes are being reinvented as a kind of border patrol, a first line of veterinary surveillance."

14. See http://news.bbc.co.uk/1/hi/world/africa/4700264.stm; and www .irinnews.org/report.asp?ReportID=51680&SelectRegion=West_Africa&Sel ectCountry=NIGERIA (both Web sites accessed May 6, 2007).

15. A spokesperson for Birdlife International thinks that the chicken trade has made this fowl the most migratory avian on the planet. Donald McNeil, "From the Chickens' Perspective, the Sky Really Is Falling," *New York Times*, March 28, 2006, D6. Anna Tsing, "Figures of Capitalist Globalization: Firm Models and Chain Links," paper presented at the University of Minnesota for "Markets in Time" study group, 2006, explores the kin relations between legal and illegal trade, resource extraction, and manufacturing that are both necessary to global capitalism and also organic to hyperexploitation of people and other species. As Marx understood, how else can accumulation be realized? There might actually be a good answer to that question, and it will have transspecific, posthumanist justice at its heart.

16. See Elizabeth Rosenthal, "Bird Flu Virus May Be Spread by Smuggling," *New York Times*, April 15, 2006, A1, A8.

17. Steven Lee Myers, "Ukraine Plugging a Porous Border: Efforts Focus on Moldavan Region's Murky Economy," *International Herald Tribune*, May 29, 2006, 3.

18. Thorleif Schjelderup-Ebbe, "Social Behavior in Birds," in *Handbook of Social Psychology*, ed. Carl Murchison (Worcester, Mass.: Clark University Press, 1935).

19. Sue Fishkoff, "When Left-Wingers and Chicken Wings Populated Petaluma," *Jerusalem Post Service*, Friday May 7, 1999, www.jewishsf.com/content/2-0-/module/displaystory/story_id/11172/edition_id/214/format/html/displaystory.html. A radio series, *Comrades and Chicken Ranchers* (www.jewishsf.com/content/2-0-/module/displaystory/story_id/3707/edition_id/66/format/html/displaystory.html, accessed May 6, 2007), and a television documentary, *A Home on the Range* (www.jewishchickenranchers.com/get/, accessed May 6, 2007), tell the story.

20. Julie Phillips, *James Tiptree, Jr.: The Double Life of Alice B. Sheldon* (New York: St. Martin's Press, 2006), 151. Thanks to Katie King for pointing me to Tiptree's life in chickens and the tie with scientific agrarian nation building for Israel. On the doleful history of scientific chicken farming, see Smith and Daniel, *The Chicken Book*, 232–300. On the animal–industrial complex, see Noske, *Beyond Boundaries*, 22–39. In ironic justice, in the early twenty-first century the Rutgers University School of Law is home to the Animal Rights Law Center.

21. Phillips, *James Tiptree, Jr.*, 284.

22. A kindly scientist's seeding a global pandemic from an airplane with a virus to exterminate the human species was the plot of Tiptree's "The Last Flight of Dr. Ain," her breakthrough story into science fiction stardom, published in 1969 in *Galaxy*. Of course, my allegorical mind races to the bird flu virus. "The Last Flight of Dr. Ain" and many of my other favorite stories are collected in James Tiptree Jr.: *Warm Worlds and Otherwise* (New York: Ballantine, 1975); *Star Songs of an Old Primate* (New York: Ballantine, 1978); and *Out of the Everywhere* (New York: Ballantine, 1981). As Racoona Sheldon, Tiptree published "Morality Meat," dealing with unfree pregnancy, a right-to-life adoption center, defective babies, and a new and very suspicious kind of meat in a nation whose entire meat industry, including chickens, had been wiped out by drought and grain diseases, in *Despatches from the Frontiers of the Human Mind*, ed. Jen Green and Sarah Lefanu (London: Women's Press, 1985), 209–34.

23. Begin with www.rbst.org.uk/ and click to a large knot of promisingly impure work to put agricultural multispecies flourishing into action.

24. The eighteenth-century philosophe Denis Diderot precedes us in understanding what watching a fertile egg can do to convince us that Western philosophy has never really been all that Western, a point Isabelle Stengers makes forcefully. In Diderot's *D'Alembert's Dream*, the philosopher says to his

interlocutor, "You see this egg? That's what enables us to overturn all the schools of theology and all temples on the earth." Denis Diderot, "A Conversation between d'Alembert and Diderot," from *D'Alembert's Dream* (*Le rêve d'Alembert*), 1769, trans. Ian Johnston, Malaspina University-College, Nanaimo, B.C., available online at www.mala.bc.ca/~Johnstoi/diderot/conversation.htm (accessed May 6, 2007). Isabelle Stengers, *Power and Invention: Situating Science*, trans. Paul Bains (Minneapolis: University of Minnesota Press, 1981), 117–18. Thanks to Stengers for pointing me to Diderot's appreciation of the egg.

11. BECOMING COMPANION SPECIES IN TECHNOCULTURE

1. Jan-Kyrre Berg Olsen and Evan Selinger, eds., *Philosophy of Technology* (n.p.: Automatic Press/VIP, December 2006). For sample replies from participants, see *www.philosophytechnology.com/*.

12. PARTING BITES

1. The northern hairy-nosed wombat can be tracked through the Wombat Information Center, www.wombania.com (accessed May 6, 2007); BIRD, the biodiversity information Web site, http://bird.net.au/bird/index.php?title =Yaminon (accessed May 6, 2007); and Tim Flannery and Paula Kendall, *Australia's Vanishing Mammals* (Sydney: R. D. Press, 1990).

2. Everyone knows that termites need their cellulose-digesting symbionts, but fewer know that grass-eating wombats have specialized guts that are home to their own species of cellulose-processing workers. See "Feeding Ecology and Diet," www.answers.com/topic/wombat (accessed May 6, 2007).

3. Working on the Queensland wombat for over ten years, Dr. Andrea Taylor of Monash University, in Melbourne, "has developed a low disturbance genetic technique to census the wombat population. Wombat hair is collected on sticky tape strung across wombat burrows and DNA in the follicle is used to identify the sex and the 'owner' of the hair" (www.yaminon.org/gallery.html, accessed December 2006). Living endangered means living in technoculture; it is a condition of flourishing, or not, on earth now for most critters. See also Andrea Taylor, "Molecular Biology Meets Conservation Biology—Australian Mammal Case Studies," *Australian Frontiers of Science*, 2003, www.science.org.au/events/ frontiers2003/Taylor.htm (accessed May 6, 2007).

4. Lynn Margulis and Dorion Sagan, "The Beast with Five Genomes," *Natural History Magazine*, June 2001, online at www.naturalhistorymag.com/ 0601/0601_feature.html.

5. Hayward, "Envisioning Invertebrates."

6. To think about other practices of reckoning, see the essential text Helen Verran, *Science and an African Logic* (Chicago: University of Chicago Press, 2001). Not coincidentally, Melbourne-based Verran writes about Aboriginal landholding, management practices, mathematics, and meanings of country among the Wik and the Yolngu. For example, see Helen Verran, "Re-imagining Land Title in Australia," *Postcolonial Studies* 1 (1998): 237–54. Verran works with Indigenous Knowledge and Resource Management in the Northern Territory (www.cdu.edu.au/centres/ik), and she writes about how Aboriginal knowledge traditions can contribute to "doing" the nature of Australia.

7. Patricia Piccinini, *In Another Life*, published on the occasion of the exhibition at the City Gallery Wellington, February 19–June 11, 2006 (Wellington, Aotearoa New Zealand: City Gallery, 2006). I draw from Piccinini's own essay, "In Another Life," 12–13, as well as from artist and writer Stella Brennan's introduction of Piccinini, "Border Patrol," 6–9. See also Patricia Piccinini's Web site (www.patriciapiccinini.net/) for more drawings of human babies meeting her fabulated companion species from the series she called Nature's Little Helpers and her short essay "About These Drawings . . ." Thanks to Lindsay Kelley for introducing me to Piccinini's work in my graduate seminar on animal studies and science studies in 2004 and to April Henderson for sending me *In Another Life* in late 2006. Jim Clifford is Henderson's PhD dissertation adviser in the History of Consciousness Department, and I like to think that the "James" sitting face-to-face with the surrogate for the wombat is the young Clifford making one of his first postcolonial critter contacts in preparation for his wonderful writing about Pacific islanders' syncretic and heterogeneous theory, culture, and politics.

8. Telling a powerful story knotted through the transatlantic world rather than through Australia and the trans-Pacific, Sidney Mintz explores sugar's symbiogenetic naturecultures in *Sweetness and Power: The Place of Sugar in Modern History* (New York: Penguin, 1986). Commodities, labor, slavery, spice, medicine, luxury, and much more are all there, but the humanist frame of Mintz's anthropology makes it harder to see all the other organisms (and other nonhumans) actively involved.

9. Consider the shaping of "new natures," complete with the assemblages of mixed native and introduced species of every place on earth by the twenty-first century, perhaps especially in Australia—where pure categories of wild, domestic, endemic, or exotic cannot do justice to an environmentalism committed simultaneously to multispecies coflourishing, heterogeneous collective memory, and complex histories. Serious projects are required to build and rebuild livable

naturecultures into the future. Origins are not accessible even in principle. See the controversial work by the Australian Tim Low: *Feral Future: The Untold Story of Australia's Exotic Invaders* (Chicago: University of Chicago Press, 2002) and *The New Nature: Winners and Losers in Wild Australia* (Sydney, Australia: Penguin, 2002). Many endangered endemics have come to depend on introduced species for resources critical to eating and reproducing, which makes "restoration" and "preservation" a bit touchy. For integration of Low's approaches with science studies, sociology, colonial and postcolonial cultural studies, and considerations of animal well-being from both ecological and rights perspectives, see Franklin, *Animal Nation*; the kookaburra example is on 230.

The anthropologist Deborah Bird Rose, *Reports from a Wild Country* (Sydney: University of New South Wales, 2004), writes about the wounded space of Australian land and people and the deep need for recuperation and reconciliation in countermodern mode. Based on many years of work with Aborigines, especially in the Northern Territory, her perspective is rooted in relentless memory of the realities of mass killings and death in the white settler colony and its replacement ecologies. I find Rose's way of working fundamental for rebuilding a more livable world. Recognizing that approaches to current environmental–ethical dilemmas must be complex and polyvalent, she also appreciates mixed and heterogeneous naturecultures across times. Indeed, her work is all about mutually interconnected webs of relationships that are always in motion. But she refuses to look away from the onrushing catastrophe embedded in past and present human-made mass death that continues to sweep up critters of every category, human and nonhuman alike. See also Deborah Bird Rose, "What If the Angel of History Were a Dog?" *Cultural Studies Review* 12, no. 1 (March 2006): 67–78. There she tracks the ongoing death work in the poisoning of dingoes and wild dogs and hanging their corpses from trees as both a reality and a figure of a world howling with grief in the notes of howling dingoes.

Although they both depend on mixed-species assemblages, I think it is safe to say that Tim Low's "feral futures" have a different resonance from the ecological ur-restoration discourses proper to reestablishing Pleistocene fauna and ecosystems in North America. Still, something is compelling about "restoring" the grasslands of the western United States and the Great Plains by "transplanting" elephants and African lions. See Eric Jaffe, "Brave Old World: The Debate over Rewilding North America with Ancient Animals," *Science News* 170 (November 11, 2006): 314–18. This could put the chronologically parochial fights among ranchers, hunters, and environmentalists about repopulation of the land by northern gray wolves into perspective!

10. Franklin, *Animal Nation*, 166–92.

11. Barad, *Meeting the Universe Halfway*, 377, 393.

12. Donna Haraway, "Situated Knowledges: The Science Question in Feminism as a Site of Discourse on the Privilege of Partial Perspective," *Feminist Studies* 14, no. 3 (1988): 575–99. I remember that feminist "standpoint theory" was not and is not about fixed positions and identities but about the relational work and play of intersectional feminist worlding, which my colleague and friend Nancy Hartsock called feminist historical materialism. I attribute her insight to her love of horses along with her love—and close reading—of Marx. Hartsock understands "becoming with" in order to "become worldly." See Sandra Harding, ed., *The Feminist Standpoint Theory Reader* (New York: Routledge, 2003).

13. Katie King, my mentor for three decades in reading feminist science fiction, wrote, "When I first saw *James (sitting)*, I thought it was an illustration for a cover for Suzette Hadin Elgin's *Native Tongue!*" Indeed. The linguist Elgin's sf novel (New York: DAW, 1984) is about twenty-third-century human women, living after the repeal of the Nineteenth Amendment to the U.S. Constitution and in the grip of the Twenty-fifth Amendment, which has rendered women legal minors. The women are linguists of the Lines, communications specialists who mediate trade contacts between humans and aliens. Considered incapable of such things, in a special language they invented called Láadan, the women nourish plans for overthrowing the established disorder and building a new world. Láadan would become a native language. For a description of the language and links, see http://en.wikipedia.org/wiki/L%C3%A1adan. My 1984 paperback cover of *Native Tongue* has a large green alien head peering benignly (?) at a diminutive blond human baby seated on a circular embroidery frame, with ranks of test tubes full of gestating embryos in the background. Indisputably (how?) female, the scaly smiling maternal alien looms awfully close to the child. Her head looks very much like a protist covered by spherical bacteria. Or like the reptilian snake head of Lord Valdemort in feminine drag in a Harry Potter movie. Joining the futuristic alien and the terran archaic is a staple trope in sf. The baby is gesturing with its left hand to its mouth—hungry? talking? Or is the baby the extraterrestrial lady's lunch? Only the feral future will tell.

14. For great pictures of this wombat species and information about the Yaminon Defense Fund, see www.yaminon.org/ (accessed December 2006). The Web site looks like a one-person operation. I would not be surprised to find a story like C. A. Sharp's if someone set out to track the examined lives of these wombats and their passionate people. The term *wombat* itself comes from

the Eora Aboriginal community that lived around the area of modern Sydney (http://en.wikipedia.org/wiki/Wombat).

15. Katie King, "Pastpresents: Knotted Histories under Globalization," in *Thinking with Donna Haraway*, ed. Ghamari-Tabrizi, in ms., 2. King's book, *Networked Reenactments: Histories under Globalization* (under review), develops her insight through examining reenactments on television (*Highlander, Xena, Nova*), in museums (the Smithsonian's Science in American Life), and in scholarly histories (historiography of seventeenth-century Quaker women and the "scientific revolution"). King is in alliance with Bruno Latour's Parliament of Things, reworked to serve flexible knowledges with feminist verve.

16. Watch how my story works as reenactment. I have telescoped times and details to tell a true fabulation. Pastpresents are crucial to doing this. Reenactments are not empirically unaccountable, but they are not positivist reconstructions either. The evidence or facts for a story are always themselves caught up in layered reenactments. Katie tells me Mischa might have described herself as pagan, and both of them wore the names of anarchist and feminist in various ways over the years (but never as Identities), but many at the birth ceremony would not have done so then or later. Cyberwitches populated the Santa Cruz Mountains a few years after the placenta feast. I regard the technofeminists and the hippie home-birth community as kin, engaged in a kind of sf spiral dance when species meet.

17. Derrida (with Jean-Luc Nancy), "'Eating Well,' or the Calculation of the Subject," 115.

18. Barad, *Meeting the Universe Halfway*, 384.

19. www.albionmonitor.com/3-10-96/ex-feralpigs.html (accessed May 7, 2007).

20. Check out the California Department of Fish and Game paper on wild pig management, www.dfg.ca.gov/hunting/pig/index.htm (accessed May 7, 2007). Feral pigs in California date from Spanish mission times. The pigs are a particular environmental disaster in places such as the Santa Cruz Island Preserve, where the Nature Conservancy and the National Parks Service launched a program in 2005 to eradicate them. Prohunt, Inc., from New Zealand was hired to do the work. Are these antipodean hunters a guardian species like Piccinini's surrogates? The pigs on the island laid waste to the vegetation crucial to cover for the island foxes. That drew golden eagles, who hunted the foxes to near extinction. The eradication program includes relocating eagles to the mainland and captive breeding and release of foxes. Native plant communities are also expected to recover. See www.nature.org/wherewework/northamerica/states/

california/press/press_sci040805.html (accessed May 7, 2007). Prohunt, Inc., established a subsidiary in Orange County, California, to operate more easily in the United States. The company specializes in wild animal management for conservation projects. Prohunt has supplied New Zealand goat-hunting dogs and expertise for the Isabella goat eradication project in the Galápagos, written an ungulate eradication plan for Cocos Island, Costa Rica, and provided advice and expertise for the eradication of goats on Gaudalupe Island, Mexico. See www.prohunt.co.nz/aboutus.htm (accessed May 7, 2007). On pig eradication on Santa Cruz Island, see www.prohunt.co.nz/newsletter.htm (accessed May 7, 2007). The ecological damage from wild pigs on the California mainland is more complex but also substantial. Hunters are not always benign in this story, put mildly. Some "sportsmen" have been known to release piglets into areas not yet inhabited by pigs to increase their hunting base.

21. For crucial knowledge, feeling, and argument, see Carol Adams, "An Animal Manifesto: Gender, Identity, and Vegan–Feminism in the Twenty-first Century," *Parallax* 12, no. 1 (2006): 120–28. She argues, "Haraway protects the dominance that ontologizes animals as edible just as the sheepdogs she celebrates protect the ontologized 'livestock'" (126). I hope I have met Adams in this book, not convinced her, but respected her crucial truths as well as my own in a nonrelativistic way. I am not sure it can be done, but the stakes are collective and not only personal.

22. Wedde, "Walking the Dog," 358.

PUBLICATION HISTORY

An excerpt of chapter 1 titled "Encounters with Companion Species: Entangling Dogs, Baboons, Philosophers, and Biologists," will also appear in *Configurations*, special issue from 2004 Society for Literature and Science meetings, forthcoming in 2007.

Sections of earlier versions of chapters 4 and 7 also appeared in *The Companion Species Manifesto* (Chicago: Prickly Paradigm Press, 2003).

Chapter 5 was revised from "Cloning Mutts, Saving Tigers: Ethical Emergents in Technocultural Dog Worlds," which was published in Sarah Franklin and Margaret Lock, eds., *Remaking Life and Death: Towards an Anthropology of the Biosciences* (Santa Fe: School of American Research Press, 2003), 293–327.

Chapter 6 was revised from "A Note of a Sportswriter's Daughter: Companion Species," which was published in Nancy Chen and Helene Moglen, eds., *Bodies in the Making: Transgressions and Transformations* (Santa Cruz, Calif.: New Pacific Press, 2006), 143–61.

An early version of chapter 8 will be published in Beatriz da Costa and Kavita Philip, eds., *Tactical Biopolitics: Theory and Practice @ Life, Science, Art* (Cambridge, Mass.: MIT Press).

An early version of chapter 8 will also be published in Marc Bekoff and Janette Nystrom, eds., *Encyclopedia of Human–Animal Relationships* (Westport, Conn.: Greenwood Publishing Group).

An earlier version of chapter 9 was published in Evan Selinger, ed., *Postphenomenology: A Critical Companion to Ihde* (Binghamton: State University of New York Press, 2006), 175–88.

An earlier version of chapter 10 was published in B. Eekelen, J. Gonzalez, B. Stötzer, and A. Tsing, eds., *Shock and Awe: War on Words* (Santa Cruz, Calif.: New Pacific Press, 2004), 23–30.

The first part of chapter 11 was expanded from "The Writer of the Companion Species Manifesto E-mails Her Dog People," in Margaretta Jolly, ed., *a/b: Auto/Biography Studies* 21, nos. 1 and 2 (2006).

The second part of chapter 11 was adapted from "Replies to Five Questions," in Jan-Kyrre Berg Olsen and Evan Selinger, eds., *Philosophy of Technology* (N.P.: Automatic Press/VIP, December 2006), www.philosophy technology.com/.

INDEX

Aborigines (Australia): "country" and, 289; dingoes and, 288, 326n15, 342n9; dugongs and Crittercam, 255; histories and naturecultures, 388n9; knowledge practices, 387n6; presence in Shark Bay, 255, 378n8; remoras and, 378n; wombats and, 389–90n14

Aborigines (West Indies): remoras and, 378n5

Acland, Gregory, 113, 114

Acquiring Genomes (Margulis and Sagan), 30–32

activism (activists); as knowledgeable actors in technoculture, 140; making facts real, 111–15; multitasking, in dog cultures, 108; role of publicity, 114, 124–27; "science for the people," 113; silencing,

108–9, 116, 118 (*see also* "Incorrigibles, the"; "Ostrich Syndrome"); volunteers, 351n35. *See also* cosmopolitics; Sharp, C. A.; worlding

Adams, Carol, 333n10; intersectionality and animals, 309n22; veganism, 299, 346n15

Adams, Mischa, 293–94

Adolphson, Pete, 118–19

Agamben, Giorgio: "anthropological machine" in philosophy, 334n16; on Heidegger's "the open," 334n16, 367n28; *Open, The*, 334n16

agility (sport), 26–27, 313n34; authority, relations of, 220–21 (*see also* authority); contact obstacles, 208–9, 365n14 (*see also* contact

Donna J. Haraway is a professor in the History of Consciousness Department at the University of California, Santa Cruz. She is the author of *The Companion Species Manifesto: Dogs, People, and Significant Otherness* and *Simians, Cyborgs, and Women: The Reinvention of Nature.*